Scottish Professional Boxing in the Fifties and Sixties

Scottish
Professional
Boxing
in the
Fifties and Sixties

by
Brian Doyle

Self Published by Brian Doyle

First published in Great Britain in 2007 by
Brian Doyle,
18 Deakin Leas,
Tonbridge,
Kent TN9 2JU.

ISBN-13   978-0-9554480-0-3

Printed by Reflections Print Ltd., Unit 5, Orchard Business Centre, Sanderson Way, Tonbridge, Kent TN9 1QG

Contents

Scottish Professional Boxing in the Fifties and Sixties

Acknowledgement

My thanks go to everyone who has helped me put this book together.

I thank my family for their support and my wife for her patience, particularly when she had to re-input all data following the expiration of my hard drive.

My particular thanks go to Michael McConnachie in Wishaw. Michael has been a boxing enthusiast since he was a youngster. In his retirement, he has compiled the records of old time Scots boxers and his contribution has been invaluable He has given up much of his time to read through and comment on the initial draft and at times he has also provided much needed encouragement.

Thank you also to my brother Jim in Portsmouth who proof read the original draft. His input has given rise to various improvements to the draft.

I wish to thank the Scottish ex-Boxers Association and their members for their help. I would particularly like to thank the Secretary, Liam McColgan, for his prolonged assistance. Thank you also to Alex Ambrose, Evan Armstrong, Ken Buchanan, John McCluskey, Cowboy McCormack, Johnny Morrissey, Bobby Neill and Derry Treanor for their time and unprintable tales.

Thank you to the staff at the Mitchell Library, The Scottish National Library and the British Newspaper Library. Thanks also to Jim Urquhart at the Aberdeen Press and Journal, Marion Strain at North Lanarkshire County Council, Neil Moffat at Dumfries and Galloway Council, Eleanor Harris at Argyll and Bute Library, John Beedle at Hawick Library, Margaret McGarry at Motherwell Heritage Centre and the helpful staff of Boxing News.

Thank you to everyone who has supplied and given permission to use photographs. It is not clear who owned copyright on certain photographs but, where copyright is known, I have obtained permission to use all photographs.

Foreword

I was born in Glasgow in 1945. I was brought up in Kirkland Street in Maryhill and I remained there until the family moved to Milton in April 1951. My earliest sporting memory is being lifted over the turnstile by my father into nearby Firhill to watch a Partick Thistle v Celtic game from his shoulders. I have no recollection of the match but I was mesmerised by the noise and the size of the crowd.

My father was not a big football fan. His sport was boxing and he talked about it incessantly throughout the fifties. Some of the boxing crowds were as large as those at football matches and I therefore had no difficulty in capturing the boxing atmosphere from my father's commentaries. He enthused most of all about the Keenan v Tuli fight at Cathkin Park. He had been a witness to one of the all-time great fights in Scotland.

I remember that we listened to the Rocky Marciano v Don Cockell world title fight on the radio in May 1955. The fight was in the middle of the night and the following day I recall describing the fight to everyone at school. My father's enthusiasm for boxing certainly rubbed off on me and, as his interest waned towards the end of the fifties, my interest grew.

I had the Boxing News on order from 1957 until the early sixties. However, my library disappeared when my over-zealous sister decided to spring clean my bedroom when I was away. Life was never the same again and I switched my allegiance from boxing to the New Musical Express.

When I became familiar with the Internet at the beginning of this century, I tried to pick up the Scottish boxing threads but found that there was very little on offer from the fifties and sixties. My desire to find out what I could about this era has taken me on a very long trek over a period of more than four years. I had no idea at the outset that this project would dominate so much of my life and for such a long period. I started by buying a host of old boxing magazines on e-bay. There followed interviews with ex-boxers from this era, numerous visits to the Mitchell Library, the National Library of Scotland and the British Newspaper Library in North West London. Most of my time, however, has been spent collating the information gathered.

This book is a summary of Scottish professional boxing in the fifties and sixties from a fan's perspective and is dedicated to the memory of my father, Dan Doyle. He was a crane operator, much of the time at the dockside in Glasgow. He was also a gambler and a drinker but a lover of the noble art. I think that he would approve of my efforts to provide a summary of the Scottish boxing scene in these golden decades.

Brian Doyle,
Tonbridge, Kent.
January 2007

Introduction

The Second World War had a devastating effect on both the UK economy and the UK population. When the war ended in 1945, people had got used to living on the barest of rations and without luxuries. The end of the war did not improve their lot and, if anything, the situation deteriorated before it improved. The population swelled as demobbed soldiers, sailors and airmen, some badly wounded and unable to work, were repatriated. Jobs were scarce and unemployment amongst the returning heroes was high.

To help make ends meet, many of the demobbed tried their luck at professional boxing and the post war years saw an unprecedented boom in the sport. Most professional boxers had full time jobs and trained in the evenings and at weekends when they were not working overtime or fighting in the ring. The boxers were termed professional because they fought for money but their fitness and ring skills did not always measure up to this terminology.

The austere conditions in Scotland in the early fifties were not helpful to professional sportsmen. Accommodation was cramped and occupying families were large. It was not unusual for a family comprising two parents and six children to occupy two rooms. The living room/ dining room/ kitchen often doubled as a second bedroom. As accommodation was unavailable or too expensive, most newly weds had no choice other than to live in the same accommodation as one set of parents. Despite the lack of privacy, babies were conceived and the cramped conditions could house three or four generations.

Bathrooms were unheard of and baths were usually taken in the main room in a portable tin bath that had to be filled with hot water. Inside toilets were a luxury. For many families, there was a communal outside toilet to be shared with several other families. Toilet paper was invariably an old Daily Record or similar publication.

Some homes did not have mains electricity until the late fifties. Coal fires in the main room were usually the source of the hot water supply and the only source of heat in the home. It was not uncommon to wake up on a wintry morning to find ice formed on the inside of windows.

With so many occupying inadequate accommodations, most of the family would go outdoors to maintain their sanity. Children would play out after school until late when they would be called in to go to bed. Older children would hang around street corners or closes until late.

Healthcare was poor and healthy eating non-existent. Tea was rationed until 1952, sugar, eggs and sweets until 1953 and cheese, meat and other fatty products until 1954. It was impossible to have a balanced diet. Parents often passed their rations on to their children as children were particularly vulnerable at this time. Infants and young children died from diseases such as whooping cough, diphtheria, scarlet fever and measles. A polio epidemic claimed the lives of several thousand children and disabled thousands more.

Male life expectancy was 63. This contrasts with the current life expectancy of 76. There was no control over pollution and the thick black smoke that filled the air was surely a contributory factor to ill health. The smoke emerged from both industrial chimneys and the multitude of domestic chimneys that burned coal.

There was no television available to the general public in 1950. The radio or wireless as it was then known was the sole home entertainment broadcast to the public. There was a choice of three channels, the Home Service, the Light Programme and the Third Programme. No working class household listened to the Third Programme which concentrated on classical music and intellectual stimulation. The Home Service was middle of the road and the Light Programme catered for the masses. Accordingly, most working class households listened to the Light. There was little live sports coverage on the wireless at this time although the Home International football matches against England, Wales and Northern Ireland were broadcast as were major world boxing title fights. To obtain football results on a Saturday and other sports news of the week, you had to tune in to Sports Report at 5 o'clock on a Saturday afternoon.

There were neither mobile telephones nor landlines in the home. The general public did not usually make telephone calls unless it was an urgent matter or long distance to a relative with a telephone. Red public telephone boxes were not always conveniently located and you could have to walk a mile or more to the nearest box, wait in the queue and hope that you were connected when your turn came. Otherwise, it was back to the end of the queue.

For those in employment, wages were paid on a Friday evening and had to last until the next week. Most income was spent on necessities such as food, accommodation and clothing. There was little left over to spend on entertainment. Holidays abroad were out of the question. A holiday was usually a visit to a relative living in another part of Scotland.

Living conditions did gradually improve in the fifties and sixties but it can be seen that the problems facing boxers at the beginning of this period were unmistakably different from those facing current day boxers.

The first chapter of this book outlines the decline of Scottish professional boxing in this era. There follows highlights each year from 1950 to 1969 and then chapters on venues, promoters and various afterthoughts.

Appendix 1 gives a summary of all Scottish promotions in the era. I have tried to be consistent with name spellings but, particularly in the early fifties, spellings seemed to vary between newspapers. Hometowns also varied between newspapers and some boxers moved to new areas in the period. I have attempted to show the same hometown throughout the Appendix.

The general rule when showing the weight is to show the weight closest to the heavier boxer. This results in some boxers alternating between weights in the Appendix.

I conclude with the fight record of all Scottish boxers who fought for major titles and their profiles. The fight records relate only to contests in the fifties and sixties but further information relating to previous and subsequent activity is given within their profiles.

No summary of managers in the era is included as the time required to collect and collate this information would have been be too great. The leading manager by a distance was Tommy Gilmour, son of promoter Jim, as illustrated by the various cuttings that follow.

The Decline in Scottish Boxing

During the post war boom, venues were filled to capacity and ticket touting was not uncommon. The boom had attracted newcomers and ex-servicemen to the sport and more amateurs were turning professional. European and American boxers now featured regularly on UK boxing bills. However, this situation did not last and professional boxing was in decline by the early fifties. There was a 24% reduction in Scottish promotions between 1950 and 1951. There was a further 63% reduction in 1952.

The main east coast venue was Edinburgh Music Hall which hosted 19 promotions in 1950, 12 in 1951 and 8 in 1952. George Miller's regular weekly shows had come to an abrupt halt when he died in April 1951. Charlie Black temporarily revived the venue in 1952 but following 2 subsequent shows in 1954, the Music Hall ceased to be used for professional boxing.

In Glasgow, the Grove Institute had provided regular Saturday night boxing for many years. The Grove promotions featured mainly journeymen but also provided an outlet for new professional talent. When the venue was destroyed by fire in May 1950, it appeared that Glasgow fans would have no regular professional boxing.

Promoters Jim Gilmour and Alex Lucas came to the rescue of Glasgow fans by running regular promotions at the St. Mungo Halls throughout 1951. However, following 2 promotions in 1952 and 1 in 1953, the St. Mungo Halls also ceased to be used as a professional venue.

The reduction in promotions cannot be blamed solely on the closure of weekly venues. Promotions at Paisley Ice Rink had fallen from 10 in 1950 to 1 in 1952. Leith Eldorado had 5 in 1950 but none in 1952. The 1952 budget had exacerbated the situation when the Chancellor announced that entertainment tax on boxing would increase substantially. In general terms, the promoter had previously paid tax of 16% of gross takings but this tax was to increase to 33%. There was little incentive for promoters in the small halls to continue and even the diehard top line promoters were wary of the future.

It was clear that promoters would now struggle to make a profit but the decline had already been apparent before the increase in entertainment tax. There were therefore other reasons why promoters were not filling the halls. Fans complained about regular changes to advertised programmes. Make no mistake, this issue caused deep resentment amongst the paying public and was a contributory factor to diminishing crowds. At the beginning of the fifties, programmes advertised by promoters very rarely materialised in their original format and it was not unusual for promoters to leak wrong information to the press or to replace leading attractions with pre-arranged substitutes at the last minute.

Promoters were not always to blame for the bill changes. At this time, there were fewer restrictions on boxers who understandably accepted whatever fights they were offered, often with little or no notice, and they would perhaps fight several times in a month or even in a week. In early 1950, Don McTaggart fought three times in one week. Two of these fights were on consecutive nights. He won at Paisley on the 8th February, at Edinburgh on the 14th and at Dundee on the 15th. Any injury sustained at Paisley could have meant withdrawal from the subsequent bills and any injury in Edinburgh would certainly have meant a late withdrawal and a promotional headache in Dundee. When a boxer pulled out of a contest, it was not always easy to obtain a suitable replacement at short notice and substitutes were often sub-standard. A certificate signed by the boxer's own GP was sufficient proof that the boxer was unable to fight and certificates often arrived on the day of the fight. A four-day gap rule between fights was subsequently introduced to ease the problem but this had little effect.

Boxers were sometimes intimidated by promoters. Matches were made without reference to a stipulated weight and a middleweight could turn up to fight at welterweight. The weight difference only came to light at the weigh-in which, due to work commitments, often took place on the evening of the contest. At this late stage, it was too late to engage a substitute in such a contest. The lighter fighter could refuse to go ahead with the fight and lose his purse including his costs and travelling expenses or proceed in what could be a huge mismatch. At the Grove in January 1950, Hugh McLellan weighed exactly 8 stones when he lost in one round to Zeke Brown who was a stone heavier. Weight differences were not always so great but it was not uncommon to find seven to ten pound weight differentials on local bills. From 1952, a rule was introduced that all contests had to be made at a stipulated weight.

Entry charges were a prime consideration in attracting the crowds. The currency back in 1950 was pounds, shillings and pence. There were 20 shillings in a pound and 12 pence in a shilling. Take home pay for manual workers would have been in the region of £6 to £8. A return ticket on the train from Glasgow to Stirling would have cost 3/4d (3 shillings and 4 pence). A similar ticket to Perth would cost 8/6d, to Dundee 11/6d and to Aberdeen 20/-. It cost 2/- to go to the Dennistoun Palais and 5/- to go into the stand at Parkhead or Ibrox.

At Firhill on 9th May 1951, the prices for the Keenan v O'Sullivan British title fight were 63/-, 42/-, 30/-, 21/- and 5/- for the terracing. A month later, there was a lower tier bill at Carntyne where prices ranged from 3/- to 10/6d with a reduced admission charge of 1/6d for schoolboys and females. The weekly charge at the St. Mungo Halls also ranged from 3/- to 10/6d at this time. In May 1953, entry prices at Saracen Park ranged from 2/6d to 21/-. In June 1954 at Motherwell, prices were 3/- to 21/-. Firhill was packed and made money for the promoter but the other promotions were loss makers. Keenan was no doubt a box office attraction. However, the inference is that there were no other major box office attractions in Scotland. As prices at the lower end were affordable and reasonably competitive, the overall product seemed to be losing its appeal.

Promoters complained of the lack of suitable venues. Winter venues had always been a problem for boxing promoters in Scotland. The restricted capacity at Scottish venues meant that promoters could not compete with London or other big city promoters for major fights during the winter season. It was more realistic to compete with the big city promoters in the summer when Scottish football grounds were available but title fights did not always take place in the summer.

City Councils were reluctant to let the bigger and better known halls out for professional boxing and most alternatives were unsuitable. Glasgow Corporation refused applications to allow professional boxing at the St. Andrew's Halls in Berkeley Street which had a 7,000 capacity and the main Glasgow venue remained the Kelvin Hall with half that capacity. Professional boxing dates at the Kelvin Hall were also restricted and had to be regularly approved by a committee and then ratified by city magistrates. Available dates were then open to bids from promoters. Having won a date, the promoter was unable to postpone if a main attraction was injured. In such cases, a suitable replacement had to be found. In 1952, three dates were approved in the early part of the year and allocated to different promoters. Charlie Black had to cancel his date which was taken up by Sammy Docherty but only after the red tape of the Kelvin Hall committee and Glasgow Corporation had been overcome. The additional capacity of the St. Andrew's Halls could have made Glasgow as competitive as Belfast and Nottingham.

All major fights in this period were in the West of Scotland. These fights took place at the largest indoor venues which were Paisley Ice Rink and the Kelvin Hall or at outdoor venues. Paisley could hold 5,000 or 5,800 with expensive modifications and the majority of indoor title fights were held there. Firhill and Cathkin could comfortably hold in excess of 20,000 spectators.

As crowds were in free fall by 1952, promoters had to come up with new ideas to win them back. Sammy Docherty had relied on Peter Keenan throughout 1951 to headline his shows and was pleased with the public response. In 1952, he ran two consecutive Kelvin Hall promotions headlined by imported American welterweight, Danny Womber. The reaction to the first bill was encouraging but the second bill which included only two Scots out of ten boxers lacked support and was a financial disaster. Sammy's future bills featured 50% Scots on average.

In the same year, at the same venue, Alex Lucas tested public reaction with a 5-fight bill featuring only Scots. The bill included three Scottish title fights and two Scottish title eliminators. The promotion was a resounding success for the fans who watched 54 rounds of boxing but it did not provide a huge financial return for the promoter. On this bill, Alex Lucas had reached agreement with Don McTaggart and Jim Travers that the winner of their eliminator should receive 60% of the purse. Alex Lucas was keen to encourage this format on future bills. His reasoning was that such a financial inducement would encourage both boxers to train hard and put on a good show. Following on from this, the idea was floated that boxers should be paid a percentage of the gate rather than a fixed purse. After deducting the promoter's expenses, the promoter would be allocated a percentage of the receipts with the balance being divided amongst the boxers in accordance with their drawing power. These were sound ideas in theory but would never be implemented.

Boxers and managers seemed slow to accept that there was a boxing decline and continued to demand unrealistic purses. Promoters reacted either by reducing their activity or by ceasing to promote. The outcome was that many Scottish boxers could not get fights in the diminishing boxing market. Some Scots looked to England for work. However, England had similar problems and there was little work available. Most who had plied their trade as preliminary fighters or at the smaller halls simply had nowhere to go and stopped boxing. Many who continued to box on a reduced scale soon lost the incentive to train regularly and remain fit and they too were lost to the sport. New blood was not attracted as there was little financial reward for the cost and effort required to function as a professional boxer. In 1953, there were 68 appearances in Scotland by Scottish professionals. This contrasted with 487 appearances in 1950.

The Kirk O'Shotts transmitter had been launched in 1952 and television in the home was new competition to professional boxing. The growth in sales of televisions over the next few years had an adverse effect on boxing crowds. Many preferred to sit in the comfort of their homes with the new entertainment rather than brave the weather and unreliable transport system to attend a boxing show in an unheated boxing arena.

As the increase in entertainment tax took hold, there was a further reduction in Scottish promotions in 1953. There were 13 promotions in that year, 13 in 1954, 11 in 1955 and 11 in 1956. The decline appeared to have been arrested. Promoters remained cautious but new and exciting talent was coming through and the future looked promising. The east coast fared reasonably well in this four-year period. In addition to the 2 promotions in Edinburgh, there were 8 at the Eldorado in Leith, 9 at the Caird Hall and a single promotion at Kirkcaldy.

On the west coast, there were 12 promotions at the Kelvin Hall, 4 at Paisley Ice Rink, 2 at Cathkin and 2 at Firhill. Peter Keenan remained the principal attraction and had 4 major title fights at these promotions. However, new attractions such as Frankie Jones, Dick Currie, John Smillie, Charlie Hill and Matt Fulton were drawing the crowds.

Entertainment tax was abolished in the budget of 9th April 1957. The move was welcomed by the boxing world but permanent damage had already been inflicted on the sport. The Scottish boxing scene had compressed since 1952 and the distinct shortage of professional boxers could not be changed overnight. Both boxers and fans had moved on but the abolition of the tax did seem to have some impact. Promotions increased to 18 in 1957 and 1958 but then fell back to 16 in 1959.

In 1957, Scotland saw Peter Keenan defend his British and Empire titles against John Smillie and Frankie Jones lose his Empire title to Dennis Adams. Scots held the British flyweight, bantamweight and featherweight titles and were well represented in all three divisions. Middleweight Cowboy McCormack appeared in 10 and light heavyweight Dave Mooney in 8 of the 18 Scottish promotions in 1957. Both were new professionals who excited the crowd. Scottish boxing was looking good at the end of 1957.

Peter Keenan defended his Empire title twice at Paisley in 1958 and Charlie Hill defended his British title against Chic Brogan in Glasgow. Scots continued to hold the flyweight, bantamweight and featherweight crowns and dominate these weights. 7 of the top 10 UK featherweights were Scottish. John McCormack was a leading middleweight and Chic Calderwood was attracting much attention although most of his boxing was in England. It is no surprise that Johnny Morrissey, John McCormack, Dave Mooney, Alex Ambrose, Peter Keenan and Billy Rafferty appeared most often on Scottish bills in 1958. They were all exciting to watch and gave the fans value for money. The Scottish contingent was augmented by the Irish connection of John Caldwell, Derry Treanor and Freddie Gilroy.

The only major title fight in Scotland in 1959 was Frankie Jones defending his British flyweight title against Alex Ambrose in February. Jones and Bobby Neill were British champions. Scotland was still well represented in the lower divisions but not in such numbers as in previous years. John McCormack had won and lost the British middleweight title. Chic Calderwood was on the verge of winning the British light heavyweight title.

It was a disappointment that the number of promotions in 1960 and 1961 dropped back to the figures of 1955 and 1956. There were 11 promotions in both 1960 and 1961. Chic Calderwood was the main draw in 1960. He won the British title, the Empire title and recorded 4 further victories, including the win over Willie Pastrano. He was now the only Scot holding a major title.

In 1961, John McCormack won the European middleweight title but fought only twice in Scotland. Calderwood remained British and Empire champion but fought only once in Scotland.

In 1962, there were no major title fights and only 6 promotions in Scotland. Calderwood remained British and Empire champion and Jackie Brown had won both the British and Empire flyweight titles. However, neither boxer fought in Scotland in 1962.

There were 8 Scottish promotions in 1963. Walter McGowan appeared on 5 occasions, winning the British and Empire titles from Jackie Brown and defending his Empire title once. Calderwood fought 3 times in Scotland before he was stripped of his titles.

In 1964, there were 6 promotions. The main draw, Walter McGowan, was now performing outside of Scotland and managed only 2 Scottish appearances. John McCormack fought twice in Scotland as did Chic Calderwood who won back his British light heavyweight title.

Walter McGowan headlined 1 of the 4 promotions in 1965. The main headliner was Cowboy McCormack against Chic Calderwood. However, none of these box office draws would ever again fight in Scotland.

Of the 8 promotions in 1966 and 6 in 1967, all but two were at the Sporting Club in the Central Hotel. This switch reflected the lack of interest shown by the general public. Peter Keenan kept the concept running as long as he could but even he conceded that there was no fan base for professional boxing and ceased promotions in May 1967. Peter Keenan had been the sole Scottish promoter since February 1964 and there was now a huge void.

There were 2 promotions in late 1968 and 1 in 1969. The initial 1968 show was well supported but the following 2 shows were not and Peter Keenan's conclusion that the Scottish public were no longer interested in attending live professional boxing was confirmed. New professional Jim Watt had fought on the last 3 Scottish bills of this era but now had to head to England to continue has career. This was a path that all Scottish professionals now had to follow if they wished to continue in boxing. Professional boxing in Scotland no longer existed at the end of the sixties.

Highlights of 1950

At the beginning of 1950, there were no Scottish boxers holding British, Empire or world titles. Scottish title holders at the commencement of the year were as follows.

Flyweight	Norman Tennant (Dundee)
Bantamweight	Eddie Carson (Edinburgh)
Featherweight	Jim Kenny (Polmont)
Lightweight	Harry Hughes (Wishaw)
Welterweight	Ginger Stewart (Hamilton)
Middleweight	Jake Kilrain (Bellshill)
Light Heavyweight	Bert Gilroy (Coatbridge)
Heavyweight	Ken Shaw (Dundee)

During the year, Ginger Stewart, Jake Kilrain and Bert Gilroy retired and Ken Shaw emigrated to New Zealand.

Flyweight

In the flyweight division, Rinty Monaghan of Northern Ireland began the year as British, Empire, European and world champion. Due to bronchial trouble, Monaghan was unable to defend his world and European titles against Honore Pratesi of France by the imposed deadline of 31st January and shortly afterwards decided to retire. All four titles were therefore vacant.

Scotland had a number of contenders for the British flyweight title. Scottish champion Norman Tennant was ranked second behind Terry Allen of Islington and Glaswegians Joe Murphy and Vic Herman were ranked sixth and eighth respectively. Although his UK ranking was number 5, Peter Keenan was thought to be the leading flyweight in Great Britain after Monaghan and Allen. Allen had beaten Monaghan on points in February 1949 and had drawn with him in Belfast in September 1949 in his challenge for all four titles in what proved to be Monaghan's final contest. Allen was therefore a strong candidate for all of the titles following Monaghan's retirement. Keenan supporters were, however, convinced that he could bring the world flyweight crown back to Scotland and eagerly looked forward to the remainder of the year.

Keenan had started the year off in January at Paisley Ice Rink against Dickie O'Sullivan of Finsbury Park. O'Sullivan had turned professional in 1944 and was still a top ranking British flyweight at the time of the contest although his weight was closer to that of a bantamweight and the match was made at 8 stone 4 pounds. Keenan performed flawlessly and disposed of his experienced opponent in 3 rounds.

Keenan next made his London debut against Jean Sneyers of Belgium. Sneyers was considered by many to be the outstanding flyweight in the world and had lost only 1 of his 19 professional contests. That defeat was in Glasgow in 1948 to Norman Tennant of Dundee when he had to retire because of a broken thumb. Keenan impressed with a close 10 rounds points victory and moved himself closer to the flyweight pinnacle.

Norman Tennant had a poor start to the year. In a hard fight made at 8 stone 6 pounds, he was outpointed over 10 rounds at the Caird Hall by fellow Dundonian and bantamweight contender Bobby Boland. He then fought Vic Herman at the same venue and was again outpointed over 10 rounds. The decision was controversial and booed by the home fans. However, Herman's claims to fight Peter Keenan in an eliminator for the British title were strengthened as was his right to meet Tennant for the Scottish title. Due to the controversy, a return match proved a big attraction to fight fans and was made at the Kelvin Hall on 8th March. Herman again proved to be the victor, this time winning on points over 8 rounds.

In late March, Peter Keenan was due to fight top European flyweight Louis Skena at Paisley Ice Rink but had to withdraw due to injury. His place on the bill was taken by Vic Herman. Herman was outclassed and lost a points verdict over 10 rounds. Given that Skena was outpointed by Jean Sneyers in the following month, it was clear that Peter Keenan was a cut above the other flyweight contenders from Scotland.

In May, Keenan fought the highly rated Maurice Sandeyron of France in a match at 8 stone 5 pounds. In another close fight, he won on points over 8 rounds. He was then matched with Vic Herman whom he had already beaten in 1949 and he defeated him again, on points over 10 rounds. When the British Boxing Board of Control left Keenan out of the flyweight eliminators for the British title but included him in the bantamweight eliminators, it was clear that Keenan's future was as a bantamweight. The flyweight eliminators were Norman Tennant v Joe Murphy and Vic Herman v Norman Lewis from Wales.

Murphy had a quiet year prior to his eliminator, winning 2 of his 3 contests and losing only to Tino Cardinale of Italy on points at Paisley. His opponent, Tennant, continued his losing sequence, losing to Cardinale on points, suffering a knockout against Black Pico and losing on points to Jimmy Pearce of Middlesbrough whom Murphy had beaten. The eliminator took place at Dundee Ice Rink on 27th September. Murphy appeared favourite but it was Tennant who gained his first win of the year after 6 consecutive defeats. The fight lasted 9 rounds before the referee stepped in to save Murphy who had a badly cut eye. Tennant had one more fight in the year, winning and reversing his previous loss against Jimmy Pearce.

Herman had points victories before and after his defeat by Peter Keenan and was in good shape when he made the journey to Porthcawl for his eliminator.

He fought well and stopped his fellow contender in the tenth round. It was now generally accepted that Herman was number 2 to Terry Allen and that he would again defeat Tennant in their final eliminator. Herman completed the year with a fine points win over Tino Cardinale and a hard earned draw against Honore Pratesi.

In late April, Terry Allen became world and European flyweight champion by outpointing Honore Pratesi at Harringay Arena. On 1st August, he lost his world title in Honolulu to Dado Marino from Hawaii. On 30th October, he lost his European title to Jean Sneyers at Nottingham.

Bantamweight

Manuel Ortiz of the USA was world bantamweight champion at the beginning of 1950. A professional since 1938, he won the title in 1942 and successfully defended 15 times before losing the title in 1947. He regained the title two months later and defended a further 4 times by the end of 1949. He had fought in Glasgow in 1949, winning on points against Jackie Paterson.

The Empire bantamweight title was held by South African Vic Toweel. He had won the title in Johannesburg in 1949 by outpointing Stan Rowan from Liverpool. Toweel had also fought Jackie Paterson in 1949, beating him on points over 10 rounds in Johannesburg.

The European champion was Spaniard Luis Romero who had won the title in 1949. In December 1949, he outpointed Bobby Boland of Dundee over 10 rounds in Barcelona.

The British champion was Danny O'Sullivan from King's Cross in London. He won the title in December 1949 beating Teddy Gardner of West Hartlepool. In 1949, he had also beaten Fernando Gagnon of Canada in an eliminator for the Empire title. Scottish contenders for the British title were Scottish champion Eddie Carson ranked 5 and Dundee's Bobby Boland ranked 6.

Eddie Carson began his professional career in 1945 and he won and defended the Scottish title in 1949. He had also fought for the Scottish flyweight title in 1949, losing on points to Norman Tennant. An eliminator series for the right to meet Carson had already been arranged. The first eliminator took place in Dundee on 2nd January and the victor was Dundonian Willie Myles, on points over 10 rounds against Kent-based Glaswegian Eddie McCormick.

Jim Dwyer from Glasgow had turned professional in 1948 and had previously outpointed Willie Myles in 1949. He repeated his victory when stopping his opponent in 5 rounds in the final eliminator at the Music Hall, Edinburgh in November. Myles had won 2 of 5 fights since winning the first eliminator in January. Dwyer looked forward to his championship meeting with Carson whom he had beaten on points over 8 rounds in October. Dwyer's overall record for the year was 5 wins in 10 contests.

In January, Bobby Boland had outpointed Norman Tennant. Boland followed up with impressive wins against Amleto Falcinelli of Italy and Fernando Gagnon of Canada. Boland had 2 further wins, a draw and 2 losses including one defeat to Maurice Sandeyron, all by the end of June.

In the same period, Carson had 7 fights. He won 5 of these fights but lost on points to European champion Luis Romero and was knocked out by Tommy Proffitt from Droylesden who had been named in the series of eliminators for the British title. Proffitt's semi-final eliminator was against Bobby Boland. The second eliminator was between Peter Keenan and Irish Champion Bunty Doran.

Keenan won his eliminator against Doran on points over 10 rounds. Although never a classic, Keenan clearly did enough to take the verdict. The contest between Boland and Proffitt took place at Newcastle in September. The result was a major disappointment for Boland who was disqualified in the fifth round. The fight was close and Boland thought he was ahead when the referee called a halt to proceedings. The final eliminator between Keenan and Proffitt was set for Paisley in November.

A dejected Boland then punched his way back into the headlines with a superb points win over British champion Danny O'Sullivan. He was then surprisingly defeated by an unknown Tunisian before ending the year with a points win over Theo Medina, the former French bantamweight champion and conqueror of Maurice Sandeyron. 1950 had been a good year for Boland but the disqualification was a serious setback.

Peter Keenan was in devastating form when he met Proffitt and he knocked the Englishman out in the second round. Keenan completed the year with a points win over Louis Skena.

As Scottish champion, Eddie Carson thought that he should have been included in the eliminators. However, he won only 3 of 6 contests in the second half of the year and his UK ranking slipped.

Danny O'Sullivan preferred a European title tilt rather than a fight for the Empire title. A further Empire eliminator was therefore arranged between Fernando Gagnon and Teddy Gardner. Gagnon was the winner in 4 rounds but he went on to lose in his title attempt against Vic Toweel in Johannesburg.

O'Sullivan fought for the European title at Harringay Arena but he was stopped by Luis Romero in 13 rounds. Toweel then became world champion when he outpointed Manuel Ortiz over 15 rounds in Johannesburg. He subsequently defended and retained both the world and Empire titles against Danny O'Sullivan, stopping the Londoner in 10 rounds. Toweel had won all of his 17 professional contests to date but had yet to fight outside of South Africa.

At the end of 1950, Keenan was ranked number one contender to O'Sullivan, Boland was number 2, Dwyer number 7 and Carson number 8. Scotland was indeed well represented in the bantamweight division.

Featherweight

Scottish champion Jim Kenny remained unchallenged throughout the year. He began the year in fine style by knocking out Tommy Burns of Stockton in 3 rounds at Paisley Ice Rink in an eliminator for the British and Empire titles held by Ronnie Clayton of Blackpool. This win surprised many and Kenny followed up with 2 good wins on points. In a highly impressive display, he then knocked out Bert Jackson of Fleetwood in Blackpool in the final eliminator for the titles. Due to an injury to Ronnie Clayton, the championship match was delayed until November. Kenny kept himself busy with 4 further hard fights, winning 3 and drawing the other. When he faced Clayton at the Albert Hall, he was unbeaten in 8 contests in 1950.

Ronnie Clayton turned professional in 1941 and although he was only 27, he had 88 professional fights behind him and had lost only 15 of these contests. He had held the titles since 1947 but had defended only twice due to a lack of top opposition. He had also been European featherweight champion but had lost his title to the current champion, Ray Famechon of France.

Most fans expected a Clayton victory and this is what they got. Kenny was handicapped as he had to have a bad bruise under his right foot cut before he entered the ring and he fractured a finger in round 3. Nevertheless, he gave a good account of himself and lost on points by the narrowest of margins.

Roy Ankrah was born in the Gold Coast, now Ghana, in 1926 but had settled in Glasgow and was a prominent figure on the Scottish fight scene. He was very popular with promoters and was kept very busy. A run of more than 100 straight wins, most of them in Africa, was ended on his London debut when he was disqualified in the third round against Jimmy Murray of Streatham. Ankrah was extremely angry at this decision as he had already floored Murray 14 times before he was disqualified. Ankrah was also a contender for the British Empire featherweight title and had been matched against Jim Kenny prior to the Clayton v Kenny fight but, much to the disappointment of all Scottish fans, the fight had to be cancelled. Ankrah took on Luis Romero in Madrid and stopped him in 6 rounds. In the year, he won 14 of 15 fights and was inundated with offers from promoters in London, Australia and the United States.

Jock Bonas, a professional since 1945, had a mixed career and was not in the same class as Jim Kenny. However, in 1950 he won 12 of his 16 fights, beating some very capable featherweights and rising to a number 7 British ranking.

Gene Caffrey of Glasgow had an amazing 23 fights in the year and incredibly all of these fights took place between January and September. He won 12, drew 2 and lost 9. One of his losses was a knockout by Roy Ankrah.

A new professional in December 1949, Don McTaggart from Paisley was undefeated after 16 fights but ended the year losing on a knockout to George Lamont of Glasgow. Another new professional, Tommy Miller from West Lothian, won all of his 6 contests.

Lightweight

Harry Hughes, a professional since 1944, had held the Scottish lightweight title since 1947 and had defended successfully twice. He had also fought for the British and European lightweight titles in 1949.

In the 1950 eliminator series for the Scottish title, Jackie Marshall from Glasgow outpointed Johnny Flannigan from Whitburn over 10 rounds at the Music Hall in Edinburgh. Marshall was in turn outpointed in the final eliminator by Jim Findlay of Motherwell at Paisley Ice Rink. Hughes defended his title at Paisley and justified his position as favourite when he ran out an easy points winner against Findlay. Hughes won 5 of his 8 fights in the year but none of his opponents were rated in the UK top 10. His highest British ranking was 5 at the beginning of the year at which time Jackie Marshall was ranked 9. However, Scotland had no top 10 fighters by the end of the year.

Jim Findlay won 4 of 7 fights in the year. Flannigan won 2 of 7. Jackie Marshall moved up to welterweight. Motherwell's Neilly Phillips was new to the paid ranks and was unbeaten in 10 fights in 1950.

Welterweight

At the beginning of 1950, Willie Whyte of Glasgow was the top Scottish welterweight and ranked number 7 challenger to British champion Eddie Thomas. Whyte was an experienced professional and had in the past held the Scottish welterweight title and fought a British welterweight title eliminator. He had also fought and lost to Jake Kilrain for the Scottish middleweight title at Celtic Park in 1949. By August he had fought 8 times, losing only 2, both to number 2 British contender Bob Frost of West Ham.

Billy Rattray had won a Scottish title eliminator in 1949 but Scottish promoters showed no interest in staging a Scottish title fight against the holder Ginger Stewart of Hamilton. When Stewart decided to retire and relinquish his title, Willie Whyte was nominated to fight Rattray for the title and the fight was staged at Dunoon in September. Rattray won the decision after a closely fought 12 round contest. Rattray lost only 1 of his 8 fights in 1950.

At the close of the year, Rattray was ranked 5 and Whyte 6 in the UK.

Middleweight

Jake Kilrain had been a professional since 1931 and was a former British welterweight champion. However, he was 36 at the beginning of the year and decided to finish his career. There were no other Scottish middleweights in the same class as Kilrain.

Light Heavyweight

Our leading light heavyweight was Bert Gilroy who had fought boxers of the calibre of Freddie Mills, Bruce Woodcock and Don Cockell. Gilroy was ranked number 6 challenger for the British title when he retired after 18 years of professional boxing. His retirement left a gap in the division as no other Scot was ranked in the British top 20.

Heavyweight

Following Ken Shaw's emigration, George Stern from Glasgow became Scotland's heavyweight hope in 1950. He was unbeaten in 5 contests in the year but defeated only one top 10 fighter. His UK ranking at the end of the year was number 6.

Left – Tommy Gilmour's boxing stable in 1951

"THE WAY TO THE STARS"

Consult Scotland's Premier Boxers' Manager

The "STAR MAKER"

★

TOMMY GILMOUR

who presents for your approval :

PETER KEENAN
British & European bantamweight champion.

WILLIE ARMSTRONG,
Scottish middleweight champion.

JOHNNY FLANNIGAN,
Scottish lightweight champion.

JIM KENNY,
Ex-featherweight champion.

HARRY HUGHES,
Ex-lightweight champion.

WILLIE WHYTE,
Ex-welterweight champion.

NEIL PHILLIPS,
Lightweight contender.

JACKIE MARSHALL,
Welterweight contender.

DANNY MALLOY,
Welterweight prospect.

JOE MURPHY,
Flyweight contender.

BILLY DIXON,
Hard-hitting welter.

JIM McMILLAN,
Classy lightweight.

BOBBY DURNAN,
Featherweight contender.

CHICK BRADY,
Featherweight prospect.

We extend a cordial invitation to boxers, managers, and all connected with the fight game. When in Glasgow, visit our well-equipped gym, where all training facilities will be provided, free of charge. All communications to :

TOMMY GILMOUR,
682 Rutherglen Road, Glasgow, C.5.
Telephone : South 1708,

Gym :
36 Olympia Street, Glasgow, S.E.
Telephone : BRI 3202.

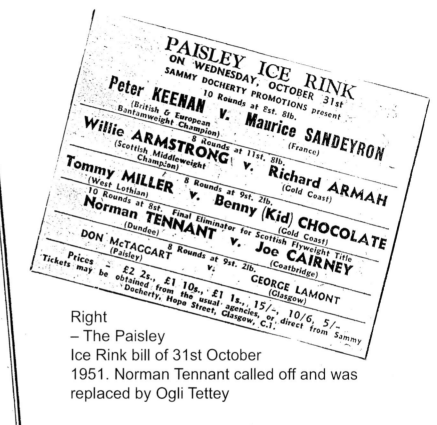

PAISLEY ICE RINK
ON WEDNESDAY, OCTOBER 31st
SAMMY DOCHERTY PROMOTIONS present

Peter KEENAN v. Maurice SANDEYRON
(British & European Bantamweight Champion) (France)
10 Rounds at 8st. 8lb.

Willie ARMSTRONG v. Richard ARMAH
(Scottish Middleweight Champion) (Gold Coast)
8 Rounds at 11st. 8lb.

Tommy MILLER v. Benny (Kid) CHOCOLATE
(West Lothian) (Gold Coast)
8 Rounds at 9st. 2lb.

Norman TENNANT v. Joe CAIRNEY
(Dundee) (Coatbridge)
10 Rounds at 8st. Final Eliminator for Scottish Flyweight Title

DON McTAGGART v. GEORGE LAMONT
(Paisley) (Glasgow)
8 Rounds at 9st. 2lb.

Prices — £2 2s., £1 10s., £1 1s., 15/-, 10/6, 5/-
Tickets may be obtained from the usual agencies, or direct from Sammy Docherty, Hope Street, Glasgow, C.1.

Right
– The Paisley
Ice Rink bill of 31st October
1951. Norman Tennant called off and was
replaced by Ogli Tettey

28

Highlights of 1951

At the turn of the year, there were no Scottish boxers holding British, Empire or European titles. Scottish title holders were as follows.

Flyweight	Norman Tennant (Dundee)
Bantamweight	Eddie Carson (Edinburgh)
Featherweight	Jim Kenny (Polmont)
Lightweight	Harry Hughes (Wishaw)
Welterweight	Billy Rattray (Dundee)
Middleweight	Vacant
Light Heavyweight	Vacant
Heavyweight	Vacant

Flyweight

In January, the final eliminator for the British flyweight title was held at Paisley Ice Rink. Norman Tennant's Scottish flyweight title was also at stake. Vic Herman continued his domination over Tennant, winning on points over 12 rounds. Herman was now Scottish title holder and in line to meet Terry Allen for the vacant British title. The title fight was arranged for 11th June at Leicester. Herman had 3 more fights before his championship date. He won all 3 of the fights which included a points win over the highly rated Frenchman Dante Bini.

Allen fought Jimmy Pearce and Henry Carpenter and beat them both on points. Prior to the title fight, Terry Allen was rematched with Dado Marino for the world title. This fight would go ahead irrespective of the result of his fight against Herman.

Six busloads of fans made the journey from Glasgow to Leicester for the Allen v Herman contest. A close contest was expected. However, Herman was not at his best and seemed in awe of his opponent who had moved in far higher boxing circles and he lost the fight on points over 15 rounds.

Norman Tennant's loss of his Scottish title was his only defeat in 5 outings in 1951. He was later nominated by the Scottish Area Council to fight Joe Cairney of Coatbridge in a final eliminator for the Scottish title. Cairney had fought his way into the British rankings and stopped Joe Murphy in 6 rounds in the first eliminator but had ended the year badly with defeats against Ghanain Ogli Tettey and Teddy Gardner of West Hartlepool, the new number one contender for the British title.

Vic Herman recovered from his defeat by Terry Allen with a points win over Henry Carpenter. He was then matched with Teddy Gardner at Newcastle in a British flyweight title final eliminator but lost on points over 12 rounds. He had 2 more fights in the year but did not win either of them.

At the end of the year Herman was ranked number 3 in the UK and number 6 in the world. Tennant was ranked 4 in the UK and 10 in the world. Cairney was number 6 in the UK and Murphy number 7.

Terry Allen failed to recover his world title from Dado Marino. He lost on points in Honolulu in November. Teddy Gardner of West Hartlepool was waiting to meet him for the British and Empire titles in 1952. Jean Sneyers relinquished his European flyweight title which was now vacant.

Bantamweight

Scottish Champion Eddie Carson had 2 fights in January winning them both in 5 rounds. His challenger for the Scottish title, Jim Dwyer, had 3 fights prior to their meeting but managed only one win. He was outpointed by higher ranked Tommy Proffitt over 10 rounds and also lost a points decision to unbeaten Scottish featherweight Tommy Miller. Carson retained his title with a points win over 12 rounds at the Kelvin Hall in March. He had 4 further fights in the year and lost only to Jean Sneyers who was too classy and stopped the Scot in the eighth. Dwyer had 2 further fights in the year but lost both.

In the lead up to his British title fight, Peter Keenan outboxed a strong Jose Rubio over 8 rounds, stopped Armand Deianna in 6 rounds and came from behind to narrowly outpoint Amleto Falcinelli over 10 rounds. Danny O'Sullivan watched the Falcinelli fight and was confident that he would beat Keenan in the title match. This match took place at Firhill on 9th May in front of a sell-out crowd. O'Sullivan had trouble making the weight and the stewards were criticised for allowing the fight to go ahead. Although Keenan knocked O'Sullivan out in round 6, he too was criticised for not finishing the fight sooner. The consensus was that O'Sullivan had lost the fight on the scales but his fights against Romero and Toweel had also taken their toll.

On the same bill, Carson beat Falcinelli on points over 10 rounds, far more decisively than Keenan had beaten the same opponent. Scottish strength in this division was emphasised by Bobby Boland who was also on the bill and notched up his second victory of the year with a hard fought 10 round points victory over Gaetan Annaloro of Tunisia to reverse his previous year defeat.

The immediate proposal was that Keenan should defend his British title against Boland but Carson protested to the Scottish Area Council that he should be considered. He argued that Boland had already had his chance and failed whilst he, as Scottish champion, had been overlooked in the recent series of eliminators and that Boland had turned down the chance to meet Carson for the Scottish title. The promoters, however, preferred a match against Boland who was a far bigger draw than Carson. Keenan was himself now looking to fight for the European title against Romero or the world title against Toweel.

Keenan's first defence was arranged against Boland and the match was approved by the British Boxing Board of Control. The fight was at Firhill on 27th June. Boland took a fight against Maurice Sandeyron in Paris in the interim and lost on a disqualification in round 4 following a clash of heads. The disqualification was a setback for Boland particularly as it followed so closely after his disqualification against Tommy Proffitt. Boland was arguably the strongest bantamweight in the UK but he did not always channel his strength in the right direction.

Peter Keenan retained his title by stopping Boland in round 12. The referee stepped in as the plucky Dundonian had a very badly cut eye. Keenan had taken advantage of slack defence in the tenth and floored Boland. Keenan then took charge but was relieved when the referee intervened. Boland was a tough fighter and had given Keenan the hardest fight of his career to date. European champion Luis Romero was introduced to the Firhill crowd before the fight and said later that he would return to defend his title against Keenan. The British Boxing Board of Control formally nominated Keenan as challenger for the European title.

Bobby Boland followed his defeat by taking a non-title match against world champion Vic Toweel in South Africa. The result was disastrous. He was knocked out in the first round and did not return to the ring in 1951.

Keenan was matched with Romero for the European title at Firhill on 5th September. Romero had also agreed a fight with Toweel for the world title in South Africa and that fight would be in jeopardy if he lost to Keenan. Romero was a worthy champion who fought regularly and had held the title since August 1949. Keenan too was highly regarded in world circles. The Scot took the title on points over 15 rounds with a brilliant boxing display and the signal was sent to Toweel that Keenan had him in his sights. Keenan had one more fight in the year, drawing with Maurice Sandeyron in a close 10 round contest at Paisley.

The British Boxing Board of Control protested in vain that Romero's fight with Toweel for the world title should not go ahead. The outcome of the match was a 15 round points win for Toweel who had still not fought outside of South Africa. At the turn of the year, Peter Keenan was ranked third in the world after Toweel and Jimmy Carruthers of Australia.

The Scottish Area Council nominated Eddie Carson for the British Title. They also announced that Billy Taylor of Stirling should meet Laurie McShane of Glasgow in a final eliminator for the Scottish title but this fight did not materialise due to lack of promoter interest. McShane did all of his fighting in England and won 5 of his 9 fights in the year. Taylor was a new professional and had won 14 of his 17 fights in the year.

The year end British rankings were Boland 3, Carson 5 and McShane 6.

Featherweight

Scottish champion Jim Kenny had turned professional in 1947 and by the end of 1949 had lost only 4 of 32 contests. He had a superb 1950, losing only to Ronnie Clayton in his British title fight, and his record at the end of 1950 was 5 defeats in 41 contests. His fortune, however, took a turn for the worse in 1951. In his first fight of the year, he was clearly beaten when he lost his Scottish title on points over 12 rounds to George Stewart of Hamilton at the Kelvin Hall. Kenny then travelled to South Africa to fight world bantamweight champion Vic Toweel and was stopped in 7 rounds. He then took on Frank Johnson from Manchester. Johnson had lost only one of 25 professional fights and was destined to become British and Empire lightweight champion. Johnson stopped Kenny in 5 rounds. 3 fights, 3 losses and a year to forget for Jim Kenny.

In April, Tommy Miller from Blackburn in West Lothian met Glaswegian George Lamont in an eliminator for the Scottish title. Miller had won 9 of his 10 professional contests and Lamont had won all of his 3 fights in 1951. Miller took the 10 round points verdict at Ayr Ice Rink. Miller disappointed in the remainder of the year winning only 2 of his subsequent 5 contests. Lamont had one more fight in the year losing on points to young Don McTaggart whom he had previously beaten. McTaggart was unbeaten in 12 fights during the year and had therefore lost only once in 27 professional contests. As he was under 21, however, he was too young to challenge for the Scottish title.

A second eliminator between Gene Caffrey and Dunfermline's Peter Guichan was due. The winner of this match was to face Miller and the eventual winner was to fight Jim Kenny in a final eliminator.

New Scottish champion George Stewart had turned professional in 1948 but had only 28 fights behind him, losing 7, prior to winning the Scottish title. He went on to box Dai Davies, the tough Welshman, in an eliminator for the British featherweight title. Stewart narrowly lost on points over 10 rounds at Firhill in September.

Jock Bonas retired from UK boxing but was to have several fights in Australia in 1952. Jim Kenny's British ranking plummeted but Tommy Miller and George Stewart were now ranked in the UK top 10.

Roy Ankrah outpointed Ronnie Clayton over 15 rounds at Earls Court to take the British Empire featherweight title in April. At the same venue in November, he outpointed British lightweight champion Tommy McGovern of Bermondsey.

Lightweight

In June, Johnny Flannigan outpointed Harry Hughes over 12 rounds at Alloa to win the Scottish lightweight title. Flannigan won 5 of 7 fights in the year and was ranked number 6 in the UK. He was stopped by future British lightweight champion Joe Lucy in his last fight of the year. Hughes had a disappointing year winning only 3 of 8 fights.

Since his Scottish title defeat at the hands of Harry Hughes, Jim Findlay from Wishaw was unbeaten in 5 fights. Findlay beat Neilly Phillips from Wishaw on points over 10 rounds in an eliminator for the Scottish lightweight title at Carntyne Stadium in Glasgow. This was only Phillip's second defeat in 17 professional contests.

Welterweight

Billy Rattray was nominated to fight Cliff Curvis of Swansea in a British welterweight title eliminator. However, Curvis proved too clever and too experienced for Rattray who was knocked out in the second round at Ayr Ice Rink in April. Rattray had previously lost 2 of 3 fights in the first quarter and did not fight again in 1951.

Willie Whyte had a mixed year winning 3 of 6 fights. He performed well when going down on points over 10 rounds to Wally Thom from Birkenhead who became British welterweight champion three months later. Whyte was nominated to fight Jackie Marshall in an eliminator for the Scottish title but Marshall retired.

Middleweight

Willie Armstrong of Port Glasgow fought as a professional for the first time in 1951. He won his first 7 fights in less than 17 rounds of boxing. In his eighth fight, he stopped Dave Finnie of Hawick in 10 rounds at the Sports Ground, Rosyth to win the vacant Scottish middleweight title. Armstrong continued his progress with 5 further wins before he was stopped in 6 rounds by top 10 middleweight Ron Crookes from Sheffield.

Heavyweight

George Stern became a professional in 1948 and had won 15 of his 17 contests by the end of 1950. Hugh McDonald also from Glasgow had been around since 1942 and his fight record read 9 wins, 16 losses, 2 draws at the end of 1950. On 22nd June, Stern won the vacant Scottish heavyweight title when McDonald was disqualified in the seventh round of their title fight at the Recreation Ground, Alloa. Stern was ranked 8 in the UK.

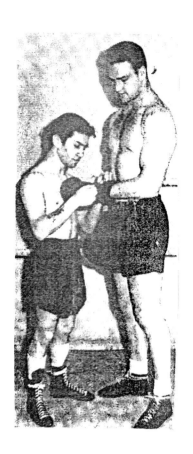

Left – On 4th April 1952, Vic Herman fought Frenchman Jean Binet at Bermondsey, South London. On the same bill was South African heavyweight Lou Strydom. His opponent was Greenock's Jock McVicar who did all of his fighting in London. Herman and Strydom were pictured together in a publicity shot. Strydom was 6 foot 7 inches and weighed in at 15 stones and 4 pounds. Herman was just over 5 foot and weighed just 8 stones and 2 pounds

Right – Jim Kenny was close to the end of his career when he was outpointed by unbeaten Sammy McCarthy at the Empress Hall, Earls Court in November 1952.

Highlights of 1952

At the beginning of 1952, Peter Keenan was the British and European bantamweight champion. No other Scots held major titles. Scottish title holders were as follows.

Flyweight	Vic Herman (Glasgow)
Bantamweight	Eddie Carson (Edinburgh)
Featherweight	George Stewart (Hamilton)
Lightweight	Johnny Flannigan (Whitburn)
Welterweight	Billy Rattray (Dundee)
Middleweight	Willie Armstrong (Glasgow)
Light Heavyweight	Vacant
Heavyweight	George Stern (Glasgow)

Flyweight

The Scottish title eliminator between Norman Tennant and Joe Cairney did not materialise. Tennant had one fight in 1952, losing on points to Johnny Black of Preston. He decided to quit boxing following this defeat and Cairney was therefore nominated to fight Vic Herman for the Scottish title.

Vic Herman was in dazzling form at the beginning of 1952. He fought 6 times in England between January and May and won each time. He returned to Glasgow to appear on the Firhill bill on 21st May against Maurice Sandeyron. Sandeyron had previously fought for the world flyweight title against Rinty Monaghan and had outpointed Terry Allen in London earlier in the year but he was now more of a bantamweight than a flyweight. Herman fought a terrific fight but the Frenchman proved too skilful and won the 10 rounds points decision. Herman's next contest was against another Frenchman, Honore Pratesi, who had fought for the world and European flyweight titles against Terry Allen. The contest was at Porthcawl and Herman took the verdict on points over 10 rounds. His next fight was his first defence of the Scottish title against Joe Cairney at the Kelvin Hall in August.

Since winning his eliminator against Joe Murphy in the previous year, Cairney had fought and lost three times. As he had lost to Ogli Tettey and Tettey had already been defeated by Vic Herman in April, a comfortable win for Herman was expected. However, in a gruelling fight that went the distance, Cairney surprisingly won the title in a very close contest. Cairney had one more contest in the year, outpointing Johnny Summers from Edinburgh. Herman also had one more contest which he won on points.

Jimmy Thomson from Glasgow had won 11 of 14 contests in 1951 and 4 of 6 in 1952. Jimmy Quinn from Kirkintilloch had won 6 of 9 in 1952. They were matched in an eliminator for the Scottish flyweight title on the Kelvin Hall bill in August. Quinn was a comfortable winner on points. At the end of 1952, Scotland had six top 10 UK flyweights. Cairney was 3, Herman 4, Murphy 6, Summers 7, Quinn 8 and Thomson 9. Summers, however, did not box again.

The European flyweight title was vacant. The title had been relinquished by Jean Sneyers who had weight difficulties and won by Teddy Gardner who had knocked out Louis Skena from France. Gardner, however, retired following his defeat by Jake Tuli from South Africa in their British Empire title fight. Terry Allen had lost his British and Empire titles to Gardner in March but regained the British title against Eric Marsden in October. The world title was now held by Yoshio Shirai of Japan.

Bantamweight

Vic Toweel was world and Empire champion. Peter Keenan was British and European champion. Keenan travelled to South Africa to fight Toweel on 26th January for the Empire and world titles. Toweel was a 3 to 1 on favourite in front of a 25,000 crowd. Unfortunately, Keenan was not at his best and was well beaten on points over 15 rounds.

Keenan's next date was at Firhill in May where he was to defend his European bantamweight crown against Jean Sneyers. Keenan had previously beaten Sneyers on points when they were both fighting as flyweights. Keenan was on top in the first 4 rounds but tragedy struck in the fifth when he tore a cartilage in his right knee and was unable to continue. The victorious Belgian promised promoter Sammy Docherty that he would return to Glasgow to defend his title against Keenan when he was fit.

Keenan's comeback fight was at Paisley Ice Rink in October. His opponent was Italian Amleto Falcinelli who was well known to Scottish fans and had previously lost to Keenan. Keenan suffered further misfortune with any eye injury that forced him to retire in the fifth round. This was to be his last fight of a year to forget. 3 fights, 3 losses. He was due to defend his British bantamweight title against Frankie Williams from Birkenhead but the fight had to be postponed until 1953.

As Laurie McShane was now fighting as a featherweight, Scottish champion Eddie Carson defended his title against challenger Billy Taylor of Stirling at the Music Hall, Edinburgh in February. He stopped Taylor in 2 rounds. He was rematched with the same opponent in his fourth defence of the title in August at the Kelvin Hall and this time knocked him out in the tenth round. Carson had 2 other fights in the year but lost both. Although nominated by the Scottish Area Council in the previous year, he was not recognised as a contender for the British title although he finished the year as number 3 challenger to Keenan. Taylor had won 14 of his 17 fights in 1951 but following his second defeat by Carson, he had just one more fight before retiring. Jim Dwyer also retired.

Bobby Boland's form faltered in 1952 and he won only 4 of his 11 contests. His British ranking dropped to 9.

Vic Toweel was sensationally deposed as world and Empire bantamweight champion in November. He was knocked out in the first round of his contest with Australian champion Jimmy Carruthers at his favourite Johannesburg venue. Jean Sneyers never did defend his European title as, due to continuing weight problems, he had to relinquish the title which remained vacant at the end of the year.

Featherweight

The Caffrey v Guichan eliminator did not take place. As Guichan retired and Caffrey's results took a tumble, Tommy Miller met Jim Kenny in the final eliminator for the Scottish featherweight title at Falkirk Ice Rink in May. Kenny had declined since reaching the peak of his form in 1950 but had won both his 1952 fights inside the distance. Miller had won 1 and drawn 2 but was still considered to be favourite to win. The fight turned into a terrific scrap which Miller won on points over 10 rounds.

The fight for the Scottish title was arranged for August at the Kelvin Hall. The fight was also to double as a semi-final eliminator for the British title. George Stewart had 4 fights in 1952 prior to his eliminator against Miller and managed only one win, against Don McTaggart. He was also to lose his title to Miller who was outstanding on the night and won easily on points over 12 rounds. Miller's opponent in the final eliminator was Freddie King from Wandsworth. Miller had 4 more hard contests before his date with King and he won them all. The final eliminator was held at the Empress Hall, Earls Court in early December and Miller was involved in yet another great fight. King hit Miller with everything but Miller came back and King was saved by the bell in the eleventh round. The unfortunate Miller, however, lost the 12 round points verdict. This was his only loss in 10 contests in the year.

Eliminators for Miller's Scottish title were held in August. Don McTaggart outpointed Jim Travers of Airdrie at the Kelvin Hall on the same August bill on which Miller won the title. McTaggart had a reasonable year, winning 6 and drawing one of his 9 contests. In the second eliminator, Chic Brady stopped fellow Glaswegian George Lamont in the first round at Kirkcaldy Ice Rink.

George Stewart had 3 more quality fights in the year but lost them all. His retirement followed. Jim Kenny did outpoint British champion Ronnie Clayton but lost 3 of 4 other fights. George Lamont had 2 fights and lost both. Lawrie McShane won 5 out of 7. Travers won 5 of 10. Miller was clearly the number one featherweight in Scotland but McTaggart was leading the challengers.

Roy Ankrah retained his Empire featherweight title against Ronnie Clayton at Nottingham in February. At the same venue in June, he was matched with European featherweight champion Raymond Famechon of France for his title in a fight that doubled as an eliminator for the world title held by New Yorker Sandy Saddler. Famechon was no stranger to the Nottingham Arena. He had originally won the European title there in 1948 against Ronnie Clayton and had also defended the title successfully at Nottingham against the same opponent in April. Ankrah was not at his best and lost the fight on points over 15 rounds. Clayton remained British champion having stopped Dai Davies in 5 rounds in his fourth defence of the title.

Lightweight

The old war horse Harry Hughes outpointed Billy Elliott from Glasgow over 10 rounds at the Music Hall, Edinburgh in an eliminator for the Scottish lightweight title in January. In February, Johnny Flannigan relinquished his Scottish title and retired due to health reasons. His announcement came two days before the final eliminator between Harry Hughes and Jim Findlay was due to take place. It was too late to alter the status of the fight and it was agreed that the eliminator should proceed. However, Hughes did not make the weight and was out of the eliminator. The fight went ahead at catchweight and Findlay won by a knockout in the third round. Findlay was then matched with Neilly Phillips for the vacant title at the Kelvin Hall in March and took the title by stopping his rival in the eighth round.

Findlay was the best Scottish lightweight around but he could not mix it with the best from England and won only 2 of his 4 further fights in the year. Both Hughes and Phillips retired before the end of the year.

Welterweight

Billy Rattray relinquished his Scottish title in July 1952 because of weight difficulties. His main rival Willie Whyte had been a professional since 1946 and was a previous holder of the title. He was now 35 but keen to win the title for a second time. He was matched against Danny Malloy from Bonnybridge who was 12 years his junior and had a record of 11 wins and 4 losses since turning professional in 1951. In August, Whyte was the victor on points over 12 rounds at Kirkcaldy Ice Rink, his experience proving to be the telling factor.

Middleweight

Willie Armstrong was unchallenged in Scotland this year. He fought only 3 times, losing once.

Heavyweight

George Stern was also unchallenged in Scotland in the year. He also fought 3 times, losing twice. His UK ranking was 9.

Highlights of 1953

At the beginning of 1953, Peter Keenan was the British bantamweight champion. No other Scots held major titles. Scottish title holders were as follows.

Flyweight	Joe Cairney (Coatbridge)
Bantamweight	Eddie Carson (Edinburgh)
Featherweight	Tommy Miller (West Lothian)
Lightweight	Jim Findlay (Motherwell)
Welterweight	Willie Whyte (Glasgow)
Middleweight	Willie Armstrong (Glasgow)
Light Heavyweight	Vacant
Heavyweight	George Stern (Glasgow)

Flyweight

On 28th January, Jimmy Quinn beat Joe Cairney on points over 12 rounds at Paisley Ice Rink to win the Scottish flyweight title. Quinn then tried his luck in the north of England but lost points decisions in both of his fights there. He returned to Scotland and, on the June bill at Firhill, he retained his Scottish title by knocking out Jimmy Thomson of Glasgow in the twelfth round. To complete his year, Quinn was enticed to Porthcawl to fight unbeaten Dai Dower who stopped him in 7 rounds.

Dower also stopped Joe Cairney in 4 rounds and outpointed Joe Murphy later in the year. Murphy fought twice only in 1953 and lost both contests. Cairney fought 3 times, lost 2 and drew 1. Thomson won 3 of 6 fights in the year.

Vic Herman won his first contest of the year and then fought Empire champion Jake Tuli to whom he lost on points over 10 rounds. There followed a trip to the Far East. He won one contest and lost one in Bangkok before travelling on to Tokyo where he was stopped in the tenth round by world champion, Yoshio Shirai. He had no further fights in 1953.

Despite the lack of activity and success of Scottish flyweights in 1953, they were all ranked in the British top 10 at the end of the year.

Terry Allen and Jake Tuli remained British and Empire champions respectively. Louis Skena was the new European flyweight champion. Yoshio Shirai successfully defended his world flyweight title twice during the year

Bantamweight

Peter Keenan duly defended his British bantamweight title for the second time. His opponent was Frankie Williams from Birkenhead and the venue was Paisley Ice Rink on 28th January. Keenan successfully held on to the title by stopping his challenger in the seventh round. This was Keenan's first success since September 1951. Next up was Stan Rowan from Liverpool at the Kelvin Hall on 18th March. The outcome of this 10 round contest which went the distance was bizarre. Rowan went to Keenan's corner at the end of the fight and the referee came over and raised his hand. However, after the referee had left the ring, he discovered that he had raised the wrong hand. The referee's card clearly showed Keenan as the winner and the MC had to announce the error and that Keenan was the winner. The original decision had been well received by the crowd but the amended result brought a storm of protest from the crowd who thought that Rowan had won.

Keenan was matched with old foe, Maurice Sandeyron, for the European bantamweight title that had been vacated by Jean Sneyers. Keenan had beaten the Frenchman in 1950 and drawn with him in 1951. The fight was at Firhill where Keenan had lost the title to Sneyers. The early rounds went Sandeyron's way. Keenan came into the contest in the fifth when a cut appeared between Sandeyron's eyes. Sandeyron came back in the later rounds but it was Keenan who finished strongest and did just enough to clinch the points verdict.

Keenan was considering offers to fight unbeaten Empire flyweight champion Jake Tuli from South Africa and Nigerian featherweight Hogan Bassey. He was, however, anxious for a showdown with world and Empire champion Jimmy Carruthers who had gone back to Johannesburg in March and given Vic Toweel a return fight. Carruthers recorded another emphatic win with a tenth round knockout in front of 32,000 people.

In Britain, the biggest draw for a British title fight would be Keenan against unbeaten John Kelly from Belfast. Kelly had 19 straight professional wins and he had just stopped Bunty Doran to win the Northern Ireland bantamweight title.

Keenan was ranked number 5 in the world after Carruthers, Robert Cohen from France, Pappy Gault from the United States and Vic Toweel. Cohen had lost only 1 of 29 fights and had beaten Pappy Gault on points in Paris in April and was the number one contender for the European title. However, when the British title defence was agreed against John Kelly in Belfast in October, the European Boxing Union agreed that the fight should also be for the European title. They also nominated Cohen to fight the winner. At this time, Keenan was negotiating a world title fight with Carruthers in Australia but had not agreed terms.

Perhaps Keenan had too much on his mind when he travelled to Belfast but he fought the most ineffective fight of his career and Kelly was crowned the new British and European champion after a 15 round points victory. Keenan had one more fight in 1953, at the Albert Hall against contender Ron Johnson of Bethnal Green. He fought cautiously but stopped his fellow contender in the seventh.

Hugh Riley from Edinburgh had turned professional in 1950. He won 7 of his first 8 contests before leaving for an extended stay in the United States and Canada. He fought in both countries and returned to Scotland to fight Eddie Carson for the Scottish bantamweight title. The contest at Leith resulted in a points win for Carson who had now defended the title 5 times. Following this defeat, Riley once again disappeared from the UK boxing scene.

Carson had lost his previous fight this year. He next took on top 10 bantamweight Jimmy Brewer of King's Cross who had lost only 7 of 41 contests. This was a risky match as Carson hoped to figure in the next series of eliminators for the British bantamweight title. However, Carson performed well to stop Brewer in 7 rounds.

Peter Keenan was ranked 2 behind Kelly and Carson was now ranked 7. Bobby Boland moved up to featherweight.

Featherweight

The Scottish featherweight division was to suffer in 1953. The final eliminator between McTaggart and Brady did not materialise as McTaggart moved up to lightweight and Brady ceased to box. Jim Kenny was nominated to fight Tommy Miller for the Scottish title but after only one fight in the year, Kenny retired due to a combination of ill health and weight problems. Miller had to travel to get fights and lost points decisions in Belfast and London. He also turned down a non-title fight against Roy Ankrah. In September, after several months of inactivity, Miller also decided to retire leaving the Scottish featherweight title vacant.

Few of the other Scottish featherweights managed to find fights in 1953. Lawrie McShane won 2 of 7. New professional, Charlie Hill, won 8 of 9 contests. His only defeat was on a disqualification for a low blow.

Roy Ankrah remained Empire featherweight champion and was unbeaten in 8 contests in the year.

Lightweight

Scottish champion Jim Findlay may have thought that he had no challengers for his title following the retirement of Harry Hughes and Neilly Phillips. However, Don McTaggart had moved up to lightweight in 1952 and was matched with Findlay for the Scottish title at Paisley Ice Rink in January. McTaggart was good enough to take the title on points over 12 rounds. Findlay subsequently retired leaving the way for McTaggart to consolidate his position as the outstanding lightweight in Scotland. He made no inroads into the British title scene, however, as he lost 3 of his 4 remaining bouts in the year.

Welterweight

Danny Malloy was rematched with Willie Whyte for the Scottish welterweight title. No Scottish promoter took the fight and the defence took place at the King's Hall, Belfast in October. Malloy exacted his revenge by stopping Whyte in the fifth round and becoming the new champion. Whyte decided to retire and this left Malloy with no competition in Scotland.

Malloy had lost to Aldgate's Lew Lazar in May. Lazar was a formidable opponent having lost only 1 of 28 professional contests and he was later to fight twice for the British and Empire titles. The defeat was therefore no disgrace. Later in the year, Malloy was knocked out in the third round by British champion Wally Thom at Leeds.

Middleweight

Willie Armstrong had a quiet year winning only 1 of 4 contests. There was no Scottish opposition on the horizon. He was ranked 9 in the UK.

Heavyweight

George Stern had 2 fights in the year, losing both. He was disqualified against Joe Bygraves who went on to become Empire heavyweight champion and who retained his title against Henry Cooper and Dick Richardson. Hugh Ferns was more active with 8 contests, winning 5. Two of his defeats were to Joe Bygraves. Hugh McDonald was inactive.

Highlights of 1954

At the beginning of 1954, there were no Scottish boxers holding British, Empire or European titles. Scottish title holders were as follows.

Flyweight	Jimmy Quinn (Kirkintilloch)
Bantamweight	Eddie Carson (Edinburgh)
Featherweight	Vacant
Lightweight	Don McTaggart (Paisley)
Welterweight	Danny Malloy (Bonnybridge)
Middleweight	Willie Armstrong (Glasgow)
Light Heavyweight	Vacant
Heavyweight	George Stern (Glasgow)

Flyweight

Jimmy Quinn retained his Scottish title against Jimmy Thomson at the Kelvin Hall in February. Thomson had to retire in the fourth round. Thomson had 3 more fights in 1954, winning 1 and losing 2.

In December, Quinn defended his title against Joe Cairney and achieved the same fourth round stoppage to retain his title. Cairney had not fought for 13 months and decided to retire following this defeat.

Vic Herman managed a creditable draw against Danny O'Sullivan at the Albert Hall in February. His final professional contest was against Peter Keenan at the Kelvin Hall on 26th May.

Joe Murphy was inactive during the year and was never again to fight in the United Kingdom.

Quinn was the only notable Scottish flyweight at the end of the year. However, aside from his two championship wins; he won only 1 fight out of 4 and was ranked number 4 in the UK at the end of the year.

Louis Skena had relinquished his European title in April owing to weight difficulties. Terry Allen unsuccessfully fought for the title in September and following this defeat, he too announced his retirement leaving the British title vacant. Welshman Dai Dower had won the Empire crown from Jake Tuli in October and was number one contender for the British title. Pascual Perez of Argentina won the world title from Yoshio Shirai in Tokyo.

Bantamweight

In January, Peter Keenan began the year with an 8 round points victory over Frenchman Robert Meunier in Nottingham. Meunier was the only man to have defeated Robert Cohen. Keenan was then matched with Eddie Carson for the Scottish bantamweight title at the Kelvin Hall on 24th February. The outcome was a 12 round points win for Keenan,

On February 27th, Robert Cohen of France convincingly won the European bantamweight title by knocking out John Kelly at the King's Hall in Belfast. The Scottish Area Council immediately nominated Keenan as sole contender to fight Kelly in a return for the British title. Another Irishman, George O'Neill, had beaten Eddie Carson in 1953 and was also a leading contender.

On 7th April, Cohen came to Glasgow and fought Eddie Carson at the Kelvin Hall. The European champion emerged from the contest with a 10 round points win. Carson fought well and came out of the fight with great credit. Peter Keenan entered the ring and challenged Cohen to defend his European title against him. George O'Neill was also on the bill but an 8 round points defeat did not help his claims for a British title fight with Kelly.

On 10th April, Kelly took on Belgian champion Pierre Cossemyns in Belfast and was knocked out in the ninth round. Two weeks later, the British Boxing Board of Control announced that Kelly should defend against Keenan. Keenan had one more contest before the title fight and that was against his old foe Vic Herman at the Kelvin Hall in May. This fight was anything but memorable and the referee had to call for more action on three separate occasions. Keenan won on points over 10 rounds but it was a poor display from both boxers.

On May 2nd, Jimmy Carruthers defended his World bantamweight title against Chamrern Songkitrat of Thailand at the National Stadium in Bangkok in front of a crowd of 55,000 in the first world title fight ever staged in Thailand. The outdoor contest was affected by heavy rain and both boxers fought in their bare feet. Carruthers was the winner on points in his third defence of the title and remained unbeaten as a professional. On May 16th, Carruthers surprisingly announced his retirement from boxing leaving both the world and Empire titles vacant.

On 18th September, Robert Cohen became world champion when he defeated Chamrern Songkitrat on points over 15 rounds at the National Stadium, Bangkok. The crowd on this occasion was 69,819. Cohen finished the year by stopping Roy Ankrah in 3 rounds in Paris in December.

There had been some concern that John Kelly could no longer make bantamweight. This worry proved unfounded and on 21st September Peter Keenan regained the British bantamweight title by knocking out Kelly in the sixth round at Paisley Ice Rink. On this occasion, he performed brilliantly. He relinquished his Scottish title and was immediately challenged for the British title by Eddie Carson. However, the British Boxing Board of Control nominated George O'Neill as the official contender and the fight was fixed for 11th December at the King's Hall, Belfast.

In his third and last fight of the year, Carson took on unbeaten Spaniard Pedro Paris at Leith Eldorado in October and lost on points over 8 rounds. Carson had lost all of his 3 fights in 1954.

Peter Keenan won well in his title defence against George O'Neill. He won on points over 15 rounds and now had his sights on Cohen for the world and European titles. The Empire title was also vacant and this was also on his hit list for 1955.

Featherweight

Chic Brogan had turned professional in 1950 and had a chequered professional career. By the end of 1953, he had 18 professional contests and had lost 8. He was nominated to fight Gene Caffrey in an eliminator for the Scottish title and won the contest on points at Edinburgh Music Hall on 23rd March. Prior to his title fight against Charlie Hill, Brogan had 8 contests in 1954, winning 4, drawing 1 and losing 3.

Before his contest with Brogan, Charlie Hill had 8 straight wins in 1954, improving his record to 16 wins in 17 outings. The title fight was at Paisley Ice Rink on 7th December. Hill was a hot favourite and justified his favouritism with a 12 round points win. He finished the year as number 5 challenger for the British title.

George Lamont had 2 fights which he lost and then retired. Laurie McShane won 1 of 4 contests.

Sammy McCarthy from Stepney had taken the British title from Ronnie Clayton at the White City Stadium in June. McCarthy was tough and had lost only 3 of 37 contests to such renowned names as Jean Sneyers, Hogan Bassey and Ray Famechon. Billy Kelly had also taken the Empire crown from Roy Ankrah in October and Ray Famechon had taken the European title from Jean Sneyers in September. Hill was a great prospect and was aiming for fights with these leading names in 1955.

Lightweight

Scottish Champion Don McTaggart received no Scottish challenge in 1954. He won his first 5 fights and then faced Central Area champion Johnny Butterworth from Rochdale. He lost the contest on points over 10 rounds in Manchester. He concluded the year with an 8 round draw in Belfast and was ranked number 7 in the UK.

Joe Lucy from Mile End had won the British lightweight title in 1953. He had only 3 fights in 1954 and lost 2 of these, both to Johnny Butterworth.

Welterweight

Scottish Champion Danny Malloy announced his retirement in August. The main contenders for the vacant title were Danny Harvey and Roy MacGregor from Glasgow and Jimmy Croll from Dundee. MacGregor had been around since 1947 but had an undistinguished professional career. Croll had been a professional since 1953 and had lost only 3 of his 17 professional contests. An eliminator between MacGregor and Croll was made at the Caird Hall in October and was something of a damp squib as Croll was disqualified in the second round for illegal use of the head.

The fight between MacGregor and Harvey for the vacant title took place at Paisley Ice Rink in December. Harvey had turned professional in 1952 and had a record of 16 wins in 20 fights. He had, however, lost to Jimmy Croll in 7 rounds. MacGregor won the title on points over 12 rounds in a highly entertaining contest. Croll had two more contests before the end of the year and won both.

Neither MacGregor nor Harvey had a British ranking but Jimmy Croll was just inside the top 10 at the year end.

Middleweight

Willie Armstrong remained unchallenged in Scotland and was ranked number 5 in the UK. He had 8 fights in the year and lost 2. One defeat was in Berlin to Gustav Scholz, the referee stopping the fight in the eighth round. Scholz entered the contest unbeaten in 54 professional fights and was a future European middleweight champion.

Heavyweight

George Stern fought twice and lost twice in the year. Hugh Ferns fought 4 times and lost 3. Hugh McDonald had 1 contest which he lost.

Highlights of 1955

At the beginning of 1955, Peter Keenan was British bantamweight champion. Scottish title holders were as follows.

Flyweight	Jimmy Quinn (Kirkintilloch)
Bantamweight	Vacant
Featherweight	Charlie Hill (Cambuslang)
Lightweight	Don McTaggart (Paisley)
Welterweight	Roy MacGregor (Glasgow)
Middleweight	Willie Armstrong (Glasgow)
Light Heavy	Vacant
Heavyweight	George Stern (Glasgow)

Flyweight

In February, Dai Dower won the British flyweight title and retained his Empire crown against Eric Marsden of St. Helens. He then won and lost the European flyweight title and successfully defended his Empire title against Jake Tuli before the end of the year. Jimmy Quinn was the Scottish champion throughout the year. He had only 3 fights during the year, all of them outside of Scotland, and he won these comfortably. Quinn had just missed out on fighting for the vacant British title but was now rated number one challenger to Dower for the title.

Dick Currie was the great Scottish flyweight hope when he made his professional debut on 10th May at the Kelvin Hall. He knocked out Mickey King of Belfast in 2 minutes 39 seconds of the first round to confirm his potential. However, he came unstuck in his second fight when he was stopped in 3 rounds following a terrific left hook to the jaw from the unranked flyweight, Bobby Robinson of Newcastle. He had 3 further fights during the year and won all of them but his reputation had already taken a knock.

Frankie Jones also turned professional in 1955. He had 3 fights in Scotland and won all of them. His second win was on points against Bobby Robinson.

Vic Glenn was born in Dundee but lived in Stepney. He was ranked number 4 in the UK but his claims to fight for the Scottish flyweight title were ignored by the Scottish Area Council.

Pascual Perez remained world Champion. Young Martin had defeated Dai Dower to win the European title.

Bantamweight

The world title holder was Robert Cohen of France. Cohen had relinquished his European title which was now vacant. Keenan had hopes of fighting for the vacant title and also of taking on Cohen. However, when Cohen suffered a broken jaw at the beginning of the year, Keenan agreed a 3-fight, 90 day tour of Australia. Following the retirement of undefeated world and Empire champion Jimmy Carruthers, Bobby Sinn was the new Australian number one and he was earmarked to be Keenan's first opponent for the vacant Empire title.

Peter Keenan had started the year with a 10 round points victory over Frenchman Dante Bini in Glasgow. On 28th March, he won the vacant British Empire title when he clearly outpointed Bobby Sinn over 12 rounds in Sydney in front of a crowd of 13,500. He was outpointed in his other fights in Australia against French Champion Andre Valignat and the experienced Italian Roberto Spina and these defeats dented his European and world title ambitions.

Following his return to Scotland, Keenan defended his British Empire title against Jake Tuli of South Africa at Cathkin Park in front of a 30,000 crowd on 14th September. Keenan was knocked down 3 times in the first round, was down several more times in the fight, suffered a badly cut eye and was well behind when he came back in round 14 with a superb punch to knock out Tuli and retain his title.

In November, Keenan outpointed the highly rated Belgian Pierre Cossemyns. His last opponent of the year was another top Frenchman, Emile Chemama, who had beaten Young Martin and Hogan Bassey as well as Sandeyron, Bini and Cossemyns. In Marseilles in December, the Scot lost a 10 round points verdict.

John Smillie arrived on the professional scene on 17th March and had 9 fights in the year, winning 8 and drawing the other. He quickly progressed up the rankings and finished the year as number 7 bantamweight in the UK.

In October, Mario D'Agata won the vacant European bantamweight title.

Featherweight

Charlie Hill was the Scottish featherweight champion at the beginning of the year. He had lost only one fight in 18 and continued on his winning ways with 5 further victories, all on points, during the year. There was paper talk of him fighting European champion, Ray Famechon of France, or fighting Billy Kelly of Belfast for his British and Empire titles. Kelly had taken the titles from Sammy McCarthy of Stepney in January. In the second half of the year, Hill was matched with former champion McCarthy in a final eliminator for the British title. The fight was, however, postponed several times following illness and injuries sustained by Hill.

As a result of the delays, the Board nominated McCarthy to fight Kelly for the title. McCarthy was, however, having weight difficulties and decided to move up to lightweight. The Board subsequently announced that Hill should face Kelly for the title. Contracts were signed in December for a January showdown in Belfast.

Hard-hitting Matt Fulton from Glasgow and Dundonian Dave Croll were up and coming featherweights. In the year, Croll was unbeaten in 6 fights. Fulton lost 2 out of 12. Chic Brogan lost all 3 of his contests in the year and reverted to bantamweight.

Ray Famechon lost his European title to Spaniard Fred Galiana in November. In the same month Billy Kelly lost his Empire title to Hogan Bassey of Nigeria.

Lightweight

On 15th December, Don McTaggart forfeited his Scottish title following his emigration to Australia.

Welterweight

Roy MacGregor was Scottish champion at the start of the year. The main contenders for the title were Jimmy Croll and Danny Harvey, both of whom were beaten by MacGregor in 1954. On 20th December, Jimmy Croll won the title when he beat MacGregor on points over 12 rounds at the Caird Hall, Dundee. Croll won 7 of his 9 fights in the year and ended the year as number 8 UK welterweight. MacGregor retired following a disqualification in his next fight in Belfast on 31st December.

Wishaw's Jimmy McGuinness won his first 8 professional fights but came unstuck in his ninth fight when he had to retire against Barnsley's Johnny Spittal whom he had already outpointed in fight number 8.

Middleweight

Scottish champion, Willie Armstrong, was given the opportunity to fight in Milan on 29th January. He was matched with top Italian Allesandro D'Ottavio to whom he lost on points over 8 rounds. Armstrong was having difficulty finding opponents at middleweight and had to take fights against light-heavyweights. He lost 3 of his 5 fights in 1955 and his British ranking fell from 5 to 8.

Heavyweight

Scottish champion, George Stern, retired early in the year to join the Glasgow police force. A regular opponent over the years was Hugh McDonald, a 17 stone giant from Glasgow who worked as a chargehand in Peter Keenan's bar. During the year, McDonald was stopped in 6 rounds by Joe Erskine and knocked out by Brian London, both formidable opponents. Hugh Ferns, the other leading Scottish heavyweight, was disqualified in the second round of his fight with Henry Cooper following a low blow. He did, however, beat Dick Richardson who was disqualified for illegal use of his head in front of a 14,000 crowd in Cardiff. Neither Scot was ranked.

Highlights of 1956

Peter Keenan remained the main man on the Scottish boxing scene and began the year as British and Empire bantamweight champion.

Flyweight

In January, Scottish Champion Jimmy Quinn's manager asked the British Boxing Board of Control to consider Quinn as the leading contender to Dai Dower for his British title. His request was rejected.

Meanwhile, Dick Currie had a disastrous start to the year. He was clearly outpointed at the Tower Circus, Blackpool by Malcolm McLeod over 8 rounds on 13th January. Frankie Jones followed him into the same ring against the same opponent on 17th February and won convincingly on points. Although this confirmed Jones above Currie in the rankings and his manager, Joe Gans, asked the Scottish Area Council to nominate Jones as the sole contender for the Scottish flyweight title, it was Dick Currie who fought and won the Scottish title on 2nd May, beating Jimmy Quinn on points over 12 rounds at the Kelvin Hall. Promoter Sammy Docherty quickly approached Dai Dower on behalf of Currie and asked for a title match which did not materialise as the Board deemed Currie to be too inexperienced to fight the world number 3 for the British title.

The Scottish Area Council had already decided that Currie's first defence should be against Jones. Both boxers had 2 more contests which they won before the championship fight took place at Firhill on 19th September. Jones beat Dave Moore and Vic Glenn. Currie beat Colin Clitheroe and Frenchman Roland Roy. The title fight was also given recognition as a final eliminator for the British title. At the end of 12 rounds, the referee awarded the fight to Jones who became the new Scottish champion. The referee's decision was condemned by the Scottish Area Council as none of the Council members agreed with the decision.

The British rankings now showed Jones as number 2 to Dower, Currie number 4, Quinn number 5 and Glenn number 6.

Jimmy Quinn followed up his fight with Dick Currie with a draw against Vic Glenn but was stopped by Len Reece in his next fight in December. Currie had one further fight, defeating Francisco Carreno of Spain. Both Quinn and Glenn retired from boxing.

Bantamweight

There was nobody to touch Peter Keenan in the UK. Keenan hinted that he would be happy to defend his titles against John Smillie or Dai Dower. Talks did take place with Dower but the Welshman was unhappy with the money on offer and thought he could obtain a bigger purse as a leading contender for the world flyweight title. Keenan's first fight of 1956 was on 22nd October in Sydney. He retained his Empire title by stopping new Australian champion

Kevin James in the second round. This was an impressive win against a southpaw who, at 5 foot 10 inches, was the tallest bantamweight in the world. He followed this in November with a 12 round points win over European number 7, Federico Scarponi of Italy, in Melbourne. In December, he fought Al Asuncion in Manila and was knocked out for the first time in his career. This defeat put paid to any hope that he had of a world title fight with Mario D'Agata of Italy who had won the title from Robert Cohen in June.

On 27th June, John Smillie outpointed George Dormer of West Ham over 10 rounds at the Kelvin Hall in a British bantamweight title eliminator. He was now in line to face Keenan but because of Keenan's travels, this fight was not to materialise until 1957. Smillie had 5 further fights in 1956 and won them all. He finished the year as number 2 British bantamweight behind Peter Keenan.

On 20th June, Malcolm Grant beat Chic Brogan on points over 12 rounds to win the Scottish bantamweight title in Glasgow. In a rematch on 19th September, Brogan outpointed Grant over 12 rounds to take the title from him. Brogan won 3 of 4 fights and Grant 5 of 6 fights in 1956. Their only defeat was against each other. Brogan had a year end ranking of 6. Malcolm Grant retired.

Billy Rafferty made his professional debut during the year and won all of his 5 fights.

Featherweight

On 4th February, Charlie Hill became the first Scot since 1937 to win the British featherweight title when he outpointed Billy Kelly of Belfast over 15 rounds in Belfast. The fight was close and Kelly thought that he had done enough to win. The home crowd also disagreed with the decision and showed their disapproval by throwing chairs and bottles and engaging in wholesale brawls resulting in a hospital count of seven. Following a complaint against the decision by the Northern Ireland Area Council, the referee was ordered to appear before the British Board of Control but the complaint was dismissed.

Hill fans and promoters were now clamouring for an Empire title tilt against Hogan Bassey. However, when the dust had settled, there was a rematch with Kelly set for Cathkin Park in August. Kelly had taken further fights before the rematch and sustained an eye injury which caused him to withdraw from the fight with Hill. Hill took 3 more summer fights and won all of them. He was then inactive until December due to a nose operation.

Matt Fulton, a close friend of Charlie Hill, was unbeaten in 6 contests in 1956 and Bobby Neill was unbeaten in 12 in his professional career when they met on 19th September at Firhill in an eliminator for the British featherweight title and also for the vacant Scottish featherweight title. Fulton was forced to retire in round 8 and Neill became Scottish champion. In his next fight, Neill stopped former European champion Ray Famechon of France.

Hill was matched with Neill in a non-title fight on 4th December at Harringay Arena in London. Sensationally, Neill battered Hill to defeat in the first round. Neill was then nominated to fight Jimmy Brown of Belfast in a final eliminator in the new year, the winner meeting Hill for the title. Hill's rematch with Kelly would not now take place. Brown had won his 19 professional fights, 16 inside the distance. Neill had won his 15 professional fights, 12 inside the distance. At the turn of the year, Neill was ranked behind Hill and Brown with Matt Fulton a further two places behind Neill.

Dave Croll lost 3 of 9 fights in the year but was not ranked.

Lightweight

Arthur Donnachie of Greenock made his professional debut in March and won all 10 of his fights in 1956.

Welterweight

Danny Harvey retired at the age of 24. Jimmy Croll lost only 1 of 8 fights in 1956 and his ranking improved to number 4 in the UK by the end of the year. Jimmy McGuinness won 5 of 7 but was still unranked.

Middleweight

The Scottish Area Council had requested that Walloping Willie Armstrong be considered as a contender for the British title held by Pat McAteer of Birkenhead despite the fact that his UK ranking was number 7. However, Armstrong was given the opportunity to fight McAteer in a non-title bout in Liverpool on May 10th. Armstrong took the fight but was outclassed and knocked out in the 4th round and that ended his chance of being considered as a contender.

Armstrong moved up to light heavyweight and was back in the ring within 3 weeks. He lost 3 of 8 fights in 1956.

Len Mullen turned professional during the year and won 3 of his 4 fights.

Left – Tommy Gilmour's boxing stable in 1957.

Above – The Nottingham Ice Rink bill of 9th December 1957.

Below – Top North of Scotland promoter George Grant.

Highlights of 1957

At the beginning of 1957, Peter Keenan was British and Empire bantamweight champion and Charlie Hill was British featherweight champion. Keenan was Britain's longest reigning title holder.

Flyweight

Dai Dower was the British and Empire flyweight champion. He was due to defend his British title against Frankie Jones but Dower had his eye on a world title shot at unbeaten Pascual Perez of Argentina. Dower also turned down an overweight match against Dick Currie. The Empire committee nominated Jones, Dennis Adams of South Africa and Pat Supple of Canada as the leading contenders for the Empire flyweight title.

On 9th March, Dick Currie decided to quit the ring as he could no longer make the flyweight limit and he had no desire to fight as a bantamweight.

On 30th March, Dower fought Perez for the world title and was knocked out in the first round. Although Dower was under contract to fight Frankie Jones in Glasgow, he decided that he could no longer combine boxing with his army duties and would not fight again until he was demobbed in late 1958. This stance was of course unacceptable to the British Boxing Board of Control and Dower was forced to relinquish his titles.

Frankie Jones won his first 3 fights of 1957. One victory was over the rugged and hard-hitting Len Reece of Cardiff in February on a cut eye decision with the Welshman ahead on points. Following the British title relinquishment by Dower, Jones was again matched with Reece, this time for the vacant British and Empire titles. The venue was the Coney Beach Arena in Porthcawl on 31st July. Despite his previous defeat, Reece was a 6 to 4 on favourite but a left hook from Jones knocked him out in the eleventh round. The performance from the new champion had been gutsy and courageous.

In his thirteenth professional contest, Jones had to defend the Empire title against Dennis Adams of South Africa and the bout was arranged for the Kelvin Hall on 23rd October. Jones won all 10 rounds of his warm up fight against Frenchman Christian Marchand and was in good shape come the time of his defence. He sparred with Pat Glancy whilst Adams sparred with Owen Reilly and Dick Currie. Adams was given no chance of winning and was on the canvas in the first round. In round 2, Jones was twice down for nine counts and never recovered. Adams smashed Jones to defeat in round 3 to take the title. A sensational fight in front of a sensational crowd and Adams promised to return to defend his title.

On 13th November, George McDade won the vacant Scottish flyweight title with a points win over 12 rounds against fellow Glaswegian Pat Glancy. Glancy won only 2 of his 6 fights in the year and was badly beaten by Terry Spinks, retiring in the third round. McDade, the smallest Scottish flyweight since Norman Tennant, also took on Spinks in Canning Town but suffered a similar fate, he too having to retire in the third round with a bad cut over his eye. McDade won 6 of 8 fights in the year. Alex Ambrose was new to the Scottish flyweight scene and won 5 of his first 6 fights.

UK rankings at the end of 1957 were Jones 1, McDade 4, Glancy 6 and Ambrose 9.

Bantamweight

In January, the Empire committee nominated John Smillie as the leading contender for the Empire bantamweight title held by Peter Keenan. The forthcoming Keenan v Smillie fight would therefore be for both the British and Empire titles. Following this announcement, Smillie suffered his first professional defeat against the tough Jimmy Carson from Belfast.

The British and Empire title match was delayed as Keenan sustained a broken finger. Keenan had not fought since December and Smillie did not manage another fight prior to their meeting on 22nd May at Firhill. Smillie performed well but Keenan was better. Smillie was a young, strong southpaw and was in the lead when the ruthless Keenan came back to stop him in the sixth and retain his crowns. He became the first Scot to win two Lonsdale Belts outright with this victory. Both boxers had 3 further fights in the year and both boxers won all 3 fights.

Johnny Morrissey, a very promising young fighter, won 6 out of 6. Billy Rafferty won 6 out of 7, losing only to unbeaten George Bowes of West Hartlepool. Dick Currie returned to the ring as a bantamweight and showed glimpses of his old self. He won 2 of 3 fights and lost the other to the dangerous Ken Langford. He had been well on top in this fight which was stopped because of a cut above his right eye.

Alphonse Halimi won the world bantamweight title from Mario D'Agata in April taking his unbeaten professional sequence to 19. He came a cropper in fight 20 against Jimmy Carson but returned to winning ways when he knocked out Scottish champion Chic Brogan in 2 rounds in September. Brogan had 3 fights previous to Halimi and won all of them. D'Agata took the European crown in October by knocking out fellow countryman Federico Scarponi. D'Agata's first defence was to be against Peter Keenan but this fight failed to materialise.

Chic Brogan relinquished his Scottish bantamweight title and moved back to featherweight. The end of year British rankings showed Smillie 3, Currie 5, Rafferty 7 and Morrissey 9. Jimmy Carson was now ranked 1 and fellow countryman Freddie Gilroy was joint 5.

Featherweight

Despite his recent defeat by Bobby Neill, Charlie Hill was nominated as leading contender for the Empire title held by Hogan Bassey.

Unbeaten Bobby Neill was due to fight Jimmy Brown of Belfast in a final eliminator for Hill's British title in his sixteenth professional contest. Matt Fulton helped the Irishman prepare for the fight which took place on 19th January in Belfast. Brown was undefeated in 19 professional fights and certainly no pushover. The outcome was too close to call and it was surprising, therefore, that Neill was well-beaten and battered and knocked out in round 8.

On the same Belfast bill, Charlie Hill was stopped in 5 rounds by Joe Quinn of Belfast. As Neill had beaten Hill in the previous month, the Irish fans were confident that Brown would become the new champion. Both Glasgow and Belfast promoters were keen to stage the contest.

Following Neill's defeat, he was challenged by Matt Fulton to fight him again for the Scottish title. Fulton then assisted Hogan Bassey in his successful Empire title defence against Percy Lewis on 1st April but lost two teeth and suffered a suspected broken jaw in the process. By May, his title aspirations had waned and he relocated to London. Neill subsequently relinquished the Scottish title.

Bobby Neill had 4 more fights in the year and won only 2 of them. In his last fight of the year, lightweight Arthur Donnachie of Greenock stopped him in the fifth at Paisley on 21st August. On 24th August, Neill was badly injured in a road accident, remained in Edinburgh Royal Infirmary until 6th September and had a plaster on his leg for three months.

Charlie Hill won fights in May and August and in October he retained his British featherweight title when he knocked out Jimmy Brown in the 10th round at Nottingham in a gutsy display that left him bleeding and tired at the end of a gruelling contest. The Nottingham bill included an appearance by Hogan Bassey who had won the world featherweight title in Paris in June. Bassey and Hill had trained together in preparation for their fights. Bassey was to relinquish his Empire title in early November.

Hill's display had opened the door to Empire and European title tilts. An Empire opportunity arose on 9th December but he was stopped in 10 rounds by Percy Lewis of Trinidad in his bid for the vacant Empire featherweight title in Nottingham. Hill took numerous counts but would not stay down and the referee had eventually to call a halt to the contest.

Johnny Kidd of Aberdeen won his first 4 professional fights. Owen Reilly of Glasgow won his first 5. John O'Brien won 5 out of 5. Dave Croll won 9, drew 2 and lost 3.

Hill, Fulton and O'Brien were the top 3 UK featherweights at the end of 1957. However, Fulton had lost 3 of his 4 fights in the year and disappeared from the boxing scene.

Lightweight

On 29th January in Belfast, Arthur Donnachie was knocked out in the first round of his fight with local boxer John McNally. This was his first professional defeat in 11 fights. He won 3 of his subsequent 5 fights and was ranked 10 in the UK at the year end.

Tommy McGuiness of Edinburgh won his first 6 professional fights.

Empire champion, Willie Toweel of South Africa, fought in Glasgow on 15th August and again on 18th September. On the first occasion, he beat Billy Kelly on points over 10 rounds in a thrilling encounter. On the second date, he also won, beating Italian Mario Calcaterra on points over 10 rounds with another brilliant display. He was a great champion and superb ring craftsman and Scottish fans were indeed fortunate to see him perform on two occasions.

Welterweight

On 12th March, Jimmy Croll fought Peter Waterman, the British welterweight champion, in London. The referee stopped the fight in the fourth round to save Croll from further punishment. Croll lost 2 of 9 fights in the year and his average British ranking for the year was 6.

Middleweight

John McCormack made his debut during the year and won 9 of his 10 fights. In the fight he lost to Jim Lynas of Coventry, he had not recovered from flu and was clearly exhausted.

Len Mullen won 4 of his 7 fights. Mullen fought only once in Scotland whereas all of McCormack's fights were in Scotland.

Light Heavyweight

Scottish middleweight champion, Willie Armstrong, now fighting at light heavyweight, outpointed future world middleweight champion Dick Tiger. His record for the year was 5 wins out of 8. He was the British number 3 behind Randolph Turpin and Arthur Howard.

Chic Calderwood made his professional debut in September and had 4 fights in the year, winning them all inside the distance. Dave Mooney won 7 out of 8.

Highlights of 1958

Flyweight

Empire champion Dennis Adams fought 7 times in 1958 and lost 5. He did retain his Empire title against Warner Batchelor, the Australian flyweight champion, in Durban but his last 4 fights of the year were in Scotland and he lost 3 of these. He was defeated by Frankie Jones and George McDade as well as the young Irish prospect John Caldwell who was based in Scotland.

British champion, Jones, had a poor year winning only 2 of his 5 fights. Jones was a true flyweight and two defeats were to opponents who were much heavier. The third loss followed a clash of heads. Alex Ambrose won 7 of his 8 fights in the year including a points win over Pat Glancy who fought only once in the year. On 2nd July, Ambrose won the Scottish flyweight title by beating the holder George McDade on points over 12 rounds in Glasgow. This fight was also an eliminator for the British flyweight title.

McDade had 3 other fights in the year. He beat Silas Boko of Nigeria and Dennis Adams but suffered a points defeat at the hands of Terry Spinks who was probably the top British flyweight at this time.

Jackie Brown of Edinburgh won his professional debut fight in October.

Terry Spinks moved up to bantamweight. John Caldwell was now ranked behind Jones, followed by Ambrose, McDade and Glancy. Caldwell was unable to fight for the British title until he was 21 in May 1959. By this time Frankie Jones would have defended against Alex Ambrose and Caldwell was likely to be the next challenger.

Bantamweight

Peter Keenan began the year with a one month suspension for failing to appear before the Scottish Area Council. The suspension was subsequently rescinded following court action by Keenan. Dick Currie was brilliant when he outpointed Frenchman Guy Schatt at the Kelvin Hall promotion in early February. Keenan and Currie were then matched at the Kelvin Hall on 5th March over 10 rounds. The fight was fairly even until round 7. Keenan then got on top and, in round 10, he had Currie down three times before the referee stepped in to stop the contest. A few weeks later, Currie retired and joined the Daily Record as a boxing correspondent.

On 2nd April, Peter Keenan retained his Empire bantamweight title by defeating South African Graham Van Der Walt on points over 15 rounds at Paisley Ice Rink. On the night, Keenan was immaculate, providing a superb and confident display for his fans. He followed this with a comfortable points win over world number 2, Billy Peacock from the USA, but was then stopped by Glasgow-based Irishman, Derry Treanor, because of a cut over his left eye. Derry Treanor won 6 of his 8 fights in the year.

On 16th October, Keenan retained his Empire bantamweight title by clearly outpointing Pat Supple of Canada, eight years his junior, over 15 rounds at Paisley. On 17th November, Keenan was outpointed over 10 rounds by world bantamweight champion, Alphonse Halimi, in Paris. He was well beaten and did not win a single round.

Johnny Morrissey continued on his winning ways in January. He won the Scottish bantamweight title by defeating Archie Downie in 4 rounds at a Hamilton Town Hall packed with 1,200 fans. He was, however, closely beaten on points at the Kelvin Hall in February by experienced Spaniard Antonio Diaz. In a return the following month at the same venue, he knocked out Diaz in the third round. Further victories followed against Terry Toole and Jimmy Carson. Morrissey had fought his way into a British bantamweight final title eliminator against hard hitting Freddie Gilroy of Belfast. The fight was at the Kelvin Hall on 17th September. Morrissey did not win a round and had to retire in the eighth with a broken jaw. 3 of Gilroy's 5 fights this year were at the Kelvin Hall but the British title fight against Keenan was arranged for the King's Hall, Belfast in January 1959.

Billy Rafferty won 5 of his 7 fights in the year including a surprise victory over Terry Spinks. The referee stopped their fight in the fifth due to a cut sustained by Spinks. The two fights lost were also down to cut eyes and included a defeat by former Scottish featherweight champion, Tommy Miller of West Lothian, who had made a comeback as a bantamweight earlier in the year. Miller won 2 out of 2 in the year.

Keenan, Gilroy and Bowes were the top ranked British bantamweights. Johnny Morrissey was temporarily omitted from the rankings. Billy Rafferty was ranked 4 and Tommy Miller 6. Derry Treanor could not at this time fight for a British title and did not appear in the rankings. John Smillie moved up to featherweight.

Featherweight

On 19th February, Chic Brogan won the Scottish featherweight title when he outpointed Owen Reilly over 12 rounds at Hamilton. Many in the crowd thought that Reilly had won and the verdict was greeted by predictable booing. In late May, Brogan narrowly outpointed John O'Brien, previously ranked number 2 contender for the British title, and this proved enough to earn him a crack at the British title.

British champion, Charlie Hill, had a relatively quiet year. On 2nd July, he defended his British title against Brogan at Cathkin Park. Brogan was cut in the first round and this troubled him throughout the fight. The cut opened up in round 10 and his corner signalled his retirement at the end of round 11. Hill retained his British title and won a Lonsdale Belt. In his only other fight of the year, Hill defeated Joe Quinn of Belfast who had surprisingly beaten him in the previous year.

Bobby Neill returned to the ring and won all of his 6 fights in impressive style although sustaining a broken jaw in his last fight. He was now looking to take on Hill for the British title. He was due to defend his Scottish title against Arthur Donnachie at Murrayfield Ice Rink in September but this clash had to be postponed following his latest injury.

John O'Brien had a poor year winning only 1 fight out of 5. Owen Reilly lost 3 out of 5 including a defeat by Bobby Neill. Johnny Kidd moved up to lightweight at the beginning of the year. John Smillie now fighting at featherweight had a mixed year, winning 3 out of 5. Dave Croll won 3 of 5

Scots dominated the featherweight rankings. Hill was ranked 1, Neill 2, Brogan 4, O'Brien 5, Smillie 7, Croll 8, and Reilly 9.

Lightweight

Empire Champion, Willie Toweel, again fought in Glasgow this year. In a major upset, he was stopped by Frenchman Guy Gracia at the Kelvin Hall on 23rd April.

On 19th November, Arthur Donnachie stopped British Empire featherweight champion Percy Lewis of Trinidad in round 6 in Glasgow. The fight had the crowd on its toes from round 3 when Donnachie began to attack. Both boxers had weighed in at 9 stone 3 pounds. Of his 3 other fights in the year, Donnachie won only one.

On 2nd April, Johnny McLaren won the Scottish lightweight title by stopping Tommy McGuiness of Edinburgh in the twelfth round at Paisley. McLaren, a professional since 1954, had lost more fights than he had won. McGuinness had won 8 of 10 contests prior to their meeting.

On 25th July, Aberdonian Johnny Kidd won the Scottish lightweight title by knocking out McLaren in the ninth round at Aberdeen. Kidd had moved up from featherweight and was unbeaten in 8 professional contests before the title fight. As Scottish champion, he won his next 2 fights but was outpointed in his last contest of the year by Spike McCormack of Belfast.

Both Donnachie and Kidd were ranked just inside the UK top 10.

Welterweight

Although Jimmy Croll had a bad year, winning only 1 of his 6 fights, he had a number 6 British ranking. He fought British lightweight champion Dave Charnley in September but had to retire in round 4 with a badly cut left cheek following a collision of heads. Croll was also stripped of his Scottish title at the beginning of the year as he refused to accept a low purse offer to defend the title.

Middleweight

John McCormack won his first 4 fights of the year. On 2nd July, he won the Scottish middleweight title by outpointing Len Mullen over 12 rounds at Cathkin Park. On 10th July, it was announced by the British Boxing Board of Control that he should fight the veteran Martin Hansen of Liverpool in an eliminator for the British title. The winner would face either Alex Buxton or Freddie Cross in a final eliminator. Prior to fighting Hansen, Cowboy outpointed Jim Lynas against whom he had suffered his only professional defeat. He then went on to outpoint Hansen over 10 rounds in Liverpool on 9th October. He completed the year with a points victory over Frenchman Jean Ruellet and was rated number 3 in the UK.

Len Mullen had one further contest in 1958 before he retired.

Light Heavyweight

Dave Mooney lost 3 of his 7 fights in the year. On 17th September, he was knocked out in the third round by Eddie Wright in a British light heavyweight title eliminator at the Kelvin Hall. On 29th October, he was stopped by Chic Calderwood in the fifth round of a one-sided fight in their Scottish light heavyweight title contest, also at the Kelvin Hall. Calderwood won all of his 11 fights in the year and was proving to be one of Scotland's finest boxing prospects.

Both Willie Armstrong and Dave Mooney retired.

Highlights of 1959

Flyweight

Alex Ambrose had done enough to get a shot at the British flyweight title held by Frankie Jones. This was to be the first time that two Scots would fight for the flyweight title. Although Jones had held the title since July 1957, he had not defended it for a variety of reasons. Fans thought that there was little to choose between the fighters. As it turned out, Jones won well on points over 15 rounds.

Both Ambrose and Jones lost to Derek Lloyd of Chingford in March and May respectively and Lloyd became a leading contender for Jones's title. Jones had one further fight in the year, beating George McDade on points. Ambrose lost 4 of his 9 fights in the year. He retained his Scottish flyweight title with a draw against George McDade but subsequently lost the title to Jackie Brown of Edinburgh, Ambrose having to retire with a severe eyebrow injury. Ambrose moved up to bantamweight.

Jones had been due to defend his British title against John Caldwell but, due to illness, the match was put back. Jackie Brown was matched with Derek Lloyd in a British flyweight title eliminator. The fight took place at Paisley Ice Rink on 21st October and Brown was the victor in the fifth round when the referee stopped the fight. Brown won all of his 6 contests in 1959 and could look forward with confidence to 1960. Brown would, however, have to wait for his title chance as the scene was set for Jones v Caldwell in 1960.

George McDade had only 2 contests in the year as did Pat Glancy. Glancy beat Alex Ambrose on a disqualification but lost to Derek Lloyd.

Empire champion Dennis Adams continued his losing streak, suffering 2 defeats in 2 contests in the year. The Empire committee nominated Jones and Caldwell as the leading challengers. Risto Luukkonen won the European flyweight title from Young Martin. Pascual Perez remained the unbeaten flyweight champion of the world. Jones was ranked number 7 in the world and John Caldwell of Belfast was ranked number 8.

Bantamweight

On 10th January, Peter Keenan defended his British and Empire bantamweight titles against Freddie Gilroy in front of a sell-out crowd at the King's Hall in Belfast. His sparring partners in the lead-up to the fight were Owen Reilly and John Smillie. Belfast was caught up in the excitement of the fight and the atmosphere was likened to that on Cup Final day. Gilroy was a hot 7 to 4 on favourite and the Irish crowd were confident of victory. It was certainly the biggest fight in Belfast since Billy Kelly was at his peak. Gilroy duly obliged his supporters by giving Keenan the worst beating of his career and the referee called a halt in the eleventh round. Gilroy was certainly a worthy successor to Keenan. The large crowd gave a noisy rendition of "When Irish Eyes are Smiling" and were joined in song by the defeated

Keenan. In recognition of his sportsmanship, the crowd spontaneously followed up with "I belong to Glasgow" and "Auld Lang Syne" and a memorable sporting night was brought to a close.

Peter Keenan began his professional boxing career in 1948 and had fought at the top level since 1951. The defeat by Gilroy was to be his last fight and he was now to turn his hand to boxing promotion. On 15th April, Gilroy fought in Glasgow and knocked out Charles Sylla in 2 rounds. He subsequently defended his Empire title, outpointed Piero Rollo of Italy to win the European bantamweight title and beat former world champion Mario D'Agata of Italy who had lost the European crown to Rollo. He was unbeaten in 20 fights by the end of 1959 and ranked number 2 contender for the world title held by Mexican Joe Becerra who had won the title from Alphonse Halimi.

Since the retirement of Peter Keenan, Scottish bantamweight prospects were in the hands of Billy Rafferty and Johnny Morrissey but they were unlikely to prove a match for the unbeaten Gilroy. Rafferty had a splendid year winning all of his 6 fights convincingly. He beat Len Reece of Cardiff in a British bantamweight title final eliminator and was on course to fight Gilroy in 1960.

Morrissey had come back well following his defeat by Gilroy in 1958 and won all of his 5 fights in 1959 including the retention of his Scottish bantamweight title against Tommy Miller who had to retire in the fifth round at Paisley. This was Tommy Miller's final professional fight.

Featherweight

The long awaited title fight between Bobby Neill and Charlie Hill took place at Nottingham Ice Rink on 13th April. The fight proved to be one of the most remarkable championship fights since the war. Neill had cuts to both eyes and Hill was on the canvas 10 times. The contest was a marvellous exhibition of courage from both men but Neill was the winner in round 9 when the referee stopped the fight. This fight marked the end of Charlie Hill's professional career.

A non-title fight was immediately arranged for Neill at Wembley on 2nd June against Terry Spinks who had now moved up to featherweight. Neill won by a knockout in the ninth round having been well behind on points.

On 1st September, Spinks lost on points to Glasgow based Derry Treanor who had also moved up to featherweight. On 15th September, John O' Brien narrowly outpointed Spinks over 12 rounds at Wembley Pool in a British featherweight title final eliminator and received a great ovation from the crowd at the end of the fight. Neill now had to defend his title against O'Brien. Neill secured a non-title fight against world champion Davey Moore of the USA who had recently conquered Hogan Bassey to take the title. Neill was destroyed in the first round with the referee having to intervene to save Neill from further punishment.

On 11th November, Dave Croll won the Scottish featherweight title by knocking out the holder Chic Brogan in the second round at Dundee. Following the defeat, Brogan retired. Croll won 5 of 6 fights in the year.

John O'Brien obtained an Empire title chance against Percy Lewis on 7th December at Nottingham Ice Rink. O'Brien inexplicably misjudged the count and the opportunity against a champion who had not fought since the previous December. Lewis retained his British Empire featherweight title by stopping O'Brien in the second round. O'Brien won 4 of his 6 fights this year. John Smillie won 3 of 5 and drew with Owen Reilly in Reilly's only fight of the year.

Johnny Kidd had a setback when he was stopped by Barney Beale from Lambeth at Manor Place Baths in London in his first fight of the year. He reverted to featherweight and won his 5 subsequent contests rising to number 7 in the UK. He was followed by Dave Croll at 8 and John Smillie at 9. John O'Brien was ranked 2 behind Bobby Neill.

Lightweight

The parents of British and Empire lightweight champion Dave Charnley were Scottish and Charnley had lived in the Motherwell area when he was a youngster. On 17th June, he made his Scottish debut as a professional at Firhill and beat Belfast's Billy Kelly in 6 rounds when Kelly was disqualified for persistently ducking too low. The decision was met with boos and a spectator was arrested for attacking the referee.

Scotland's leading lightweight, Arthur Donnachie, lost 2 contests and retired. Johnny McLaren fought twice and lost twice. Tommy McGuinness had one win out of 4 fights.

Welterweight

Jimmy Croll failed to win any of his 3 fights and moved up to middleweight.

Middleweight

John McCormack was due to fight Freddie Cross in a final eliminator for the British middleweight title held by Terry Downes. However, Cross withdrew from the contest and, in preference, undertook a tour of Australia. Downes therefore had to defend his title against McCormack.

Downes already had a contest for 24th February at Wembley against French middleweight champion Michel Diouf. Downes lost this fight in the fifth, having to retire with a cut eye. As a result of this injury, the title fight was postponed until June and then until September. McCormack took on Diouf at Paisley Ice Rink in March and outpointed him in his hardest professional fight to date. Cowboy had 4 other fights in 1959 prior to the September showdown, all of which he won convincingly.

On 15th September, the contest with Downes took place at Wembley. McCormack had no answer to the body punching of Downes and was floored 12 times. Despite this, John McCormack won the British middleweight title when Downes was disqualified in the eighth round. This was a disappointing end to the fight and the decision was greeted by loud booing from the crowd. In the aftermath, Downes mouthed that he did not want to fight McCormack again and McCormack retorted that he had got no satisfaction from winning by a disqualification. Downes purse was withheld until the circumstances were considered by the stewards who decided to withhold £100.

A return fight was arranged for 3rd November. In this contest, Downes came back from the brink of defeat to regain his title by stopping McCormack in the eighth round after putting Cowboy down 5 times.

Light Heavyweight

Chic Calderwood won all of his 8 fights in the year taking his professional tally to 23 fights, 23 wins of which 17 were inside the distance. Notable victories included knocking out Yolande Pompey who had fought Archie Moore for the world title in 1956 and stopping Jack Whittaker of Warwick in the seventh round in a final eliminator for the vacant British light heavyweight championship. Calderwood was now the leading light heavyweight in the UK.

Yvon Durelle of Canada was the Empire champion. The leading contenders were Mike Holt of South Africa and Johnny Halafihi of Tonga who had drawn in a final eliminator at Earls Court in November. When Durelle subsequently gave up the title due to weight difficulties, the Empire committee ruled that the pair should be matched for the vacant title.

Calderwood was set to fight for the British title in 1960. He was also eyeing a meeting with the winner of the Holt v Halafihi contest.

Highlights of 1960

Flyweight

Frankie Jones recommenced training in January following some time out with jaundice. His first fight of the year did not take place until 20th May. He beat Eddie Barraclough in 7 rounds but his overall performance did not impress. His next outing was on 15th August against Ron "Ponty" Davies in Aberdare. In a disappointing performance, he narrowly lost on points over 10 rounds. He then chose to fight the Venezuelan Champion, Ramon Arias, in Caracas on 31st August and was knocked out in the seventh round.

Number one challenger John Caldwell had a contrasting start to the year. He knocked out former European flyweight champion Young Martin in 3 rounds on 9th February and outpointed the current European champion Risto Luukkonen of Finland over 10 rounds on 23rd February. Next, he outpointed the French flyweight champion Rene Libeer on 31st May.

The outcome of the British title fight between Jones and Caldwell was predictable. Caldwell took the title on 8th October with a third round knockout. Although only 27, Jones decided to retire from professional boxing. Caldwell had one further fight and win, against Christian Marchand, before the end of the year and was now ranked amongst the top 3 flyweights in the world.

Unbeaten Jackie Brown was now the top Scottish flyweight. He won 5 fights between January and May and in June he fought Italian Mario D'Agata, the former world bantamweight champion. The venue was Firhill Stadium. Although trailing, Brown finished strongly and gained a 10 round points win in the greatest victory of his career. Next up, he was contracted to fight Scottish bantamweight champion Johnny Morrissey of Newarthill at Paisley Ice Rink on 10th August. This turned out to be a fantastic fight for the spectators with Brown just shading the points verdict over 8 rounds. His final opponent of the year was Derek Lloyd of Chingford. Surprisingly, he lost his unbeaten record to Lloyd, a man whom he had previously beaten comprehensively. Brown retired in the fifth with a damaged wrist.

George McDade won 4 of 7 fights in the year including a 10 round points win over Pat Glancy at the Central Hotel, Glasgow on 10th March in a Scottish flyweight title eliminator. Glancy lost all 3 of his fights in 1960.

At the end of the year, Caldwell was a worthy British champion. Dennis Adams remained a poor Empire champion. He retained his title by knocking out fellow countryman Les Smith in the first round of their fight in Durban in July. This was his first win in more than two years. Luukkonen remained the European champion. Pone Kingpetch of Thailand had deposed Pascual Perez as world flyweight champion during the year.

Bantamweight

Both Billy Rafferty and Freddie Gilroy remained inactive in the lead-up to their battle for the British, Empire and European bantamweight titles on 19th March in Belfast but both were in superb physical condition when they entered the ring. Rafferty had spent many rounds sparring with John Caldwell and Derry Treanor. However, it was Gilroy who stormed into the lead, winning the first 6 rounds. The courageous Rafferty fought back and was only slightly behind when the referee stopped the fight in the thirteenth round on account of his damaged right eye. The gallant Rafferty received a thunderous ovation for his gutsy performance. Gilroy's unbeaten tally was now 21.

Johnny Morrissey made his first appearance of the year on March 9th at the Kelvin Hall. His opponent was Dwight Hawkins from Los Angeles. The American constantly threw low punches and was disqualified by referee Jake Kilrain in the fifth. This unsatisfactory decision prompted the inevitable storm of boos and fights amongst the crowd. Morrissey next travelled to Wembley Pool where he took on the unbeaten Roy Beaman from Brixton on 31st May. Beaman was something of a sensation and had won his first 12 fights in style. However, Beaman lost his record to Morrissey whose superior skill saw him win decisively on points over 8 rounds.

Freddie Gilroy fought Mexican Ignacio Pina in Manchester on 25th April and surprisingly lost his unbeaten record. The Mexican outboxed Gilroy over 10 rounds. Billy Rafferty was then invited to fight Pina at Belle Vue, Manchester on 9th June. This proved to be an all-action fight from the first bell. Pina was a skilled ring craftsman and a difficult opponent for Rafferty. However, the battling Scot split open Pina's right eyebrow in the sixth round and took control, emerging as a winner on points over 10 rounds. This was probably Rafferty's greatest victory to date. Gilroy was at the fight and later congratulated Rafferty in his dressing room. He promised to give Rafferty a return fight in the future.

In July, Johnny Morrissey refused to defend his Scottish bantamweight title against Alex Ambrose as the purse on offer was unacceptable. He subsequently relinquished the title and signed to meet Jackie Brown. Brown won the fight on points as mentioned above. Morrissey had one more fight in the year, against fellow contender George Bowes of Hesleden to whom he lost on points over 8 rounds.

The world bantamweight title had been won by Mexican Joe Becerra in 1959. He had knocked out reigning champion Alphonse Halimi and he repeated the feat in February 1960. He successfully defended the title again in May but was surprisingly knocked out by a fellow countryman in August and promptly announced his retirement. The world bantamweight title was therefore vacant. London promoter Mickey Duff announced that he wanted a Rafferty-Pina match for the world title. Fellow promoter Jack Solomons announced that he would be seeking a Gilroy-Halimi match for the title. Another contender was Italian bantamweight champion Piero Rollo. A recognised title match was eventually made between Gilroy and Halimi and it was staged at

Wembley on 25th October. It was a very close contest but the points decision went to Halimi.

Gilroy forfeited the European bantamweight title when he took on the world title fight with Halimi. Billy Rafferty had taken a fight with Piero Rollo in Cagliari on 30th October. Originally intended as yet another match for the world title, the fight was contracted over 15 rounds. In the fight subsequently labelled an unofficial eliminator for the world and European titles, the Italian took an early lead but characteristically Rafferty fought back and the fight went the distance. Although the contest was very close, Rafferty's badly cut eye perhaps counted against him and the verdict was given to the Italian.

In November, it was announced that Rafferty should fight George Bowes in a final eliminator for the British bantamweight title. These were the top two challengers to Gilroy who, it was rumoured, had weight problems and was contemplating a move up to featherweight.

Alex Ambrose had a mixed year. He stopped Len Reece and outpointed John Agwu and Eddie O'Connor. He had to retire against Roy Beaman with an eye injury and was outpointed over 10 rounds by Piero Rollo. He finished the year as number 6 British bantamweight just behind Johnny Morrissey and Roy Beaman.

Featherweight

Bobby Neill was due to defend his British featherweight title against John O'Brien at Nottingham on 1st February. However, in the middle of January, O'Brien concluded that he had had enough of boxing and decided to retire. He was 22 years old. The following week, he said that he might not retire after all but towards the end of the month, he again changed his mind and formally notified the British Boxing Board of Control of his retirement. The Board refused to accept his resignation as he had contracted to fight Neill and ordered him to appear before them. At that meeting, the Board withdrew his licence. Promoter Reg King also sued O'Brien for the loss that he incurred.

Bobby Neill defeated substitute Alberto Serti from Italy on points over 10 rounds. In April, he stopped another Italian, Germain Vivier, in 5 rounds and in June he knocked out Jimmy Carson of Belfast in the third round.

Johnny Kidd fought Terry Spinks in London on 26th January in an eliminator for Neill's title. Spinks had lost only 4 of 33 professional contests. Three of these defeats had come against Scots, Billy Rafferty, Bobby Neill and John O'Brien, and the fourth against Glasgow based Derry Treanor. Kidd fought the greatest fight of his life but Spinks was declared the winner on points over 12 rounds. The decision was close and was greeted with booing. An exhausted Spinks was elated that he had broken his Scottish jinx and looked forward to a rematch with Bobby Neill for the British title.

Johnny Kidd came back with a 10 round points win over South African Sexton Mabena in March but was then stopped in 8 rounds by American Tommy

Tibbs in May. On June 21st, he was matched with Bobby Neill at the Albert Hall in a non-title fight. He was slightly ahead on points when the fight was stopped in the fifth round in his favour. Neill had sustained a badly gashed right eye and the referee deemed the injury too dangerous to continue. Although Spinks was the number one challenger to Neill, Kidd was close behind as was Derry Treanor who had now been granted British citizenship.

The British title fight between Neill and Spinks was staged in London on 27th September. Neill lost in controversial circumstances when the referee stopped the fight in the seventh round. Although Neill had a minor cut over his left eyebrow, it had not caused any problem to the boxers. A rematch was quickly agreed. The rematch purse was £5,000 winner-take-all and the venue was Wembley on 22nd November. Spinks was again victorious and knocked Neill out in the fourteenth round. Neill collapsed after the fight and was rushed to Wembley General Hospital. He was operated upon to remove a blood clot and he remained in hospital until 16th December. The second fight with Spinks was Bobby Neill's last fight and he retired at the age of 27.

Johnny Kidd fought Scottish featherweight champion Dave Croll in London on 15th November. Croll had already lost to Derry Treanor, Terry Spinks and Phil Jones. It was a surprise, therefore, when Croll sensationally knocked out Kidd in the second round. Croll refused a rematch with Kidd as he thought that it would jeopardise any chance that he had of a fight with Spinks. Croll did not fight again in the year. Kidd took on Love Allotey of Ghana and was outpointed over 8 rounds so that his stock as a leading challenger to Spinks had diminished considerably. Derry Treanor who was having difficulty finding opponents, had one further fight in 1960 which he also won and he ended the year as top Scottish challenger, just ahead of Croll and Kidd.

John Smillie won 4 of 8 contests in the year but retired from boxing in the UK. He moved to Australia where he had some later success.

George Judge had turned professional in 1959 and by the end of 1960 he had won 8 of 11 fights.

Lightweight

Jimmy Gibson of Dunfermline made his professional debut on 28th January. He won his first 3 fights convincingly and was then matched with former Scottish champion Johnny McLaren. He won this fight on points over 8 rounds but was disqualified in his next fight against Jim Jordan of Belfast. There followed two more victories and then a points loss to Maurice Cullen of Shotton. He was then nominated by the Scottish Area Council for a Scottish lightweight title match against Alex McMillan from Glasgow. McMillan had won 5 of his 6 professional fights.

Gibson outpointed McMillan over 12 rounds at Paisley on 2nd November to take the title. Both boxers had one further contest in the year but they were both losers.

Welterweight

Tommy McGuinness of Edinburgh had been a professional since 1957. He lost a Scottish lightweight title fight in 1958 and had a better than average professional record. Jimmy McGuinness from Wishaw had turned professional in 1955 and had won 16 of his 21 professional fights. The namesakes were matched for the Scottish welterweight title in Glasgow on 10th March 1960. The outcome was a win for Jimmy on points over 12 rounds. This marked the end of Tommy's career. Jimmy had one more fight in the year which he lost. Neither boxer had been ranked in the UK top 10.

Middleweight

John McCormack began his campaign on 9th March at the Kelvin Hall. He outclassed his opponent Tommy Tagoe of Ghana and the referee stopped the contest in the third round. His next outing was in Milan on 19th June against top Italian Giancarlo Garbelli. Cowboy did very well to win on points over 10 rounds. At Paisley Ice Rink on 10th August, he performed brilliantly against Midland Area champion George Aldridge from Market Harborough. Aldridge was floored three times before the referee called a halt to the fight in the ninth round.

Then it was off to Berlin to face the formidable European champion Gustav Scholz. Scholz had been a professional since 1948 and had lost only 1 of 83 professional contests. The iron man of Germany won a very close 10 round points verdict in front of ten thousand fans amid a storm of booing. Cowboy received a fantastic reception from the German fans in appreciation of his efforts. Cowboy concluded the year with a 10 round points win over George Benton of the USA at Paisley Ice Rink.

This had been a good year for McCormack following the loss of his British title in the previous year. Terry Downes had defended the title successfully against Welshman Phil Edwards and won his 4 further fights in the year and he was looking towards Empire champion Dick Tiger and Gustav Scholz in 1961. Cowboy was the number one challenger for the British title and could look forward to a meeting with Phil Edwards in an eliminator for the title.

Jimmy Croll retired.

Light Heavyweight

Chic Calderwood had served his professional apprenticeship in winning all of his 23 fights in the previous 28 months. His big moment arrived on 28th January at Paisley Ice Rink when he faced Arthur Howard for the vacant British light heavyweight championship. He took his opportunity stopping his opponent in round 13 and became the first Scot to hold the title. The world was now his oyster. Fights were suggested for the vacant Empire title against Johnny Halafihi, the European title against Erich Schoeppner and then the world title against Archie Moore.

However, the vacant Empire title match was between Halafihi and South African Mike Holt with the winner to defend against Calderwood. The pair fought a dull and dreary draw on 25th April at Nottingham. When Calderwood signed to meet Halafihi at Firhill on 9th June, the Empire committee ruled that the fight should be for the Empire title with the winner to defend against Holt. Holt protested to no avail.

At Firhill, the rain fell heavily for the first 7 rounds during which time the Tongan held his own. He tired in the later rounds and was cut badly and the referee stopped the fight in the twelfth round. Calderwood had become the first Scot to win the Empire light heavyweight title.

Calderwood was back in the ring on 10th August at Paisley Ice Rink against American Joey Armstrong who was pounded to defeat in 8 rounds. Calderwood was now ranked in the world top 10. At number 3 in the rankings was boxing maestro Willie "the Wisp" Pastrano of Miami. Pastrano was only 24 but had fought professionally more than 70 times, many against heavyweights, losing only 7. The pair signed to meet at the Kelvin Hall on 16th September in an eagerly anticipated fight. Calderwood's world rating seemed on the generous side and it was expected that Pastrano would emerge as the victor.

Pastrano was well ahead in the early stages as a result of his lightning punches. Calderwood seemed to have no answer in the early rounds but he did come back with that pounding left that he possessed and, with the crowd behind him, he clawed his way back into the fight. The fight was very close and Pastrano had a very good tenth and last round which made him the winner in his eyes. However, the verdict was given to Calderwood. This was a sensational victory that was celebrated by the Scottish boxing fraternity who were convinced that they had a future world champion in their midst.

The newspapers let it be known that the next step should be for the world title against Moore. Approaching the winter, any contest would have to be indoors but there was not a venue in Scotland that would be able to support such a contest. Moore asked for £65,000 plus expenses for the fight but this kind of money was beyond even the top London promoters' reach and Calderwood would have to go to the United States to get the fight.

Erich Schoeppner had a prior claim on the title as his title fight with Moore was postponed because Moore did not make the weight. Calderwood wanted to fight Schoeppner for the European title and have the contest recognised as a final eliminator for the world title. The German let it be known that he did not want to fight Calderwood. He was willing to fight only Moore. The National Boxing Association then stripped Moore of the title for failing to make the weight against Schoeppner and announced that Harold Johnson of the USA, Schoeppner, Pastrano and Calderwood were the contenders for the vacant title. Other boxing bodies, however, continued to acknowledge Moore as champion.

Calderwood continued his winning sequence on 2nd November at Paisley where he outclassed the German Rolf Peters in 4 rounds. Archie Moore attended the fight as a guest of promoter Peter Keenan who had not given up hope of bringing him to Glasgow to meet Calderwood.

Calderwood finished the year at Wembley with a win over Sonny Ray from Chicago who had a ranking of 12 in the world. Calderwood won 8 of the 10 rounds in a convincing display that enhanced his world ranking. Unfortunately he had broken his nose in two places and this was to delay his next fight.

Towards the end of the year and following rumours of a Johnson/ Calderwood title match, Willie Pastrano asked for a return with Calderwood in Glasgow. Pastrano's title claims had been damaged following a points defeat by fellow American Jesse Bowdry. Schoeppner also changed his mind about fighting Chic and offered to put his title at stake against him.

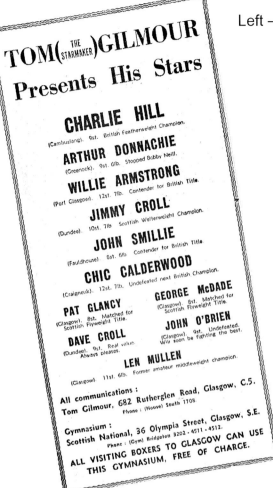

Left – Tommy Gilmour's boxing stable in 1958

TOM (THE STARMAKER) GILMOUR
Presents His Stars

CHARLIE HILL
(Cambuslang). 9st. British Featherweight Champion.

ARTHUR DONNACHIE
(Greenock). 9st. 6lb. Stopped Bobby Neill.

WILLIE ARMSTRONG
(Port Glasgow). 12st. 7lb. Contender for British Title.

JIMMY CROLL
(Dundee). 10st. 7lb. Scottish Welterweight Champion.

JOHN SMILLIE
(Fauldhouse). 8st. 6lb. Contender for British Title.

CHIC CALDERWOOD
(Craigneuk). 12st. 7lb. Undefeated next British Champion.

PAT GLANCY
(Glasgow). 8st. Matched for Scottish Flyweight Title.

GEORGE McDADE
(Glasgow). 8st. Matched for Scottish Flyweight Title.

DAVE CROLL
(Dundee). 9st. Real value. Always pleases.

JOHN O'BRIEN
(Glasgow). 9st. Undefeated. Will soon be fighting the best.

LEN MULLEN
(Glasgow). 11st. 6lb. Former amateur middleweight champion.

All communications :
Tom Gilmour, 682 Rutherglen Road, Glasgow, C.5.
Phone : (House) South 1708.

Gymnasium :
Scottish National, 36 Olympia Street, Glasgow, S.E.
Phone : (Gym) Bridgeton 3202 - 4511 - 4512.

ALL VISITING BOXERS TO GLASGOW CAN USE THIS GYMNASIUM, FREE OF CHARGE.

Right – The Paisley Ice Rink bill of 28th August 1958. There were no late bill changes.

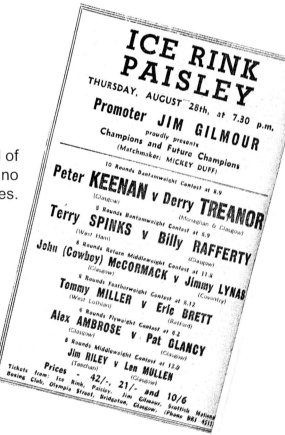

ICE RINK PAISLEY

THURSDAY, AUGUST 28th, at 7.30 p.m.

Promoter **JIM GILMOUR**
proudly presents
Champions and Future Champions
(Matchmaker: MICKEY DUFF)

10 Rounds Bantamweight Contest at 8.9
Peter **KEENAN** v Derry **TREANOR**
(Glasgow)   (Monaghan & Glasgow)

8 Rounds Bantamweight Contest at 8.9
Terry **SPINKS** v Billy **RAFFERTY**
(West Ham)   (Glasgow)

8 Rounds Return Middleweight Contest at 11.8
John (Cowboy) **McCORMACK** v Jimmy **LYNAS**
(Glasgow)   (Coventry)

8 Rounds Featherweight Contest at 8.12
Tommy **MILLER** v Eric **BRETT**
(West Lothian)   (Retford)

8 Rounds Flyweight Contest at 8.2
Alex **AMBROSE** v Pat **GLANCY**
(Glasgow)   (Glasgow)

8 Rounds Middleweight Contest at 12.9
Jim **RILEY** v Len **MULLEN**
(Teechan)   (Glasgow)

Prices " 42/-, 21/- and 10/6
Tickets from: Ice Rink, Paisley. Jim Gilmour, Scottish National
Boxing Club, Olympia Street, Bridgeton, Glasgow. (Phone BRI 4511)

Highlights of 1961

Flyweight

Jackie Brown was pleased to hear that South Africa had left the Commonwealth in March 1961. This political decision meant that Dennis Adams was no longer the British Empire title holder and the title was vacant. British champion John Caldwell was not interested in this title as he was aiming for the world title. The obvious match seemed to be Jackie Brown against Derek Lloyd. Despite his recent defeat to Lloyd, Brown was ranked behind Caldwell and before Lloyd. Brown had won a British flyweight title eliminator in 1959 but still awaited his fight with the champion.

Brown was wanted for a fight with world bantamweight champion Alphonse Halimi in Tunis in March but he opted to take a fight with British and Empire bantamweight champion Freddie Gilroy at Paisley on 12th April. Many thought that Gilroy was past his best but his 10 pound weight advantage proved too much for Brown who was knocked out in the fourth round.

Brown returned to winning ways with an 8 round points win over Brian Cartwright from Birmingham on 15th May. He returned to the same Newcastle arena on 12th June against Eddie Barraclough of Rotherham. The referee ordered both boxers out of the ring in the fifth round for failing to fight. Brown spent the 5 rounds backing away from his opponent and his purse was withheld.

The European flyweight crown passed from Risto Luukkonen to Salvatore Burruni of Italy on 29th June. Burruni's first defence was looking like Jackie Brown but the British Boxing Board of Control refused to sanction Brown's participation following his most recent poor display. Derek Lloyd got the fight but lost in 6 rounds in August and this marked the end of his professional career.

John Caldwell stepped up to bantamweight and relinquished his British flyweight title. The British and Empire titles were now vacant.

Brown fought in August against Aberdonian Ollie Wylie whom he outpointed over 6 rounds. He then took on former European bantamweight champion and world number 6 bantamweight Piero Rollo in Cagliari but was knocked out in the sixth round.

Walter McGowan began his professional career at the Kelvin Hall on 9th August when he stopped George McDade in 3 rounds. McDade decided to quit professional boxing as he could see no future for himself in the sport. On 22nd September at Hamilton Town Hall, McGowan outpointed Eddie Barraclough over 8 rounds. His next opponent at Paisley Ice Rink on 25th October was Jackie Brown. Brown remained a top flyweight and this was surely a contest too soon for the new Benny Lynch. The fight was close and could have gone either way but the points decision over 8 rounds went to

Brown. Pandemonium followed the decision and fighting broke out in the crowd as coins and missiles were thrown.

Brown was now back in favour and was nominated to fight number 2 contender Brian Cartwright for the vacant British flyweight title. McGowan had one more fight, defeating West Ham's Brian Bissmire on points. McGowan ended the year as UK number 3 behind Brown and Cartwright.

Danny Lee from Port Glasgow turned professional in February and was unbeaten in 8 fights at the end of 1961. He was nominated to fight Jackie Brown for the Scottish flyweight title. He also signed to meet Walter McGowan early in the 1962 and ended the year as UK number 7.

Johnny Mallon from Glasgow was another new professional who won his 3 fights in the year. Pat Glancy was inactive.

Bantamweight

Freddie Gilroy remained British and Empire champion but he was clearly beaten in his May fight with Belgian Pierre Cossemyns for the vacant European bantamweight title. A few days later, his fellow countryman John Caldwell outpointed Alphonse Halimi to become world bantamweight champion. Halimi had beaten Gilroy to take the title in October 1960. Caldwell repeated the result in the return in October and the former Lennoxtown resident was now unbeaten in 25 fights.

Billy Rafferty's final eliminator against George Bowes was put back until April as Bowes was injured in a warm-up fight. When Bowes entered the ring at the King's Hall in Belfast, he had lost only 3 of 31 professional contests. His losses had been to Gilroy, Cossemyns and Len Reece. There was little to choose between the fighters. In Rafferty's only fight of the year, he narrowly defeated Bowes on points over 12 rounds to set up a return title fight with Gilroy.

Rafferty was due to meet Gilroy at the King's Hall in Belfast on 7th October for the British and Empire titles but Gilroy had to call off injured. Rafferty was offered a 10 round fight with John Caldwell but turned the offer down. He also called off an overweight fight with Eder Jofre, the holder of the American version of the world bantamweight title, due to a lack of fitness. Rafferty was ranked in the world top 10 throughout the year.

Alex Ambrose had 3 contests and won all of them and finished the year as number 5 British bantamweight.

In his last bantamweight contest before moving up to featherweight, Johnny Morrissey stopped Tommy Burgoyne of Halton in April. However, Burgoyne did enough in the year to merit a December ranking of 9 in the UK.

Featherweight

Terry Spinks was the British champion at the beginning of the year. Top challenger was Welshman Howard Winstone. Winstone won the title from Spinks in May and continued on his winning ways for the remainder of the year. His professional record now read 27 contests and 27 wins.

Johnny Kidd's first opponent of the year was the experienced Nigerian Roy Jacobs who had recently drawn with Terry Spinks and lost narrowly to Howard Winstone. Kidd seemed to have done enough to win but the decision was a draw. Both Kidd and Jacobs next appeared on the April Paisley bill. Jacobs outpointed George Judge. Kidd was matched with fellow contender Derry Treanor whom British featherweights had been avoiding. Kidd was well beaten on points. In May, Treanor outpointed Belgian featherweight champion Jean Renard over 8 rounds and in November he stopped Manchester's Freddie Dobson in 7 rounds. It was a good year for Derry Treanor, 3 fights and 3 wins. He had fought only 4 times in the previous two years but had won them all. He ended the year as number one challenger to Howard Winstone and was nominated to meet him for his British title in the new year.

Johnny Kidd fought again in April. He was outpointed by unbeaten Kenny Field from Shoreditch and decided to move back to lightweight. George Judge lost 3 of his 9 fights in the year and ended the year as joint UK number 9. New professional Bobby Fisher won 4 of his 5 fights and shared the number 9 ranking with Judge. Fisher had fought Judge twice, losing the first on points but winning the return by a second round knockout. Dave Croll was inactive throughout the year and was dropped from the rankings. Johnny Morrissey had only one contest as a featherweight in the year, losing a points decision to Kenny Field.

John O'Brien applied to the British Boxing Board of Control for a licence but his application was rejected. Owen Reilly had not fought since 1959. He won his first 3 fights in 1961 but retired following a defeat by Roy Beaman.

Lightweight

By the end of May Jimmy Gibson had fought 6 times, winning 4. One loss was to the unbeaten Johnny Cooke from Liverpool and the other, to Phil McGrath of Halifax, was a travesty. London based Dave Higgins from Fife had fought 6 times since turning professional and had won all of them. The pair were matched for Gibson's Scottish lightweight title at the National Sporting Club in London on 26th June. Gibson retained his title when Higgins had to retire in the ninth round. Higgins had one further fight in the year but he was knocked out in the first round by Johnny Cooke. He subsequently disappeared from the boxing scene.

The Scottish Area Council had announced that eliminators for the Scottish lightweight title should be held between Johnny Kidd, Dave Higgins, Sammy McSpadden and Alex McMillan. No promoter made an offer for any of the eliminators but an offer was made and approved for Gibson to defend against Johnny Kidd. Gibson was unbeaten in 3 fights since defeating Higgins. Since his loss to Derry Treanor, Kidd had won 2 of his 3 fights. On 27th November, Kidd won the title by outpointing Gibson over 12 rounds in London. It was an exciting contest between two evenly matched boxers but it was a pity that the fight had not been staged in Scotland. Both boxers were ranked in the UK top 10.

Sammy McSpadden was unbeaten in 14 fights at the end of 1961. He was based in Fulham and had fought only once in his native Scotland.

Welterweight

Scottish champion Jimmy McGuinness retired. Ian McKenzie from Ayr won his first 3 professional fights.

Middleweight

The final eliminator for the British middleweight title between Cowboy McCormack and Phil Edwards of Cardiff was held at Paisley Ice Rink on 22nd February. McCormack worked and sparred with Randolph Turpin in the lead up to the fight. In a tough contest, Cowboy built up a commanding lead by the eighth round but Edwards put Cowboy down 3 times and McCormack had to work hard to take the decision on points. At the Kelvin Hall on 10th May, McCormack easily outpointed Michel Diouf over 10 rounds.

McCormack then signed with London based manager Al Phillips. His next fight was at Wembley Empire Pool on 11th July. His opponent was Nigerian Sandy Luke whom he beat on points over 8 rounds. On the same bill Terry Downes won the world middleweight title by stopping defending champion Paul Pender in the ninth round. Downes still held the British middleweight title.

Downes did not fight again in 1961. Cowboy was matched with Dutch middleweight Harko Kokmeier for the European middleweight title on 17th October at Wembley Empire Pool. He knew that a win could to lead to a possible rematch with Downes. Cowboy won the title on points over 15 rounds, winning every round. Cowboy was back in demand. George Aldridge challenged him and Phil Edwards was willing to fight for expenses only but Cowboy signed for a series of fights abroad.

Willie Fisher of Craigneuk was a new professional. He won all of his 8 contests in 1961. Another new professional, Willie Hart of Glasgow won his first 2 fights.

Light Heavyweight

Chic Calderwood was matched with Jesse Bowdry in February. However, Bowdry was nominated by the National Boxing Association to fight Harold Johnson for the world title and the bill was cancelled. At Miami Beach on 7th

February, Johnson stopped Bowdry in the ninth round to become NBA world champion. At the same time, Ring Magazine named Calderwood as number one contender to Moore.

Calderwood signed to meet Von Clay from Philadelphia at Wembley on 7th March. He was not a top ranker and it is likely that he was underestimated by Calderwood. Von Clay was an uncouth fighter but he caught Calderwood early on and broke his vulnerable nose and Chic had to box defensively to protect the damage to his nose and last the distance. Von Clay was given the verdict on points but Calderwood received a standing ovation from the crowd for his brave performance. The sting in the tail was that Von Clay then fought Harold Johnson for the World title on 24th April. Johnson stopped him in the second round.

Calderwood's first professional defeat had seen him drop down the world rankings. There was no UK competition at light heavyweight and Calderwood had to look at heavyweights as he sought to re-establish himself. The first stop in his comeback was in Liverpool. His opponent was Liverpudlian Dave Rent who had fought most of his professional career in the United States, often as a heavyweight. Chic came back in style and stopped his opponent in the seventh round. His next opponent at the Kelvin Hall was heavyweight Jim Cooper to whom he gave away a stone in weight. The outcome was a 10 round draw. The crowd booed the decision as it was clear to most that Cooper had won. Henry Cooper was at the ringside and thought that his brother had won 8 of the 10 rounds.

Calderwood was ordered to defend his British title against Southern Area champion Stan Cullis of Bristol but this contest was postponed because of back problems suffered by Calderwood following a sparring session with former Empire heavyweight champion Joe Bygraves. Calderwood also signed to defend his Empire title against Johnny Halafihi but this fight had to be postponed as Halafihi was injured. Calderwood agreed a fight in Detroit against Henry Hank who was ranked number 6 world middleweight but was fighting as a light heavyweight. The fight was scheduled for 15th December. Hank, the 2 to 1 on favourite, outpointed Calderwood over 10 rounds. Chic was well beaten although a section of the crowd booed the decision.

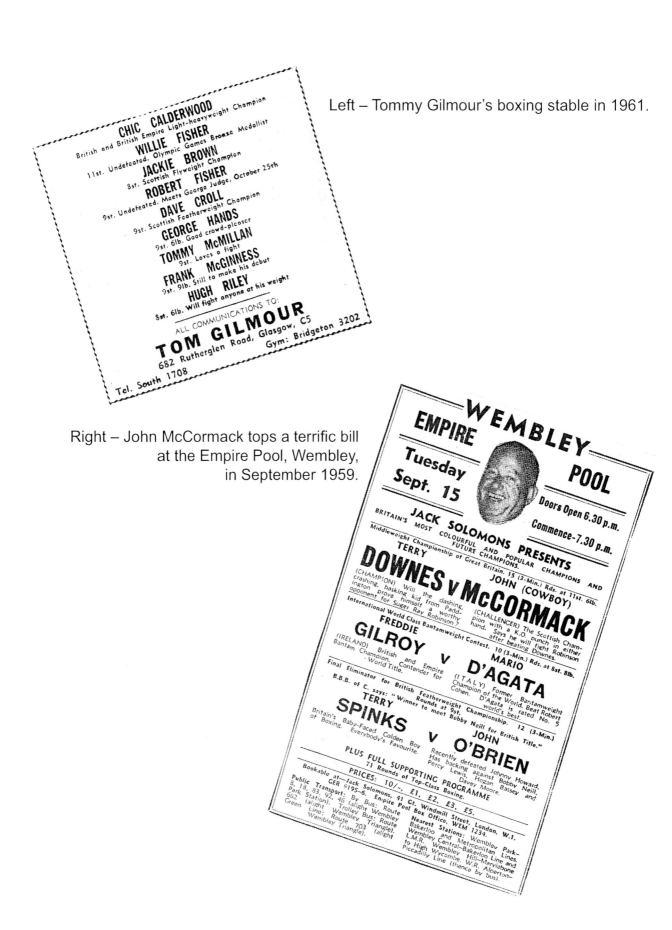

Left – Tommy Gilmour's boxing stable in 1961.

Right – John McCormack tops a terrific bill
at the Empire Pool, Wembley,
in September 1959.

80

Highlights of 1962

Flyweight

Jackie Brown fought Birmingham's Brian Cartwright for the British flyweight title in Birmingham on 27th January. Brown emerged victorious with a comfortable win on points over 15 rounds. Brown was now eyeing Salvatore Burruni's European flyweight title. He was also linked with an Empire title fight against top Australian Rocky Gattelarri or Lloyd Gordon of Canada.

Danny Lee was due to meet Walter McGowan at the Kelvin Hall on 31st January. However, McGowan was injured and the fight was postponed. Lee took on Ernie Butterworth of Manchester in March and stopped him in 6 rounds. Peter Keenan wanted to match Lee against Brown for the British title but his terms were not good enough for Brown.

Lee eventually met McGowan at the Kelvin Hall on 14th June. McGowan was the points winner over 8 rounds and he followed this up with 3 more wins, all inside the distance, against continental and American opposition.

Danny Lee returned to the ring in October but surprisingly lost to Belfast's Alex O'Neill. He was matched with Johnny Mallon for the vacant Scottish flyweight title at the National Sporting Club in London on 8th November. In his three 1962 fights to date, Mallon had lost to George Bowes, Alex O'Neill and Orizu Obilaso of Nigeria and he was also to lose his fourth against Lee. Lee became Scottish flyweight champion with a points win over 10 rounds.

Pat Glancy fought twice in the year, winning the first and losing the second. This marked the end of his boxing career.

Jackie Brown's second fight of the year was in August. His opponent was the former European champion Risto Luukkonen and the venue was Helsinki. Brown was knocked out in the fourth round. On his return to the UK, he turned down an offer to defend his title against Walter McGowan. He took two further fights in London and won both of them. He was then matched with Orizu Obilaso for the vacant Empire flyweight title at the National Sporting Club on 10th December.

Masahiko "Fighting" Harada of Japan won the world flyweight title from Pone Kingpetch in October. Jack Solomons immediately made an offer to Harada to defend against Walter McGowan. When this was turned down, Solomons turned his attention to Burruni but was again unsuccessful. Jackie Brown was busy and he too was not interested in McGowan who would have to wait.

The 10th December was another glory night for Jackie Brown. Although he was down for a 9 count in the second, he tamed the Nigerian to take the Empire flyweight title on points over 15 rounds. He ended the year as British and Empire flyweight champion but knew that he would have to defend his titles against Walter McGowan in the coming year.

Bantamweight

In May 1961, Freddie Gilroy was on the verge of quitting after losing the European bantamweight title to Pierre Cossemyns whom he had previously knocked out. He had not fought since and it was rumoured that he had weight problems in the lead up to the defence of his British and Empire bantamweight titles against Billy Rafferty in Belfast on 3rd March. Rafferty had not fought since winning the title eliminator against George Bowes in April 1961. Despite the lay offs, both boxers were in peak condition As always, Rafferty fought courageously but Gilroy was always ahead and, in the twelfth round, Rafferty was knocked out for the first time in his career. Rafferty had previously announced that he would quit if he lost and he was true to his word.

Edinburgh's Lewie Mackay found himself elevated to number 5 UK bantamweight following a win over Dai Corp and a draw with Don Weller. Tommy Burgoyne had lost twice to Corp and twice to Alex Ambrose in the period to October and had managed only 2 wins in 8 contests. The two met for the vacant Scottish bantamweight title at the Kelvin Hall on 14th November. Neither boxer was in the same class as Alex Ambrose who was not interested in the Scottish title. Burgoyne won the title, stopping Mackay in the eighth round.

Alex Ambrose had a mixed year losing 4 of his 8 fights.

Featherweight

In January, Derry Treanor became ill with shingles when training for his British featherweight title fight with Howard Winstone and the fight was rearranged for Wembley on 10th April. On the night, Winstone was well ahead when Treanor had to retire at the end of the fourteenth round. Winstone quoted that this fight had been the hardest fight of his unbeaten 29 fight career. This fight also marked the end of Derry Treanor's boxing career.

Johnny Morrissey made his first appearance in 9 months against Bobby Fisher of Craigneuk at Govan Town Hall on 27th February. Fisher had done well since turning professional in the previous year but Morrissey was a tough, experienced fighter and the match was too soon for Fisher who was knocked out in the second round. Fisher was to fight 7 more times in the year. He lost only one, on a disqualification. He outfought and outpunched Terry Spinks at the Majestic Ballroom in Finsbury Park in his best victory of the year. He had redeemed himself by the year end and was challenging for the British title.

Johnny Morrissey went from strength to strength. He was a worthy winner against Empire featherweight champion Floyd Robertson whom he stopped in 8 rounds. He outpointed Americans Gene Fossmire and Pablo Acevedo and Frenchman Rene Barriere and he fought a draw with Phil Lundgren of Bermondsey.

Dave Croll and George Judge retired. John O'Brien was granted a licence and won 2 of 4 fights in the year. In his first fight for two and a half years, he was stopped by Kenny Field in 3 rounds and then he was stopped by George Bowes in 6 rounds. He had fought fairly well in these fights but was very rusty. His next two fights showed a marked improvement. He stopped Andy Doherty in 2 rounds and then stopped Phil Lundgren, rated number 2 in the UK. He finished the year as British number 5 just behind Morrissey and Fisher.

Lightweight

Johnny Kidd began 1962 with a fine 10 round points win over Spike McCormack in Belfast. However, he lost his 5 subsequent fights in the year. Jimmy Gibson competed twice only, winning one and losing one.

Sammy McSpadden was from Newarthill but fought mainly in London as he was unable to find fights on Scottish bills. He was unbeaten in 14 professional fights at the end of 1961 and continued his progress in 1962. He fought and won 7 further contests in the year In February, he was ranked number 5 in the UK. In March, following his defeat of Shotton's Maurice Cullen, he was elevated to number one challenger to Dave Charnley. Cullen had already been nominated to fight Johnny Cooke of Bootle in a final eliminator for the British lightweight title so that McSpadden's title aspirations had to be shelved. Cullen outpointed Cooke at Liverpool in October.

Alex McMillan and Johnny McLaren retired.

Welterweight

Ian McKenzie continued his bright professional start of the previous year. He won 7 of his 8 fights in the year.

Middleweight

Cowboy McCormack started his year on 5th January in freezing Frankfurt. He was defending his European title against German Heini Freytag who was a 2 to 1 on favourite with the bookies. The bookies got it wrong this time. Cowboy gave his opponent a boxing lesson and won the fight on points over 15 rounds.

Next stop was Copenhagen to defend against the Dane Chris Christensen. Cowboy was on a promise of a fight against former world champion Gene Fullmer at Madison Square Gardens if he won convincingly. His preparation for the fight was not good and he was 9 pounds overweight at a test weigh-in. However, he did make the weight and the fight went ahead on schedule. When the fight was brought to a halt in the fourth round, bottles and glasses showered the ring and there was fighting in the crowd. The disruption lasted approximately 10 minutes during which time the result was not known. Order was restored when the verdict was announced. The verdict was that Cowboy had been disqualified and that Christensen was the new European champion.

The official reason for the disqualification was that Cowboy hit his opponent whilst the referee was still counting. The Dane had risen at 5 but the referee continued to count despite the fact that the compulsory 8 count did not apply in European title fights. An immediate return was not in the offing for Cowboy and Christensen took on and lost his title to unbeaten Laszlo Papp of Hungary on 16th May.

Cowboy wanted a match with Papp but first he had to fulfil his engagement against world number 4 middleweight Henry Hank at the Kelvin Hall on 14th June. McCormack crashed his way into the world rankings by trouncing the American on points.

In the following months, Laszlo Papp avoided McCormack whom he considered to be too dangerous. The world scene was dominated by American-based fighters who were not interested in fighting Cowboy. Terry Downes had lost his world middleweight title and was ordered to defend his British middleweight title against McCormack. Downes was struggling to make middleweight and showed no interest in defending his title against McCormack. The British Boxing Board of Control therefore stripped Downes of the title and decided that Cowboy must fight George Aldridge of Market Harborough for the vacant title. The winner would meet Laszlo Papp for the European title. The fight was scheduled for Manchester on 26th November.

Cowboy was in great demand and was offered top fights in Vienna, Paris, London and New York. His next fight, however, was at the Kelvin Hall in September when he outpointed American Ike White over 10 rounds. As the date of the title fight approached, it was clear that Cowboy was struggling with his fitness and in making the weight. The Scottish Area Council suggested a postponement but this suggestion was dismissed by the Board and Cowboy had to lose in excess of 10 pounds in the days prior to the fight. Aldridge knocked Cowboy out in the sixth round but it appeared that the last gasp weight reduction was the cause of Cowboy's defeat.

Willie Fisher won 5 of his 6 fights in the year and his British ranking was 7 at the end of the year. However, Willie Hart won only 2 of 5 fights.

Light Heavyweight

Chic Calderwood defended his British and Empire titles against Stan Cullis of Bristol at the National Sporting Club in London on 12th February. Cullis was no match for the champion and was knocked out in the ninth round. During the fight, Calderwood sustained a broken bone in his hand and was unable to fight for some months.

His next contest was a defence of his Empire title against Tongan Johnny Halafihi at Newcastle on 4th June. With a combination of boxing skill and powerful punching, Calderwood retained his title with a 15 round points victory but he was again injured and had to postpone his next arranged fight with Giulio Rinaldo of Italy for the vacant European light heavyweight title.

The fight was rescheduled for September. The venue was the Palazzo Dello Sport in Rome. Rinaldo was a hot favourite and thought to be invincible in Rome. He had beaten world champion Archie Moore in Rome but had lost the rematch in the USA. The fight lasted 15 rounds and Calderwood was the clear winner but predictably Rinaldo was given the decision. The crowd booed and jeered the verdict which should have gone to Calderwood.

Calderwood broke his hand again in October and did not fight again in 1962. He was ranked eighth in the world at the end of 1962.

PROMOTER AND BOXER

ARTICLES OF AGREEMENT

(For the use of Members of the B.B.B. of C. only)

Where alternatives appear in italics they must all except one be struck out.

An Agreement made this 6th day of APRIL 19 62 between
JOHN MORRISSEY of GLASGOW
(hereinafter called the Promoters) of the one part
and GUS DEMMY PROMOTIONS of
(hereinafter called the Boxer) of the other part

All blank spaces must be completed before signature.

WHEREBY IT IS AGREED THAT:

1. The Boxer shall appear and box at FREE TRADE HALL on the afternoon/evening of MONDAY APRIL 9th 1962 in a contest of 10 rounds of 3 minutes each round against FLOYD ROBERTSON of GHANA & BELFAST or such substitute Boxer (hereinafter called the opponent Boxer) as hereinafter provided in accordance with the Boxing Rules of the B.B.B. of C.

2. The Boxer shall weigh-in at 9 stone 2 lb. at 1— p.m. at FREE TRADE HALL on the date of the contest. If overweight the Boxer shall be allowed one hour to make the agreed weight. If he is then overweight he shall pay a weight forfeit to the opponent Boxer of £ 5

3. The Promoter shall provide in his agreement with the opponent Boxer that the opponent Boxer shall weigh-in at 9 stone 2 lb. (under similar conditions to the Boxer) and if overweight the opponent Boxer shall pay a weight forfeit to the Boxer of £ 5

4. The Promoter shall be responsible for the collection and payment of weight forfeits. The payment of forfeit money as above shall in no way prevent the Board or Area Council taking any action they deem necessary under REGULATIONS 15 and 22.

5. If the opponent Boxer shall be not more than 1 lb. above the stipulated weight, the Boxer will box him and shall be paid the agreed weight forfeit.

6. In the event of the Boxer failing to appear and box or to weigh-in as provided above (except under circumstances set out under Clause 15A of this Agreement), in consequence of which the contest does not take place, he shall pay to the Promoter the sum of £ damages and any such additional amount as may be assessed by the Board or Area Council after being satisfied that such additional damages have been incurred.

7. In the event of the Promoter failing to supply a duly qualified opponent he shall pay to the Boxer £ damages and any such additional amount that may be assessed by the Board or Area Council after being satisfied that such additional damages have been incurred.

8A. In consideration for boxing as above the Promoter shall pay to the Boxer the sum of £ 150-0-0 per cent. of the Gross Receipts if he wins the said contest, £ 150-0-0 or per cent. of the Gross Receipts if he loses, and £ 150-0-0 or per cent. of the Gross Receipts if the said contest is drawn. For the purpose of this Agreement it is agreed that Gross Receipts do not include Entertainment Tax, and any fee payable in respect of Broadcast, Television or Film(s).

8B. The Promoter shall deduct such sum as may be payable in accordance with REGULATION 20, PARAGRAPH 38 (A) and (B) of the B.B.B. of C. REGULATIONS and shall forthwith pay to the B.B.B. of C. the moneys so deducted.

9. In the event of an Agreement being entered into for the said contest to be Broadcast or Televised, whether by the B.B.C. or any other person, firm or corporation, either in Great Britain or elsewhere, the Promoter shall pay to the Boxer 23½ per cent. of the fee or fees so received. In the event of the contest being filmed 23½ per cent. of the fee shall be paid to the Boxer. Fees in respect of Broadcast, Television or Film(s) shall be treated as being separate and apart from the purse money mentioned in Clause 8.

In cases of Television or Broadcast of boxing contests where the fee is paid for a period of time as distinct from a specific contest 47½ per cent. of the fee is to be divided among the Boxers concerned in the Broadcast or Television. In the event of any dispute arising from the allocation of such fees the sum payable to the Boxers shall be forwarded by the Promoter within twenty-four hours of receipt, to the Board or Area Council concerned, who shall decide in their absolute discretion as to the allocation.

10. The Boxer shall on the signing of this Agreement deposit the sum of £ with the Board or Area Council as a guarantee of his appearance and his compliance with the conditions. In the event of the contest taking place, the sum deposited shall be returned to the Boxer.

11. The Referee shall be appointed by the Board or Area Council of the B.B.B. of C.

12. The Boxer shall not box publicly or in any Boxing Booth days before the date of the contest without the consent in writing of the Promoter.

13. The Boxer, within eight hours of the contest, shall be certified in a fit condition to box by a duly qualified Medical Officer appointed by the Promoter, or, if called upon to do so by the Board, Area Council or the Promoter at any time by a Medical Officer appointed by the Board or an Area Council.

14. The Boxer shall from the date hereof until the contest conform in all respects to the reasonable arrangements made by the Promoter for, or in any way concerning, the contest, and shall not be guilty of any act or conduct calculated or which might reasonably be expected to render him unfit to carry out the terms of this Contract in all respects and will carry out all reasonable requirements of the Promoter which are put forward for the success of the contest and the fitness of the Boxer.

NOTE.—Promoters, Managers and Boxers should particularly note lines 4 and 5 of the first paragraph of Clause 9.

One hundred and fifty pounds all in

Johnny Morrissey's contract for his fight with Floyd Robertson

Highlights of 1963

At the beginning of 1963, Jackie Brown was the British and Empire flyweight champion and Chic Calderwood was the British and Empire light heavyweight champion.

<u>Flyweight</u>

Jackie Brown had a January fight in Manchester against Belfast's Alex O'Neill whom he stopped in 7 rounds. This was a fine win as the rugged O'Neill was just behind Walter McGowan in the British rankings. McGowan then faced Frenchman Bernard Jubert at the Kelvin Hall on 31st January and had a convincing points victory over 8 rounds.

Brown had agreed to defend his Empire title in Australia against Rocky Gattelarri. However, the British Boxing Board of Control stopped him from taking this fight because of his impending British title fight. He had also taken a February fight in Manchester and another in Paris against the tough Tunisian Felix Brami. These fights were also due to take place before his defence against McGowan on 20th March. As a result of injury, however, Brown had to withdraw from both of these contests. He was also upset that French champion Rene Libeer had been nominated to fight Salvatore Burruni for the European title. His reasoning was that he had beaten Walter McGowan who had beaten Libeer

Brown finally faced McGowan at Paisley Ice Rink on 2nd May in an encounter eagerly awaited by all of the British boxing public. A world title fight with Pone Kingpetch possibly awaited the winner. Brown was the harder puncher but McGowan oozed class and was very fast. It was McGowan who won a hard fight with a twelfth round knockout. There was no doubt that he was ahead on points and that the courageous Brown seemed to tire towards the end. McGowan was the new British and Empire champion.

McGowan returned to Paisley in June and performed magnificently to stop American champion and world number 6 Ray Perez of Honolulu with a dazzling boxing display. He turned down a non-title fight with Salvatore Burruni but took on the unknown Kid Solomon of Jamaica and put his Empire title at stake. McGowan stopped his man in the ninth round of a one sided fight to retain his British Empire flyweight title.

Jackie Brown did not fight again until September when he travelled to Paris to take on Felix Brami. He lasted only 3 rounds before the referee stopped the fight. He finished the year with a points victory over Kid Solomon and would in future fight as a bantamweight.

Hiroyuki Ebihara of Japan was the new world champion following his defeat of Pone Kingpetch. In October, McGowan was named by the European Boxing Union as official challenger for the European flyweight title held by Burruni. He was also ranked number 4 in the world. He was due to fight Pascual Perez at Paisley in November but the former world champion called off and was replaced by Ric Magramo of the Phillipines. McGowan was a convincing points winner over Magramo and took a further step towards a fight for the world title.

Danny Lee won only 2 of 5 fights in the year. He fought Rocky Gattelarri in Sydney in May but was stopped in the fifth round. Johnny Mallon won 1 of 2 and moved up to bantamweight.

Bantamweight

Alex Ambrose travelled to Paris to take on Felix Brami on 21st March. He lost the contest on points over 10 rounds and retired from the sport. Lewie Mackay had quit boxing following a kidney complaint. Tommy Burgoyne was now the leading Scottish bantamweight. He fought 6 times in the year, winning only 2 but these were against top 10 bantamweights. He finished the year ranked 8 in the UK.

Evan Armstrong from Ayr made had a winning professional debut at Paisley Ice Rink in November.

Featherweight

At the Kelvin Hall on 31st January, Johnny Morrissey attempted to become the sixth Scot to win the British featherweight title. The champion, Howard Winstone, was a classy boxer and took control of the fight from the early stages. In an inspired display, he stopped the plucky Scot in the eleventh round to retain his title. Morrissey fought only once more in the year. The result was a draw against the highly rated Dennis Adjei of Ghana. Morrissey had agreed a return fight with Freddie Gilroy in March but a nose injury forced Gilroy to withdraw from Jack Solomon's Glasgow bill and he was replaced by Adjei.

Bobby Fisher was just behind Johnny Morrissey in the rankings and had been matched with Billy Calvert of Sheffield in a final eliminator for the right to fight Winstone. The venue was the Kelvin Arena on 28th February. Fisher was on top throughout the contest but was knocked out in the tenth round when he was caught by a sucker punch.

John O'Brien outpointed Con Mount Bassie on the same bill. This followed his revenge win over George Bowes in Blackpool. O'Brien was now looking to be the Scot who might be most likely to give Winstone a contest. O'Brien flew to Milan where he faced Italian Champion Lino Mastellaro on 5th April. Mastellaro had fought a 15 round draw with European champion Gracieux Lamperti in the previous year and he was a top fighter. The 10 rounds points decision went against O'Brien but he fought well.

Gracieux Lamperti had lost his European title in 1962 to Italian Alberto Serti and Serti defended his title against Howard Winstone in Cardiff on 9th July. Winstone stopped Serti in the fourteenth round to become European champion. He then successfully defended both his European and British featherweight titles against Billy Calvert on 20th August

Bobby Fisher had fought once since losing to Calvert and had won the fight convincingly. He next agreed to fight John O'Brien at Paisley Ice Rink on 12th September. Labelled an unofficial eliminator for the British and European titles, victory went to O'Brien who stopped Fisher in the second round. Winstone agreed to defend his titles against O'Brien subject to the approval of the British Boxing Board of Control. Approval followed and the contest was arranged for the National Sporting Club in London on 9th December. The venue sparked controversy as the NSC was a private members club and any championship fight had to be staged at a public venue. The Board allowed the venue to proceed as contracts had been signed in good faith. Winstone once again showed his class winning clearly on points over 15 rounds. O'Brien was courageous and fought well but was beaten by a true champion.

Bobby Fisher fought 3 more times in the year and won 2, against Dennis Adjei and lower ranked Mick Greaves. His end of year UK ranking had dropped to 10 whereas Morrissey and O'Brien were still top 3.

Lightweight

Sammy McSpadden extended his unbeaten run with 2 wins in March. He headed off to Madison Square Gardens in New York for his next fight against the highly rated Italian American Johnny Bizzaro. McSpadden tasted defeat for the first time, losing a 10 round points decision, but gained many admirers in the USA. He returned to the UK determined to win a fight against Dave Charnley for the British lightweight title which Charnley had held since 1957. McSpadden received numerous offers of fights in the United States, South Africa and Australia but opted to fight on in his old London stamping ground in September. He returned with a points victory over Spike McCormack.

The world lightweight champion was Carlos Ortiz of Puerto Rico. Ortiz was in London on 10th October to fight Maurice Cullen who had already lost to McSpadden. McSpadden got a slot on the same bill against Sugar Ramos of Cuba who was the world featherweight champion. Cullen lost on points and McSpadden was stopped in 2 rounds. The referee was a bit hasty in stopping the fight but, although McSpadden was not disgraced, there was a clear gap in class between the Ramos and the Scot.

McSpadden then took off to South Africa to fight the South African lightweight champion Stoffel Steyn and was outpointed over 10 rounds in Johannesburg on 2nd November. He had gained much experience in the year but his 3 defeats had seen his British ranking remain at 3 and a British title chance continued to elude him.

Johnny Kidd fought 5 times, won 2 and retired. Jimmy Gibson moved up to welterweight.

Welterweight

Ian McKenzie moved up to middleweight. Three new welterweights appeared on the scene. Norrie McCulloch from Glasgow won his first 6 fights. Andy Wyper from Newmilns won his first 5 fights and drew his sixth. Don McMillan from Glasgow won 3 of his 4 fights. His defeat was to Wyper. The Scottish Area Council ruled that Wyper should fight either McCulloch or McMillan for the Scottish welterweight title. Peter Keenan opted to sign up McMillan against Wyper for the title in the new year.

Jimmy Gibson fought twice, won one and had a British ranking of 9 for most of the year. However, he would not fight again.

Middleweight

Willie Hart won 4 of 6 fights in the year. He fought Ian McKenzie for the vacant Scottish middleweight title on 30th May at the Kelvin Hall but lost on points over 10 rounds. McKenzie won 2 of 5 fights in the year. Willie Fisher won only 2 of 6 in the year but one victory was an 8 round points win over Ian McKenzie on 28th November. Fisher was ranked between 6 and 7 in the UK throughout the year and was the only ranked Scot at the year end.

Light Heavyweight

John McCormack moved up to light heavyweight but had one fight only in 1963. He fought at Wembley Pool on 10th September against Central Area middleweight champion Harry Scott from Liverpool. The referee stopped the fight in favour of Scott in the fifth round after McCormack had been on the canvas 7 times. McCormack was in decline and Scott would not have been allowed in the same ring when Cowboy was at his peak. McCormack was banned for 2 months and fined £25 for putting on such an inept performance.

Chic Calderwood began the year on 14th January with a 10 round points win over heavyweight Ray Shiel. He turned down a fight with former European light heavyweight champion Eric Schoeppner but accepted a fight with Jose Torres, the unbeaten and highly rated Puerto Rican. However, Calderwood fractured a bone in his hand during an exhibition bout in January and the Torres fight was cancelled.

Calderwood was back in the ring at the Kelvin Hall on 21st March when he convincingly outpointed American Tommy Fields over 10 rounds. There was now talk of Calderwood facing Californian Wayne Thornton in an eliminator for the world title. The title was held by Harold Johnson but he was due to defend against Willie Pastrano on 1st June. Calderwood fought his old American adversary Von Clay at the Kelvin Hall on 30th May. Von Clay had lost a world title fight to Johnson 1961 following his defeat of Calderwood. This time Calderwood was an easy winner against a disappointing Von Clay. On the next evening, Willie Pastrano became the new light heavyweight champion of the world.

Calderwood next appeared at Paisley Ice Rink on 27th June. His opponent was American Eddie Cotton who was number 3 contender to Pastrano. A world title fight was a distinct possibility if he beat Cotton. However, Calderwood lost to Cotton on points but it was a close contest. There was fighting amongst spectators and coins, bottles and beer cans were thrown following the disputed decision. Calderwood was offered a contest at Madison Square Gardens against Henry Hank or Wayne Thornton but he chose to defend his British and Empire titles against Ron Redrup of West Ham in Blackpool on 30th July. He won every round and stopped Redrup in the eleventh but damaged both of his hands in the process

He was next due to fight American Freddie Mack at Newcastle but tore a stomach muscle and was hospitalised for ten days. A fight was meantime arranged against former European middleweight champion Gustav Scholz in Dortmund on 16th November. The winner of this contest was expected to face Giulio Rinaldi for Rinaldi's European title. After he signed for the fight with Scholz, the European Boxing Union ruled that Rinaldi should defend against Scholz despite the fact that Calderwood had been number one contender for 6 months. In Dortmund, Calderwood fought abysmally and was well beaten on points over 10 rounds. Calderwood's world ranking had improved from 8 to 7 during the year but he dropped out of the top 10 following the Scholz defeat. He also forfeited his British and Empire titles as a result of a conviction for assault.

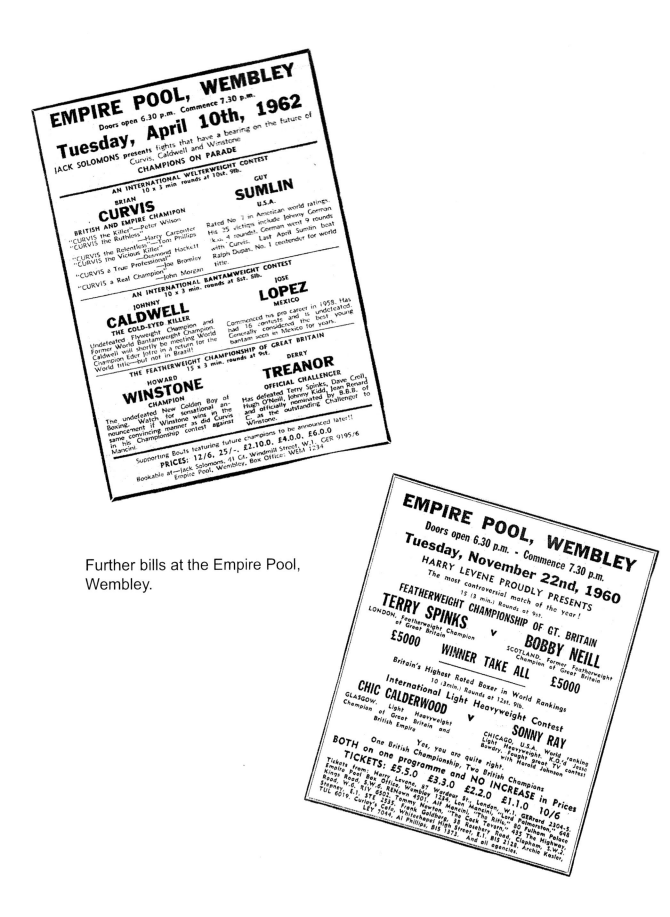

Further bills at the Empire Pool, Wembley.

Highlights of 1964

At the beginning of 1964, Walter McGowan was British and Empire flyweight champion. No other Scots held major titles.

Flyweight

Walter McGowan was due to fight Salvatore Burruni for the European flyweight title in early 1964. Burruni had won the title in June 1961 from Risto Luukkonen and had successfully defended the title against Derek Lloyd, Ben Ali, Pierre Rossi and Rene Libeer. He was unbeaten in 4 years, had lost only 3 of 66 contests in 7 years and would be a formidable opponent for McGowan.

Burruni called off the fight with McGowan because of weight problems. He had won 2 warm-up contests in January but was 9 pounds over the flyweight limit and there was therefore a chance that he would be stripped of his title before he fought McGowan. In February, he weighed 8 stone 6 pounds when he outpointed Brian Cartwright over 10 rounds. He was due to fight Jackie Brown on 6th March but called off with a mystery injury. The contest was rescheduled for 25th March and Burruni scaled 8 stone 8 pounds at the weigh-in. However, Brown was barred from fighting because of an ear infection.

McGowan had taken a contest at 8 stone 8 pounds against Risto Luukkonen who was now European bantamweight champion and had suffered only 4 losses in 35 contests. The venue was Paisley Ice Rink on 4th March and Walter proved too fast for his most famous victim to date. Luukkonen was teased and tormented throughout the contest in what was a spectacular victory for Walter. He won clearly despite conceding height, weight, reach and experience to his 32 year old opponent.

The contest with Burruni had been rescheduled for 24th April at Palazzo Dello Sport in Rome. There was a worry that some fiasco would be contrived in advance of the contest because of the champion's weight difficulties. This did not happen and the champion weighed in under the limit. The fight lasted 15 rounds and the Italian was battered and bruised by the final bell but he had come back strongly in the closing stages to clinch the verdict. McGowan had fought tremendously well but his opponent's strength, stamina and experience proved just too much for the Scot who accepted the verdict graciously. McGowan left the ring with the cheers of the normally partisan crowd ringing in his ears in recognition of his fine display. It was apparent that McGowan required more experience at this level if he was to challenge Pone Kingpetch who had regained the world flyweight title.

When back in Scotland, Walter had to consider his future. A tour of the Far East or the USA was suggested as was a contest with John Caldwell or a defence of his Empire title in Australia against Rocky Gattelarri. In the end, he opted to take on Natalio Jiminez of the Dominican Republic at Paisley on 3rd September. Jiminez had lost only to Burruni, Gattelarri and world number 5 Efren Torres. Walter won well, outboxing his opponent in virtually every round. He had one more outing in the year, stopping Spanish flyweight champion Luis Rodriguez in 2 rounds.

McGowan had made continued progress in the year. His world ranking had improved to 6 by the year end.

Danny Lee moved up to bantamweight during the year.

Bantamweight

Scottish bantamweight title holder Tommy Burgoyne defended his title against Jackie Brown at the National Sporting Club in London on 24th February. Brown took the title with a comfortable points win over 10 rounds. He was so delighted with his win that he danced a jig of victory but slipped and twisted his ankle which put his fight with Burruni on 6th March in doubt. The contest was rescheduled but, as mentioned above, Brown was unable to fight because of an ear infection. His next arranged contest was with Alan Rudkin on 16th June in what was considered to be a final eliminator for the British and Empire bantamweight titles now held by John Caldwell. Brown had also to withdraw from this contest because of a lump on his groin and a boil on his thigh. The injury-prone Brown was now being considered a bad risk by promoters.

He did fight at Porthcawl against Welshman Glyn Davies on 28th July and recorded a convincing 8 round points win. His third and final contest of the year was against British and Empire bantamweight champion and former world bantamweight champion John Caldwell at Paisley Ice Rink on 11th November. Jackie Brown completely outboxed John Caldwell in what was undoubtedly the best performance of his career but had to be content with a draw over 10 rounds.

Tommy Burgoyne won 1 of 9. Danny Lee lost both of his fights. Johnny Mallon retired. Evan Armstrong was fighting mainly as a featherweight.

The year end British rankings saw Jackie Brown at number 3, Danny Lee at 7 and Tommy Burgoyne at 9.

Featherweight

John O'Brien was Scotland's top featherweight but had great difficulty in finding British opponents. He did not fight between December 1963 when he lost in his bid to lift the British title and December 1964 when he fought the rugged Ghanain Dennis Adjei. Both were leading Empire featherweights and it was likely that the winner would be matched with Empire champion Floyd Robertson, also a Ghanain. O'Brien outclassed Adjei with a superb display and the referee had to stop the fight in the seventh round following a flurry of left hooks from the Scot.

Although ranked just behind champion, Howard Winstone, O'Brien had been ignored by the British Board of Control which announced George Bowes v

Frankie Taylor as a final eliminator. Perhaps his 12 month period of inactivity had led to the snub.

Next ranked Scot was Johnny Morrissey who had one contest which he won. However, Johnny then retired as he was having weight difficulties.

Next in line was Bobby Fisher. Fisher had 4 contests in the year but lost 2 of them. He was knocked out by Ghanain Joe Tetteh and was stopped in one round by world number 4 featherweight Rafiu King of Nigeria.

Evan Armstrong won 7 of 9 contests and ended the year as British number 8, one place behind Bobby Fisher. He had been stopped by Fisher in September.

Lightweight

Sammy McSpadden was Scotland's leading lightweight. On 17th January, he fought South African champion Stoffel Steyn in Capetown and was outpointed over 10 rounds. In his next fight in Durban on 14th February, he stopped the former South African champion Charlie Els. McSpadden was now struggling to make lightweight and stepped up to welterweight. Scotland had no other lightweights in the British rankings.

Welterweight

In July, Sammy McSpadden outpointed Ricky McMasters from Jamaica and in November, he outpointed Johnny Cooke of Bootle who was a leading challenger to Brian Curvis for the British and Empire welterweight titles.

The Scottish welterweight title fight between Andy Wyper and Don McMillan was held at Govan Town Hall on 21st January. Wyper emerged the victor when McMillan had to retire with a badly cut mouth in the seventh round. Wyper followed up with 4 more victories. Due to a lack of suitable UK opponents, Wyper was matched with his first continental opponent at the National Sporting Club in London on 5th October. Wyper's style was all out attack from the first bell but this tactic did not work against Spaniard Jose Medrazo in October. Wyper sustained a cut eye and suffered his first loss when the referee had to stop the fight in the fifth round. A rematch was arranged in November but astonishingly neither boxer appeared at the weigh-in and the match was cancelled. In December, Wyper was outpointed by Sean Doyle from Barnsley. Two successive defeats meant that Wyper's reputation had taken a knock.

Don McMillan had been unlucky in his fight with Wyper. He had 5 further fights in the year and won them all and was moving back up the ratings.

Norrie McCulloch won his first 3 fights of the year but lost to Liverpool's Brian McCaffrey in his final fight.

Scotland was well represented in the welterweight division but only British number 8 Sammy McSpadden and number 10 Andy Wyper were recognised at the top level.

Middleweight

Willie Hart had a good year winning all 4 of his fights. In contrast, Scottish middleweight champion Ian McKenzie lost all 3 of his fights in the year. Willie Fisher won one out of 3 and remained the top ranked Scottish middleweight.

Light Heavyweight

Chic Calderwood had forfeited his British and Empire titles when he was imprisoned for three months for assault. Old foes Giulio Rinaldi and Willie Pastrano were now the European and world light heavyweight champions respectively. Whilst Chic Calderwood was in Saughton Prison, his great rival John McCormack had stepped up from middleweight to light heavyweight. In January, Cowboy knocked out Empire contender Joe Louis from Nigeria in the first round at Govan Town Hall and five minutes elapsed before the Nigerian regained consciousness.

At the end of January, Calderwood was released from prison. He was ordered to appear before the British Boxing Board of Control on 12th February. His licence could have been revoked but the Board chose to suspend him for 3 months and to severely reprimand him as to his future conduct. Calderwood had expected the worst and was accordingly delighted at the outcome. Fight offers were in abundance and he had sufficient time to consider these carefully.

Cowboy McCormack took on Crewe's Malcolm Worthington at Paisley Ice Rink on 4th March and knocked him out in the first round. This was another impressive finish by Cowboy against a high ranking British light heavyweight. Unfortunately, McCormack was injured in May and did not fight again in 1964. He had been due to appear on the same Kelvin Hall bill on 28th May as Terry Downes and the Chic Calderwood comeback.

Calderwood made a cautious return against Alan Harmon of Jamaica who decided that he had suffered enough after 6 rounds of a one-sided fight and did not come out for the seventh. There had been some slow-handclapping during the fight because of the lack of good action. In contrast, the Downes fight was all action. Downes pummelled the highly-rated American Eddie Zaremba and was a worthy points winner over 10 rounds.

Downes, Calderwood and McCormack were the top 3 light heavyweights in the UK. Downes had no interest in the British title and had set his sights on Willie Pastrano's world title despite the fact that he was not in the world rankings. Calderwood wanted back his British title and McCormack wanted Calderwood.

Calderwood next took on the durable Freddie Cross from Nuneaton, ranked number 8 in Britain. At Porthcawl on 28th July, Cross did no more than give Chic a valuable workout and the Scot was a clear points winner over 8 rounds. Calderwood was then awarded a British title fight against Bob Nicholson of Farnborough. At Paisley Ice Rink on 9th November, Calderwood won back the British title with a straightforward win, the referee stopping the fight in the seventh round.

On 30th November, Willie Pastrano retained his world light heavyweight title in Manchester by stopping Terry Downes in the eleventh round. Calderwood was at the ringside. Peter Keenan subsequently asked Pastrano to defend against Calderwood whom Pastrano rated as a very good fighter. Refusing an £18,000 cash offer, Pastrano told Keenan that he would not defend in Glasgow as he had felt intimidated by the crowd in his previous fight with Calderwood. He had never been so happy losing a fight as he could not comprehend what would have happened if he had won.

Downes wanted a rematch. However, the Scottish Area Council let it be known that it would contest any rematch. The Council felt that Downes should first face Calderwood for the British title rather than be allowed a rematch. In any case, Pastrano was not interested in fighting Downes again and disappeared back to the USA with his title.

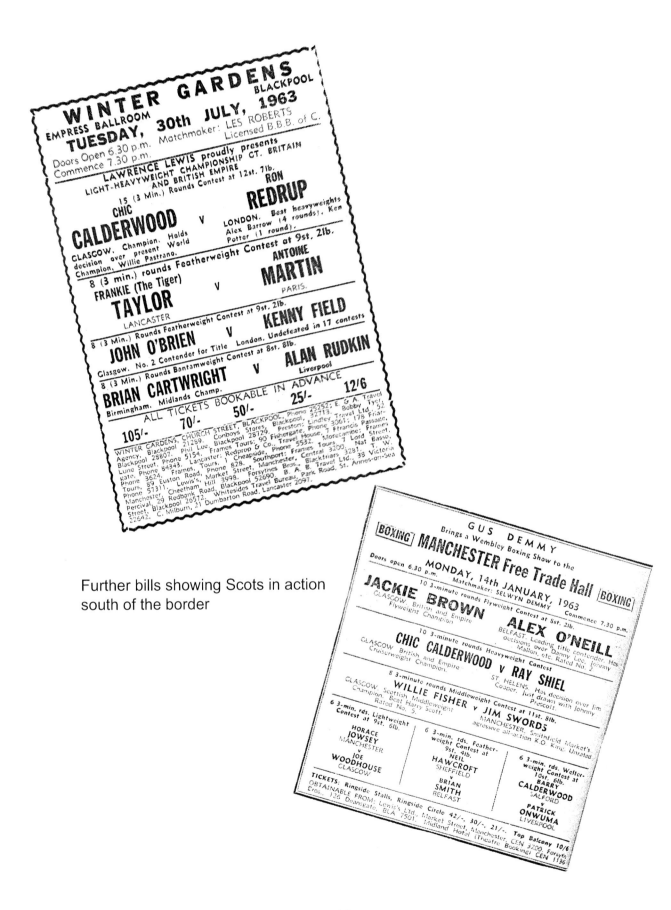

Further bills showing Scots in action south of the border

Highlights of 1965

Flyweight

Walter McGowan was British and Empire flyweight Champion but had no UK opposition on these fronts and had to take on bantamweights throughout 1965. He was brilliant in January when he stopped Londoner Mick Hussey in 3 rounds at Solihull. He next fought at the Royal Albert Hall in February against the tough Tunisian bantamweight Felix Brami, unbeaten in 28 fights, and ranked world number 6. As the hard punching Brami had knocked out 14 of his opponents to date, many of the media thought that a similar fate awaited McGowan. However, on the night, Walter's all-round performance was a revelation. His brilliant display showed why he was considered to be the fastest and slickest flyweight/ bantamweight in the world. He was a clear victor on points over 10 rounds and was a cut above any opponent that Brami had previously met. This was undoubtedly McGowan's greatest victory to date.

World champion Pone Kingpetch had been enticed from Thailand to Rome to defend his title against 32 year old European champion Salvatore Burruni on 23rd April. McGowan watched Burruni win the title on points with ease. McGowan had been booked on to the same bill against the vastly experienced Italian bantamweight champion, Federico Scarponi. However, the Italian called off and was substituted by the undistinguished Ghanain Benny Lee whom McGowan had no trouble defeating on points over 10 rounds, despite conceding 8 pounds to the Ghanain.

Burruni subsequently relinquished his European title. Rene Libeer of France beat Paul Chervet of Switzerland to take the vacant title in June.

London promoter Jack Solomons had been promised that Burruni's first defence would be against McGowan in London. However when problems arose, Solomons arranged for Brazilian world bantamweight champion Eder Jofre to defend against McGowan in September. This was subject to Jofre retaining his title against Fighting Harada of Japan on 18th May but as Jofre was unbeaten in 50 fights, this did not seem likely. As a warm-up, McGowan was matched with world number 5 bantamweight Jose Medel of Mexico. This was a dangerous match and a loss would upset McGowan's world title plans.

Former world flyweight champion Harada outpointed Jofre in Japan and McGowan was stopped in the sixth round by Medel. McGowan displayed his customary speed and skill but these qualities did not prove to be enough against a heavier and harder-hitting opponent and Medel was clearly ahead when the referee stopped the fight. The September match with Jofre was now off and it was back to the drawing board for McGowan.

In early July, McGowan was matched with Tommaso Galli who had won the Italian bantamweight title from Federico Scarponi in June, but the fight was called off late. He was back in the ring at Paisley in August. He fought American Ron Jones who had previously beaten Jackie Brown comprehensively. Walter won the first 5 rounds but emerged from a clinch in the sixth with a nasty eye cut. It was not clear whether the damage had been inflicted by a punch or the head of Jones. Nevertheless, it was the end for Walter who had to have 8 stitches inserted in the wound. Jones was complimentary in victory. He acknowledged that McGowan was the fastest and most difficult opponent that he had ever met and he was sure that McGowan would one day be world flyweight champion. As a result of his injury, McGowan did not fight again until December.

Salvatore Burruni knocked out Rocky Gattelarri in December in the first defence of his world title.

John McCluskey joined the professional ranks during the year and won his first 2 fights.

Bantamweight

Jackie Brown began the year with wins inside the distance in February and March. He was at the ringside at Nottingham on 22nd March to see Alan Rudkin's gutsy performance in winning the British and Empire bantamweight titles from John Caldwell. Brown returned to Scotland and in his next fight he outclassed Spaniard Ramon Casal, again inside the distance. Peter Keenan matched Brown with world number 6 Ron Jones of Chicago on his Paisley bill on June 10th. This was a great opportunity for Brown but he was unfortunately knocked out in the second round by Jones. Brown had 2 further fights in the year and won them both. He finished the year ranked 4 in the UK behind Rudkin, Caldwell and Monty Laud. Danny Lee retired. Tommy Burgoyne won only one of 8 and disappeared from the rankings.

Jose Medel had already beaten the new world champion Fighting Harada and looked likely to become the next world champion. In June, Medel was named number one contender for the world title. However, Harada sidestepped the Mexican and defended against Alan Rudkin in Tokyo in November. He retained the title with a points victory.

Italian Tommaso Galli won the European bantamweight title from Ben Ali in August. He was unbeaten in 19 contests when he made a voluntary defence of the title against Walter McGowan. In Rome on 3rd December, McGowan outboxed Galli and was a clear winner but the result was declared a draw so that the Italian retained the title. The reaction of the crowd to the decision mirrored that of the press who, to a man, thought that McGowan had been robbed of the decision.

Featherweight

Fiery John O'Brien's first outing of the year was in Glasgow on 4th February. His opponent was number 4 world ranked Nigerian Rafiu King. O'Brien fought well and was on top after 4 rounds. However, in the fifth the referee stopped the fight in favour of King as a result of a one inch cut sustained by O'Brien. Angry fans roared their disapproval to what was a disappointing ending to a great contest.   The loss put paid to an O'Brien return against Howard Winstone.

O'Brien's next appearance was in front of 16,000 fans at Earls Court on 7th September on the Howard Winstone v Vicente Saldivar's World title bill. He knocked out his opponent Jesus Saucedo of Mexico, Saldivar's sparring partner, in the fourth round with a devastating left hook.   The Mexican remained on the canvas for 4 minutes receiving medical treatment and unfortunately died later from the injuries sustained in the fight.   O'Brien decided to continue boxing and travelled to Mexico for his last fight of the year. He was stopped in the eighth round by Mexican champion Mario Diaz who was ranked world number 6. O'Brien was well-beaten and was never in the fight.

Evan Armstrong had 8 fights in the year and won 7 of them. His sole defeat to Coventry's Tony Riley was a surprise but he put the record books straight by stopping Riley in their return.   He was due to fight Bobby Fisher for the vacant Scottish title but the contest was cancelled due to illness and never did take place.   The best performance of his career to date was in November when he stopped former number one contender George Bowes. He finished the year ranked British number 5, just one place behind John O'Brien.

Bobby Fisher dropped out of the rankings due to inactivity.

Lightweight

Ken Buchanan had his first professional fight in September.   He won the contest convincingly in the second round and went on to record further wins in his next 4 fights.

Welterweight

Sammy McSpadden was the leading contender for the British and Empire welterweight titles held by Swansea's Brian Curvis. In February, he was due to fight fellow Scot Don MacMillan but McSpadden had to withdraw due to illness and did not manage a contest until early June. At the Empire Pool, Wembley, his opponent was the talented and unbeaten Moroccan Nessim Cohen whom McSpadden skilfully outpointed over 10 rounds. Next stop was Johannesburg and Willie Ludick of South Africa who was ranked number 4 welterweight in the world. The South African champion had outpointed Brian Curvis in April and was virtually unbeatable in his homeland. A victory would have propelled McSpadden up the rankings but fortune did not smile on the Scot who was outpointed over 10 rounds.

McSpadden remained in South Africa to take on Fraser Toweel who had lost to Ludick on several occasions.   The outcome was another 10 round points defeat. McSpadden fought well in both contests but it was very difficult to go to South Africa in the sixties and win a points decision.   Undeterred, McSpadden returned to Fulham where he was soon notified that he was to fight Brian Curvis for the British and Empire titles.

McSpadden was the first Scot in 26 years to fight for the British welterweight title and he was keen to emulate the achievements of Jake Kilrain. Curvis had lost a points decision for the world welterweight title in the previous year against Emile Griffith but retained a ranking of 4 in the world. The match was at Sophia Gardens, Cardiff on 25th November and Curtis was the overwhelming favourite. McSpadden fought bravely but his courage was not enough to thwart Curvis whose punches seemed to land on McSpadden's jaw with sickening regularity. In the end, Sammy was well beaten when the referee stepped in to stop the fight in the twelfth round.

Don MacMillan won 2 of his 4 fights in the year. One defeat was to Scottish welterweight champion Andy Wyper whose career had faltered in 1964. The fight at Govan Town Hall was a classic and a close encounter with Wyper edging the decision, probably due to MacMillan being on the canvas 3 times. Wyper had 2 further fights in the year, winning one and losing one. Norrie McCulloch lost twice and did not fight again.

Despite three consecutive losses, McSpadden remained number 2 to Curvis. Don McMillan was number 8.

Middleweight

Willie Hart was outpointed over 10 rounds by Jim Swords of Manchester in an eliminator for the British middleweight title in January. He next fought in August at Paisley where he knocked out Scottish middleweight champion Ian McKenzie. He was then outpointed over 10 rounds by unbeaten Johnny Pritchett of Bingham. Within 2 months of this contest, Pritchett defeated Wally Swift to become British middleweight champion. In his final contest of the year, Hart outpointed Central Area middleweight champion Harry Scott of Liverpool over 10 rounds. 4 quality contests saw Hart remain a contender amongst British middleweights at the end of 1965. His year end ranking was 7.

Willie Fisher won 2 of 4. Ian McKenzie managed only a draw in 3 contests. Both boxers were ranked just outside the UK top 10.

Light Heavyweight

In January, Chic Calderwood fought an unimpressive Otha Brown from Miami at the Albert Hall in London. Calderwood's performance was also below par and the crowd booed throughout the contest which ended when Brown retired at the end of round 8. In view of the shortage of UK opposition at light heavyweight, it was decided that Calderwood would take on heavyweights. This strategy was to rebound on Calderwood.

In early February, Calderwood fought the vastly experienced and dangerous American Freddie Mack to whom he gave 10 pounds. Despite a cut eye in the first round following a head clash, Calderwood built up a substantial points lead. However, he was caught with a left hook in round 8 and did not recover.

Mack moved in and pummelled Calderwood and the Scot was knocked out for the first time in his career. Peter Keenan was keen to arrange a rematch but Calderwood realised that he was not a heavyweight and declined the offer. Calderwood came back in May with a convincing 10 round points victory over another dangerous opponent, number 10 ranked Johnny Persol from Brooklyn.

Cowboy McCormack returned to the ring at Govan in April. He had been out of action for almost a year following an ankle operation. He had an impressive win stopping Frenchman Bernard Quellier in the sixth round.

The fight that the whole of Scotland awaited was set for 10th June at Paisley Ice Rink. McCormack's lack of activity meant Calderwood was favourite. Calderwood was also physically larger and had sparred more for this fight than any other. McCormack cut Calderwood's eyebrow in the first round which he clearly won. Calderwood had a better second round but McCormack concentrated on the cut eyebrow and blood began to pour from the wound. The referee had no option other than to stop the fight and declare McCormack the winner. It was an unfortunate end to a contest that had promised so much. A disconsolate Calderwood offered McCormack an immediate return with the title at stake but due to various injuries Calderwood did not box again in 1965.

McCormack too did not box again in 1965. He had signed to meet Giulio Rinaldi in Rome for the Italian's European light heavyweight title at the end of November. The Italian, however, called off the fight. McCormack's world ranking at the year end was 14 and Calderwood's was 11.

On the world scene, Willie Pastrano was deposed as light heavyweight champion by Jose Torres of Puerto Rico. Torres had been due to fight Calderwood in 1963 but the fight had not materialised because of injury to Calderwood.

A 1964 Manchester bill showing that Scots continued to
ply their trade in England

Highlights of 1966

Flyweight

Walter McGowan remained British and Empire flyweight champion and continued to fight at both flyweight and bantamweight. He started the year on 6th January against Italian Nevio Carbi in London. Although not at his best, he was comfortably ahead when the referee stopped the fight in his favour as a result of cuts around the Italian's eyes. In February, McGowan signed to meet Salvatore Burrunl for his world flyweight title in London. Burruni subsequently lost a 10 round points decision to Chartchai Chionoi in Bangkok and required time for his injuries to heal before he met McGowan.

On 28th March, McGowan took on bantamweight Ernesto Mirando of Argentina and defeated him on points over 8 rounds. His fight with Burruni was at Wembley Pool on 14th June and it proved to be a night to remember. McGowan was at his brilliant best and had improved tremendously since he last fought Burruni. He punched with authority and was a clear points winner at the end of 15 rounds. He was now the world flyweight champion. Under pressure from the British Boxing Board of Control, McGowan relinquished his British and Empire flyweight titles in November.

McGowan agreed to defend his world title for the princely sum of £10,000 plus expenses against Chartchoi Chionoi. The contest was on 30th December in the steamy humidity of Bangkok and McGowan had found it hard to prepare properly in the intense heat. He began the contest like a whirlwind and soon built up a points lead. However, the Thai's left jab began to find its mark as McGowan felt the effects of the heat and Chionoi went on to dictate the fight. Following a punishing right cross which left McGowan covered in blood, the referee stepped in to end the contest in favour of the Thai in round 9. McGowan accepted defeat graciously and, in a sporting gesture warmly appreciated by the crowd, he lifted and paraded Chionoi around the ring to the accompaniment of loud cheers. It was a sad end to a wonderful year for Walter.

George Hind turned professional during the year and won his first 8 contests. John McCluskey won all of his 5 fights taking his unbeaten professional run to 7. At the end of the year, the top 3 UK flyweights were McGowan, McCluskey and Hind.

Bantamweight

British and Empire bantamweight champion Alan Rudkin had fought and won 3 times before the end of March. His next contest was a defence against Walter McGowan. Due to an injury to Rudkin, the fight was delayed until 6th September at Wembley Pool. The fight was eagerly awaited by fans throughout the UK and it proved to be well worth the wait. In a thrilling contest, McGowan emerged the winner on points after 15 closely fought rounds. There was little in it, Rudkin having dominated the early rounds and McGowan coming back midway through the contest. In September 1966,

McGowan was the British and Empire bantamweight champion as well as the world, British and Empire flyweight champion.

In November, McGowan took on Spanish bantamweight champion Jose Bisbal who had lost points decisions to Alan Rudkin and Howard Winstone. Another superb performance saw Walter stop the Spaniard in 5 rounds.

Evan Armstrong lost his first fight of the year to the British number 3 featherweight Brian Cartwright of Birmingham. He conceded 6 pounds in this contest. He moved back to bantamweight and redeemed himself thereafter, winning all of his 7 further contests. In August, Armstrong was deemed to be too good for most British bantamweights and the British Boxing Board of Control banned him from fighting UK bantamweights other than Alan Rudkin and Jackie Brown. In September, he knocked out Jackie Brown in the fourth round to win the Scottish bantamweight title. Brown had dominated the fight and had shown that Armstrong was not yet at the same level as the top bantamweights but Brown was caught by three devastating punches that ended the fight. Jackie Brown had one further fight in the year, losing to George Bowes, before retiring. Evan Armstrong was the main challenger to Walter McGowan after Alan Rudkin.

Featherweight

John O'Brien remained the top Scottish featherweight. He was inactive throughout the year but signed to meet Floyd Robertson for the Empire title in early 1967. Howard Winstone had failed in his quest for the world title against Vicente Salivar in 1965 and Robertson similarly failed against the Mexican early in 1966. O'Brien was capable of mixing it with the best and was confident that he could win the Empire title from Robertson who had been ranked in the world top 10 in 1966. O'Brien was ranked 2 in the UK behind Winstone.

Lightweight

Ken Buchanan had 11 contests and won them all. His unbeaten professional run was now 16 wins. He was now ranked number 5 in the UK and was due to fight John McMillan for the Scottish title, vacant since 1963, in the new year.

Welterweight

Sammy McSpadden followed up his unsuccessful attempt to win the British title with a visit to Sweden in June. He lost an 8 round points decision to the local fighter Stig Walterson in Gothenburg. He had 2 further fights in London but lost both on points. This series of defeats prompted his retirement at the end of 1966.

Andy Wyper, the miner from Galston, had suffered from defective eyesight since he defeated Don MacMillan in 1965. His recovery saw him return to the ring for the first Sporting Club bill in Glasgow in April. He was back with a bang and stopped Darkie Smith of Wolverhampton in 2 rounds. The Scottish champion next appeared at the Anglo American Sporting Club in London two weeks later. At the weigh-in, his opponent Dennis Pleace of Cardiff was almost 3 pounds overweight but Wyper agreed to proceed with the fight to ensure that the show was not cancelled. Wyper won on points over 8 rounds in a disputed decision. Two weeks later, Wyper was stopped in 7 rounds by Peckham-based Jamaican Don Davis. He sustained a broken nose and did not return to the ring in 1966.

Don McMillan impressed when he narrowly outpointed Don Davis over 10 rounds in June. Although he was now considered to be the top Scottish welterweight, he had little chance of a contest against Brian Curvis for the British title. He outclassed Chris McAuley of Larne over 8 rounds in October and 7 days later lost an 8 round points decision to Shaun Doyle, the Central Area welterweight champion and a leading contender for the British title. He concluded the year with a disappointing draw against Fred Powney of Doncaster. His year end UK ranking was 9.

Middleweight

Willie Hart began 1966 with an 8 round points win over Gary Chippendale of Bristol. Following this win he had to take a lengthy break from the sport because of high blood pressure. He returned to training towards the end of the year but did not fight again.

Willie Fisher and Ian McKenzie were inactive.

Light Heavyweight

Chic Calderwood demolished Derek Richards of London in one round in January. In February, he stopped Alfredo Vogrig of Italy in 3 rounds. A further contest was arranged for March against Jose Menno of Argentina. Calderwood was not as sharp as usual and was caught with some sucker punches and sustained an eye injury which led to the referee stopping the fight in favour of the Argentinian in the tenth round. Calderwood was angry with this defeat and decided against any further warm-ups before his British light heavyweight title fight with Cowboy McCormack.

Barney Eastwood won the right to stage the title fight in Belfast. However, when it was announced that McCormack had damaged his shoulder in training and would not be able to recommence training until May, Calderwood took on American Dick Hall in April. Calderwood won on points but the fight was thought to be the worst fight seen in the United Kingdom for many years. The crowd jeered and booed throughout the contest and pelted the ring with coins and newspapers.

In early May, Calderwood was nominated to fight Italian Piero Del Papa for his European light heavyweight title. Del Papa had defeated fellow countryman Giulio Rinaldi in March to take the title much to the consternation of John McCormack whose title fight with Rinaldi had been cancelled in November

1965. The British Board of Control ruled that Calderwood must defend against McCormack before he fought Del Papa. However, when Barney Eastwood abandoned his plans to stage the fight, the Board decided to cancel the title fight and told McCormack that he now had to face Irishman Young McCormack in an eliminator. This left Calderwood free to take on Del Papa and the contest was arranged for 17th August at Lignano.

At the Albert Hall on 28th June, Cowboy was outpointed over 10 rounds by Young McCormack who was 10 years his junior. The fight was close but Cowboy had run out of steam and retirement beckoned.

Calderwood was the number 7 challenger to Jose Torres. Del Papa was rated number 3. Calderwood could not afford to lose to the Italian if he was to have a tilt at the world title. After 6 rounds, the contest was even and both men were cut and bleeding. However, torrential rain made the ring slippery and dangerous and the referee had to halt the fight and declare a no contest. Calderwood received his full purse and was still on course for a world title fight.

Calderwood's world title chance came unexpectedly on 15th October in San Juan. However, the outcome was a disappointment. Chic was knocked out in round 2 by a right cross of which he had no recollection. Calderwood returned to the UK and agreed terms to defend his British title against Young McCormack in early 1967. However, on 13th November Calderwood was killed in a car crash.

Highlights of 1967

Flyweight

On 16th January, John McCluskey became the third successive Scot to hold the British flyweight title. He succeeded in only his eighth professional fight when he knocked out Tony Barlow of Manchester in 8 rounds. He returned to Manchester in February and won well on points over 10 rounds against Spaniard Manolin Alvarez. He moved on to Wembley in March to record the tenth win of his career against Lachy Linares of the Dominican Republic.

Unbeaten Italian Fernando Atzori won the European flyweight title in January when he defeated Frenchman Rene Libeer. Peter Keenan enticed the Italian to Glasgow on 11th May to take on John McCluskey. Atzori was unbeaten in 16, McCluskey unbeaten in 10. The Italian won a close 10 round points decision. Atzori defended successfully against Rene Libeer and Fritz Chervet before the end of 1967.

John McCluskey next travelled to Sweden in November to face the Swedish flyweight and bantamweight champion Jan Persson. McCluskey returned with a 10 round points victory under his belt.

George Hind's unbeaten run came to an end. He lost 2 of 4 contests in the year.

Chartchai Chionoi successfully defended his world title in July in Bangkok but he had not yet fought outside of Asia. Walter McGowan attended the fight and had been introduced to the crowd. Jack Solomons persuaded Chionoi to come to London to defend his title against Walter McGowan at the Empire Pool on 19th September. McGowan won the first 6 rounds but, following a clash of heads, his eyebrow split and the referee had to stop the fight in the seventh round. McGowan had put everything into this fight but had been thwarted by his old injury hoodoo.

Bantamweight

Walter McGowan remained British and Empire champion. The Spaniard Mimoun Ben Ali was European champion and Masahiko "Fighting" Harada of Japan was world champion. Harada had won the title from Eder Jofre in 1965 and successfully defended against Jofre and Alan Rudkin. On 3rd January, he retained his title against Mexican Jose Medel.

In January, McGowan was ordered to defend his British title against Alan Rudkin. The winner was to defend against the winner of the eliminator between Evan Armstrong and Jim McCann from Belfast. Rudkin, however, opted to take a European tilt at Ben Ali.

McGowan took on Osamu Miyashita of Japan in March at the World Sporting Club in London. He was in great form and comfortably outpointed his opponent over 10 rounds. In his next fight in May, he was again in dazzling form, winning each of the 10 rounds against Frenchman Giancarlo Centa. Rudkin in the meantime had been unsuccessful in his attempt to win the European bantamweight title.

Next up for McGowan was the French bantamweight champion, Antoine Porcel. Porcel had been nominated with Rudkin by the European Boxing Union as the challengers for Ben Ali's European title. Rudkin had failed and Porcel was now recognised as the number one challenger. At the World Sporting Club in July, McGowan put on yet another impressive display winning every round against the Frenchman.

Early in the year, Evan Armstrong had an impressive win over Ghanain Benny Lee in 2 rounds. His next fight was against Jim McCann in the final eliminator for the British bantamweight title. At Paisley on 11th May, Armstrong was in great form and was well ahead when the Irishman had to retire in the fifth round with a cut eyebrow. Armstrong had one further fight, in October, and boxed an 8 rounds draw with Patrick Mambwe of Zambia. Armstrong was number 3 in the UK after McGowan and Rudkin and number 15 in the world.

Due to injury, McGowan was unable to fight Rudkin in 1967. Rudkin came back to the ring in December and knocked out Ron Jones in 2 rounds.

Featherweight

John O'Brien flew to Accra in Ghana to meet Floyd Robertson on 28th January for the British Empire featherweight title. However, there was a dispute over the weigh-in and O'Brien refused to go ahead with the fight. O'Brien had been taken to the wrong weigh-in venue and by the time that the correct venue was found, Robertson had weighed-in and left. O'Brien then weighed-in but as both boxers were not present at the time of the weigh-in, it was declared void. O'Brien was persuaded to remain in Ghana and the fight was rearranged for 3rd February. Robertson made the weight at the second attempt and defended his title in front of 15,000 fans. O'Brien dictated the fight from the first bell, shocking the home crowd into silence. He was well ahead by round 11. When the bell sounded for the twelfth round, Robertson remained on his stool and O'Brien was declared the new champion.

O'Brien injured his knee and was unable to accept a defence against New Zealander Toro George. He did not fight again until November due to a lack of suitable or willing opponents. He travelled to Melbourne to defend his Empire title against Australian featherweight champion Johnny Famechon who had lost only 4 of his 44 fights and was a dangerous opponent. O'Brien was pleased to have fellow-Scot but now Melbourne resident John Smillie in his corner. However, Famechon outboxed the Scot who had three gashes over his eyes when the referee stopped the fight at the end of the eleventh round.

Howard Winstone had been unsuccessful in two further world title fights against Vicente Saldivar of Mexico. By taking these contests, Winstone forfeited his European featherweight title but O'Brien was not nominated to fight for this title. Ironically, Saldivar retired following his battles with Winstone and the world featherweight title was vacant. O'Brien remained the number 1 UK challenger to Howard Winstone.

Hugh Baxter of Glasgow won 5 of his 7 fights in the year before he was paired with Jimmy Revie of Stockwell in an eliminator for the new British junior lightweight title. Revie proved too strong for the Glaswegian who had to retire in the eighth round with a cut eye.

Bobby Fisher was once a leading contender for the British featherweight title and he too moved to junior lightweight in the hope of an early tilt at the title. He won 3 of his 4 fights in the year but his loss to Brian Cartwright meant that Cartwright was included in the eliminators rather than Fisher.

New professional Tommy Glencross won his 5 fights.

Lightweight

The fight for the vacant Scottish lightweight title took place in Glasgow on 23rd January. Ken Buchanan took the title with a 10 round points verdict over John McMillan. By the end of 1967, Buchanan had taken his unbeaten professional run to 23. His final fight of the year was a comfortable 12 round points victory over Spike McCormack of Belfast in a final eliminator for the British lightweight title.

Welterweight

Don McMillan had 4 fights and lost one and was ranked British number 10. Andy Wyper managed only one fight in January which he lost and he did not box again. Malcolm McKenzie of Edinburgh won his first 6 professional fights.

Middleweight

Willie Fisher was disqualified after 4 rounds against Derek Cowper in a final eliminator for the Scottish middleweight title. He retired later in the year. Cowper won 2 of 5 fights in the year.

Cathkin Park in 2004

Highlights of 1968

Flyweight

John McCluskey began the year with hopes of a rematch with Fernando Atzori, this time for the Italian's European title. His first outing of the year was against Zambia's Kid Miller who had not won a fight since relocating to Europe in 1967. McCluskey made short work of the Zambian by knocking him out in the second round. He then won each of the 8 rounds when he faced Spanish flyweight champion Fabian Bellanco at the Empire Pool, Wembley. His long awaited tilt at the European flyweight title was to take place in Naples in June. Atzori's unbeaten record had been lost in Mexico City against Octavio Gomez in January but he had since returned to winning ways against Fabian Bellanco. McCluskey was unsuccessful against the Italian who knocked the Scot out in round 4. As a result of this defeat, McCluskey had no chance of a world title fight against Chartchai Chionoi. To progress, he needed more experience against continental opposition.

The British Boxing Board of Control ordered McCluskey to defend his British flyweight title against Walter McGowan and also nominated McGowan to fight for the European flyweight title. McGowan, however, announced that he would fight only as a bantamweight in the future and would not fulfil his flyweight commitments. He relinquished his Empire flyweight title.

Due to a lack of suitable flyweights, McCluskey had to take on bantamweights. In his next fight, he was outpointed by bantamweight Johnny Clark of Walworth. He then travelled to Berne to meet European flyweight contender Fritz Chervet. McCluskey was a clear points winner but, as often happened in Europe, the 10 round points decision was given to the local fighter.

McCluskey had gone into his European title fight ranked number 16 in the world. However, following 3 successive defeats, his stock had fallen.

George Hind managed only one fight and he was defeated by London bantamweight Johnny Fitzgerald.

Bantamweight

On 10th January, 34 year old Salvatore Burrini won the European bantamweight title from Ben Ali. The following day, Walter McGowan had a lengthy operation on his forehead and his eyes and remained out of action until May. When Howard Winstone won the vacant world featherweight title on 23rd January, Jack Solomons was keen for him to defend his title against McGowan. When Lionel Rose of Australia won the world bantamweight title from Fighting Harada in Tokyo in late February, Solomons also cabled Rose a huge offer to defend against McGowan. However, McGowan first had to successfully defend his British and Empire bantamweight titles against Alan Rudkin.

The title defence was promoted by Harry Levene at Belle Vue, Manchester on 13th May. McGowan had not fought since contesting the world flyweight title in September 1967. Rudkin had good wins in December and January and had been sparring with McGowan's close friend, John McCluskey. McGowan's inactivity showed in his sluggish start to the contest. However, he picked up momentum and finished the thrilling 15 round contest in great style. His slow start, however, may have cost him the narrow decision which went to Rudkin. McGowan had 3 more fights in the year and won them all. His world ranking was 9 at the end of the year, one behind Rudkin.

Scottish champion Evan Armstrong was now ahead of McGowan as a challenger for the British title. Armstrong had 3 good wins in the early part of the year before flying to Mexico to face world number 13 Jose Medel who was one of the hardest hitting bantamweights in the world. Medel had fought 93 professional contests and had lost a world title fight with Fighting Harada in 1967. This was a major step up in class for Armstrong but he was up to the challenge and performed remarkably well on the night. Although the Mexican finished the contest with cuts over both eyes, he was given the 10 round points decision. The 16,000 Mexican crowd greeted the decision with loud whistles and Armstrong was carried shoulder high from the ring. He certainly made an impression on the local fans.

He was offered a further fight in Mexico against Ruben Olivares who was unbeaten in 38 professional contests. Armstrong had to turn this fight down as he had agreed to meet world number 2 bantamweight Jesus Castillo, yet another Mexican, in Los Angeles on 28th August. Castillo proved too good for Armstrong who was stopped in the second round. On the same bill Lionel Rose outpointed Jose Medel on points over 10 rounds. In December, Rose retained his world title outpointing Castillo.

In November, Armstrong took on Empire contender Bob Allotey of Ghana. He unfortunately lost the contest as a result of a cut eye. As the year drew to a close, Armstrong had been waiting for more than 19 months for his British title shot following his final eliminator victory.

Featherweight

John O'Brien was finding it more and more difficult to find opponents. When Howard Winstone won the world title in January, it was expected that he would have to relinquish his British title as had been the ruling with Walter McGowan and John Caldwell. Winstone had already forfeited the European title. O'Brien took the matter up with the British Board of Control but received no satisfactory response and when Winstone lost his world title to Jose Legra in July, he was still British champion.

In September, O'Brien had his first fight of the year against Daniel Vermandere who had lost only one of 26 contests in France. At the National Sporting Club in London, O'Brien battered the Frenchman to defeat in 5 rounds. The following month, the same treatment was handed out to Ray Opoku of Guyana who was no match for the Scot.

In October, O'Brien's challenge to British junior lightweight champion, Jimmy Anderson, for his title was ignored. However, he then became the Board's official nominee to fight for the European featherweight title and was also nominated to fight Jimmy Revie of Stockwell in a British featherweight title final eliminator.

In June, Bobby Fisher travelled to Edmonton in Canada to face the highly rated Canadian featherweight champion Billy McGrandle. O'Brien had turned down McGrandle due to a knee injury received when playing football. Fisher performed well but lost the contest on points over 10 rounds. On his return to the UK, he won 2 of his 3 fights, losing only to Southern Area bantamweight champion Brian Packer on points. McGrandle's next fight was for the British Empire featherweight title against Johnny Famechon but he was knocked out by the champion in the twelfth round. Fisher was back in the UK rankings at number 5.

Hugh Baxter had a disappointing year losing all 3 of his fights. Tommy Glencross won both of his fights, taking his unbeaten record to 7.

Lightweight

Ken Buchanan was the first Scot in 19 years to fight for the British lightweight title. His opponent was Maurice Cullen of Shotton. Cullen had held the title since 1965 and was an awkward and experienced opponent. At the Anglo American Sporting Club in London on 19th February, Buchanan won the title with a wonderful, controlled performance, knocking the champion out in the eleventh round. Despite his new status, Buchanan was in no rush to challenge the world's top lightweights. He consolidated his growing reputation with 4 further impressive victories in the year.

He won each of the 8 rounds against Leonard Tavarez, the French Senegalese fighter. He easily outpointed Londoner Ivan Whiter over 8 rounds. He outpointed the vastly experienced Cuban Angel Garcia over 10 rounds and he stopped Tunisian Ameur Lamine in 3 rounds. Unbeaten Buchanan was now ranked in the world top 10. Sammy Docherty was keen to match Buchanan against John O'Brien but this fight never materialised.

Jim Watt made his professional debut in October and won both his professional contests inside the distance.

Welterweight

Malcolm McKenzie won his first 3 contests of the year and was nominated to fight Vic Andreetti of Hoxton in an eliminator for the British junior welterweight title. Andreetti had lost the inaugural fight for the title in February 1968. The eliminator took place in May at the Anglo American Sporting Club in London. Andreetti proved too strong for the Scot who suffered his first professional defeat when the referee stopped the contest in the eighth round. McKenzie had 4 more fights, losing 2.

Don McMillan had a more successful year. He began the year in South Africa where he drew with the unbeaten Transvaal middleweight champion Pierre Fourie and lost on points to Fraser Toweel. On his return to the UK, McMillan rattled up 4 successive wins against reasonable opposition and remained in the UK top 10.

Middleweight

Both Derek Cowper and Ian McKenzie retired.

Heavyweight

Terry Feeley was new on the heavyweight scene. He won 3 of 5 fights in 1967 and 6 of 8 in 1968.

Highlights of 1969

Flyweight

John McCluskey had held the British title unchallenged for more than 2 years. However, Tony Barlow of Manchester was nominated to fight McCluskey for the title. McCluskey first had a date in Johannesburg against South African bantamweight Mike Buttle to whom he conceded 7 pounds. McCluskey came through the bout unscathed and was a convincing points winner over 10 rounds. He was also untroubled in his title defence and stopped the gallant Mancunian in the thirteenth round.

There followed speculation that McCluskey would fight Johnny Fire of Zambia or Nigerian Orizo Olibaso for the Empire title, that he would return to South Africa to meet 34 year old Dennis Adams , that he would undergo a 3 fight tour of Japan and that he would fight Rudkin, McGowan and Clark who were the top 3 UK bantamweights. None of these fights happened. Instead, he easily stopped leading British contender Glyn Davies in 5 rounds, he inflicted the first defeat on the Mexican Arturo Leon in Texas and he outpointed Fritz Chervet in his grudge return in Zurich.

George Hind was inactive throughout the year.

Bantamweight

In April, Walter McGowan returned to the ring against French featherweight champion Michel Houdeau to whom he conceded 6 pounds. At the World Sporting Club in London, McGowan bombarded the Frenchman with various combinations leading the referee to intervene in the fourth round when Houdeau sustained a cut eye. McGowan was due to meet Salvatore Burruni for the European bantamweight title but the Italian sought and was granted a postponement in June. In April, he had retained his title against Frenchman Pierre Vetroff. On 24th July, however, Burruni announced his retirement from boxing, leaving the European title vacant and McGowan without a title fight.

McGowan took a contest in San Remo against Italian featherweight Umberto Simbola whom he totally outclassed on points over 8 rounds. In his third and final fight of the year, he again won in style against Antonio Chiloiro, another Italian featherweight.

The European Boxing Union matched Italian Franco Zurli with Spaniard Ben Ali for the vacant European bantamweight title which Zurli won on points. McGowan had designs on the title but he was behind Alan Rudkin in the pecking order. In March, Rudkin was outpointed by Lionel Rose in his world and Empire bantamweight title fight. Rose then lost the world title to Ruben Olivares of Mexico. In December, Rudkin fought again for the world title against the Mexican in Los Angeles but was stopped in 2 rounds.

At long last, Evan Armstrong's big chance came in Manchester on 9th June when he faced Alan Rudkin for the British bantamweight title. He put up a brave fight but had to retire in the eleventh round. He had 2 further fights this year and won both of them.

McGowan and Armstrong remained the leading contenders for Rudkin's British title.

Featherweight

John O'Brien had been matched with 21 year old Jimmy Revie of Stockwell in a final eliminator for Howard Winstone's British title. However, when Winstone announced his retirement, the match was for the vacant British featherweight title. Revie, whose father hailed from Shettleston, had lost only 1 of 20 and that was against Jimmy Anderson in his attempt on the British junior lightweight title in 1968. O'Brien was vastly experienced and had mixed it with the best. At the World Sporting Club in March, Revie's aggressive style won him the first 2 rounds. O'Brien came back in the third and had Revie in trouble. In round 4, Revie hit O'Brien with a series of jabs and both of O'Brien's eyes began to swell. The referee had no option other than to halt the fight in the fifth round as both of O'Brien's eyes were virtually closed.

O'Brien returned to the ring in August. He travelled to South Africa and had two fine wins there. One victory was against Arnold Taylor who went on in the seventies to win the WBA bantamweight title. Towards the end of the year, O'Brien was nominated to fight Jimmy Anderson for the British junior lightweight title.

Hugh Baxter fought Jimmy Bell of Kilmarnock for the Scottish featherweight title at the National Sporting Club in London in April. Bell was the victor on points over 10 rounds. Having won his first 5 fights of the year, Bell travelled to Belgium and stopped Belgian champion Jean De Keers in 4 rounds. The Belgians liked Bell and he returned to Brussels in December but he lost a disputed points decision to Algerian Ould Makloufi.

Baxter fought in Cagliari in August but lost a points decision to future European lightweight champion Antonio Puddu. His record for the year was 3 wins and 3 losses.

Bobby Fisher won 2 of 4. Tommy Glencross improved his record to 11 wins in 11 fights.

Scotland was well represented in the featherweight division. O'Brien remained the number one contender but Fisher was number 4, Bell number 5 and Baxter number 6.

Lightweight

British champion Ken Buchanan started the year off superbly with a 10 round points win over the Puerto Rican Frankie Narvaez. Narvaez had previously beaten world champion Carlos Cruz and was ranked number 6 in the world.

In February, Buchanan stopped New Yorker Mike Cruz in 4 rounds and in March he convincingly outpointed Jose Luis Torcida from Spain.

Carlos Cruz lost his world title to Armando Ramos of Los Angeles. Buchanan was matched with Cruz at Nottingham in July and a victory would virtually ensure Buchanan being elevated to the number one challenger. A few days prior to the fight, Cruz withdrew with a sprained ankle. He was replaced by American Jerry Graci who had been stopped in 7 rounds by Ramos in May. Graci was no match for Buchanan who stopped him in the first round. The withdrawal of Cruz was a blow to Buchanan although tempered somewhat when the European Boxing Union ordered Pedro Carrasco of Spain to defend his European lightweight title against Buchanan.

Buchanan briefly retired from the sport following a contractual wrangle with his manager but was in magnificent form when he returned to the ring in November against Italian Vincenzo Pitardi whom he stopped in 2 rounds. His fight with Carrasco was postponed and indeed would never take place. Buchanan was ranked number 6 world lightweight behind the likes of Ramos, Cruz, Ismael Laguna and Carrasco.

Jim Watt had difficulty obtaining fights in 1969. He had 3 more contests and won all of them impressively. He was rated UK number 5 at the end of the year.

New professional Johnny Cheshire won 6 of his 8 fights in the year.

Welterweight

Don McMillan continued to campaign as Scotland's leading welterweight but managed only one win in 6 during the year. His British ranking was 11. Malcolm McKenzie fought once and won.

Heavy

Terry Feeley fought once in the year, losing to future champion Joe Bugner.

Left – Peter Keenan in boxing pose.

Above – Dick Knox, Vincent O'Kine and Charlie Hill pose before winning their contests at Lanarkshire Sports Stadium in June 1954

Above – Alex Ambrose leaving Glasgow Central Station to do his National Service in 1955, seen off by Peter Keenan.

Below – Alex Ambrose and Johnny Morrissey.

Johnny Kidd and Johnny McLaren in their Scottish lightweight title fight at
Linksfield Park, Aberdeen in July 1958
(courtesy of the Aberdeen Press and Journal)

Above: Billy Rafferty in boxing pose.

Johnny Morrissey winning his return fight against Antonio Diaz in March 1958.

Another victory for Cowboy McCormack.

Alex Ambrose prior to his meeting with Roy Beaman in 1960

Chic Calderwood displaying his Lonsdale Belt.

Above – Cowboy McCormack on the attack.

Below – The famous McMillan brothers with their mother.

A gathering of Scottish boxers plus one guest, some past their peak.
John McCulloch, Danny Harvey, Bobby Boland, Peter Keenan, Billy Rafferty, Alan
Rudkin, Bobby Neill, Walter McGowan and Chic Brady.

John McCluskey in boxing pose.

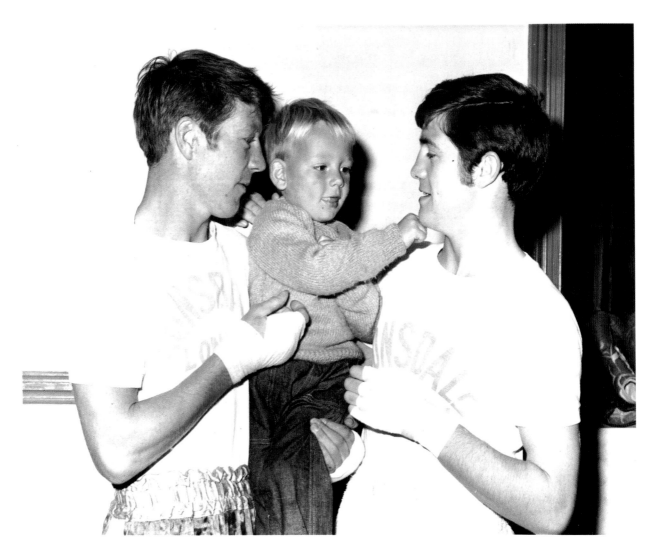

Evan Armstrong with son, Evan, and Johnny Chesire.

Evan Armstrong with Lonsdale Belt.

Ken Buchanan and Jim Watt after their British title fight.

Evan Armstrong's Testimonial at Ayr Racecourse in 2004

Above – Cowboy McCormack, Evan, Evan's brother, Dick McTaggart and
Andy Wyper.

Below – Alan Rudkin, Joe Kelly, a friend, John McCluskey, Evan,
Walter McGowan

Ken Buchanan and Cowboy McCormack at Evan Armstrong's Testimonial.

Below – Bobby Neill in 2004 with Liam McColgan, Secretary of the
Scottish Ex-Boxers Association.

Professional Boxing Venues

Glasgow, Kelvin Hall

The Kelvin Hall in Glasgow was the leading indoor venue of Scottish professional boxing in the fifties and sixties. The Kelvin Hall was originally built in 1927 and was converted in 1987 to house the Museum of Transport and the Kelvin Hall International Sports Arena. It is situated at 1,445 Argyle Street in the West End of the city and opposite Kelvingrove Art Gallery and Museum.

Boxing promotions at the Kelvin Hall were restricted by Glasgow magistrates. There were a total of 40 promotions in the fifties and 13 in the sixties. There was at least one promotion in each year until 1965 but there were no promotions after 1965. The most promotions in any one year were 8 in 1958.

Despite the Kelvin Hall label as the most prestigious indoor arena in Scotland, the Hall witnessed very few championship fights in the period. The capacity of the Hall was 3,500 / 4,000 which was significantly less than Paisley Ice Rink. In 1957, Frankie Jones lost his British Empire flyweight title to Dennis Adams and in 1963 Johnny Morrissey failed in his bid to win the British featherweight title from Howard Winstone. Alex Ambrose's debut at the Kelvin Hall was in 1959 when he lost on points to Frankie Jones in his challenge for Jones's British flyweight title.

Of the Scottish boxers whose records are listed in Appendix 2, only Ken Buchanan, John McCluskey and Bobby Neill did not fight professionally at the Kelvin Hall in this era. Renowned British boxers such as John Caldwell, Ronnie Clayton, Freddie Gilroy and Terry Downes made appearances as did world famous fighters such as Robert Cohen, Willie Pastrano and Willie Toweel. Former world champion Jackie Paterson also fought there in 1950.

It was Johnny Morrissey who made most appearances at the Kelvin Hall. He fought there 16 times between 1957 and 1963. Cowboy McCormack featured 12 times between 1957 and 1962. Dick Currie managed 11 appearances between 1954 and 1958.

The leading Kelvin Hall promoter in this era was undoubtedly Sammy Docherty who held 22 promotions between 1952 and 1959 plus 1 joint promotion with Jim Gilmour. Peter Keenan had 9 promotions between 1960 and 1965. Alex Lucas held 10 promotions between 1952 and 1956.

Glasgow, Central Hotel

The Central Hotel is one of the oldest hotels in Glasgow. The front entrance is at 99 Gordon Street and forms part of the fabric of Glasgow Central station. The hotel has now been renamed the Quality Hotel.

Charity promotions were held at the Banquetting Hall in 1959, 1960 and 1961. These shows were known as Champagne and Cabaret nights and were based on the increasingly popular Sporting Club formats. In 1960, the main bout was a Scottish welterweight title clash between the McGuinnesses, Jim of Wishaw and Tommy of Edinburgh, supported by a Scottish flyweight title eliminator between Pat Glancy and George McDade. The paying guests were treated to 36 rounds of boxing which left little time for the cabaret.

Peter Keenan revived the Sporting Club idea and ran 12 shows between 1966 and 1967. The Club had 350 to 400 members who paid 50 guineas annual membership. John McCluskey, Evan Armstrong, Jackie Brown and Ken Buchanan made appearances on the Keenan bills. A well-known personality or team from the world of sport or show business would feature as a guest at each show.

Glasgow, Govan Town Hall

Govan Town Hall was situated on Govan Road and bordered by Summertown Road, Carmichael Street and Merryland Street on the south west side of Glasgow. The building was opened in 1901. The concert hall entrance was in Summertown Road with a maximum seating capacity of 2,500. The building is currently undergoing a refurbishment programme to create a base for facility and production companies in the film and media industry.

Although the Hall was not the top Glasgow venue, it was a popular venue with boxers. There were 9 promotions at the Hall between 1955 and 1969. Peter Keenan promoted 4 times and George Lucas twice. Cowboy McCormack made most appearances. He featured on bills in 1957, 1964 and 1965. Andy Wyper won the vacant Scottish welterweight title against Don McMillan in 1964. Other leading boxers who fought at Govan Town Hall were Jackie Brown, John Smillie, Frankie Jones, Billy Rafferty, Derry Treanor, Johnny Morrissey, Matt Fulton and Evan Armstrong.

Glasgow, Kelvin Arena

The Kelvin Arena formerly the Kelvin Cinema was situated at 1,067/1,073 Argyle Street. When it opened, it was a newly built, modern arena and could accommodate 2,000 fans. There were 3 promotions at the Arena in 1961 and 1 in 1963. Unfortunately with the decline in Scottish boxing, the Arena was never filled at these promotions.

The most attractive contest at the Arena was in 1963 when Bobby Fisher lost the final eliminator for the British featherweight title to Billy Calvert. Derry Treanor, Alex Ambrose, John O'Brien and Walter McGowan featured at the Kelvin Arena as did Henry Cooper's twin brother Jim. Jimmy Gibson appeared on 3 of the 4 shows.

Glasgow, Grove Street Institute

The Grove Institute was an Evangelical Christian Hall situated at 80/82 Grove Street, just north of St. George's Cross. The Grove hosted regular indoor promotions on Saturday nights. In 1950, there were 19 promotions between

7th January and 13th May. Following the last promotion on 13th May, fire destroyed the building on Sunday morning. The building was never restored and Glasgow fans were deprived of their only weekly venue. The bill usually comprised five six round fights or four such fights plus an exhibition. Peter Keenan, Maurice Sandeyron and Vic Herman boxed exhibitions at the Grove in 1950.

Glasgow, St. Mungo Halls

This venue was located in the south side of Glasgow, just off Ballater Street at 140 Moffat Street in Hutchesontown. Regular Saturday shows commenced in December 1950. The shows were similar to the Grove and the venue was difficult to access. Various promoters ran shows but not one could make a financial success of the venue. There were 28 promotions between September 1950 and February 1953.

Glasgow, Whiteinch Borough Town Hall

The Town Hall was built in 1894 and situated in Inchlee Street close to Victoria Park. The Hall hosted one 5-fight promotion in 1959. All of the contests went the distance and participants included Jackie Brown, Dave Croll and Arthur Donnachie.

Glasgow, Firhill Stadium

Firhill Stadium in Glasgow has been the home of Partick Thistle Football Club since 1909. The stadium is situated north of the city centre in Firhill Road. Firhill was the premier outdoor venue of Scottish boxing in the fifties and attracted crowds of 30,000 to the top line promotions. There were 11 promotions in the period. The boxer making most appearances at Firhill was Peter Keenan who appeared in 8 of the 11 promotions. Hamilton featherweight, George Stewart, appeared 5 times between 1950 and 1952. Sammy Docherty promoted 8 of the 11 shows.

Peter Keenan appeared in 6 title fights at Firhill. In 1951, he won the British bantamweight title against Danny O'Sullivan, defended the title against Bobby Boland and then won the European title against Luis Romero. In 1952, he lost the European title to Jean Sneyers and in 1953 regained the title against Maurice Sandeyron. In 1957, he retained his British and Empire bantamweight titles against John Smillie. Keenan returned to Firhill in 1960 as promoter when Chic Calderwood won the British Empire light heavyweight title against Johnny Halafihi.

Glasgow, Cathkin Park

When it was opened in 1884, the ground was known as Hampden Park but renamed New Cathkin Park when the current Hampden Park was opened in 1903. It had been the home of Queens Park before the team moved to the new ground. The ground then became the home of Third Lanark Athletic Club and was renamed Cathkin Park. Third Lanark played in the Scottish First

Division for many years until 1965 but, sadly, the club was bankrupted in 1967. The ground passed into the hands of Glasgow Parks Department which has developed the ground into a municipal park. The football ground remains as does some of the terracing.

Cathkin Park had long been a boxing venue before 1950. There were promotions in 1955, 1956 and 1958. The 1955 promotion featured the unforgettable British Empire title fight between Peter Keenan and Jake Tuli and the 1958 promotion included Charlie Hill's British featherweight title defence against Chic Brogan. Peter Keenan, Chic Brogan and Matt Fulton fought on 2 of the 3 bills.

Glasgow, Carntyne Greyhound Stadium

Carntyne Stadium was close to Parkhead Hospital and lay between Myreside Street and Shettleston Road. A one-off promotion was held here in June 1951 featuring a Scottish lightweight title eliminator between Jim Findlay and Neilly Phillips.

Glasgow, Saint Anthony's Football Ground

The football ground was the home of Saint Anthony's Football Club and was located at Helen Street in Govan and close to Ibrox Stadium. There was one promotion at this venue in June 1950. My friend, Michael McConnachie, is sure that this promotion was at Carntyne Greyhound Stadium. He may be right but my research shows that the bill was in Govan.

Glasgow, Saracen Park

Saracen Park is situated at Hawthorn Street, Possilpark in the north of Glasgow. The ground is the home of Ashfield Football Club and has also been used for greyhound racing and speedway by Glasgow Giants and Glasgow Tigers. There was a single promotion at this venue in 1953.

Aberdeen, Linksfield Park.

The only Aberdeen promotion in this era was at Linksfield Park in July 1958 when local boy Johnny Kidd won the Scottish lightweight title against Johnny McLaren. The bill attracted a crowd of 2,500. Linksfield Park is located at Linksfield Road, a short distance from the city centre, and is now known as the Chris Anderson Stadium.

Alloa, Recreation Park.

Alloa Athletic Football Club was founded in 1878 and moved to Recreation Park in 1895. The sole promotion at this venue was in June 1951. The promotion featured contests for the Scottish lightweight title between Johnny Flannigan and Harry Hughes and the Scottish heavyweight title between George Stern and Hugh McDonald.

Ayr Ice Rink

The Ice Rink was opened in March 1939. It was situated at Beresford Terrace and had a capacity in excess of 4,000. The Rink was demolished in 1972.

Charlie Black promoted here in September 1950 and April 1951. The 1951 bill included an eliminator for the British welterweight title between Billy Rattray and Cliff Curvis plus a Scottish featherweight title eliminator between George Lamont and Tommy Miller. Paisley's Don McTaggart appeared on both bills.

Banff, Deveronvale Park

The home of Deveronvale Football Club saw a one-off promotion in July 1959 as part of the MacDuff Gala week. There were 2 contests, a novice heavyweight competition and exhibition bouts from Peter Keenan and Tommy Cavan.

Coatbridge, Greyhound Stadium.

The Coatbridge Greyhound Stadium in Ellis Street was opened in December 1949 with covered accommodation for more than 3,000 spectators. The promoters of the stadium were the Beattie brothers, five of them in total. Brothers Andrew and George obtained promoter licences and there were four promotions there in July / August 1950.

A further promotion was held here in June 1960. In the main bout, John Smillie defeated George Judge.

The site is now the headquarters of Coatbridge Police and Coatbridge Health Centre.

Dumfries Drill Hall

The Drill Hall in Newall Terrace was built in 1890. The venue has been renamed the Loreburn Drill Hall and has a current capacity of 1,400. There was one promotion here in August 1950 and another in May 1960.

Dundee, Caird Hall

The Caird Hall is located at City Square in the centre of Dundee. The building was completed in 1923 with funds provided by local entrepreneur Sir James Key Caird. The concert hall had a seating capacity of 3,300.

There were 16 promotions at the Caird Hall in the fifties but none in the sixties. 11 promotions were by George Grant, 3 by Mont Leslie and there were single promotions from Alex Lucas and Peter Keenan. It was at the Caird that Jimmy Croll won the Scottish welterweight title in 1955 and brother Dave won the Scottish featherweight title in 1959. Jimmy Croll fought 11 times and brother Dave 7 times at the venue. Other regular performers were Norman Tennant, Johnny Davidson, Sammy Welsh and Peter Cain.

Dundee Ice Rink

The Ice Rink was used when the Caird Hall was not available. The Ice Rink was located in Kingsway and had a capacity of 2,000. There were two promotions by George Grant in 1950 when the rink was the home of Dundee Tigers Ice Hockey team. Sammy Welsh and Peter Guichan appeared on both promotions. The second bill saw Norman Tennant stop Joe Murphy in a British flyweight title eliminator.

Dundee, Premierland

The Premierland was situated in William Lane. George Grant arranged for the building of this indoor stadium which was ready for use in 1951. There were 2 promotions in 1951 and 2 in 1952. A previous temporary construction had existed before the war and housed several promotions. The initial 1951 promotion attracted a full house in excess of 2,000 with hundreds turned away. Tommy Croll and Peter Cain were on all 4 bills. Jimmy Croll was on 3 of the bills.

Dunoon, Castle Gardens

The Pavilion in Dunoon Castle Gardens was burnt down in April 1949. The Council temporarily erected two large hangars which were used until the Queen's Hall was built in 1958. One of the hangars was the venue of the sole promotion by Jim Gilmour in September 1950 which was headlined by a Scottish welterweight title fight between Billy Rattray and Willie Whyte. The capacity of the venue was approximately 1,000.

Dunoon, Recreation Park

Recreation Park was adjacent to Black Park and is the site of the present Dunoon Stadium. There was a one-off promotion here in 1950. Withdrawals and non-appearances resulted in a 2 fight bill bolstered by a Peter Keenan exhibition.

Edinburgh Music Hall

The Music Hall is set within the Assembly Rooms at 54 George Street in the centre of Edinburgh. The Music Hall was opened in 1843 and continues to flourish in the 21st century. Although the capacity was limited to around 1,500, there were regular promotions until the early fifties. For such a small venue, the promotions were of a remarkably high standard. In 1950, there were 19 promotions. The number reduced to 12 in 1951 and 8 in 1952. There were no promotions in 1953 and only 2 in 1954. No further promotions were held at the Music Hall.

The bills usually comprised 4 or 5 contests of 6 to 8 rounds. Scottish bantamweight champion, Eddie Carson, was a regular headliner. The biggest attraction at the Music Hall was the Scottish bantamweight title encounter between Eddie Carson of Edinburgh and Billy Taylor of Stirling in February 1952. There were also 2 Scottish title eliminators in 1950. Jackie Marshall from Glasgow outpointed Johnny Flannigan from Whitburn in a lightweight eliminator and Jim Dwyer from Glasgow stopped Willie Myles from Dundee in a bantamweight eliminator.

Another regular was Paisley's Don McTaggart who was unbeaten in 10 contests at the venue.

Falkirk Ice Rink

The Ice Rink opened in 1938 and had a capacity in excess of 4,000. The old ice rink is now the Forth Centre in Grangemouth Road and recently became an indoor market. There were promotions in 1950, 1952 and 1957. Charlie Black promoted in 1950 and Jim Gilmour promoted in 1952 and 1957. In 1952, Jim Kenny fought Tommy Miller in a Scottish featherweight title eliminator. Jim Kenny also appeared on the 1950 bill. Other notable boxers on these bills were Roy Ankrah, Chic Brogan, Jimmy Croll, Alex Ambrose, Frankie Jones, John Smillie, Danny Malloy and Chic Calderwood. There was generally a fleet of buses that left St. Enoch Square in Glasgow to attend these promotions but the promotions were poorly supported.

Greenock Town Hall

The Town Hall at Clyde Square dates back to 1886. There were 4 promotions between 1953 and 1959. Hugh Ferns boxed at the venue in 1953 and promoted in 1957 and 1959. The leading contest was the Scottish flyweight title fight between George McDade and Pat Glancy in 1957. Dave Croll and Alex Ambrose each featured on 2 bills.

Hamilton Town Hall

The Town Hall is currently undergoing a major refurbishment but it was a popular venue for boxers in this era with a capacity for 1,200 fans. There were 11 promotions at the venue between 1957 and 1968. Promoters attracted the cream of Scottish boxing such as Alex Ambrose, Chic Brogan, Chic Calderwood, Ken Buchanan, Walter McGowan, Sammy McSpadden, Johnny Morrissey, John O'Brien, Billy Rafferty and Jim Watt. Johnny Morrissey and Owen Reilly appeared on 4 bills. Bobby Fisher appeared on 3, 1 in 1961 and 2 in 1968.

Hawick Town Hall

The Town Hall was opened in 1886 and has a seating capacity of 500. There were 2 promotions in March/April 1951. The initial bill featured local middleweight Dave Finnie.

Irvine Meadow Football Ground

There was a one-off 6 fight promotion on a chilly night in May 1960. The bill included Alex Ambrose and John Smillie.

Kilwinning, Abbey Park

Abbey Park is the home of Kilwinning Rangers Football Club. George Lucas was responsible for the sole promotion in July 1954 with a bill headlined by Charlie Hill. The show was postponed for one day due to heavy rain and the attendance on the next night was poor.

Kirkcaldy Ice Rink

Kirkcaldy Ice Rink is situated in Rosslyn Street in the Gallatown district of Kirkcaldy. The rink was opened in 1938 and a crowd of 4,500 attended an ice hockey match to mark the opening of the rink. There were promotions in 1952 and 1953 by Jim Gilmour and George Grant respectively. The 1952 promotion featured the Scottish welterweight title fight between Willie Whyte and Danny Malloy and a Scottish featherweight title eliminator between Chic Brady and George Lamont. Dunfermline's Peter Guichan and Lochgelly's Johnny Drummond appeared on the bill. The 1953 bill included local boy Johnny Beveridge and Reggie Watson from Kennoway.

Jim Gilmour's grandson, Tommy, brought professional boxing back to the Ice Rink with promotions in 2005 and 2006.

Leith, Eldorado

The Eldorado Ballroom was situated just across the road from Leith Hospital. There were 19 promotions there between 1950 and 1960 when promotions ceased. The biggest fight of the era was when fellow Edinburgh boxers Eddie Carson and Hugh Riley fought for the Scottish bantamweight title in 1953. The return in 1956 produced a no contest when both boxers failed to provide any action. Jackie Brown and Eddie Phillips made 4 appearances at the venue. Billy Rafferty and John McCormack appeared twice. The final bill in 1960 included Jackie Brown, John Smillie, Jimmy Gibson and Johnny McLaren.

The building became derelict and was destroyed by fire in 1984.

Motherwell, Lanarkshire Sports Stadium

The stadium was purpose built on the site of a derelict pit bing near Milton Street as a speedway track. Motherwell Eagles began to use the track in 1950. The stadium had a capacity of almost 60,000 including cover for 5,000. George Lucas was responsible for the sole promotion in Motherwell in June 1954 with a bill headlined by Charlie Hill. The stadium has since been demolished but the site remains as playing fields.

Paisley Ice Rink

Paisley Ice Rink was situated in East Lane in the east side of the town. The site was formerly the home of Abercorn Football Club and the Ice Rink was opened to the public in the nineteen forties. The building closed as an Ice Rink in 1970 and closed permanently in 1973. The site is now a supermarket. The Ice Rink was second only to the Kelvin Hall in terms of promotions. There were 48 promotions in the period, 5 fewer than the Kelvin Hall.

Peter Keenan fought for titles 4 times at Paisley and promoted the remaining 3 title contests that were seen at the Ice Rink. Paisley was a good venue for Keenan. In 1953, he defended his British bantamweight title against Frankie Williams. In 1954, he won back his British bantamweight title from John Kelly. In 1958, he retained his British Empire bantamweight title against both Graham Van Der Walt and Pat Supple. Keenan fought at Paisley Ice Rink 17 times losing only 2, to Derry Treanor and Amleto Falcinelli.

In 1960, Chic Calderwood won the British light heavyweight title against Arthur Howard. In 1963, Walter McGowan won the British and Empire titles against Jackie Brown and retained his Empire title against Kid Solomon.

The legendary Sugar Ray Robinson was on a 1964 bill and Cassius Clay took part in an exhibition in 1965.

The capacity of the Ice Rink was in the region of 5,000. In 1950, Sammy Docherty arranged for the entire ice surface to be covered with timber in order to increase the capacity to 7,000 for the Keenan / Proffitt fight. However, the magistrates limited the crowd to 5,800.

Portobello Town Hall

The Town Hall is situated in Portobello High Street. The Main Hall which could accommodate between 750 and 800 people saw 2 promotions in April 1952.

Rosyth Sports Ground

A one-off promotion in August 1951 included a Scottish middleweight title fight between Willie Armstrong and Dave Finnie.

Scottish Boxing Promoters

In the period 1950 to 1969, there were 318 boxing promotions in Scotland. Almost 50% of the total promotions, 155 to be precise, were held between 1950 and 1952. There were 75 promotions in 1950, 57 in 1951 and 23 in 1952. In the 9 year period 1953 to 1961, promotions numbered between 11 and 18 in each year. Subsequent to 1961, promotions were in single figures and dropped to lows of 2 in 1968 and 1 in 1969. There was therefore a remarkable contrast between the 75 promotions held in 1950 and the single promotion held in 1969.

Many promoters lost heavily on their initial promotion and were not heard of again. Others lasted a few shows before they realised that there were easier and more reliable ways of making a living. Scotland was lucky to have a number of seasoned promoters in this era and, leaving aside joint promotions, the leading promoters in the period were as shown in the following table. Peter Keenan led the way with 53 promotions.

Keenan Peter	53
Docherty Sammy	41
Gilmour Jim	34
Miller George	31
Lucas Alex	31
Black Charlie	23
McMillan Johnny	20
Grant George	18
Black Harry	11

A list of promoters in surname alphabetical order follows.

BEATTIE Andrew

Andrew Beattie promoted once at Paisley in 1950. Despite several call-offs, a good bill was provided. Perhaps the hassle, the poor financial return and the fact that brother George had also lost money was enough to make Andrew Beattie a one-off promoter.

BEATTIE George

George Beattie promoted at Coatbridge 4 times in summer of 1950. The series met with limited success and the promoter decided to concentrate on greyhound racing which was more popular with the public.

BLACK Charlie

Charlie Black was the leading west coast promoter in 1950. In addition to 7 promotions at Paisley Ice Rink, he also promoted at Ayr Ice Rink, Falkirk Ice Rink, the Kelvin Hall and Firhill in that year. Danny McKay, Don McTaggart and Neilly Phillips were regulars on Charlie Black promotions and each featured 5 times in the 1950 promotions.

Between January and April 1951, he had 2 bills at the Kelvin Hall, one at Paisley and one at Ayr. Each bill had at least a British title eliminator or a Scottish title fight and Glasgow featherweight, George Lamont, appeared on each bill. Black took a step back from promoting at this stage. Edinburgh Music Hall promoter, George Miller, had died in April 1951 and Black, seeing the lack of activity in Edinburgh, considered moving future promotions to the east coast. He concluded a 7-show deal at the Music Hall which he ran between January and March 1952. The bills were typically 5-fight bills with 6 or 7 Scots on each bill. In February 1952, Eddie Carson headlined in a Scottish bantamweight title fight against Billy Taylor of Stirling.

Black returned to the Music Hall with a bill in September. He had intended to run some further shows but decided to give up his licence after 25 years blaming the heavy tax on boxing, the lack of suitable venues and the scarcity of future talent as his reasons. Black promoted 23 shows between 1950 and 1952 and was an important figure in the profession at this time.

BLACK Harry

Harry Black was an Edinburgh promoter. He was responsible for 11 shows between 1951 and 1957, 9 at Leith Eldorado and 2 at Edinburgh Music Hall. He promoted the all-Edinburgh Scottish title fight between Eddie Carson and Hugh Riley at the Eldorado in October 1953 and the Scottish title eliminator between Chic Brogan and Gene Caffrey at the Music Hall in March 1954. Eddie Carson headlined several times and bills included Cowboy McCormack, Billy Rafferty and Charlie Hill. He also jointly promoted at the Eldorado with Sammy Docherty in December 1956 and Peter Keenan in 1960.

BLYTH George

George Blyth managed one promotion in October 1957. The show at Hamilton Town Hall was memorable for all of the wrong reasons. October 1957 was the height of the Asian flu epidemic and Johnny Morrissey was a late withdrawal from the 5 fight bill because of flu. Charlie Currie from Coatbridge was overweight for his contest with Andy Baird of Birmingham and Baird refused to go ahead with the fight. John O'Brien was due to fight Billy Allport of Walsall but Allport failed to show. The promoter was now down to two contests. Experienced Dundee featherweight Dave Croll was due to fight Belfast bantamweight Billy Skelly who had a dismal record. This was an obvious mismatch and the crowd were unlikely to be thrilled with a short, one-sided contest. Blyth persuaded bantamweight Billy Rafferty who was in the audience to replace Croll. There was a 45 minute delay before the show commenced with the main fight between Matt Fulton and Spike McCormack from Belfast. Fortunately, the crowd saw a cracking contest between the boxers which the Irishman shaded. When the MC announced that the second contest was to be the final bout of the evening, there was pandemonium in the hall with the crowd baying for Blyth's blood.

Disappointed fans were told to retain their tickets for half price entry at the next Hamilton show. There was, however, to be no next show for Blyth who lost his promoter's licence as a result of the fiasco.

BROWN George

George Brown promoted a show in Dumfries in 1960 using Glasgow and North of England boxers. It was not a financial success and was a one-off.

BUTLER Dan T

Dan T Butler became prominent in 1951. His first promotion was at Leith Eldorado in January with a 4-fight bill of Scots against Mancunians. This was supposedly the first of a series of fortnightly shows but was not a huge success. The Edinburgh scene at the time was dominated by George Miller and Butler decided to switch to Hawick where he ran promotions in successive weeks in March / April. He used boxers from the borders and the North East of England but Hawick did not appear to be interested in professional boxing and the disillusioned Butler soon gave up his licence. George Miller died in mid-April but Butler had tasted enough of the promotion business to know that it was not for him.

COLLINS Jackie

Jackie Collins was responsible for outdoor promotions at Alloa and Rosyth in 1951. In his first promotion in Alloa, there were 2 Scottish title fights. Johnny Flannigan outpointed Harry Hughes for the Scottish lightweight title and George Stern beat Hugh McDonald on a disqualification in a heavyweight title contest. Collins followed up with a Scottish middleweight title fight at Rosyth where Willie Armstrong stopped Dave Finnie.

DOCHERTY Peter

Peter Docherty operated as PD Promotions. He held 2 Kelvin Hall bills in 1950 and a Paisley Ice Rink bill in 1951. He enticed Maurice Sandeyron to fight on both Kelvin Hall bills, against Bobby Boland and Peter Keenan. Peter Docherty bills were always of a high standard.

DOCHERTY Sammy

Sammy Docherty has been known as both a loveable rogue and a crook. He was a well-known Glasgow bookmaker and Scotland's leading boxing promoter in the fifties. His first promotion in 1950 had been at the St. Mungo Halls in September. His 2 other shows that year were at Paisley Ice Rink and included Peter Keenan's British bantamweight title eliminator against Tommy Proffitt. 2 Paisley bills featuring Peter Keenan in early 1951 and 3 open air promotions at Firhill followed. The Firhill promotions were also headlined by Peter Keenan who won the British title against Danny O'Sullivan, defended against Bobby Boland and won the European title against Luis Romero. The open air shows had been very lucrative for Sammy Docherty.

Docherty held only one winter promotion in 1951, again at Paisley and headlined by Peter Keenan. He switched from Paisley to the Kelvin Hall in 1952 and held two uninspiring bills in the early part of the year. Docherty complained of the lack of Scottish box office attractions and American welterweight Danny Womber topped both bills. The second bill featured only 2 Scots out of 10 boxers and lacked the support of fans.

Docherty was back at Firhill in May with Peter Keenan who lost his European title to Jean Sneyers. The change in the rate of entertainment tax meant that Sammy did not promote again until April 1954 when he put on an excellent bill headlined by Eddie Carson against Robert Cohen at the Kelvin Hall. He was unhappy with the financial outcome and delayed his next promotion until February 1955 when he returned to the Kelvin Hall with Peter Keenan as top of the bill.

It was 1956 before Sammy was back to his best. In all three of his 1956 promotions at the Kelvin Hall, box office attractions Dick Currie and Matt Fulton appeared. The biggest promotion of the year was by Sammy at Firhill. Top of the bill was Dick Currie against Frankie Jones in a British flyweight title eliminator. The match was also for the Scottish flyweight title. In support, Matt Fulton took on Bobby Neill in an eliminator for the British featherweight title and for the Scottish featherweight title. Chic Brogan also fought Malcolm Grant for the Scottish bantamweight title. Docherty finished 1956 with a joint promotion with Harry Black at Leith Eldorado.

1957 was a busy year. Docherty returned to Paisley Ice Rink for one show in April and there were 5 shows at the Kelvin Hall. The October bill saw Frankie Jones lose his Empire title to Dennis Adams. Willie Toweel appeared on two of the bills. However, Docherty relied very much on crowd favourites Cowboy McCormack, Johnny Morrissey, Dave Mooney and Dick Currie at this time. There were also 2 Firhill promotions. On the May bill, Peter Keenan fought John Smillie for the British and Empire bantamweight titles.

1958 was also a busy year for Docherty. There were excellent promotions at Hamilton Town Hall in January and February, each headlined by a Scottish title fight. There were 7 promotions at the Kelvin Hall. The regular Scottish boxers on these shows were Johnny Morrissey, Derry Treanor and Dave Mooney. Future world bantamweight champion John Caldwell had his first 6 professional fights on these bills and fellow countryman and future opponent and world bantamweight contender Freddie Gilroy appeared on 3 of the bills. The highlights at the Kelvin Hall were a shock defeat for Willie Toweel, Peter Keenan's long awaited fight with Dick Currie, Chic Calderwood against Dave Mooney for the Scottish light heavyweight title and Johnny Morrissey against Gilroy in a British bantamweight title eliminator.

In 1959, Docherty held 3 promotions at the Kelvin Hall and one at Firhill. John Caldwell appeared on each bill and Billy Rafferty and Johnny Morrissey were again on hand to strengthen the bills. Dave Charnley also appeared on a strong Firhill bill. The pick of the Kelvin Hall matches was Frankie Jones and Alex Ambrose for the British flyweight title and Billy Rafferty's British bantamweight title eliminator against Len Reece. There was also a joint promotion with Jim Gilmour at the Kelvin Hall in November in aid of Cancer Research.

Peter Keenan had converted to promoter in 1959 and had proved a worthy rival as number one promoter to Sammy Docherty. After his final Kelvin Hall show on 28th October 1959, Docherty decided that boxing promotion was no longer for him. His protégé, John Caldwell, was unbeaten in 14 and would keep him involved in boxing. However, Docherty unexpectedly made a promotional comeback in 1968 with 2 further bills at Hamilton Town Hall. Jim Watt and Bobby Fisher appeared on both bills and Ken Buchanan and John O'Brien also featured. The first bill was an outstanding success but the second bill was not supported and Sammy Docherty again retired as a promoter.

In all, Sammy Docherty promoted 39 times in the fifties and twice in the sixties. 22 of his promotions were at the Kelvin Hall, 8 at Firhill, 6 at Paisley, 4 at Hamilton and 1 at the St Mungo Halls.

Sammy Docherty was a shrewd and tough business man. He made many great promotions in Scotland before going on to manage future world champion John Caldwell. As indoor venues in Scotland had insufficient capacity to allow him to compete with the leading British promoters, he applied for a promoter's licence in Northern Ireland. His plan was to use the 8,000+ capacity King's Hall with leading Scottish boxers such as Peter Keenan. His application was, however, refused. In the mid-fifties, he formed a partnership with Belfast promoter George Connell with a view to matching Peter Keenan with Robert Cohen. The match did not materialise and the partnership was subsequently dissolved.

Docherty sometimes made the front pages rather than the back pages of newspapers. One week before his September 1951 bill at Firhill, he was fined £30 or three months imprisonment for customs offences relating to nylon stockings. He opted to pay the fine. There was also a prolonged court case to determine whether he had paid £9,000 or £90,000 cash into his bank account. The poor bank clerk had receipted the larger amount in error. Sammy thought that his ship had arrived in Glasgow but the beaks ruled otherwise. His main headlines were in 1967 when John Caldwell's civil action questioned what had happened to his earnings when Sammy was his manager. Needless to say, Sammy emerged unscathed form the confrontation.

ELDORADO Promotions

Edinburgh had been deprived of boxing since September 1952 when this syndicate promoted in Leith in May 1953. The dream of future shows on a regular basis did not materialise following the lack of support for the initial show.

ELLIOT Charlie

Charlie Elliot's one and only promotion was at Greenock Town Hall in September 1956. Local boxers Arthur Donnachie and Tony McCrorey featured. Billy Rafferty and Dave Croll won all Scottish bouts in the remaining contests. The bill was supplemented by a Peter Keenan exhibition with John O'Brien and Frankie Jones. Elliot was aware that he would lose money even if he managed a full house. He did lose money on a good show and he did not achieve a full house and became yet another disillusioned promoter.

FERNS Hugh

Former Scottish heavyweight, Hugh Ferns, made promotional appearances at Greenock Town Hall in November 1957 and August 1959. The initial bill boasted a Scottish flyweight title fight between George McDade and Pat Glancy. Alex Ambrose, Dave Croll and local lightweight Bobby Kane appeared on the second bill. A novice heavyweight competition and exhibitions supplemented the 4 fight bill which produced 17 rounds of boxing.

GERAGHTY Mike

Mike Geraghty, a Larkhall publican, promoted only once. The venue was Hamilton Town Hall in February 1964. There was a 6-fight bill headed by Johnny Morrissey. The bill included 8 Scots and 4 Belfast boxers and the promotion was well supported.

GILMOUR Jim

Jim Gilmour's first promotion in 1950 was at Dunoon. The main contest was a Scottish welterweight title fight between Willie Whyte and Billy Rattray. There was also a test promotion at the St Mungo Halls just before Christmas.

In 1951, Gilmour began regular promotions at the St Mungo Halls where he promoted 18 times before ceasing operations at the Halls on 3rd November 1951. The attendance at these shows was poor indicating that fight fans were no longer interested in this type of bill and promoter Gilmour had lost money on each show.

In 1952, he ran shows at Falkirk and Kirkcaldy. The Falkirk bill saw Jim Kenny take on Tommy Miller for the Scottish featherweight title and the Kirkcaldy bill saw Willie Whyte take on Danny Malloy for the vacant Scottish welterweight title. These promotions were not financially successful and Jim Gilmour ceased to operate after his Kirkcaldy show in August 1952.

Gilmour returned in 1957 with 2 excellent promotions at Paisley Ice Rink and a high quality bill at Falkirk Ice Rink. The Falkirk crowd saw Frankie Jones, Chic Calderwood, Alex Ambrose, John Smillie and Tommy McGuinness record victories. The Paisley bills starred Peter Keenan supported on both occasions by Arthur Donnachie and Willie Armstrong. Bobby Neill, Charlie

Hill, Johnny Kidd, Alex Ambrose, Chic Calderwood and Billy Rafferty also appeared.

In 1958, Gilmour promoted 4 times at Paisley, once at Hamilton and once at Cathkin Park. The Cathkin bill included the British featherweight title fight between Charlie Hill and Chic Brogan, the Scottish flyweight title fight between Alex Ambrose and George McDade and the Scottish middleweight title fight between Cowboy McCormack and Len Mullen. The Paisley bills were all top quality and included Peter Keenan's defences of his Empire bantamweight title against Pat Supple and Graham Van Der Walt, the Scottish lightweight title fight between Johnny McLaren and Tommy McGuinness, Derry Treanor's defeat of Peter Keenan and Billy Rafferty's defeat of Terry Spinks.

Gilmour's first promotion of 1959 saw a switch of venue to Whiteinch in Glasgow. Despite the small venue, the bill included Jackie Brown, Dave Croll, Hugh Riley and Arthur Donnachie. There followed 2 Kelvin Hall bills. Both bills featured Cowboy McCormack and Alex Ambrose whose Scottish flyweight title fight with George McDade ended in a draw. The promotion on 28th May was Jim Gilmour's last promotion.

Jim Gilmour also jointly promoted a charity bill with Sammy Docherty at the Kelvin Hall in November 1958. He died in October 1963.

GRANT George

George Grant started life as a newsboy and graduated to a bookmaker with 7 betting shops in Dundee and Angus. He had promoted since 1934 and was the top promoter in the North East of Scotland. He had promoted world flyweight champion Jackie Paterson at Hampden Park 3 times in the forties.

He put on his first bill of the fifties at the Caird Hall, Dundee on 2nd January 1950. In all, he promoted 4 times in 1950, twice at the Caird Hall and twice at Dundee Ice Rink. At this time Dundee boasted leading Scottish boxers such as Norman Tennant, Bobby Boland, Willie Myles and Billy Rattray, all of whom featured on George Grant bills. The September bill at Dundee Ice Rink included the British flyweight title eliminator between Norman Tennant and Joe Murphy.

He promoted once at the Caird Hall and twice at Premierland in 1951. The Croll brothers featured for the first time and became the main attraction of these shows.

There were 11 further promotions between 1952 and 1955. The Premierland had been specially built by Grant to host boxing promotions but this was used only twice in 1952. One promotion was at Kirkcaldy Ice Rink with the remaining 8 at the Caird Hall. His final promotion at the Caird Hall on 20th December 1955 saw Jimmy Croll lift the Scottish welterweight title with a 12 round points win over Roy MacGregor.

George Grant announced his retirement on 1st January 1956. He cited a lack of personalities as the principle reason that he did not run more promotions.

HAMILTON Dick

Dick Hamilton ran shows in successive weeks at Portobello Town Hall in April 1952. The first show was a 4-fight show featuring Edinburgh boxers against boxers from the North East of England and was reasonably successful. The second show was reduced to 3 fights and was unsuccessful.

HANNAH Finlay

Finlay Hannah promoted twice. The promotions were at Hamilton Town Hall and Govan Town Hall in 1957. The Hamilton bill was originally 6 fights but was reduced to 5 when Archie Downie's opponent failed to show. Two 6 rounders went the distance but Johnny Morrissey, Owen Reilly and Charlie Currie all stopped their opponents early and the crowd saw only 20 rounds of boxing. The Govan bill was a 4-fight bill again featuring Morrissey and Reilly as well as Matt Fulton. Early stoppages meant that the crowd saw only 14 rounds of boxing. The 4-contest bill was supplemented by an exhibition between Dick Currie and Dennis Adams.

Finlay Hannah died in a motor accident near Uddingston in March 1959.

HUGHES Pat

Pat Hughes first and only promotion was at Irvine Meadow Football ground in May 1960. An entertaining 6-fight bill included Alex Ambrose, John Smillie, George McDade and Jimmy Gibson.

KEENAN Peter

Peter Keenan retired from boxing in January 1959. It had been alleged that Keenan financed promotions prior to 1959 but no punitive action was ever taken by the Scottish Area Council as there was no evidence of any wrongdoing. His first official promotion was in March 1959 and he went on to assume the mantle of leading Scottish promoter in his era. He promoted 53 times between 1959 and 1967 and jointly promoted once with Harry Black. Of 63 Scottish boxing promotions in the sixties, Peter Keenan promoted 46 plus 1 with Harry Black.

Keenan's main venue was Paisley Ice Rink where he put on 21 promotions between 1959 and 1967. There were 9 promotions at the Kelvin Hall, 4 at Govan Town Hall, 2 at Hamilton Town Hall, 2 at the Kelvin Arena and single promotions at the Caird Hall, Firhill and Deveronvale Park. Towards the end of his promotional career, Keenan concentrated mainly on his promotions at the Central Hotel. There were 12 promotions at the Central Hotel between 1966 and 1967.

In his first year as a promoter, he put on Scottish title fights at flyweight, bantamweight and featherweight and British title eliminators at flyweight and light heavyweight. In 1960, he put on a Scottish lightweight title fight and 3 massive Chic Calderwood fights. In January, it was the British light heavyweight title fight with Arthur Howard. In June, it was the Empire light heavyweight title fight with Johnny Halafihi and in September, it was the memorable fight with Willie Pastrano.

In 1963, he promoted the McGowan versus Brown British and Empire flyweight title fight and the McGowan Empire defence against Kid Solomon. In 1964, he promoted the Calderwood British title fight against Bob Nicholson. He also brought the legendary Sugar Ray Robinson to his September Paisley bill. In 1965, he brought together Chic Calderwood and John McCormack.

In the period to 1965, both Jackie Brown and Chic Calderwood featured on 16 Peter Keenan promotions. John McCormack appeared on 13, Walter McGowan on 11 and George Judge on 10. Other boxers who appeared regularly on Keenan promotions were Willie and Bobby Fisher, Alex Ambrose, Johnny Morrissey, Jimmy Gibson and Danny Lee.

At the Central Hotel, Derek Cowper appeared on 8 of the 12 promotions, George Hind on 7 and Tommy Connor on 5. The September 1966 bill included the Scottish bantamweight title fight between Evan Armstrong and Jackie Brown and the January 1967 bill included the Scottish lightweight title fight between Ken Buchanan and John McMillan.

Although Keenan appeared to be a successful promoter, he suffered the same fate as other promoters at many of his shows. If crowds did not turn out to see quality bills, there was little chance of making the promotion pay. Keenan kept Scottish boxing alive in his time as a promoter despite the obvious deterioration of the Scottish boxing scene. He could not continue to subsidise the sport that he loved and turned his promotional skills to wrestling which was attracting larger crowds than boxing. The Scottish boxing public should be grateful to Peter Keenan for his contribution to the sport between 1959 and 1967.

KELLY Johnny

Johnny Kelly had been involved in boxing since the thirties. He had been a second to both Benny Lynch and Jackie Paterson and was confident that his shows at the Kelvin Arena would revive Scottish boxing. His 2 promotions at the Kelvin Arena in May 1961 were, however, financial flops. The talented Jimmy Gibson featured on both bills but could not be connected with the poor turn out at the modern arena.

LESLIE Mont

Mont Leslie made a promotional comeback to promote 3 times at the Caird Hall, Dundee between September 1950 and January 1951. Local fighters

Norman Tennant, Al Gallacher and Johnny Davidson appeared on all of the bills.

LEVER Jerry

On 3 occasions, Jerry Lever organised champagne and supper boxing shows at the Central Hotel for charity. The 4-fight March 1960 bill provided 36 rounds of boxing including the Scottish welterweight title fight between Tommy McGuinness and Jim McGuinness and a Scottish flyweight title eliminator between George McDade and Pat Glancy. The May 1959 and November 1961 bills were less attractive and provided only 18 and 17 rounds of boxing respectively. At prices ranging from 10 to 100 guineas, the shows were not a great financial success. They did, however, sow the seed for a Scottish National Sporting Club in the head of Peter Keenan.

LUCAS Alex

Although born in Edinburgh, Alex Lucas had left the east coast and had promoted at Glasgow and Paisley since 1946. His family business, Lucas Furniture, in Jamaica Street, Glasgow was his full-time occupation and he looked upon promoting as a hobby. He did not promote in 1950 but put on a show at Carntyne Greyhound Stadium in 1951. The innovative promoter introduced a boy's gate at the lowly price of 1/6d and offered reduced admission to women. The 4-fight bill included 7 Scots and a Scottish lightweight title eliminator. He also promoted 5 times at the St Mungo Halls in 1951.

In 1952, he put on 3 shows at the Kelvin Hall, 2 at St Mungo Halls and one in Paisley. His 5-fight August bill at the Kelvin Hall was all-Scottish and included 3 Scottish title fights and 2 Scottish title eliminators. It had been a long time since a programme of such variety and strength had been seen in Scotland. All of the fights went the distance and a total of 54 rounds were boxed.

There was another top bill at Paisley in January 1953 which provided 42 rounds of boxing. Peter Keenan defended his British bantamweight title against Frankie Williams and there were 2 Scottish title fights. A Kelvin Hall bill followed. His third promotion of the year was at Firhill where Peter Keenan beat Maurice Sandeyron in a European bantamweight title fight. Again there was Scottish title fight in support. There was a disappointing attendance at Firhill and Lucas suffered a substantial monetary loss. The remainder of the year was disappointing for Lucas as he was unable to compete with Belfast in bidding for the Keenan versus Kelly fight and he was also unable to offer Keenan a warm-up for this fight because of the lack of a suitable venue.

2 promotions at the Kelvin Hall and 2 at Paisley followed in 1954. The top bout was Peter Keenan's rematch with John Kelly for the British bantamweight title. There were, however, also 5 Scottish title fights on these bills. Charlie Hill fought on all 4 bills which were packed with top action.

There were also outdoor shows at Motherwell and Kilwinning in the summer of 1954. Charlie Hill and Dick Knox featured on both bills.

He ran a 6-fight bill at Govan Town Hall in early 1955. There followed 3 bills at the Kelvin Hall and bills at Paisley and Cathkin Park. Cathkin Park witnessed the Keenan versus Tuli Empire title battle in front of a crowd of 30,000.

There were promotions in Govan, Dundee and Cathkin Park in 1956. His last promotion was at the Kelvin Hall and featured the British bantamweight title eliminator between John Smillie and George Dormer.

It was a sad blow to Scottish boxing when Alex Lucas died suddenly on 8th August 1956 in a Glasgow hospital aged 61. He had supported Scottish boxing following the increase in Entertainment Tax despite finding himself in the red in many of his shows. He had taken his shows to different parts of the country and had given newcomers a chance at smaller venues whilst continuing to put on bills of the highest standard at the leading venues.

McGUINNESS Tommy

Tommy McGuinness was the brother of Jim McGuinness who had won the Scottish welterweight title in 1960. He made his promotional debut at Hamilton Town Hall in April 1961. 7 Scots on the bill were supplemented by 3 Belfast boxers. Johnny Morrissey, Jimmy Gibson, Sammy McSpadden, Owen Reilly and Willie Fisher were all successful in a good night of boxing. McGuinness quit as a promoter after this show.

McMILLAN Johnny

Johnny McMillan was the regular promoter at the Grove in the early fifties. He ran 19 shows between 1st January 1950 and his final show on 13th May 1950. This promoter and venue gave young Scottish talent the chance to box professionally at a nursery level. In June 1950, he promoted a 7-fight bill for local charities at Saint Anthony's Football Ground in Govan.

McQUEEN Ken

Ken McQueen held 5 promotions at the Eldorado in Leith in early 1950. His last 3 promotions featured very few Scots despite the fact that there was a vast quantity of Scots available for action at all levels.

MILLER George

George Miller was the number one Edinburgh promoter in the early fifties and it was mainly due to him that Edinburgh was a centre of regular boxing at this time. Miller had first staged shows before the war at the Oddfellows Hall and the Prom at Portobello. He operated regularly at Edinburgh Music Hall each year between September and March with great success until his untimely death at home in Portobello on 17th April 1951. He ran 31 promotions in the period January 1950 to March 1951 and the promotions were of a consistently high standard for such a small venue. The top contests in this period were 2 Scottish title eliminators, Jackie Marshall against Johnny Flannigan in March 1950 and Willie Myles against Jim Dwyer in November 1950.

MURRAY Johnny

Johnny Murray promoted at Govan Town Hall in 1957. His one-off bill was attractive and included leading boxers such as Billy Rafferty, Derry Treanor, John McCormack and Dave Mooney.

NEILL Andy

Andy Neill was the father of Bobby Neill and he had arranged a promotion at the 6,000 capacity Murrayfield Ice Rink in September 1958 to be headlined by Bobby against Pierre Cossemyns or Arthur Donnachie and supported by a Scottish title fight between Chic Brogan and John Smillie. However, when Bobby Neill broke his jaw in early September, the promotion was not financially viable and was cancelled.

Andy Neill's sole promotion was at Leith Eldorado in November 1958. The promotion comprised 4 contests of 8 rounds, all of which went the distance. A good bill saw local boxer Hugh Riley beat Danny McNamee. Alex Ambrose, Dave Croll and John Smillie also appeared and were winners.

NESS John

Glasgow business man John Ness was the final promoter in this era. His only promotion was at Govan Town Hall in 1969.

REA Ernie

Local bookmaker, Ernie Rea, put on an outdoor show at Coatbridge Greyhound Stadium in June 1960. This was to be his only promotion. Local boxer Johnny McLaren featured but the main contest was between John Smillie and George Judge.

ROBERTSON Jackie

Jackie Robertson, a well-known Dumfries welterweight, was credited as promoter of the Dumfries promotion in August 1950.

RUSSELL Bob

Bob Russell ran a promotion at Dunoon Recreation Park in July 1950. He hoped to catch the Glasgow holiday crowd but the promotion was ruined by poor weather and the non-appearance of headliner Billy Dickson's opponent. There were only 2 contests and 12 rounds of boxing.

SOLOMONS Jack

Jack Solomons was the premier promoter in the history of British boxing. His original application to promote in Scotland had been turned down in the late fifties. However, a further application in 1960 was successful and he left his London Empire to promote twice in 1962 and twice in 1963 at the Kelvin Hall. However, his wish to revitalise Scottish boxing did not meet with the approval of his rival Peter Keenan. Solomon's 4 promotions were within a 7 month period between September 1962 and March 1963. Johnny Morrissey appeared on all 4 bills and Ian McKenzie on 3. Walter McGowan was a main attraction appearing on the first 3 bills and Chic Calderwood bolstered the final bill. The highlight of the promotional sequence was Howard Winstone's British featherweight title defence against Johnny Morrissey in January 1963.

TOWNSLEY Ralph

Ralph Townsley held his only promotion at Linksfield Stadium, Aberdeen in July 1958. The main attraction was Aberdonian Johnny Kidd winning the Scottish lightweight title from Johnny McLaren but the 5-fight bill was a good one and it is a pity that there were no further shows from this promoter.

WILSON Jimmy

Jimmy Wilson held 3 promotions in 1953. He promoted at the St Mungo Halls and at Greenock Town Hall in February and at Saracen Park in May. Wilson had hoped to recoup the February losses at Saracen Park but lost several hundred pounds on the outdoor bill despite fine weather and a minimum entrance charge of 2/6d. He subsequently gave up his promoter's licence.

Some Afterthoughts

In the period 1st January 1950 to 31st December 1969, 22 major title fights were staged in Scotland as follows.

World Titles   -   0
European Titles   -   3
Empire Titles   -   8
British Titles   - 11

9 of the title fights were at Paisley, 8 at Firhill, 3 at the Kelvin Hall and 2 at Cathkin.

Sammy Docherty promoted 8 of the contests, Peter Keenan 6, George Lucas 4, Jim Gilmour 3 and Jack Solomons 1.

Only two contests were for double titles. Keenan v Smillie and McGowan v Brown were both for the British and Empire titles.

Peter Keenan fought for 12 of the 22 titles.

All of the European title fights featured Peter Keenan. He won the European bantamweight title on 5th September 1951 from Luis Romero. He then lost the title on 21st May 1952 to Jean Sneyers and regained the title on 17th June 1953 from Maurice Sandeyron. All of the contests were at Firhill. Sammy Docherty promoted the first two fights and Alex Lucas the third.

Paisley Ice Rink hosted four of the Empire title fights. Two were held at Firhill, one at Cathkin and one at the Kelvin Hall. Peter Keenan fought in four of the contests and promoted three. He won the Empire bantamweight title at Cathkin on 14th September 1955 when he beat Jake Tuli. He retained the title against John Smillie at Firhill on 22nd May 1957 and at Paisley against Graham Van Der Walt and Pat Supple on 2nd April 1958 and 16th October 1958 respectively.

At Paisley, Keenan promoted Walter McGowan's British Empire title wins on 2nd May 1963 against Jackie Brown and 12th September 1963 against Kid Solomon. He was also the promoter on 9th June 1960 at Firhill when Chic Calderwood defeated Johnny Halafihi to lift the Empire light heavyweight crown.

On 23rd October 1957, Frankie Jones lost his Empire flyweight title to Dennis Adams at the Kelvin Hall. Sammy Docherty promoted this and also the Keenan v Smillie fight. Alex Lucas promoted the Keenan v Tuli fight and Jim Gilmour promoted the Keenan fights at Paisley.

In the period 1950 to 1969, British title contests featuring Scots numbered 41. Of the 41 contests, 30 were held outside of Scotland. There were 2 contests in Wales, 7 in Belfast and 21 in England. There were 6 all-Scottish fights for the British title as follows.

Flyweight	Jones v Ambrose
	McGowan v Brown
Bantamweight	Keenan v Boland
	Keenan v Smillie
Featherweight	Hill v Brogan
	Hill v Neill

All of these fights took place in Scotland other than Hill v Neill.

The number of appearances by Scottish fighters at each weight was as follows.

Flyweight	10
Bantamweight	15
Featherweight	13
Lightweight	1
Welterweight	1
Middleweight	3
Light Heavyweight	4

The British flyweight title was held by Frankie Jones from 31st July 1957 to 8th October 1960. Jackie Brown, Walter McGowan and John McCluskey held the title between them from 27th February 1962. The title was therefore held by Scots for just over 11 of the 20 years in the period of review.

Peter Keenan held the British bantamweight title from 9th May 1951 to 3rd October 1953 and again from 21st September 1954 to 10th January 1959. Walter McGowan held the title from 6th September 1966 to 13th May 1968. The title was therefore held by Scots for just over 8 years 5 months in the period.

Charlie Hill held the British featherweight title from 4th February 1956 until 13th April 1959 and Bobby Neill from 13th April 1959 until 27th September 1960. The title was therefore held by Scots for almost 4 years 8 months.

Ken Buchanan held the British lightweight title from 19th January 1968.

Cowboy McCormack held the British middleweight title for 49 days.

Chic Calderwood held the British light heavyweight title for almost 6 years. He first won the title on 28th January 1960 but it was forfeited in late 1963. He regained the title in November 1964 and held it until his death in November 1966.

Of the British titles contested in Scotland, two were at flyweight, five were at bantamweight, two were at featherweight and two were at light heavyweight. Frankie Jones retained his British flyweight title against Alex Ambrose at the Kelvin Hall on 5th February 1959. Walter McGowan's victory against Jackie Brown in September 1963 was also for the British flyweight title.

The five British bantamweight title fights were won by Peter Keenan. The Empire victory over John Smillie was also for the British title. Other victories were against Danny O'Sullivan, Bobby Boland, Frankie Williams and John Kelly. Three of the fights were at Firhill and promoted by Sammy Docherty. The other two were at Paisley Ice Rink and promoted by Alex Lucas.

Charlie Hill defended his British featherweight title on 2nd July 1958 against Chic Brogan at Cathkin Park. Jim Gilmour promoted the fight. At the Kelvin Hall on 31st January 1963, Johnny Morrissey failed to win the British featherweight title from Howard Winstone. Jack Solomons was the promoter.

Peter Keenan promoted both light heavyweight contests at Paisley Ice Rink. Chic Calderwood defeated Arthur Howard on 28th January 1960 and Bob Nicholson on 11th November 1964.

Only 3 Scots fought for world titles in this era. Peter Keenan lost to Vic Toweel in 1952, Chic Calderwood lost to Jose Torres in 1966 and Walter McGowan beat Salvatore Burruni before losing twice to Chartchai Chionoi.

Appendix 1

A complete list of professional promotions in Scotland between 1950 and 1969

<u>1950</u>

02/01/1950	Caird Hall	Promoter – George Grant	
Bantam	Dickie Dunn (Dundee)	lost pts 6	Al Callacher (Dundee)
Bantam	Bobby Boland (Dundee)	win pts 10	Norman Tennant (Dundee)
Bantam	Willie Myles (Dundee)	win pts 10	Eddie McCormick (Deal)
	(Scottish Bantamweight Title Final Eliminator)		
Feather	Harry McCabe (Dundee)	lost pts 6	Jimmy Dunn (Glasgow)
Light	Pat McKay (Edinburgh)	win rsf 2	Johnny Davidson (Dundee)
Middle	Gus McPhee (Perth)	lost rsf 4	Jim Gallacher (Glencraig)

07/01/1950	Grove Institute	Promoter – Johnny McMillan	
Feather	Zeke Brown (Jamaica)	win ret 1	Hugh McLellan (Campbelltown)
Light	Harry Lucas (Edinburgh)	win pts 4	Hal Crosby (Tipton)
Middle	Alex Dobbins (Glasgow)	win pts 6	Jack Brown (Doncaster)
Welter	Tom McGoldrick (Perth)	lost pts 6	Jim Craig (Dundee)

10/01/1950	Edinburgh Music Hall	Promoter – George Miller	
Fly	Pat McCambridge (Glasgow)	lost ko 3	Wal Marcel (France)
Feather	Vernon Sollas (Jamaica)	drew 8	George Lamont (Glasgow)
Feather	Zeke Brown (Jamaica)	win ret 2	Owen Durkins (Glasgow)
Welter	Joe Baillie (Glasgow)	lost pts 8	Frankie Naro (Dumbarton)
Welter	Tom McGoldrick (Perth)	lost pts 6	Ginger Scott (Edinburgh)

14/01/1950	Grove Institute	Promoter – Johnny McMillan	
Feather	Danny Woods (Clydebank)	win pts 6	Lewis Goodwin (Jamaica)
Feather	Harry McCabe (Dundee)	lost pts 6	Hal Crosbie (Tipton)
Feather	Pat McCambridge (Glasgow)	win rsf 4	Bob Donaldson (Glasgow)
Light	Harry Lucas (Edinburgh)	win pts 6	Jack Docherty (Jamaica)
Light	Tommy Miller (Glasgow)	lost pts 4	Jackie Ryan (Blackpool)

17/01/1950	Edinburgh Music Hall	Promoter – George Miller	
Fly	Andy McCulloch (Glasgow)	win pts 6	Jeff Oscroft (Notts)
Bantam	Glyn Evans (Doncaster)	win ko 2	George Johnson (Leeds)
Feather	Jim Dwyer (Glasgow)	win ret 3	Budge Johnson (Lincoln)
Feather	Sam Donegan (Glasgow)	lost pts 4	Bob Donaldson (Glasgow)
Welter	Tommy Jones (Derby)	lost pts 8	Ginger Roberts (Whitley Bay)

18/01/1950	Paisley Ice Rink		Promoter – Charlie Black	
Fly	Peter Keenan (Glasgow)	win ko 3	Dickie O'Sullivan (London)	
Feather	Don McTaggart (Paisley)	win rsf 3	Billy Moore (Clydebank)	
Feather	George Stewart (Hamilton)	lost pts 6	George Lamont (Glasgow)	
Light	Jim Findlay (Motherwell)	win pts 8	Hugh Smith (Sunderland)	
Light Heavy	Bert Gilroy (Coatbridge)	win pts 8	Gerry McDermott (Dublin)	

19/01/1950	Leith Eldorado		Promoter – Ken McQueen	
Bantam	Dickie Dunn (Dundee)	win pts 6	Pat Maguire (Glasgow)	
Feather	Teddy Peckham (Bournemouth)	lost rsf 8	Jock Bonas (Edinburgh)	
Feather	Mick Day (Glasgow)	lost pts 8	Peter Fay (Bournemouth)	
Light	Pat Kelly (Perth)	lost pts 8	Harry Legge (Bournemouth)	
Light	Pat McKay (Edinburgh)	win pts 4	Johnny Kildare (Newarthill)	

21/01/1950	Grove Institute		Promoter – Johnny McMillan	
Fly	Jim Wallace (Glasgow)	win rsf 2	Joe Harvey (Paisley)	
Fly	Hugh McLellan (Campbelltown)	win ko 2	Pat McCambridge (Glasgow)	
Light	Hal Crosbie (Tipton)	lost pts 6	Jackie Ryan (Blackpool)	
Light	Pat Kelly (Perth)	win pts 6	Ollie Fleming (Jamaica)	
Welter	Alex Dobbins (Glasgow)	lost pts 6	Jack Brown (Doncaster)	

28/01/1950	Grove Institute		Promoter – Johnny McMillan	
Fly	Pat McCambridge (Glasgow)	win pts 4	Jim Wallace (Glasgow)	
Feather	Danny Woods (Clydebank)	lost ret 3	Zeke Brown (Jamaica)	
Light	Harry Lucas (Edinburgh)	win rsf 4	Frankie Brown (Dumbarton)	
Light	Pat McKay (Edinburgh)	win rsf 4	Johnny Kildare (Newarthill)	
Middle	Alec Nimmo (Edinburgh)	lost rsf 2	Jack Brown (Doncaster)	

31/01/1950	Edinburgh Music Hall		Promoter – George Miller	
Bantam	Eddie Carson (Edinburgh)	win pts 8	Vernon Sollas (Jamaica)	
Feather	Hal Crosbie (Tipton)	lost pts 6	Zeke Brown (Jamaica)	
Light	Tommy Miller (Glasgow)	drew 6	Harry Lucas (Edinburgh)	
Welter	Jim Scott (Edinburgh)	drew 6	Ginger Scott (Edinburgh)	
Middle	Alex Dobbins (Glasgow)	win pts 6	Jack Brown (Doncaster)	

04/02/1950	Grove Institute		Promoter – Johnny McMillan	
Fly	Jim Wallace (Glasgow)	lost rsf 3	Andy McCulloch (Glasgow)	
Feather	Billy Moore (Clydebank)	win pts 6	Pat Cahill (Dundee)	
Feather	Hal Crosbie (Tipton)	win pts 6	Zeke Brown (Jamaica)	
Light	Tommy Miller (Glasgow)	win ko 1	Robert Lang (Glasgow)	
Welter	Jim Craig (Dundee)	win pts 6	Jim Scott (Edinburgh)	

08/02/1950	Paisley Ice Rink	Promoter – Charlie Black	
Feather	George Lamont (Glasgow)	lost pts 6	Roy Ankrah (West Africa)
Feather	Jim Kenny (Polmont)	win ko 3	Tommy Burns (Stockton)
	(British and Empire Featherweight Title Eliminator)		
Feather	Don McTaggart (Paisley)	win rsf 5	Andy McCulloch (Glasgow)
Light	Jackie Marshall (Glasgow)	lost pts 8	Solly Cantor (Canada)
Light	Johnny Flannigan (Whitburn)	lost ko 1	Laurie Buxton (Watford)
09/02/1950	Leith Eldorado	Promoter – Ken McQueen	
Fly	Johnny Summers (Edinburgh)	lost pts 8	Jimmy Pearce (Middlesbrough)
Feather	Jock Bonas (Edinburgh)	win pts 8	Jim Dwyer (Glasgow)
Feather	Mick Day (Glasgow)	win ko 1	Jimmy Thompson (Newcastle)
Light	Harry Lucas (Edinburgh)	win rsf 3	Hugh Docherty (Glasgow)
Welter	Danny McKay (Edinburgh)	win ko 7	Joe White (Carlisle)
11/02/1950	Grove Institute	Promoter – Johnny McMillan	
Bantam	Owen Durkins (Glasgow)	win pts 6	Pat Maguire (Glasgow)
Light	Harry Lucas (Edinburgh)	drew 6	Johnny Davidson (Dundee)
Light	Billy Kid Andrews (Dundee)	win rsf 3	Tommy Miller (Glasgow)
Light	Frankie Brown (Dumbarton)	win ret 2	Pat Kelly (Perth)
Welter	Alex Dobbins (Glasgow)	win pts 6	Billy Stevens (Tilliiecoutry)
14/02/1950	Edinburgh Music Hall	Promoter – George Miller	
Bantam	Jack Horseman (West Hartlepool)	lost pts 8	Vernon Sollas (Jamaica)
Bantam	Eddie Carson (Edinburgh)	win pts 8	Jimmy Webster (London)
Feather	Don McTaggart (Paisley)	win ret 1	Chic Watson (Edinburgh)
Feather	Roy Ankrah (West Africa)	win pts 6	Zeke Brown (Jamaica)
15/02/1950	Caird Hall	Promoter – George Grant	
Fly	Vic Herman (Glasgow)	win pts 10	Norman Tennant (Dundee)
Bantam	Bobby Boland (Dundee)	win rsf 3	Roy Ball (Wales)
Feather	Don McTaggart (Paisley)	win pts 4	Pat Walsh (Perth)
Welter	Billy Rattray (Dundee)	dnc 6	Alex Dobbins (Glasgow)
Welter	Jim Craig (Dundee)	drew 6	Ginger Scott (Edinburgh)
18/02/1950	Grove Institute	Promoter – Johnny McMillan	
Feather	Billy Moore (Clydebank)	win pts 6	Benny Lacey (Glasgow)
Welter	Pat McKay (Edinburgh)	win pts 6	George Cameron (Glasgow)
Middle	Dave McLaren (Comrie)	win ko 1	Jack Brown (Doncaster)
Light Heavy	Scotty O'Hara (Glasgow)	win ko 1	Alec Nimmo (Edinburgh)
Light Heavy	Jock McCusker (Glasgow)	win ret 4	Frankie Martin (Glasgow)
25/02/1950	Grove Institute	Promoter – Johnny McMillan	
Fly	Joe Harvey (Paisley)	win rsf 1	Jim Wallace (Glasgow)
Light	Zeke Brown (Jamaica)	win pts 6	Jackie Ryan (Hamilton)
Welter	Jim Scott (Edinburgh)	win pts 6	Johnny Davidson (Dundee)
Welter	Alex Dobbins (Glasgow)	win pts 6	Billy Stevens (Tilliecoutry)

28/02/1950	Edinburgh Music Hall		Promoter – George Miller	
Bantam	Andy McCulloch (Glasgow)	win pts 6	Dickie Dunn (Dundee)	
Feather	Roy Ankrah (West Africa)	win rsf 4	Len Shaw (Sheffield)	
Feather	Don McTaggart (Paisley)	win dis 5	Zeke Brown (Jamaica)	
Welter	George Cameron (Glasgow)	lost pts 6	Ginger Scott (Edinburgh)	
Welter	Billy Stevens (Tilliecoutry)	lost rsf 4	Jimmy Molloy (Liverpool)	

02/03/1950	Leith Eldorado		Promoter – Ken McQueen	
Bantam	Al Gallacher (Dundee)	win pts 6	Joe Quinn (Belfast)	
Feather	Jock Bonas (Edinburgh)	win pts 8	Dave Lloyd (Wales)	
Feather	Mick Day (Glasgow)	win rsf 3	Bill Greenfield (Burnley)	
Welter	Tommy Armour (Belfast)	drew 8	Ginger Roberts (Whitley Bay)	

04/03/1950	Grove Institute		Promoter – Johnny McMillan	
Feather	Owen Durkins (Glasgow)	lost rsf 1	Johnny Hale (London)	
Feather	Benny Lacey (Glasgow)	win pts 6	Pat Maguire (Glasgow)	
Welter	Jim Scott (Edinburgh)	win pts 6	Ginger Scott (Edinburgh)	
Welter	Alex Dobbins (Glasgow)	win pts 6	Dave McLaren (Comrie)	
Middle	Frankie Martin (Glasgow)	lost ko 2	Jack Brown (Doncaster)	

07/03/1950	Edinburgh Music Hall		Promoter – George Miller	
Bantam	Vernon Sollas (Jamaica)	win pts 8	Willie Myles (Dundee)	
Bantam	Eddie Carson (Edinburgh)	win pts 8	Ronnie Bissell (Yorks)	
Light	Tommy Campbell (Dundee)	win pts 6	Tommy Miller (Glasgow)	
Light	Jim Scott (Edinburgh)	win rsf 1	Benny Moran (Dumbarton)	

08/03/1950	Kelvin Hall		Promoter – Peter Docherty	
Fly	Vic Herman (Glasgow)	win pts 8	Norman Tennant (Dundee)	
Bantam	Bobby Boland (Dundee)	lost pts 8	Maurice Sandeyron (France)	
Feather	George Lamont (Glasgow)	lost pts 6	George Stewart (Hamilton)	
Light	Jim Findlay (Motherwell)	win pts 6	Morry Jones (Liverpool)	
Welter	Alex Dobbins (Glasgow)	lost rsf 5	Billy Stevens (Tilliecoutry)	
Heavy	George Stern (Glasgow)	win pts 6	Hugh McDonald (Glasgow)	

10/03/1950	Falkirk Ice Rink		Promoter – Charlie Black	
Fly	Joe Murphy (Glasgow)	win rsf 5	Micky McLaughlin (Belfast)	
Feather	Jim Kenny (Polmont)	win pts 10	Stan Gossip (Hull)	
Feather	Roy Ankrah (West Africa)	win rsf 5	Peter Morrison (Hull)	
Welter	Ginger Scott (Edinburgh)	win pts 6	George Cameron (Glasgow)	
Welter	Danny McKay (Edinburgh)	win rsf 6	Ginger Stewart (Hamilton)	

11/03/1950	Grove Institute		Promoter – Johnny McMillan	
Bantam	Billy Moore (Clydebank)	win pts 6	Harry Lucas (Edinburgh)	
Light	Tommy Miller (Glasgow)	win pts 6	Peter Collins (Edinburgh)	
Light	Hal Crosby (Tipton)	win pts 6	Zeke Brown (Jamaica)	
Light Heavy	Colin McKinlay (Dumbarton)	win pts 6	Jock McCusker (Glasgow)	
Light Heavy	John Alexander (Motherwell)	win ko 3	Scotty O'Hara (Glasgow)	

14/03/1950	Edinburgh Music Hall		Promoter – George Miller
Bantam	Joe Collins (Sunderland)	lost rsf 2	Mick Day (Glasgow)
Light	Johnny Flannigan (Whitburn)	win pts 8	Hugh Smith (Sunderland)
Light	Tommy Miller (Glasgow)	drew 6	Billy Bird (Sunderland)
Light Heavy	John Alexander (Motherwell)	lost rsf 2	Wally Diamond (Jamaica)

18/03/1950	Grove Institute		Promoter – Johnny McMillan
Bantam	Pat Maguire (Glasgow)	win rsf 2	Dickie Dunn (Dundee)
Feather	Billy Moore (Clydebank)	lost ko 4	Zeke Brown (Jamaica)
Light	Pat Kelly (Perth)	win ko 3	Frankie Brown (Dumbarton)
Welter	Ginger Scott (Edinburgh)	win pts 6	Tommy Mount (Motherwell)
Welter	Billy Stevens (Tilliecoutry)	win pts 8	Dave McLaren (Comrie)

21/03/1950	Edinburgh Music Hall		Promoter – George Miller
Bantam	Vernon Sollas (Jamaica)	win pts 8	Peter Harvey (Pontefract)
Light	Harry Lucas (Edinburgh)	win pts 6	Zeke Brown (Jamaica)
Welter	Jim Scott (Edinburgh)	lost pts 6	Johnny Fitzpatrick (Doncaster)
Middle	Jimmy Ingle (Dublin)	win pts 8	Billy Carroll (Doncaster)

22/03/1950	Paisley Ice Rink		Promoter – Charlie Black
Fly	Vic Herman (Glasgow)	lost pts 10	Louis Skena (France)
Feather	Don McTaggart (Paisley)	win ko 2	Max Brady (Lurgan)
Light	Johnny Smith (Clydebank)	lost pts 8	Laurie Buxton (Watford)
Welter	Danny McKay (Edinburgh)	drew 8	Ezzie Reid (Jamaica)
Light Heavy	Jock Todd (Ayr)	lost pts 8	Tommy Carswell (London)

25/03/1950	Grove Institute		Promoter – Johnny McMillan
Feather	Robert Lang (Glasgow)	win ko 1	Sam Donegan (Glasgow)
Feather	Pat Maguire (Glasgow)	lost pts 4	Pat McCoy (Galway)
Light	Mickey Foyle (Coatbridge)	win ko 3	Harry Lucas (Edinburgh)
Light	Pat Kelly (Perth)	win rsf 5	Peter Collins (Edinburgh)
Middle	Billy Stevens (Tilliecoutry)	win pts 6	Alex Dobbins (Glasgow)

28/03/1950	Edinburgh Music Hall		Promoter – George Miller
Bantam	Eddie Carson (Edinburgh)	win rsf 8	Mick Day (Glasgow)
Bantam	Andy McCulloch (Glasgow)	win pts 6	Pat Maguire (Glasgow)
Light	Jackie Marshall (Glasgow)	win pts 10	Johnny Flannigan (Whitburn)
	(Scottish Lightweight Title Eliminator)		
Welter	Jim Scott (Edinburgh)	lost ko 5	Dave McLaren (Comrie)

01/04/1950	Grove Institute		Promoter – Johnny McMillan
Feather	Pat Maguire (Glasgow)	lost pts 4	Pat McCoy (Galway)
Light	Billy Mack (Glasgow)	win rsf 4	Robert Lang (Glasgow)
Welter	Dave McLaren (Comrie)	win ko 2	Benny Moran (Dumbarton)
Middle	Billy Stevens (Tilliecoutry)	win ko 2	Alec Gibson (Larkhall)
Middle	Colin McKinlay (Dumbarton)	win pts 6	Jack Brown (Doncaster)

08/04/1950	Grove Institute	Promoter – Johnny McMillan	
Feather	Harry McCabe (Dundee)	lost ko 2	Joe McArdle(Chester)
Feather	John Kenny (Glasgow)	lost pts 6	Jimmy Dickson (Glasgow)
Light	Mickey Foyle (Coatbridge)	win pts 6	Ted Ansell (Jamaica)
Light	Ginger Scott (Edinburgh)	win ko 4	Jackie Socks (Chester)
Welter	Frankie Naro (Dumbarton)	win ko 2	Tony Reilly (Dundee)
13/04/1950	Leith Eldorado	Promoter – Ken McQueen	
Fly	Mickey McLaughlin (Belfast)	lost pts 8	Billy Hazelgrove (Brighton)
Bantam	Al Gallacher (Dundee)	lost ko 2	Jimmy Thompson (Newcastle)
Bantam	Vernon Sollas (Jamaica)	lost pts 8	Jackie Quinn (Belfast)
Light	Gordon Goodman (Bournemouth)	win pts 8	Pat Kelly (Perth)
14/04/1950	Kelvin Hall	Promoter – Charlie Black	
Fly	Vic Herman (Glasgow)	win pts 8	Jacques Louni (France)
Feather	Jim Kenny (Polmont)	win pts 10	Stan Rowan (Liverpool)
Feather	Mick Day (Glasgow)	lost ko 8	Stan Salter (Deptford)
Light	Neilly Phillips (Motherwell)	win ko 4	George Cameron (Glasgow)
Welter	Billy Rattray (Dundee)	lost rsf 1	Eric McQuade (Downham)
Welter	Danny McKay (Edinburgh)	win ko 2	Ezzie Reid (Jamaica)
15/04/1950	Grove Institute	Promoter – Johnny McMillan	
Bantam	Sid Charles (Bolton)	lost pts 6	Tommy Smyth (Glasgow)
Feather	Jimmy Dickson (Glasgow)	win ko 1	Ron Hammersley (Bolton)
Feather	Pat McCoy (Galway)	lost pts 6	Frank Jones (Bolton)
Light	Sammy Welsh (Dundee)	win pts 6	Jackie Socks (Chester)
20/04/1950	Leith Eldorado	Promoter – Ken McQueen	
Feather	Gene Caffrey (Glasgow)	lost ko 5	Roy Ankrah (West Africa)
Feather	Teddy Peckham (Bournemouth)	lost pts 8	Stan Gossip (Hull)
Feather	Denny Dennis (Dublin)	win pts 6	Zeke Brown (Jamaica)
Light	Gordon Goodman (Bournemouth)	win pts 8	Pat Kelly (Perth)
Light	George Cameron (Glasgow)	lost ko 3	Mias Johnson (Jacksdale)
22/04/1950	Grove Institute	Promoter – Johnny McMillan	
Fly	Joe Cairney (Coatbridge)	drew 8	Tommy Smyth (Glasgow)
Feather	Pat McCoy (Galway)	win rsf 1	Jimmy Dickson (Glasgow)
Light	Frank Tierney (Glasgow)	lost rsf 3	Barney McGee (Glasgow)
Middle	Alex Dobbins (Glasgow)	win pts 6	Colin McKinlay (Dumbarton)
Middle	Bobby Brown (Dunfermline)	lost ret 3	Jack Brown (Doncaster)
26/04/1950	Paisley Ice Rink	Promoter – Charlie Black	
Fly	Joe Cairney (Coatbridge)	lost pts 8	Frank McCoy (Belfast)
Fly	Joe Murphy (Glasgow)	lost pts 8	Tino Cardinale (Italy)
Light	Neilly Phillips (Motherwell)	win ko 2	Johnny Kildare (Newarthill)
Light	Jim Findlay (Motherwell)	win pts 10	Jackie Marshall (Glasgow)
	(Scottish Lightweight Title Eliminator)		

29/04/1950	Grove Institute	Promoter – Johnny McMillan	
Feather	Gene Caffrey (Glasgow)	win pts 6	Jim Dwyer (Glasgow)
Light	Mickey Foyle (Coatbridge)	win pts 6	Johnny Ford (Newcastle)
Light	Sammy Welsh (Dundee)	lost pts 6	Johnny Martin (Newcastle)
Light Heavy	John Alexander (Motherwell)	win ko 6	Alex O'Neill (Belfast)
06/05/1950	Grove Institute	Promoter – Johnny McMillan	
Light	Billy Dickson (Glasgow)	lost ret 3	Billy Kid Andrews (Dundee)
Light	Pat McCoy (Galway)	win pts 6	Zeke Brown (Jamaica)
Middle	Billy Black (Glasgow)	win pts 6	Tommy Mount (Motherwell)
Light Heavy	Jock McCusker (Glasgow)	drew 6	Scotty O'Hara (Glasgow)
10/05/1950	Kelvin Hall	Promoter - Peter Docherty	
Fly	Joe Cairney (Coatbridge)	win pts 8	Charles Bohbot (Morocco)
Fly	Peter Keenan (Glasgow)	win pts 8	Maurice Sandeyron (France)
Bantam	Eddie Carson (Edinburgh)	win ko 2	Jackie Paterson (Ayrshire)
Feather	George Stewart (Hamilton)	win pts 8	Jim Healy (Manchester)
Light	Jim Findlay (Motherwell)	win pts 8	Morry Jones (Liverpool)
13/05/1950	Grove Institute	Promoter – Johnny McMillan	
Fly	Stan Herman (Glasgow)	lost pts 6	Jim Roche (Dublin)
Light	Jim Scott (Edinburgh)	lost pts 6	Jackie Socks (Chester)
Light	Louis Silvers (Dundee)	lost ko 6	Jimmy Dickson (Glasgow)
Welter	Billy Ross (Methil)	win pts 6	Billy Dickson (Glasgow)
Welter	Sammy Welsh (Dundee)	win ko 3	Joe McArdle (Chester)
31/05/1950	Firhill	Promoter – Charlie Black	
Fly	Peter Keenan (Glasgow)	win pts 10	Vic Herman (Glasgow)
Feather	Jock Bonas (Edinburgh)	lost rsf 2	George Stewart (Hamilton)
Light	Johnny Carrington (Nottingham)	win pts 6	Mickey Foyle (Coatbridge)
Light	Johnny Flannigan (Whitburn)	win ret 1	Gerry Smythe (Belfast)
Light	Neilly Phillips (Motherwell)	win ko 5	Charlie Nelson (Belfast)
Welter	Danny McKay (Edinburgh)	lost rsf 5	Jeff Tite (Spratton)
14/06/1950	Dundee Ice Rink	Promoter – George Grant	
Bantam	Bobby Boland (Dundee)	win dis 5	Alvaro Nuvoloni (Italy)
Feather	Peter Guichan (Dunfermline)	win pts 8	Al Young (Jamaica)
Feather	Pat Walsh (Perth)	lost ko 3	Ronnie Gill (London)
Light	Roy MacGregor (Glasgow)	lost pts 6	Sammy Welsh (Dundee)
Middle	Jim Gallacher (Glencraig)	lost ko 2	Richard Armah (West Africa)

21/06/1950	Saint Anthony's Football Ground	Promoter – Johnny McMillan	
Fly	Skeets Gallagher (Renton)	win ko 1	Eric Whyte (Crewe)
Fly	Stan Herman (Glasgow)	win pts 6	Syd Charles (Bolton)
Feather	Pat McCoy (Galway)	win pts 6	Benny Lacey (Glasgow)
Feather	Par Maguire (Glasgow)	win pts 6	Billy Moore (Clydebank)
Feather	Bob Donaldson (Glasgow)	lost pts 6	John Kenny (Glasgow)
Light	Sammy Welsh (Dundee)	win pts 6	Jim Scott (Edinburgh)
Welter	Joe Cassidy (Glasgow)	win ret 6	Jim Cullery (Glasgow)

01/07/1950	Coatbridge Greyhound Stadium	Promoter – George Beattie	
Fly	Stan Herman (Glasgow)	lost pts 6	Sid Charles (Bolton)
Feather	Pat King (Coatbridge)	drew 4	Billy Walker (Coatbridge)
Light	Mickey Foyle (Coatbridge)	win pts 6	Sammy Welsh (Dundee)
Light	Billy Dickson (Glasgow)	win rsf 5	Jim Mount (Motherwell)
Light	Jim Findlay (Motherwell)	lost dis 7	Johnny Flannigan (Whitburn)

06/07/1950	Paisley Ice Rink	Promoter – Charlie Black	
Fly	Joe Murphy (Glasgow)	win pts 8	Jimmy Pearce (Middlesbrough)
Bantam	Peter Keenan (Glasgow)	win pts 10	Bunty Doran (Belfast)
	(British Bantamweight Title Eliminator)		
Feather	Tommy Miller (West Lothian)	win ret 5	Harry Crocker (Leeds)
Feather	Don McTaggart (Paisley)	win pts 6	Laurie McShane (Glasgow)
Welter	Danny McKay (Edinburgh)	lost pts 10	Eric McQuade (Downham)
Heavy	Jack Bennett (Paisley)	lost ko 1	Don Campbell (Elgin)

19/07/1950	Coatbridge Greyhound Stadium	Promoter – George Beattie	
Feather	Don McTaggart (Paisley)	win pts 6	Hal Crosbie (Tipton)
Feather	Jim Kenny (Polmont)	win pts 10	Dai Davies (Skewen)
Light	Harry Hughes (Wishaw)	win pts 8	Hugh Smith (Sunderland)
Light	Pat McKay (Edinburgh)	win pts 6	Joe Welsh (Glasgow)
Light Heavy	Jock Todd (Ayr)	lost rsf 2	Charel Baert (Newcastle)

21/07/1950	Dunoon Recreation Park	Promoter – Bob Russell	
Feather	Billy Walker (Coatbridge)	win pts 6	Pat McSorley (Baillieston)
Light	Mickey Foyle (Coatbridge)	drew 6	Zeke Brown (Jamaica)

04/08/1950	Dumfries Drill Hall	Promoter – Jackie Robertson	
Welter	Jackie Robertson (Dumfries)	win pts 8	Jack Harding (Carlisle)
Welter	George Cameron (Glasgow)	win pts 8	Duggie Paul (Dumfries)
Welter	Bobby Hamilton (Dumfries)	win ko 7	Billy King (Carlisle)
Middle	Matt Nelson (Dumfries)	drew 8	Jock Mack (Carlisle)
Middle	Jimmy Lang (Glasgow)	win rsf 2	Lexy West (Dumfries)

09/08/1950	Coatbridge Greyhound Stadium		Promoter – George Beattie	
Fly	Joe Cairney (Coatbridge)	win pts 8	Jackie Foster (London)	
Bantam	Billy Taylor (Stirling)	win pts 6	Tommy White (Bolton)	
Feather	George Stewart (Hamilton)	lost pts 8	Peter Guichan (Dunfermline)	
Light	Neilly Phillips (Motherwell)	win pts 6	Ted Ansell (Jamaica)	
Light	Harry Hughes (Wishaw)	win pts 8	Hugh Smith (Sunderland)	

23/08/1950	Coatbridge Greyhound Stadium		Promoter – George Beattie	
Feather	Jock Bonas (Edinburgh)	win pts 8	Dal Davies (Skewen)	
Feather	Jim Kenny (Polmont)	drew 8	Tom Bailey (Liverpool)	
Light	Neilly Phillips (Motherwell)	win ko 3	Mickey Foyle (Coatbridge)	
Welter	Billy Dickson (Glasgow)	lost ret 6	Jimmy Nolan (Canada)	

01/09/1950	Paisley Ice Rink		Promoter – Charlie Black	
Fly	Joe Cairney (Coatbridge)	win pts 6	Johnny Summers (Edinburgh)	
Fly	Hugh Riley (Edinburgh)	win pts 6	Micky McLaughlin (Belfast)	
Feather	Tommy Miller (West Lothian)	win pts 6	Arthur Jarrett (Jamaica)	
Light	Neilly Phillips (Motherwell)	drew 6	Hugh Mackie (British Guiana)	
Light	Harry Hughes (Wishaw) (Scottish Lightweight Title)	win pts 12	Jim Findlay (Motherwell)	
Light Heavy	John Alexander (Motherwell)	win pts 6	Jock Todd (Ayr)	
Light Heavy	Don Campbell (Elgin)	win ko 3	Matt Locke (Belfast)	

06/09/1950	Caird Hall		Promoter – Mont Leslie	
Fly	Norman Tennant (Dundee)	lost pts 8	Jimmy Pearce (Middlesbrough)	
Bantam	Al Gallacher (Dundee)	win ret 5	Billy Moore (Clydebank)	
Feather	George Stewart (Hamilton)	win pts 8	Black Bond (Jamaica)	
Light	Johnny Davidson (Dundee)	lost pts 6	Poker Law (Dumbarton)	
Heavy	George Stern (Glasgow)	win ret 3	Hugh McDonald (Glasgow)	

13/09/1950	St Mungo Halls		Promoter – Sammy Docherty	
Fly	Eddie Fitzsimmons (Liverpool)	lost pts 6	Jimmy Thomson (Glasgow)	
Bantam	Billy Taylor (Glasgow)	lost pts 8	Ron Perry (Manchester)	
Feather	Nelson Blackburn (Paisley)	win pts 4	Eddie Wright (Paisley)	
Feather	Jock Bonas (Edinburgh)	win pts 8	Peter Guichan (Dunfermline)	
Feather	Mick Day (Glasgow)	win pts 6	Benny Lacey (Glasgow)	

14/09/1950	Ayr Ice Rink		Promoter – Charlie Black	
Bantam	Eddie Carson (Edinburgh)	lost pts 8	Arturo Paoletti (Italy)	
Feather	Jim Kenny (Polmont)	win pts 8	Mario Lutti (Italy)	
Feather	Don McTaggart (Paisley)	win pts 6	Ivor Davies (Wales)	
Light	Johnny Flannigan (Whitburn)	lost pts 8	Selwyn Evans (Wales)	
Light Heavy	Don Campbell (Elgin)	win pts 6	Ken Wyatt (Wales)	

21/09/1950	Castle Gardens Pavilion, Dunoon	Promoter – Jim Gilmour	
Fly	Hugh Riley (Edinburgh)	win pts 6	Jim Roche (Dublin)
Bantam	Al Gallacher (Dundee)	drew 6	Billy Taylor (Stirling)
Feather	Nelson Blackburn (Paisley)	win ko 1	Bobby Durnan (Glasgow)
Light	Johnny Flannigan (Whitburn)	lost pts 8	Zeke Brown (Jamaica)
Welter	Billy Rattray (Dundee) (Scottish Welterweight Title)	win pts 12	Willie Whyte (Glasgow)

27/09/1950	Dundee Ice Rink	Promoter - George Grant	
Fly	Norman Tennant (Dundee) (British Flyweight Title Eliminator)	win rsf 9	Joe Murphy (Glasgow)
Bantam	Willie Myles (Dundee)	win pts 8	Ron Perry (Stalybridge)
Feather	Peter Guichan (Dunfermline)	lost pts 8	Jackie Turpin (Leamington)
Light	Sammy Welsh (Dundee)	win pts 6	John Devlin (Glasgow)
Middle	Peter Cain (Dundee)	win ko 1	Jack Slavin (Dunfermline)

03/10/1950	Edinburgh Music Hall	Promoter – George Miller	
Bantam	Eddie Carson (Edinburgh)	lost pts 8	Jim Dwyer (Glasgow)
Feather	Jock Bonas (Edinburgh)	win pts 8	Chris Kelly (Liverpool)
Light	Johnny Flannigan (Whitburn)	win pts 8	Hugh Smith (Sunderland)
Welter	Jim Craig (Dundee)	lost rsf 3	Jim Scott (Edinburgh)

04/10/1950	Paisley Ice Rink	Promoter – Andrew Beattie	
Fly	Joe Cairney (Coatbridge)	win pts 8	Mickey McKay (South Africa)
Fly	Vic Herman (Glasgow)	win pts 8	Tino Cardinale (Italy)
Feather	Nelson Blackburn (Paisley)	win ret 2	Pat Maguire (Glasgow)
Feather	George Stewart (Hamilton)	lost ret 6	Dai Davies (Skewen)
Welter	Willie Whyte (Glasgow)	win pts 8	Alan Wilkins (Wales)

10/10/1950	Edinburgh Music Hall	Promoter - George Miller	
Feather	Mick Day (Glasgow)	lost ko 2	Manny Francis (Gold Coast)
Feather	George Lamont (Glasgow)	win rsf 4	Ronnie Sinclair (Preston)
Light	Sammy Welsh (Dundee)	lost pts 6	Tommy Robinson (Preston)
Light	Jackie Marshall (Glasgow)	win ret 1	Les Darnell (Sunderland)

17/10/1950	Edinburgh Music Hall	Promoter – George Miller	
Fly	Hugh Riley (Edinburgh)	win pts 6	Paddy Hardy (Dublin)
Fly	Stan Herman (Glasgow)	lost dis 4	Terry McHale (Liverpool)
Feather	Pat McCoy (Galway)	win pts 6	Eddie Larty (Gold Coast)
Light	Harry Hughes (Wishaw)	win dis 2	Morry Jones (Liverpool)
Welter	Billy Dickson (Glasgow)	win pts 6	Jim Scott (Edinburgh)

24/10/1950	Edinburgh Music Hall	Promoter – George Miller	
Feather	Tommy Miller (West Lothian)	win rsf 6	Peter Morrison (Hull)
Feather	Mannie Francis (Gold Coast)	win ko 1	Harry Tate (Belfast)
Feather	Vernon Sollas (Jamaica)	lost pts 6	Mick Day (Glasgow)
Welter	Danny McKay (Edinburgh)	win rsf 2	Ron Davies (Spratton)

31/10/1950	Edinburgh Music Hall		Promoter – George Miller
Fly	Hugh Riley (Edinburgh)	win pts 6	Johnny Black (Preston)
Feather	George Lamont (Glasgow)	win pts 6	Don Scott (Carlisle)
Feather	Billy Taylor (Stirling)	lost pts 6	Pat McCoy (Galway)
Light	Walter Black (Edinburgh)	win ko 2	Peter Collins (Edinburgh)
Welter	Jackie Marshall (Glasgow)	lost pts 8	Les Rendle (Hull)

07/11/1950	Edinburgh Music Hall		Promoter – George Miller
Bantam	Eddie Carson (Edinburgh)	win pts 8	Mannie Francis (Gold Coast)
Bantam	Vernon Sollas (Jamaica)	lost ko 6	Brian Jelley (Bury)
Feather	Don McTaggart (Paisley)	win pts 6	Derek Smith (Manchester)
Light	Billy Elliott (Glasgow)	win ko 1	John Devlin (Glasgow)
Light	Johnny Brown (Edinburgh)	win ko 1	Tommy Sullivan (Lanark)

14/11/1950	Edinburgh Music Hall		Promoter – George Miller
Bantam	Willie Myles (Dundee)	lost rsf 5	Jim Dwyer (Glasgow)
	(Scottish Bantamweight Title Eliminator)		
Feather	Tommy Miller (West Lothian)	win rsf 2	Vernon Sollas (Jamaica)
Feather	Billy Moore (Clydebank)	lost rsf 2	Pat McCoy (Galway)
Welter	Johnny Brown (Edinburgh)	lost ko 5	Dave Bauldry (Motherwell)
Welter	Jim Scott (Edinburgh)	win dis 3	George Cameron (Glasgow)

15/11/1950	Paisley Ice Rink		Promoter – Sammy Docherty
Bantam	Peter Keenan (Glasgow)	win ko 2	Tommy Proffitt (Droylesden)
	(British Bantamweight Title Eliminator)		
Bantam	Chic Brogan (Clydebank)	win pts 4	Benny Lacey (Glasgow)
Feather	Nelson Blackburn (Paisley)	lost pts 6	Jack Lillias (Manchester)
Light	Billy Elliott (Glasgow)	win dis 2	Morry Jones (Liverpool)
Light	Harry Hughes (Wishaw)	lost ret 6	Allan Tanner (British Guiana)

28/11/1950	Edinburgh Music Hall		Promoter – George Miller
Fly	Jimmy Thomson (Glasgow)	lost ret 4	Ogli Tettey (Gold Coast)
Fly	Mark Harrison (West Hartlepool)	lost pts 6	Hugh Riley (Edinburgh)
Bantam	Eddie Carson (Edinburgh)	win pts 8	Billy Daniels (Bow)
Feather	Don McTaggart (Paisley)	win pts 6	Don Scott (Carlisle)
Welter	Jim McLean (Edinburgh)	lost pts 6	Dave Bauldry (Motherwell)

28/11/1950	Caird Hall		Promoter – Mont Leslie
Fly	Norman Tennant (Dundee)	win pts 8	Jimmy Pearce (Middlesbrough)
Bantam	Al Gallacher (Dundee)	win rsf 5	Pat Maguire (Glasgow)
Light	Johnny Davidson (Dundee)	lost pts 6	Jimmy Dunn (Glasgow)
Light	Sammy Welsh (Dundee)	win ko 1	Benny Moran (Dumbarton)
Welter	Johnny Smith (Clydebank)	lost pts 4	Alex Dobbins (Glasgow)

05/12/1950	Edinburgh Music Hall	Promoter - George Miller	
Feather	Tommy Miller (West Lothian)	win pts 6	Alf Smith (Manchester)
Feather	Nelson Blackburn (Paisley)	lost pts 6	Pat McCoy (Galway)
Welter	Jim McLean (Edinburgh)	win pts 6	Ginger Scott (Edinburgh)
Welter	Danny McKay (Edinburgh)	lost pts 8	Jackie Marshall (Glasgow)

12/12/1950	Edinburgh Music Hall	Promoter – George Miller	
Fly	Ogli Tettey (Gold Coast)	win pts 6	Mickey Roche (Dublin)
Fly	Hugh Riley (Edinburgh)	win pts 6	Sid Charles (Bolton)
Feather	Mick Day (Glasgow)	win pts 6	Johnny Finnigan (Manchester)
Feather	Pat McCoy (Galway)	win pts 6	Billy Taylor (Stirling)
Light	Sammy Welsh (Dundee)	win pts 6	Paddy Gordon (Manchester)
Welter	Jim McLean (Edinburgh)	win pts 6	Alex Dobbins (Glasgow)
Welter	Dave Fisher (Wishaw)	win ko 1	Johnny Brown (Edinburgh)

13/12/1950	Paisley Ice Rink	Promoter – Charlie Black	
Bantam	Peter Keenan (Glasgow)	win pts 8	Louis Skena (France)
Bantam	Chic Brogan (Clydebank)	win pts 4	Mickey King (Belfast)
Feather	George Lamont (Glasgow)	win ko 5	Don McTaggart (Paisley)
Feather	Tony Lombard (South Africa)	win pts 8	Hugh Mackie (British Guiana)
Light	Neilly Phillips (Motherwell)	win rsf 1	Vince Marshall (Manchester)
Light Heavy	Don Campbell (Elgin)	win pts 6	Ken Lobben (Jamaica)

23/12/1950	St Mungo Halls	Promoter – Jim Gilmour	
Bantam	Billy Taylor (Stirling)	win pts 6	Andy McCulloch (Glasgow)
Feather	Bobby Durnan (Glasgow)	win rsf 3	Eddie Wright (Paisley)
Feather	George Lamont (Glasgow)	win rsf 3	Ronnie Howard (Bolton)
Light	Johnny Flannigan (Whitburn)	win rsf 1	Ronnie Grebb (Liverpool)
Middle	Brodie Angles (Burntisland)	win ko 4	Peter Cameron (Australia)

27/12/1950	Paisley Ice Rink	Promoter – Sammy Docherty	
Fly	Jimmy Thomson (Glasgow)	drew 6	Ogli Tettey (Gold Coast)
Bantam	Bobby Boland (Dundee)	win pts 8	Theo Medina (France)
Light	Neilly Phillips (Motherwell)	drew 8	Billy Elliott (Glasgow)
Welter	Jackie Marshall (Glasgow)	win pts 8	Danny McKay (Edinburgh)

1951

01/01/1951	Caird Hall	Promoter – Mont Leslie	
Fly	Norman Tennant (Dundee)	win pts 8	Glyn David (Wales)
Feather	Al Gallacher (Dundee)	win rsf 1	Harry McCabe (Dundee)
Light	Johnny Davidson (Dundee)	win pts 6	Louis Silvers (Dundee)
Light	Sammy Welsh (Dundee)	win pts 8	Pat Kelly (Perth)
Welter	Billy Kid Andrews (Dundee)	lost ret 5	Joe Baillie (Glasgow)

09/01/1951	Edinburgh Music Hall	Promoter – George Miller	
Bantam	Eddie Carson (Edinburgh)	win ko 5	Mannie Francis (Gold Coast)
Feather	Pat McCoy (Galway)	lost pts 6	Brian Jelley (Bury)
Light	Walter Black (Edinburgh)	win ret 2	Colin Booth (Manchester)
Welter	Billy Dickson (Glasgow)	lost pts 6	Harry Warner (London)
Welter	Dave Fisher (Wishaw)	win pts 6	Dave Bauldry (Motherwell)
13/01/1951	St Mungo Halls	Promoter – Jim Gilmour	
Feather	Bobby Durnan (Glasgow)	win rsf 3	Jimmy Dunn (Glasgow)
Welter	Jimmy Lang (Glasgow)	lost ret 1	Tom McGoldrick (Perth)
Welter	Jim Scott (Edinburgh)	lost pts 8	Johnny Smith (Clydebank)
Middle	Willie Whyte (Glasgow)	win ko 5	Alex Dobbins (Glasgow)
16/01/1951	Edinburgh Music Hall	Promoter – George Miller	
Bantam	Mark Harrison (West Hartlepool)	win pts 6	Hugh Riley (Edinburgh)
Feather	Al Gallacher (Dundee)	win pts 6	Vernon Sollas (Jamaica)
Feather	Don McTaggart (Paisley)	win dis 4	Alf Smith (Manchester)
Welter	Dave Bauldry (Motherwell)	lost ko 2	Freddie Cooke (Crewe)
Welter	Jim Scott (Edinburgh)	lost rsf 4	Ginger Roberts (Whitley Bay)
17/01/1951	Paisley Ice Rink	Promoter – Charlie Black	
Fly	Vic Herman (Glasgow)	win pts 12	Norman Tennant (Dundee)
	(Scottish Flyweight Title and British Flyweight Title Eliminator)		
Feather	Jim Dwyer (Glasgow)	lost pts 8	Tommy Miller (West Lothian)
Feather	George Lamont (Glasgow)	win pts 8	Dave Lloyd (Swansea)
Light	Neilly Phillips (Motherwell)	win ret 1	Ken Millard (Swansea)
Welter	Billy Rattray (Dundee)	lost pts 8	Luigi Valentini (Italy)
18/01/1951	Leith Eldorado	Promoter – Dan T Butler	
Fly	Johnny Summers (Edinburgh)	lost pts 8	Bernard Marshall (Manchester)
Light	Mickey Foyle (Coatbridge)	win rsf 4	Dave Simmons (Manchester)
Welter	Pat McKay (Edinburgh)	lost rsf 5	Ken Maynard (Manchester)
Welter	Johnny Smith (Clydebank)	win ko 1	Paddy Gordon (Manchester)
20/01/1951	St Mungo Halls	Promoter - Jim Gilmour	
Fly	Jimmy Thomson (Glasgow)	win pts 6	Stan Herman (Glasgow)
Feather	Billy Taylor (Stirling)	win ret 2	Pat McCoy (Galway)
Feather	Chic Brogan (Clydebank)	lost dis 3	Pat Dunlop (Belfast)
Light	Harry Hughes (Wishaw)	win ret 4	Jackie Wakelam (Leeds)
Light	Frank McKenna (Belfast)	win pts 6	Jackie Pollard (Leeds)
23/01/51	Edinburgh Music Hall	Promoter – George Miller	
Bantam	Eddie Carson (Edinburgh)	win rsf 5	Roy Ball (Wales)
Feather	Vernon Sollas (Jamaica)	win ko 1	Len Marshall (Liverpool)
Feather	Don McTaggart (Paisley)	drew 6	Brian Jelley (Bury)
Feather	Pat Cahill (Dundee)	lost rsf 3	Derek Smith (Manchester)

27/01/1951	St Mungo Halls		Promoter – Jim Gilmour
Bantam	Andy McCulloch (Glasgow)	drew 6	Jim Martin (Belfast)
Bantam	Billy Taylor (Stirling)	win rsf 2	Billy Birch (Belfast)
Light	Neilly Phillips (Motherwell)	win pts 8	Ted Ansell (Jamaica)
Light	Johnny Davidson (Dundee)	win ko 1	Billy Jackson (Belfast)
Middle	Alex Dobbins (Glasgow)	win pts 6	Joe Baillie (Glasgow)
30/01/1951	Edinburgh Music Hall		Promoter - George Miller
Fly	Mark Harrison (West Hartlepool)	drew 6	Bernard Marshall (Manchester)
Fly	Jimmy Thomson (Glasgow)	win ko 1	George Wilson (Hartlepool)
Feather	Tommy Miller (West Lothian)	win rsf 3	Johnny Finnigan (Manchester)
Feather	Ron Parry (Stalybridge)	win dis 5	Pat McCoy (Galway)
Welter	Jim McLean (Edinburgh)	lost pts 6	Dave Fisher (Wishaw)
03/02/1951	St Mungo Halls		Promoter – Jim Gilmour
Bantam	Andy McCulloch (Glasgow)	win pts 6	Stan Herman (Glasgow)
Feather	Bobby Durnan (Glasgow)	win ko 2	Peter Dunlop (Belfast)
Light	Johnny Flannigan (Whitburn)	lost ret 3	Harry Lewis (Bradford)
Welter	Johnny Smith (Clydebank)	drew 8	Don Stacey (South Elmshall)
Middle	Willie Armstrong (Port Glasgow)	win ko 1	John Weir (Belfast)
06/02/1951	Edinburgh Music Hall		Promoter – George Miller
Bantam	Jackie Bryce (Airdrie)	win ko 2	Vernon Sollas (Jamaica)
Feather	Roy Thomas (Jamaica)	lost pts 6	Brian Jelley (Bury)
Feather	Don McTaggart (Paisley)	win rsf 6	Alf Smith (Manchester)
Feather	Seaman McCormack (Rothesay)	lost rsf 3	Pat McCoy (Galway)
Welter	Tommy Hinson (Dagenham)	win pts 8	Ginger Roberts (Whitley Bay)
07/02/1951	Premierland, Dundee		Promoter – George Grant
Bantam	Willie Myles (Dundee)	win pts 8	Jackie Paterson (Ayrshire)
Feather	Al Gallacher (Dundee)	win ret 4	Mickey King (Belfast)
Feather	Tommy Croll (Dundee)	win rsf 5	Pat Walsh (Perth)
Light	Jimmy Croll (Dundee)	win rsf 1	Louis Silvers (Dundee)
Middle	Peter Cain (Dundee)	win pts 6	Brodie Angles (Burntisland)
10/02/1951	St Mungo Halls		Promoter – Jim Gilmour
Light	Harry Hughes (Wishaw)	win pts 8	Jackie McGouran (Dublin)
Light	Sammy Welsh (Dundee)	lost pts 8	Rae Brown (Belfast)
Welter	Billy Dickson (Glasgow)	win rsf 6	Ginger Walsh (Dublin)
Light Heavy	Don Campbell (Elgin)	win ko 3	Peter Day (Liverpool)
13/02/1951	Edinburgh Music Hall		Promoter – George Miller
Fly	Pat McCambridge (Glasgow)	lost ko 1	Eric Whyte (Crewe)
Fly	Bernard Marshall (Manchester)	win ko 2	Tony Eaton (Huddersfield)
Feather	Tommy Miller (West Lothian)	win pts 8	Gene Caffrey (Glasgow)
Feather	Billy Taylor (Stirling)	win ko 5	Al Gallacher (Dundee)
Welter	Johnny Smith (Clydebank)	win pts 8	Harry Warner (Ashton)
Welter	Jim Scott (Edinburgh)	lost rsf 5	Billy Dickson (Glasgow)

14/02/1951	Paisley Ice Rink	Promoter – Sammy Docherty	
Fly	Joe Cairney (Coatbridge)	win rsf 2	Frank Tierney (Glasgow)
Bantam	Jackie Bryce (Airdrie)	win pts 6	Andy McCulloch (Glasgow)
Bantam	Peter Keenan (Glasgow)	win pts 8	Jose Rubio (Spain)
Light	Billy Elliott (Glasgow)	dnc 5	Jim Findlay (Motherwell)
Welter	Danny McKay (Edinburgh)	win ret 3	Johnny Downes (Newcastle)
17/02/1951	St Mungo Halls	Promoter – Jim Gilmour	
Fly	Jimmy Thomson (Glasgow)	win rsf 6	Andy McCulloch (Glasgow)
Bantam	Billy Taylor (Stirling)	win rsf 5	Jim Martin (Belfast)
Light	Johnny Davidson (Davidson)	win ko 5	Mickey Foyle (Coatbridge)
Welter	Johnny Smith (Clydebank)	lost pts 8	Bobby Peart (South Elmsall)
Middle	Willie Armstrong (Port Glasgow)	win ko 1	Tommy Stewart (Belfast)
20/02/1951	Edinburgh Music Hall	Promoter – George Miller	
Fly	Bernard Marshall (Manchester)	drew 6	Johnny Black (Preston)
Feather	Don McTaggart (Paisley)	win ret 6	Johnny Finnigan (Manchester)
Feather	Brian Jelley (Bury)	win pts 6	Joe Bird (Liverpool)
Light	Harry Hughes (Wishaw)	lost pts 8	Vince Marshall (Manchester)
21/02/1951	Premierland, Dundee	Promoter – George Grant	
Feather	Peter Guichan (Dunfermline)	lost ret 4	Zeke Brown (Jamaica)
Feather	Jimmy Dunn (Glasgow)	lost pts 6	Tommy Croll (Dundee)
Feather	Jimmy Croll (Dundee)	lost ko 2	Don Scott (Carlisle)
Light	Sammy Welsh (Dundee)	win pts 6	Sammy Parry (Manchester)
Middle	Peter Cain (Dundee)	win rsf 1	Eric Metcalfe (Norwich)
24/02/1951	St Mungo Halls	Promoter – Jim Gilmour	
Fly	Jimmy Thomson (Glasgow)	win pts 6	Andy McCulloch (Glasgow)
Feather	Nelson Blackburn (Paisley)	win ret 1	Owen Durkins (Glasgow)
Welter	Ginger Roberts (Whitley Bay)	drew 8	Johnny Smith (Clydebank)
Welter	Sammy Welsh (Dundee)	lost ko 1	Billy Dickson (Glasgow)
27/02/1951	Edinburgh Music Hall	Promoter – George Miller	
Fly	Hugh Riley (Edinburgh)	win pts 6	Jimmy Jennings (Clapton)
Feather	Pat Maguire (Glasgow)	win pts 6	Eddie Wright (Paisley)
Welter	Pat McKay (Edinburgh)	lost pts 6	Dave Fisher (Wishaw)
Welter	Jackie Marshall (Glasgow)	lost pts 8	Kay Kalio (Nigeria)
Welter	Johnny Smith (Clydebank)	drew 8	Ginger Roberts (Whitley Bay)
28/02/1951	Kelvin Hall	Promoter – Charlie Black	
Feather	George Stewart (Hamilton) (Scottish Featherweight Title)	win pts 12	Jim Kenny (Polmont)
Feather	George Lamont (Glasgow)	win pts 8	Hugh Mackie (British Guiana)
Welter	Willie Whyte (Glasgow)	lost ko 5	Luigi Valentino (Italy)
Middle	Willie Armstrong (Port Glasgow)	win rsf 4	Reuben Blairs (Jamaica)
Light Heavy	Don Campbell (Elgin)	win ko 5	Wally Diamond (Jamaica)

03/03/1951	St Mungo Halls	Promoter – Jim Gilmour	
Fly	Jimmy Thomson (Glasgow)	win pts 6	Billy Baker (Birmingham)
Feather	Jimmy Dunn (Glasgow)	lost dis 5	Bert Donaldson (Birmingham)
Light	Johnny Davidson (Dundee)	win rsf 2	Jim O'Brien (Belfast)
Welter	Danny Malloy (Bonnybridge)	win rsf 2	Ken Gordon (Leeds)
Middle	Peter Cain (Dundee)	lost pts 6	Johnny Thompson (Belfast)
06/03/1951	Edinburgh Music Hall	Promoter – George Miller	
Fly	Mark Harrison (West Hartlepool)	lost pts 6	Paddy Hardy (Dublin)
Feather	Nelson Blackburn (Paisley)	win rsf 3	Joe Bird (Liverpool)
Feather	Tommy Croll (Dundee)	lost pts 6	Vince Flynn (Leeds)
Light	Harry Hughes (Wishaw)	lost pts 8	Vince Marshall (Manchester)
10/03/1951	St Mungo Halls	Promoter – Jim Gilmour	
Fly	Jimmy Thomson (Glasgow)	win rsf 3	Jimmy Orr (Belfast)
Bantam	Chic Brogan (Clydebank)	win ko 1	Joe Lancaster (Leeds)
Feather	Bobby Durnan (Glasgow)	win rsf 6	Joe Wilding (Leeds)
Welter	Danny Malloy (Bonnybridge)	win pts 6	Dave Fisher (Wishaw)
Middle	Willie Armstrong (Port Glasgow)	win pts 6	Eddie Conner (Manchester)
13/03/1951	Edinburgh Music Hall	Promoter – George Miller	
Fly	Joe Cairney (Coatbridge)	win pts 6	Jim Roche (Dublin)
Bantam	Billy Taylor (Stirling)	win rsf 5	Jackie Bryce (Airdrie)
Feather	Don McTaggart (Paisley)	win ko 3	Charlie Simpkins (Leeds)
Feather	Gene Caffrey (Glasgow)	lost pts 8	Tommy Miller (West Lothian)
17/03/1951	St Mungo Halls	Promoter – Jim Gilmour	
Fly	Andy McCulloch (Glasgow)	lost ret 3	Sid Charles (Bolton)
Bantam	Chic Brogan (Clydebank)	win ko 6	John Kenny (Glasgow)
Feather	Nelson Blackburn (Paisley)	win rsf 1	Paddy Burke (Dublin)
Light	Johnny Davidson (Dundee)	win pts 6	Al Thomas (Liverpool)
Welter	Billy Dickson (Glasgow)	drew 6	Kit Pompey (Liverpool)
20/03/1951	Edinburgh Music Hall	Promoter – George Miller	
Fly	Billy Baker (Birmingham)	win rsf 4	Eric White (Crewe)
Feather	Jock Bonas (Edinburgh)	win pts 8	Hugh Mackie (British Guiana)
Feather	Nelson Blackburn (Paisley)	win rsf 2	Mick Day (Glasgow)
Welter	Pat McKay (Edinburgh)	lost pts 6	Dave Fisher (Wishaw)
21/03/1951	Kelvin Hall	Promoter – Charlie Black	
Bantam	Billy Taylor (Stirling)	win rsf 5	Mickey King Belfast)
Bantam	Eddie Carson (Edinburgh) (Scottish Bantamweight Title)	win pts 12	Jim Dwyer (Glasgow)
Feather	George Lamont (Glasgow)	win pts 8	Billy Daniels (Bow)
Light	Danny Robertson (Glasgow)	lost ko 1	Hugh Smyth (Belfast)
Welter	Jeff Tite (Spratton)	win pts 8	Luigi Valentini (Italy)
Middle	Peter Cain (Dundee)	lost ko 1	Jackie Hughes (Belfast)

23/03/1951	Town Hall, Hawick		Promoter – Dan T Butler
Feather	Don Scott (Carlisle)	lost pts 6	Pat McCoy (Galway)
Welter	Walter Black (Edinburgh)	lost rsf 3	Lawrie Davies (Nigeria)
Middle	Billy Geddes (Langholm)	win ko 4	Freddie Horseman (Carlisle)
Middle	Dave Finnie (Hawick)	lost pts 8	Alf O'Neill (Newcastle)

24/03/1951	St Mungo Halls		Promoter – Jim Gilmour
Bantam	Billy Taylor (Stirling)	win ko 5	Ron Perry (Stalybridge)
Feather	Pat Maguire (Glasgow)	win rsf 3	Charlie White (Folkestone)
Light	Johnny Davidson (Dundee)	lost pts 6	Gordon Riding (Lancaster)
Welter	Pat McKay (Edinburgh)	win pts 4	Roy Evans (Leeds)
Welter	Billy Dickson (Glasgow)	lost pts 6	Phil Mellish (Stalybridge)

27/03/1951	Edinburgh Music Hall		Promoter – George Miller
Fly	Jimmy Thomson (Glasgow)	win pts 6	Eddie Fitzsimmons (Liverpool)
Feather	John Kenny (Glasgow)	drew 6	Eddie Wright (Paisley)
Feather	Don McTaggart (Paisley)	win pts 6	Black Bond (Jamaica)
Welter	Jackie Marshall (Glasgow)	drew 8	Rocco Long (South Africa)

28/03/1951	Paisley Ice Rink		Promoter – Sammy Docherty
Bantam	Peter Keenan (Glasgow)	win pts 10	Amleto Falcinelli (Italy)
Feather	Roy Ankrah (West Africa)	win pts 8	Bernard Pugh (Liverpool)
Feather	Nelson Blackburn (Paisley)	win pts 6	Pat McCoy (Galway)
Welter	Danny McKay (Edinburgh)	lost pts 8	Rees Moore (Luton)
Heavy	Hugh McDonald (Glasgow)	drew 6	George Nuttall (Stockport)

31/03/1951	St Mungo Halls		Promoter – Jim Gilmour
Fly	Jimmy Thomson (Glasgow)	win pts 6	Sid Charles (Bolton)
Bantam	Chic Brogan (Clydebank)	win pts 6	John Kenny (Glasgow)
Feather	Billy Taylor (Stirling)	win pts 6	Pat McCoy (Galway)
Feather	Pat Maguire (Glasgow)	win ret 4	Eddie Wright (Paisley)
Light	Neilly Phillips (Motherwell)	win ko 1	Billy Donnellan (St Helens)

06/04/1951	Town Hall, Hawick		Promoter – Dan T Butler
Feather	Pat McCoy (Galway)	win pts 6	Don Scott (Carlisle)
Welter	Johnny Brown (Edinburgh)	lost ko 1	John McCauley (Gateshead)
Welter	Joe White (Carlisle)	win pts 6	Johnny Johnston (Gareshead)

07/04/1951	St Mungo Halls		Promoter – Alex Lucas
Bantam	Billy Taylor (Stirling)	win rsf 1	John Kenny (Glasgow)
Feather	Bobby Durnan (Glasgow)	win pts 6	Pat Maguire (Glasgow)
Feather	Johnny Murphy (Glasgow)	lost rsf 4	Jackie Pollard (Leeds)
Light	Neilly Phillips (Motherwell)	win pts 6	Charlie Fawcett (Leeds)
Welter	Jackie Marshall (Glasgow)	win rsf 4	Frank Brady (Leeds)

14/04/1951	St Mungo Halls	Promoter – Alex Lucas	
Feather	Nelson Blackburn (Paisley)	lost pts 6	Billy Kelly (Derry)
Light	Danny Robertson (Glasgow)	win ko 1	Billy Kane (Newcastle)
Light	Harry Hughes (Wishaw)	win pts 6	Jimmy Ford (Brancepeth)
Welter	Dave Bauldry (Motherwell)	win pts 6	Pat McKay (Edinburgh)
Middle	Alex Dobbins (Glasgow)	win pts 6	Alf O'Neill (Newcastle)

19/04/1951	Leith Eldorado	Promoter – Harry Black	
Fly	Jimmy Quinn (Kirkintilloch)	win ko 3	Andy McCulloch (Glasgow)
Feather	Pat McCoy (Galway)	win pts 6	Don Scott (Carlisle)
Light	Johnny Davidson (Dundee)	lost pts 6	Jimmy Ford (Brancepeth)
Welter	George Frost (Mexborough)	win ko 1	Joe White (Carlisle)
Middle	Alf O'Neill (Newcastle)	win pts 6	Ginger Roberts (Whitley Bay)
Middle	Syd Cameron (Edinburgh)	drew 4	Jimmy Cowan (Carlisle)

21/04/1951	St Mungo Halls	Promoter – Alex Lucas	
Welter	Dave Bauldry (Motherwell)	lost rsf 2	George Armstrong (Canada)
Bantam	Billy Taylor (Stirling)	win rsf 4	Billy Smith (Bangor)
Light	Billy Kelly (Derry)	win ko 1	Jackie Malloy (Liverpool)
Welter	Johnny Flannigan (Whitburn)	win pts 6	Al Thomas (British Guiana)
Welter	Ginger Roberts (Whitley Bay)	drew 6	Kit Pompey (Jamaica)

23/04/1951	Caird Hall	Promoter – George Grant	
Feather	Dave Croll (Dundee)	win ko 2	Jack Hartley (Barnsley)
Light	Jimmy Croll (Dundee)	win ko 1	Johnny Ross (Barnsley)
Welter	Sammy Welsh (Dundee)	lost pts 6	Derek Smith (Manchester)
Middle	Peter Cain (Dundee)	win pts 6	Lawson Thain (Aberdeen)

28/04/1951	St Mungo Halls	Promoter – Alex Lucas	
Fly	Ogli Tettey (Gold Coast)	win pts 6	Freddie Orr (Belfast)
Fly	Jimmy Thomson (Glasgow)	win pts 6	Jimmy Orr (Belfast)
Feather	Nelson Blackburn (Paisley)	lost ko 4	Jimmy Griffen (Belfast)
Light	Billy Elliott (Glasgow)	win ko 3	Charlie Fawcett (Leeds)
Light Heavy	Don Campbell (Elgin)	lost ret 6	Bill Jackson (Jamaica)

30/04/1951	Ayr Ice Rink	Promoter – Charlie Black	
Bantam	Billy Taylor (Stirling)	win ko 1	Billy Skelly (Belfast)
Feather	George Lamont (Glasgow)	lost pts 10	Tommy Miller (West Lothian)
	(Scottish Featherweight Title Eliminator)		
Feather	Don McTaggart (Paisley)	win pts 6	Billy Kelly (Derry)
Light	Danny Robertson (Glasgow)	win ko 4	Johnny Davidson (Dundee)
Welter	Billy Rattray (Dundee)	lost ko 2	Cliff Curvis (Swansea)
	(British Welterweight Title Eliminator)		

05/05/1951	St Mungo Halls	Promoter – Alex Lucas	
Feather	Chic Brady (Glasgow)	win ko 1	Tommy Burns (Belfast)
Light	Johnny Flannigan (Whitburn)	win ko 3	Tom Hamilton (Belfast)
Middle	Willie Armstrong (Port Glasgow)	win ko 1	Jackie Hughes (Belfast)

09/05/1951	Firhill		Promoter – Sammy Docherty

Fly	Joe Cairney (Coatbridge)	win rsf 5	Billy Barnes (Belfast)
Bantam	Peter Keenan (Glasgow)	win ko 6	Danny O'Sullivan (London)
	(British Bantamweight Title)		
Bantam	Eddie Carson (Edinburgh)	win pts 10	Amleto Falcinelli (Italy)
Bantam	Bobby Boland (Dundee)	win pts 10	Gaetan Annaloro (Tunisia)
Feather	George Stewart (Hamilton)	drew 8	Denny Dawson (Sheffield)
Welter	Jackie Marshall (Glasgow)	win pts 8	Rees Moore (Luton)

15/06/1951	Carntyno Groyhound Stadium	Promoter Alox Lucas

Fly	Jimmy Quinn (Kirkintilloch)	win pts 6	Ogli Tettey (Gold Coast)
Feather	Don McTaggart (Paisley)	win pts 6	Pat McCrorey (Greenock)
Feather	Don McQueen (Dumbarton)	win dis 3	Nelson Blackburn (Paisley)
Light	Jim Findlay (Motherwell)	win pts 10	Neilly Phillips (Motherwell)
	(Scottish Lightweight Title Eliminator)		

22/06/1951	Alloa Recreation Park	Promoter – Jackie Collins

Feather	Peter Guichan (Dunfermline)	win rsf 2	Pat Kelly (Perth)
Light	Frank Gillulley (Alloa)	lost ret 5	Pat Shields (Glasgow)
Light	Johnny Flannigan (Whitburn)	win pts 12	Harry Hughes (Wishaw)
	(Scottish Lightweight Title)		
Welter	Danny Malloy (Bonnybridge)	win rsf 2	Tommy Mount (Motherwell)
Heavy	George Stern (Glasgow)	win dis 7	Hugh McDonald (Glasgow)
	(Scottish Heavyweight Title)		

27/06/1951	Firhill		Promoter – Sammy Docherty

Fly	Joe Cairney (Coatbridge)	win rsf 6	Joe Murphy (Glasgow)
	(Scottish Flyweight Title Eliminator)		
Bantam	Peter Keenan (Glasgow)	win rsf 12	Bobby Boland (Dundee)
	(British Bantamweight Title)		
Feather	Harry Gilliland (Kilmarnock)	win pts 4	Don McQueen (Dumbarton)
Feather	George Stewart (Hamilton)	win pts 8	George Mousse (France)
Light	Tommy McMenemy (Belfast)	lost pts 8	Alan Tanner (British Guiana)
Middle	Willie Armstrong (Port Glasgow)	win rsf 3	Sammy Sullivan (Preston)

03/08/1951	Rosyth Sports Ground	Promoter – Jackie Collins

Bantam	Billy Taylor (Stirling)	win pts 6	Jim Dwyer (Glasgow)
Welter	Danny Malloy (Bonnybridge)	lost pts 6	Jimmy Muirhead (Newcastle)
Middle	Willie Armstrong (Port Glasgow)	win rsf 10	Dave Finnie (Hawick)
	(Scottish Middleweight Title)		

05/09/1951	Firhill		Promoter – Sammy Docherty

Bantam	Peter Keenan (Glasgow)	win pts 15	Luis Romero (Spain)
	(European Bantamweight Title)		
Feather	George Stewart (Hamilton)	lost pts 10	Dai Davies (Skewen)
	(British Featherweight Title Eliminator)		
Feather	Tommy Miller (West Lothian)	win pts 8	Dante Ventura (Italy)
Light	Tommy McMenemy (Belfast)	lost pts 8	Allan Tanner (British Guiana)
Middle	Willie Armstrong (Port Glasgow)	win rsf 1	Jimmy James (London)

19/09/1951	Paisley Ice Rink	Promoter – Peter Docherty	
Feather	Jim Travers (Airdrie)	win ko 1	Don McQueen (Dumbarton)
Feather	Roy Ankrah (West Africa)	win rsf 5	Jean Machterlinck (Belgium)
Feather	Don McTaggart (Paisley)	win ko 5	Harry Gilliland (Kilmarnock)
Welter	Danny Malloy (Bonnybridge)	win rsf 3	Jim Brogden (Manchester)
Middle	Willie Armstrong (Port Glasgow)	win ret 5	Jackie Wilson (Belfast)
29/09/1951	St Mungo Halls	Promoter – Jim Gilmour	
Fly	Jimmy Thomson (Glasgow)	win pts 6	Dennis Sale (Northwich)
Feather	Jim Travers (Airdrie)	win rsf 2	Jackie Reine (York)
Light	Johnny Flannigan (Whitburn)	win ko 6	Danny Delaney (York)
Welter	Danny Malloy (Bonnybridge)	win pts 6	Len Ashworth (Burnley)
06/10/1951	St Mungo Halls	Promoter – Jim Gilmour	
Feather	Pat Maguire (Glasgow)	win rsf 6	John Kenny (Glasgow)
Feather	Jim Bird (Manchester)	win rsf 1	Bobby Dodoo (West Africa)
Light	Jim Findlay (Motherwell)	win pts 6	Ken Maynard (Manchester)
Light	Neilly Phillips (Motherwell)	win pts 8	Ted Ansell (Jamaica)
Light	Jim McMillan (Paisley)	win ko 1	Tommy Sullivan (Lanark)
13/10/1951`	St Mungo Halls	Promoter – Jim Gilmour	
Fly	Jimmy Thomson (Glasgow)	lost ret 4	Jeff Oscroft (Notts)
Feather	Danny Robertson (Glasgow)	win ko 1	Teddy Mitchell (Jamaica)
Feather	Chic Brady (Glasgow)	win ko 1	Tony Hardwicke (Derby)
Light	Jim McMillan (Paisley)	win ko 2	Ron Tyson (Manchester)
Welter	Danny Malloy (Bonnybridge)	win ret 4	Harry Warner (Ashton)
20/10/1951	St Mungo Halls	Promoter – Jim Gilmour	
Bantam	Pat Maguire (Glasgow)	win ko 3	George Pithie (Edinburgh)
Light	Neilly Phillips (Motherwell)	win pts 8	Jackie Wakelam (Leeds)
Welter	Bobby Kilpatrick (Kilmarnock)	win ko 2	Colin Booth (Manchester)
Welter	Dave Fisher (Wishaw)	win pts 6	Paddy Gordon (Manchester)
Heavy	Hugh Ferns (Greenock)	win pts 6	Len Brown (Harrow)
27/10/1951	St Mungo Halls	Promoter – Jim Gilmour	
Bantam	Pat Maguire (Glasgow)	win pts 6	Eric White (Crewe)
Feather	Jim Travers (Airdrie)	drew 6	Jim Bird (Manchester)
Light	Jim Findlay (Motherwell)	win ko 4	Jackie Wakelam (Leeds)
Welter	Dave Fisher (Wishaw)	win ko 2	Johnny Brown (Edinburgh)
31/10/1951	Paisley Ice Rink	Promoter – Sammy Docherty	
Fly	Joe Cairney (Coatbridge)	lost pts 8	Ogli Tettey (Gold Coast)
Bantam	Peter Keenan (Glasgow)	drew 10	Maurice Sandeyron (France)
Feather	Tommy Miller (West Lothian)	lost pts 8	Benny Chocolate (Gold Coast)
Feather	Don McTaggart (Paisley)	win pts 6	George Lamont (Glasgow)
Middle	Willie Armstrong (Port Glasgow)	win pts 8	Richard Armah (West Africa)

03/11/1951	St Mungo Halls		Promoter – Jim Gilmour

Bantam	Billy Taylor (Stirling)	win ko 4	Ron Perry (Stalybridge)
Feather	Pat Maguire (Glasgow)	win pts 6	John Kenny (Glasgow)
Bantam	George Pithie (Edinburgh)	win rsf 5	Johnny Noble (Manchester)
Middle	Alex Dobbins (Glasgow)	lost ko 5	Jack Brown (Doncaster)

1952

15/01/1952	Edinburgh Music Hall		Promoter – Charlie Black

Light	Danny Robertson (Glasgow)	win ko 1	John Watson (Glasgow)
Light	Harry Hughes (Wishaw)	win pts 10	Billy Elliott (Glasgow)
	(Scottish Lightweight Title Eliminator)		
Welter	Johnny Brown (Edinburgh)	lost pts 6	Ginger Scott (Edinburgh)
Welter	Danny Cunningham (Methil)	win rsf 4	Dave McLaren (Comrie)

22/01/1952	Edinburgh Music Hall		Promoter – Charlie Black

Fly	Jimmy Quinn (Kirkintilloch)	win pts 8	Sid Hiom (Nottingham)
Feather	Jim Travers (Airdrie)	lost pts 8	Denny Dawson (Sheffield)
Feather	Don McTaggart (Paisley)	win dis 4	Hugh Mackie (British Guiana)
Welter	Ginger Scott (Edinburgh)	win pts 6	Peter Collins (Edinburgh)
Welter	Johnny Brown (Edinburgh)	lost ko 1	Bobby Kilpatrick (Kilmarnock)

20/02/1952	Kelvin Hall		Promoter – Sammy Docherty

Feather	Bobby Boland (Dundee)	lost dis 6	Benny Chocolate (Gold Coast)
Feather	Don McTaggart (Paisley)	lost pts 8	Alby Tissong (South Africa)
Light	Danny Robertson (Glasgow)	win pts 4	Rae Brown (Belfast)
Light	Jim Findlay (Motherwell)	win ko 3	Harry Hughes (Wishaw)
	(Scottish Lightweight Title Final Eliminator)		
Welter	Bob Frost (West Ham)	lost pts 8	Danny Womber (USA)
Heavy	George Stern (Glasgow)	win dis 5	Lou Strydom (South Africa)

26/02/1952	Edinburgh Music Hall		Promoter – Charlie Black

Bantam	Eddie Carson (Edinburgh)	win ret 2	Billy Taylor (Stirling)
	(Scottish Bantamweight Title)		
Feather	Don McTaggart (Paisley)	win pts 8	Hugh Mackie (British Guiana)
Feather	Billy Cameron (Edinburgh)	lost ret 1	Pat Maguire (Glasgow)
Welter	Syd Cameron (Edinburgh)	lost pts 6	Lawson Thain (Aberdeen)
Welter	Charlie Currie (Coatbridge)	win rsf 3	Roy Anderson (Carlisle)

04/03/1952	Edinburgh Music Hall		Promoter – Charlie Black

Fly	Johnny Summers (Edinburgh)	win ret 4	Sid Hiom (Nottingham)
Fly	Jimmy Quinn (Kirkintilloch)	win pts 8	Sid Charles (Bolton)
Welter	Jim Scott (Edinburgh)	lost pts 6	Jim Mount (Motherwell)
Welter	Bobby Kilpatrick (Kilmarnock)	win ko 2	Billy Davenport (Bolton)
Middle	Eddie Phillips (Edinburgh)	drew 8	Rocco King (Askern)

05/03/1952	Kelvin Hall		Promoter – Alex Lucas
Fly	Jimmy Thomson (Glasgow)	win pts 6	Eddie Fitzsimmons (Liverpool)
Light	Jim Findlay (Motherwell)	win rsf 8	Neilly Phillips (Motherwell)
	(Vacant Scottish Lightweight Title)		
Welter	Danny Malloy (Bonnybridge)	win dis 8	Kit Pompey (Jamaica)
Middle	Willie Armstrong (Port Glasgow)	lost pts 8	Bob Cleaver (Middlesbrough)

11/03/1952	Edinburgh Music Hall		Promoter – Charlie Black
Feather	Tommy Miller (West Lothian)	drew 8	Denny Dawson (Sheffield)
Feather	Jim Travers (Airdrie)	win pts 8	Len Shaw (Sheffield)
Light	Danny Robertson (Glasgow)	lost pts 6	George Kelly (Doncaster)
Welter	Lawson Thain (Aberdeen)	win pts 6	Tommy Mount (Motherwell)
Light Heavy	Harry Ott (Edinburgh)	win pts 6	Johnny Zedd (Doncaster)

18/03/1952	Edinburgh Music Hall		Promoter – Charlie Black
Feather	Don McTaggart (Paisley)	win pts 8	Brian Jelley (Bury)
Light	Danny Robertson (Glasgow)	win rsf 4	Ron Tyson (Manchester)
Welter	Bobby Kilpatrick (Kilmarnock)	win ko 1	Bob Kehoe (Lancaster)
Welter	Charlie Currie (Coatbridge)	win pts 8	Harry Warner (Ashton)

25/03/1952	Edinburgh Music Hall		Promoter – Charlie Black
Fly	Johnny Summers (Edinburgh)	win pts 8	Jimmy Quinn (Kirkintilloch)
Feather	Tommy Miller (West Lothian)	win dis 4	Glyn Evans (Doncaster)
Feather	John Kenny (Glasgow)	lost rsf 3	Irvin Newton (Doncaster)
Welter	Lawson Thain (Aberdeen)	win ko 5	Paddy Gordon (Manchester)
Heavy	Hugh Ferns (Greenock)	win pts 6	Frank Elrington (Sheffield)

05/04/1952	St Mungo Halls		Promoter – Alex Lucas
Fly	Jimmy Quinn (Kirkintilloch)	win pts 8	Jeff Oscroft (Notts)
Fly	Jimmy Thomson (Glasgow)	win ko 7	Jackie Allen (Manchester)
Bantam	Chic Brogan (Clydebank)	win ko 2	Johnny Bartles (Nottingham)
Feather	Jim Kenny (Polmont)	win dis 4	Hugh Mackie (British Guiana)
Heavy	Hugh McDonald (Glasgow)	lost pts 6	Jock Thoms (Mansefield)

08/04/1952	Portobello Town Hall		Promoter – Dick Hamilton
Welter	Alex Sloan (Broxburn)	win ko 3	John McCauley (Gateshead)
Welter	Syd Cameron (Edinburgh)	win rsf 4	Jack Wiles (Newcastle)
Welter	Jim McLean (Edinburgh)	lost pts 6	Sammy Gibbison (Newcastle)
Middle	Eddie Phillips (Edinburgh)	win pts 8	Patsy Dodds (Newcastle)

15/04/1952	Portobello Town Hall		Promoter – Dick Hamilton
Light	Alex Sloan (Broxburn)	lost rsf 1	Paddy Gordon (Manchester)
Welter	Syd Cameron (Edinburgh)	win ko 5	Peter Collins (Edinburgh)
Welter	Harry Warner (Ashton)	win pts 8	Johnny Cross (Bolton)

19/04/1952	St Mungo Halls	Promoter – Alex Lucas	
Fly	Jimmy Quinn (Kirkintilloch)	win rsf 3	Andy McCulloch (Glasgow)
Bantam	Chic Brogan (Clydebank)	win ko 2	Dickie Gunn (Dundee)
Feather	Jim Kenny (Polmont)	win ret 4	Brian Jelley (Bury)
Feather	Chic Brady (Glasgow)	win ko 1	Pat McGrory (Greenock)
Welter	Tommy Mount (Motherwell)	win pts 6	Syd Cameron (Edinburgh)

23/04/1952	Kelvin Hall	Promoter – Sammy Docherty	
Feather	George Stewart (Hamilton)	lost pts 8	Alby Tissong (South Africa)
Light	Alan Tanner (British Guiana)	win pts 8	Maurice Mauny (France)
Welter	Bob Frost (West Ham)	lost pts 8	Danny Womber (USA)
Middle	Jack Brown (Doncaster)	lost ko 2	Billy Wells (South Africa)
Heavy	George Stern (Glasgow)	lost rsf 3	Lou Strydom (South Africa)

23/04/1952	Premierland, Dundee	Promoter – George Grant	
Light	Tommy Croll (Dundee)	win ko 2	Jack Hartley (Barnsley)
Light	Sammy Welsh (Dundee)	lost pts 6	Derek Smith (Manchester)
Welter	Jimmy Croll (Dundee)	win ko 1	Johnny Ross (Barnsley)
Middle	Peter Cain (Dundee)	win pts 6	Lawson Thain (Aberdeen)

02/05/1952	Falkirk Ice Rink	Promoter – Jim Gilmour	
Bantam	Chic Brogan (Clydebank)	win pts 6	Ron Perry (Stalybridge)
Feather	Jim Kenny (Polmont)	lost pts 10	Tommy Miller (West Lothian)
	(Scottish Featherweight Title Eliminator)		
Light	Neilly Phillips (Motherwell)	win pts 6	Jock McCreadie (Doncaster)
Welter	Danny Malloy (Bonnybridge)	win pts 8	Ernie Vickers (Middlesbrough)
Light Heavy	Don Campbell (Elgin)	lost rsf 3	Ben Swordfish (West Africa)

07/05/1952	Premierland, Dundee	Promoter – George Grant	
Fly	Johnny Lynch (Dundee)	lost rsf 2	Benny Lloyd (Rhyl)
Bantam	Skeets Gallagher (Renton)	win ko 2	Dave Banks (Hexham)
Light	Tommy Croll (Dundee)	win rsf 4	Ian Wilson (Glasgow)
Middle	Peter Cain (Dundee)	win ko 2	Patsy Dodds (Newcastle)

21/05/1952	Firhill	Promoter – Sammy Docherty	
Fly	Vic Herman (Glasgow)	lost pts 10	Maurice Sandeyron (France)
Bantam	Peter Keenan (Glasgow)	lost ko 5	Jean Sneyers (Belgium)
	(European Bantamweight Title)		
Feather	George Stewart (Hamilton)	win pts 8	Don McTaggart (Paisley)
Light	Neilly Phillips (Motherwell)	win pts 6	Danny Robertson (Glasgow)
Welter	Billy Wells (South Africa)	lost pts 8	Peter Fallon (Birkinhead)
Welter	Charlie Currie (Coatbridge)	win pts 6	Sammy Hamilton (Belfast)

12/08/1952	Kirkcaldy Ice Rink	Promoter – Jim Gilmour	
Feather	Chic Brady (Glasgow) (Scottish Featherweight Title Eliminator)	win rsf 1	George Lamont (Glasgow)
Feather	Peter Guichan (Dunfermline)	win pts 8	Len Shaw (Sheffield)
Welter	Jimmy Croll (Dundee)	win rsf 3	Johnny Drummond (Lochgelly)
Welter	Willie Whyte (Glasgow) (Vacant Scottish Welterweight Title)	win pts 12	Danny Malloy (Bonnybridge)
20/08/1952	Kelvin Hall	Promoter – Alex Lucas	
Fly	Joe Cairney (Coatbridge) (Scottish Flyweight Title)	win pts 12	Vic Herman (Glasgow)
Fly	Jimmy Quinn (Kirkintilloch) (Scottish Flyweight Title Eliminator)	win pts 10	Jimmy Thomson (Glasgow)
Bantam	Eddie Carson (Edinburgh) (Scottish Bantamweight Title)	win ko 10	Billy Taylor (Stirling)
Feather	Tommy Miller (West Lothian) (Scottish Featherweight Title)	win pts 12	George Stewart (Hamilton)
Feather	Don McTaggart (Paisley) (Scottish Featherweight Title Eliminator)	win pts 10	Jim Travers (Airdrie)
17/09/1952	Kelvin Hall	Promoter – Alex Lucas	
Bantam	Charlie Mannion (West Hartlepool)	lost ko 3	Chic Brogan (Clydebank)
Bantam	Eddie Carson (Edinburgh)	lost pts 8	Glyn Evans (Doncaster)
Feather	Don McTaggart (Paisley)	win pts 8	Denny Dawson (Sheffield)
Feather	Jim Kenny (Polmont)	win pts 10	Ronnie Clayton (Blackpool)
Welter	Bobby Kilpatrick (Kilmarnock)	lost rsf 4	Harold Palmer (Doncaster)
Welter	Willie Whyte (Glasgow)	win pyts 8	Joe Corcoran (Huddersfield)
18/09/1952	Edinburgh Music Hall	Promoter – Charlie Black	
Fly	Joe Cairney (Coatbridge)	win pts 8	Johnny Summers (Edinburgh)
Feather	Tommy Miller (West Lothian)	win pts 8	Jacques Lesseine (Belgium)
Feather	Jim Travers (Airdrie)	win pts 8	Brian Jelley (Bury)
Light	Walter Black (Edinburgh)	win ret 4	Tommy Cavan (Glasgow)
Welter	Jimmy Croll (Dundee)	win ret 4	Billy Davenport (Bolton)
15/10/1952	Paisley Ice Rink	Promoter – Alex Lucas	
Fly	Jimmy Quinn (Kirkintilloch)	lost rsf 6	Ogli Tettey (Gold Coast)
Bantam	Chic Brogan (Clydebank)	lost ret 3	Manny Francis (Gold Coast)
Bantam	Peter Keenan (Glasgow)	lost ret 5	Amleto Falcinelli (Italy)
Feather	Jim Kenny (Polmont)	win pts 8	Rolly Blyce (Trinidad)
Welter	Tommy Cochrane (Paisley)	lost rsf 4	Tommy Mount (Motherwell)

1953

28/01/1953	Paisley Ice Rink		Promoter – Alex Lucas

Fly	Jimmy Quinn (Kirkintilloch) (Scottish Flyweight Title)	win pts 12	Joe Cairney (Coatbridge)
Bantam	Peter Keenan (Glasgow) (British Bantamweight Title)	win rsf 7	Frankie Williams (Birkinhead)
Light	Don McTaggart (Paisley) (Scottish Lightweight Title)	win pts 12	Jim Findlay (Motherwell)
Welter	Vincent O'Kine (West Africa)	win pts 6	Ernie Vickers (Middlesbrough)
Welter	Danny Harvey (Glasgow)	win dis 5	John Watson (Glasgow)

04/02/1953	St Mungo Hall		Promoter – Jimmy Wilson

Fly	Ogli Tettey (Gold Coast)	win rsf 3	Johnny Lang (Bolton)
Light	Tommy McGuinness (Craigneuk)	win rsf 6	Jackie Standring (Ashton)
Light	Tommy Cavan (Glasgow)	win pts 6	Mickey Stasak (France)
Welter	Vincent O'Kine (West Africa)	win rsf 2	Phil Mellish (Stalybridge)
Middle	Johnny Douglas (Glasgow)	win dis 4	Peter Cain (Dundee)

20/02/1953	Greenock Town Hall		Promoter – Jimmy Wilson

Feather	John Kenny (Glasgow)	win pts 4	Pat Maguire (Glasgow)
Light	Tommy McGuinness (Craigneuk)	win ko 2	Jock McCreadie (Doncaster)
Welter	Tommy Cochrane (Paisley)	lost ko 4	Les Steinhelber (Ayr)
Middle	Willie Armstrong (Port Glasgow)	win ko 2	Jim Lindley (Doncaster)
Heavy	Hugh Ferns (Greenock)	win pts 6	Frank Walshaw (Barnsley)

18/03/1953	Kelvin Hall		Promoter – Alex Lucas

Fly	Jimmy Thomson (Glasgow)	win rsf 3	Billy Baker (Birmingham)
Bantam	Peter Keenan (Glasgow)	win pts 10	Stan Rowan (Liverpool)
Feather	Jim Kenny (Polmont)	win pts 8	Lou Jacobs (Belgium)
Light	Tommy McGuinness (Craigneuk)	win pts 6	Billy Cobb (Chesterfield)
Welter	Danny Harvey (Glasgow)	win pts 8	Harold Palmer (Doncaster)

31/03/1953	Caird Hall		Promoter – George Grant

Bantam	Ogli Tettey (Gold Coast)	win pts 8	Paddy Hardy (Dublin)
Light	Johnny Beveridge (Kirkcaldy)	win ko 2	Tommy Cavan (Glasgow)
Welter	Roy MacGregor (Glasgow)	win ret 4	Bamber Gaye (West Africa)
Welter	Jimmy Croll (Dundee)	drew 8	Jack Armstrong (West Africa)
Welter	Danny Harvey (Glasgow)	win pts 6	Harry Warner (Ashton)

04/05/1953	Leith Eldorado		Promoter – Eldorado Promotions

Feather	Jim Travers (Airdrie)	win dis 6	Hugh Mackie (British Guiana)
Welter	John McAuley (Gateshead)	win rsf 3	Alex Sloan (Broxburn)
Welter	Sammy Gibbison (Newcastle)	win pts 6	Syd Cameron (Edinburgh)
Middle	Jim McLean (Edinburgh)	win pts 6	Tommy Cochrane (Paisley)

27/05/1953	Caird Hall		Promoter – George Grant

Fly	Ogli Tettey (Gold Coast)	win ko 1	Paddy Hardy (Dublin)
Feather	Pat Maguire (Glasgow)	lost pts 6	Art Beloc (Cumberland)
Feather	Freddie Bancroft (Cockermouth)	win rsf 6	Tommy Croll (Dundee)
Light	Johnny Beveridge (Kirkcaldy)	win rsf 6	Mickey Stasak (France)
Welter	Jimmy Croll (Dundee)	win rsf 4	Ken Maynard (Manchester)
Welter	Sammy Welsh (Dundee)	win rsf 4	Gus McPhee (Perth)

27/05/1953	Saracen Park		Promoter – Jimmy Wilson

Fly	Jimmy Thomson (Glasgow)	lost pts 8	Mickey Roche (Chester)
Light	Danny Robertson (Glasgow)	win pts 6	Joe Farricker (Manchester)
Welter	Danny Malloy (Bonnybridge)	lost pts 8	Lew Lazar (Aldgate)
Middle	Willie Armstrong (Port Glasgow)	lost rsf 10	Gordon Hazell (Bristol)
Light Heavy	Marshall Bell (Leith)	lost ret 5	Dennis Lockton (Manchester)

17/06/1953	Firhill		Promoter – George Lucas

Fly	Joe Cairney (Coatbridge)	drew 8	Henry Carpenter (London)
Fly	Jimmy Quinn (Kirkintilloch) (Scottish Flyweight Title)	win ko 12	Jimmy Thomson (Glasgow)
Bantam	Peter Keenan (Glasgow) (European Bantamweight Title)	win pts 15	Maurice Sandeyron (France)
Feather	Charlie Hill (Cambuslang)	win pts 6	Art Beloc (Cumberland)
Feather	Roy Ankrah (West Africa)	win pts 10	Jacques Dumesnil (France)
Light	Don McTaggart (Paisley)	win pts 8	Dick Ashcroft (Manchester)

13/10/1953	Leith Eldorado		Promoter – Harry Black

Bantam	Eddie Carson (Edinburgh) (Scottish Bantamweight Title)	win pts 12	Hugh Riley (Edinburgh)
Light	Walter Black (Edinburgh)	lost ko 2	Johnny Beveridge (Kirkcaldy)
Welter	Syd Cameron (Edinburgh)	win ko 2	Tex Williams (Newcastle)
Light Heavy	Marshall Bell (Leith)	win ko 3	Harry Greb (Carlisle)

27/10/1953	Caird Hall		Promoter – George Grant

Light	Reggie Watson (Kennoway)	win pts 6	Johnny Skelly (Shipley)
Light	Johnny Beveridge (Kirkcaldy)	win rsf 6	Johnny Delmore (Leeds)
Welter	Jimmy Croll (Dundee)	win pts 8	Peter Smith (Huddersfield)
Middle	Peter Cain (Dundee)	win ko 7	Ivor Hutton (Bacup)
Light Heavy	Marshall Bell (Leith)	drew 6	Jackie Abbott (Huddersfield)

01/12/1953	Leith Eldorado		Promoter – Harry Black

Bantam	Eddie Carson (Edinburgh)	win rsf 7	Jimmy Brewer (Kings Cross)
Light	Billy Timmins (Huddersfield)	win pts 6	Johnny Skelly (Shipley)
Middle	Peter Cain (Dundee)	win ret 5	Terry Dolan (Wakefield)
Light Heavy	Johnny Douglas (Glasgow)	drew 6	Jackie Abbott (Huddersfield)

15/12/1953	Kirkcaldy Ice Rink		Promoter – George Grant

Light	Reggie Watson (Kennoway)	win pts 6	Al Lindon (Birmingham)
Light	Hugh Cullen (Edinburgh)	lost rsf 3	Dal Willis (Jamaica)
Light	Johnny Beveridge (Kirkcaldy)	lost ko 2	Ted Ansell (Jamaica)
Welter	Jimmy Croll (Dundee)	win ko 6	Eric Skidmore (Wednesbury)
Light Heavy	Marshall Bell (Leith)	win ret 4	Dennis Lockton (Manchester)

1954

26/01/1954	Leith Eldorado		Promoter – Harry Black

Light	Mickey Foyle (Coatbridge)	win ko 2	Reggie Watson (Kennoway)
Light	Brian Jelley (Bury)	win ko 1	John Watson (Glasgow)
Welter	Eddie Phillips (Edinburgh)	win pts 8	Charlie Currie (Coatbridge)
Middle	Peter Cain (Dundee)	win pts 6	Johnny Douglas (Glasgow)
Light Heavy	Marshall Bell (Leith)	lost pts 6	Neville Rowe (Australia)

24/02/1954	Kelvin Hall		Promoter – Alex Lucas

Fly	Jimmy Quinn (Kirkintilloch) (Scottish Flyweight Title)	win ret 4	Jimmy Thomson (Glasgow)
Bantam	Peter Keenan (Glasgow) (Scottish Bantamweight Title)	win pts 12	Eddie Carson (Edinburgh)
Feather	Charlie Hill (Cambuslang)	win rsf 5	Billy Smith (Bangor)
Feather	Johnny Murphy (Glasgow)	lost pts 6	John Kenny (Glasgow)
Welter	Eddie Phillips (Edinburgh)	win ko 5	John Watson (Glasgow)
Welter	Charlie Currie (Coatbridge)	lost ko 4	Jim Brogden (Manchester)

02/03/1954	Caird Hall, Dundee		Promoter – George Grant

Feather	John Kenny (Glasgow)	win pts 6	Billy Nelson (Lancaster)
Feather	Chic Brogan (Clydebank)	win pts 8	Billy Taylor (Stirling)
Welter	Jimmy Croll (Dundee)	win pts 10	Alf Danahar (London)
Welter	Eddie Phillips (Edinburgh)	win ret 5	Ernie Vickers (Middlesbrough)
Middle	Peter Cain (Dundee)	win ko 4	Peter Regan (Huddersfield)

23/03/1954	Edinburgh Music Hall		Promoter – Harry Black

Feather	John Kenny (Glasgow)	win ko 1	Les Darcy (Middlesbrough)
Feather	Chic Brogan (Clydebank) (Scottish Featherweight Title Eliminator)	win pts 10	Gene Caffrey (Glasgow)
Feather	Billy Taylor (Stirling)	win ko 2	Ken Scott (Gateshead)
Light	Don McTaggart (Paisley)	win rsf 8	Jackie Colpitts (Prudhoe)
Middle	Syd Cameron (Edinburgh)	drew 6	Bob Conway (Stockton)

30/03/1954	Edinburgh Music Hall		Promoter – Harry Black

Feather	Charlie Hill (Cambuslang)	win ret 5	Bobby Dodoo (West Africa)
Feather	George Lamont (Glasgow)	win pts 8	Hugh Mackie (British Guiana)
Welter	Willie Ferguson (Falkirk)	lost pts 6	Billy Taylor (Thornaby)
Middle	Willie Armstrong (Port Glasgow)	lost pts 8	Abe Quartey (Gold Coast)
Middle	Peter Cain (Dundee)	win pts 6	Tommy Colcliffe (London)

07/04/1954	Kelvin Hall	Promoter – Sammy Docherty	
Bantam	Eddie Carson (Edinburgh)	lost pts 10	Robert Cohen (France)
Bantam	George O'Neill (Belfast)	lost pts 8	Ron Johnson (London)
Feather	John Kenny (Glasgow)	lost rsf 2	John McNally (Belfast)
Light	Gerry Smythe (Belfast)	lost rsf 3	Lahaouri Godih (France)
Welter	Danny Malloy (Bonnybridge)	lost rsf 5	Mickey O'Neill (Belfast)
Welter	Jimmy Croll (Dundee)	win rsf 7	Danny Harvey (Glasgow)
26/05/1954	Kelvin Hall	Promoter – Alex Lucas	
Bantam	Peter Keenan (Glasgow)	win pts 10	Vic Herman (Glasgow)
Feather	Charlie Hill (Cambuslang)	win pts 8	Freddie King (Wandsworth)
Feather	George Lamont (Glasgow)	lost pts 8	Joe King (Belfast)
Welter	Danny Harvey (Glasgow)	win pts 8	Eddie Phillips (Edinburgh)
	(Scottish Welterweight Title Final Eliminator)		
Middle	Willie Armstrong (Port Glasgow)	drew 8	Ron Crookes (Sheffield)
30/06/1954	Lanarkshire Sports Stadium	Promoter – Alex Lucas	
Fly	Jimmy Thomson (Glasgow)	win pts 6	Billy Dorris (Perth)
Feather	Charlie Hill (Cambuslang)	win ret 6	Jacques Lesseine (Belgium)
Light	Don McTaggart (Paisley)	win pts 8	Brian Jelley (Bury)
Light	Dick Knox (Motherwell)	win rsf 2	Johnny Leabody (Belfast)
Welter	Vincent O'Kine (West Africa)	win ko 4	Tommy McMenemy (Belfast)
24/07/1954	Abbey Park, Kilwinning	Promoter – Alex Lucas	
Fly	Jimmy Quinn (Kirkintilloch)	win pts 8	Paddy Hardy (Dublin)
Feather	Charlie Hill (Cambuslang)	win pts 8	Gene Caffrey (Glasgow)
Light	Dick Knox (Motherwell)	win rsf 3	Ken Smith (Leeds)
Light	Bobby Kilpatrick (Kilmarnock)	lost ret 1	George Spence (York)
21/09/1954	Paisley Ice Rink	Promoter – Alex Lucas	
Bantam	Peter Keenan (Glasgow)	win ko 6	John Kelly (Belfast)
	(British Bantamweight Title)		
Feather	John Kenny (Glasgow)	win rsf 4	Johnny Grubb (Dunoon)
Feather	Chic Brogan (Clydebank)	win ko 1	Sammy Fisher (Belfast)
Feather	Charlie Hill (Cambuslang)	win pts 8	Henk Klok (Holland)
Light	Dick Knox (Motherwell)	win pts 6	George Spence (York)
18/10/1954	Caird Hall, Dundee	Promoter – George Grant	
Feather	Dave Croll (Dundee)	win ko 5	Dave Savage (Glasgow)
Feather	Matt Fulton (Glasgow)	win rsf 4	Denis Cahill (Belfast)
Light	Johnny McLaren (Coatbridge)	win pts 6	Johnny Murphy (Glasgow)
Light	Don McTaggart (Paisley)	win ko 1	Neville Tatlow (Manchester)
Welter	Jimmy Croll (Dundee)	lost dis 2	Roy MacGregor (Glasgow)
Middle	Peter Cain (Dundee)	lost rsf 4	Tommy Hilton (Rochdale)

26/10/1954	Leith Eldorado	Promoter – Harry Black	
Bantam	Eddie Carson (Edinburgh)	lost pts 8	Pedro Paris (Spain)
Feather	Matt Fulton (Glasgow)	win rsf 6	Peter Masters (Belfast)
Light	Don McTaggart (Paisley)	win pts 8	Tommy McMenemy (Belfast)
Light	Johnny McLaren (Coatbridge)	win ko 4	Johnny Spittal (Barnsley)
Welter	Danny Harvey (Glasgow)	win ko 4	Jackie Colpitts (Prudhoe)

07/12/1954	Paisley Ice Rink	Promoter – Alex Lucas	
Fly	Jimmy Quinn (Kirkintilloch) (Scottish Flyweight Title)	win ret 4	Joe Cairney (Coatbridge)
Feather	Charlie Hill (Cambuslang) (Scottish Featherweight Title)	win pts 12	Chic Brogan (Clydebank)
Feather	Teddy Peckham (Bournemouth)	win ko 3	George Lamont (Glasgow)
Welter	Jimmy Croll (Dundee)	win pts 8	Bobby Johnson (Plymouth)
Welter	Roy MacGregor (Glasgow) (Scottish Welterweight Title)	win pts 12	Danny Harvey (Glasgow)
Middle	Willie Armstrong (Port Glasgow)	win pts 8	George Dilkes (London)

1955

14/02/1955	Caird Hall, Dundee	Promoter - George Grant	
Feather	Matt Fulton (Glasgow)	win ko 2	Teddy Barker (Swindon)
Light	Dave Croll (Dundee)	drew 6	Johnny McLaren (Coatbridge)
Welter	John Watson (Glasgow)	win rsf 3	Billy Press (Belfast)
Welter	Jimmy Croll (Dundee)	lost ko 2	Paul King (Torquay)
Welter	Roy MacGregor (Glasgow)	win pts 8	Bobby Johnson (Plymouth)

22/02/1955	Kelvin Hall	Promoter – Sammy Docherty	
Bantam	Peter Keenan (Glasgow)	win pts 10	Dante Bini (France)
Bantam	Eddie Carson (Edinburgh)	lost rsf 4	Ola Enoch (Nigeria)
Light	Allan Tanner (British Guiana)	win ret 2	Cyril Evans (Welwyn Garden City)
Light	Steve Apollo (Cyprus)	win rsf 3	Billy Graham (Belfast)
Light	Jim Stratton (Glasgow)	win rsf 6	Johnny Davidson (Dundee)
Welter	Roy MacGregor (Glasgow)	lost rsf 2	Sammy Hamilton (Belfast)

17/03/1955	Govan Town Hall	Promoter – Alex Lucas	
Bantam	John Smillie (Fauldhouse)	win ko 1	Benny Vaun (Belfast)
Bantam	Jim Cresswell (Glasgow)	win ko 3	Harry Friel (Belfast)
Feather	Matt Fulton (Glasgow)	win ko 2	Dave Welsh (Belfast)
Light	Dick Knox (Motherwell)	win pts 6	Jim Feeney (Belfast)
Light	Jim Stratton (Glasgow)	win rsf 1	Harry Stanford (Belfast)
Welter	Jim McGuinness (Wishaw)	win ko 4	Jim O'Brien (Belfast)

22/04/1955	Eldorado, Leith	Promoter – Harry Black	
Bantam	John Smillie (Fauldhouse)	win pts 6	Ernie Savery (Dunstable)
Bantam	Jim Cresswell (Glasgow)	win rsf 3	Billy Dorris (Perth)
Feather	Matt Fulton (Glasgow)	win ko 3	Alf Cottam (Preston)
Light	Dave Croll (Dundee)	drew 6	Andy Monahan (Southport)
Light	Dick Knox (Motherwell)	win pts 6	Johnny McLaren (Coatbridge)
Welter	Jim McGuinness (Wishaw)	win pts 6	Ron Barnard (Carlisle)
10/05/1955	Kelvin Hall	Promoter – Alex Lucas	
Fly	Dick Currie (Glasgow)	win ko 1	Mickey King (Belfast)
Bantam	John Smillie (Fauldhouse)	win rsf 3	Billy Gibson (Doncaster)
Feather	Charlie Hill (Cambuslang)	win pts 8	Flaviano Ciancarelli (Italy)
Feather	Matt Fulton (Glasgow)	win ko 5	Don Martin (Formby)
Light	Dick Knox (Motherwell)	win ko 4	Andy Monahan (Southport)
Welter	Jim McGuinness (Wishaw)	win pts 6	Johnny Delmore (Leeds)
02/06/1955	Kelvin Hall	Promoter – Alex Lucas	
Fly	Dick Currie (Glasgow)	lost rsf 3	Bobby Robinson (Newcastle)
Bantam	John Smillie (Fauldhouse)	win pts 6	Dave Robins (London)
Feather	Charlie Hill (Cambuslang)	win pts 8	Jacques Bataille (France)
Feather	Matt Fulton (Glasgow)	win pts 8	Sammy O'Dell (Nigeria)
Light	Dick Knox (Motherwell)	win pts 8	Derek John (Catford)
30/06/1955	Kelvin Hall	Promoter – Alex Lucas	
Fly	Frankie Jones (Plean)	win pts 6	Ken Langford (Slough)
Bantam	John Smillie (Fauldhouse)	win rsf 5	Jimmy Brewer (Kings Cross)
Bantam	Don Coshirel (Alderney)	win pts 6	Ernie Savery (Dunstable)
Feather	Matt Fulton (Glasgow)	lost rsf 3	Malcolm Ames (Croydon)
Feather	Charlie Hill (Cambuslang)	win pts 8	Denny Dawson (Sheffield)
Light	Peter Hill (Dagenham)	win ret 6	Derek John (Catford)
14/09/1955	Cathkin Park	Promoter – Alex Lucas	
Fly	Frankie Jones (Plean)	win pts 6	Bobby Robinson (Newcastle)
Bantam	Peter Keenan (Glasgow)	win ko 14	Jake Tuli (South Africa)
	(British Empire Bantamweight Title)		
Feather	Charlie Hill (Cambuslang)	win pts 8	Ken Lawrence (Southampton)
Feather	Matt Fulton (Glasgow)	win rsf 3	Tommy Higgins (Hanley)
Feather	Sammy McCarthy (Stepney)	win ko 3	Andre Younsi (France)
11/10/1955	Caird Hall	Promoter – George Grant	
Feather	Dave Croll (Dundee)	win pts 6	Teddy Barker (Swindon)
Light	Tony McCrorey (Greenock)	win pts 6	Tony Russell (Leeds)
Welter	Jimmy Croll (Dundee)	win rsf 5	Paul King (Torquay)
Welter	Eddie Phillips (Edinburgh)	won rsf 2	Charlie Currie (Coatbridge)
Welter	Johnny Davidson (Dundee)	win pts 6	Sammy Welsh (Dundee)

03/11/1955	Paisley Ice Rink		Promoter – Alex Lucas
Fly	Frankie Jones (Plean)	win pts 8	Eddie O'Connor (Dublin)
Bantam	Peter Keenan (Glasgow)	win pts 10	Pierre Cossemyns (Belgium)
Feather	Matt Fulton (Glasgow)	win pts 8	Charlie Tucker (Camberwell)
Light	Johnny McLaren (Coatbridge)	win ko 3	Bobby Spittal (Barnsley)
Welter	Jim McGuinness (Wishaw)	win pts 6	Johnny Spittal (Barnsley)

20/12/1955	Caird Hall		Promoter – George Grant
Light	Tony McCrorey (Greenock)	win pts 6	Willie Ferguson (Falkirk)
Light	Dave Croll (Dundee)	win ko 1	Harry Hunter (Belfast)
Light	Johnny McLaren (Coatbridge)	win pts 6	Matt Tolan (Leeds)
Welter	Dick Knox (Motherwell)	win ret 4	Ray Danbridge (Leeds)
Welter	Jimmy Croll (Dundee) (Scottish Welterweight Title)	win pts 12	Roy MacGregor (Glasgow)

1956

21/03/1956	Govan Town Hall		Promoter – Alex Lucas
Fly	Frankie Jones (Plean)	win rsf 5	Dave Moore (Belfast)
Bantam	Jim Cresswell (Glasgow)	drew 6	Danny McNamee (Dundee)
Feather	Dave Croll (Dundee)	win ret 4	Jimmy McAteer (London)
Light	Tony McCrorey (Greenock)	lost rsf 6	Roy Mann (Gold Coast)
Light	Arthur Donnachie (Greenock)	win rsf 3	Jackie Horseman (West Hartlepool)
Welter	Jim McGuinness (Wishaw)	lost pts 6	Harry Haydock (Gold Coast)

27/03/1956	Leith Eldorado		Promoter – Harry Black
Bantam	Billy Rafferty (Glasgow)	win pts 6	Danny McNamee (Dundee)
Bantam	Eddie Carson (Edinburgh) (Scottish Bantamweight Title)	dnc 6	Hugh Riley (Edinburgh)
Light	Arthur Donnachie (Greenock)	win ret 2	Johnny Murphy (Glasgow)
Welter	Danny Harvey (Glasgow)	win dis 4	Eddie Phillips (Edinburgh)
Light Heavy	Joe Dodds (Edinburgh)	lost pts 6	Johnny Douglas (Glasgow)

28/04/1956	Caird Hall		Promoter – Alex Lucas
Bantam	Jim Cresswell (Glasgow)	win pts 6	Danny McNamee (Dundee)
Feather	Charlie Hill (Cambuslang)	win pts 8	Flaviano Ciancarelli (Italy)
Feather	Dave Croll (Dundee)	lost pts 6	Pat McCairn (Bethnal Gren)
Welter	Jimmy Croll (Dundee)	win pts 8	Eddie Phillips (Edinburgh)
Middle	John Woolard (Glasgow)	win pts 6	Johnny Davidson (Dundee)

02/05/1956	Kelvin Hall		Promoter – Sammy Docherty
Fly	Dick Currie (Glasgow) (Scottish Flyweight Title)	win pts 12	Jimmy Quinn (Kirkintilloch)
Bantam	Chic Brogan (Clydebank)	win rsf 7	Paul Dunne (Liverpool)
Bantam	Malcolm Grant (Glasgow)	win pts 8	Don Armagh (Gold Coast)
Light	Matt Fulton (Glasgow)	drew 8	Sammy Bonnici (Malta)
Light	Tony McCrorey (Greenock)	lost pts 6	Sammy Cowan (Belfast)

16/05/1956	Kelvin Hall	Promoter – Sammy Docherty	
Fly	Dick Currie (Glasgow)	win rsf 5	Colin Clitheroe (Preston)
Fly	Jimmy Quinn (Kirkintilloch)	drew 8	Vic Glenn (Stepney)
Bantam	Billy Rafferty (Glasgow)	win rsf 6	Jack Sala (Nigeria)
Feather	Matt Fulton (Glasgow)	win pts 8	Alby Tissong (South Africa)
Welter	Danny Harvey (Glasgow)	win pts 8	Joe Rufus (Nigeria)

20/06/1956	Cathkin Park	Promoter – Alex Lucas	
Fly	Dick Currie (Glasgow)	win pts 8	Roland Foy (France)
Bantam	Malcolm Grant (Glasgow) (Scottish Bantamweight Title)	win pts 12	Chic Brogan (Clydebank)
Feather	Matt Fulton (Glasgow)	win rsf 3	JimFisher (Belfast)
Welter	Danny Harvey (Glasgow)	lost pts 8	Charlie Cosgrove (Belfast)
Middle	John Woolard (Glasgow)	win ret 2	Cliff Garvey (Newry)

27/06/1956	Kelvin Hall	Promoter – Alex Lucas	
Fly	Frankie Jones (Plean)	win pts 8	Vic Glenn (Stepney)
Bantam	Billy Rafferty (Glasgow)	win pts 6	Jim Cresswell (Glasgow)
Bantam	John Smillie (Fauldhouse) (British Bantamweight Title Eliminator)	win pts 10	George Dormer (West Ham)
Feather	Charlie Hill (Cambuslang)	win rsf 10	Ken Lawrence (Southampton)
Feather	Bobby Coote (Clydebank)	win rsf 1	Billy Graham (Belfast)

05/09/1956	Greenock Town Hall	Promoter – Charlie Elliot	
Bantam	Billy Rafferty (Glasgow)	win pts 8	Jim Cresswell (Glasgow)
Feather	Dave Croll (Dundee)	win pts 8	Bobby Coote (Clydebank)
Light	Arthur Donnachie (Greenock)	win pts 8	Ray Akwei (Gold Coast)
Light	Tony McCrorey (Greenock)	win pts 6	Derek Clark (Burnley)

19/09/1956	Firhill	Promoter – Sammy Docherty	
Fly	Frankie Jones (Plean) (Scottish Flyweight Title and British Flyweight Title Final Eliminator)	win pts 12	Dick Currie (Glasgow)
Bantam	Chic Brogan (Clydebank) (Scottish Bantamweight Title)	win pts 12	Malcolm Grant (Glasgow)
Bantam	Archie Downie (Glasgow)	win pts 6	Danny McNamee (Dundee)
Feather	Bobby Neill (Edinburgh) (Vacant Scottish Featherweight Title/ British Featherweight Title Eliminator)	win ret 8	Matt Fulton (Glasgow)
Light	Bobby Kilpatrick (Kilmarnock)	lost rsf 4	Jim Fisher (Belfast)

31/10/1956	Kelvin Hall	Promoter – Sammy Docherty	
Fly	Dick Currie (Glasgow)	win pts 10	Francesco Carreno (Spain)
Bantam	Malcolm Grant (Glasgow)	win pts 8	Archie Downie (Glasgow)
Feather	Matt Fulton (Glasgow)	win pts 8	Francis Bonnardel (France)
Middle	John Woolard (Glasgow)	win pts	Johnny Stansfield (South Africa)
Light Heavy	Jim Reilly (Twechar)	win ko 2	Jack Scott (Preston)

14/12/1956	Leith Eldorado		Promoters – Sammy Docherty and Harry Black	
Bantam	Archie Downie (Glasgow)	win pts 8	Don Armagh (Gold Coast)	
Bantam	Malcolm Grant (Glasgow)	win pts 8	Paul Dunne (Liverpool)	
Bantam	Billy Rafferty (Glasgow)	win pts 6	Derry Treanor (Glasgow)	
Welter	Eddie Phillips (Edinburgh)	drew 8	Billy Corbett (Carrickfergus)	
Light Heavy	Dave Mooney (Wishaw)	win pts 6	Jack Scott (Preston)	

1957

20/02/1957	Kelvin Hall		Promoter – Sammy Docherty	
Fly	Frankie Jones (Plean)	win rsf 8	Len Reece (Cardiff)	
Bantam	Archie Downie (Glasgow)	win ret 4	Malcolm Grant (Glasgow)	
	(Scottish Bantamweight Title Eliminator)			
Feather	Matt Fulton (Glasgow)	lost pts 8	Aryee Jackson (Ghana)	
Middle	John McCormack (Glasgow)	win pts 6	Dudley Cox (Bournemouth)	
Light Heavy	Dave Mooney (Wishaw)	win ko 1	Johnny Ewart (Carlisle)	

26/03/1957	Leith Eldorado		Promoter – Harry Black	
Feather	Billy Adams (Newcastle)	win ret 3	Colin Clough (Blackpool)	
Light	Tommy McGuinness (Edinburgh)	win ko 2	Ken Scott (Gateshead)	
Welter	Walter Black (Edinburgh)	lost dis 1	Geoff Hollingsworth (Bradford)	
Middle	John McCormack (Glasgow)	win ko 1	Cliff Garvey (Newry)	
Middle	John Woolard (Glasgow)	win pts 6	Eddie Phillips (Edinburgh)	

10/04/1957	Paisley Ice Rink		Promoter – Sammy Docherty	
Fly	Frankie Jones(Plean)	win rsf 10	Malcolm McLeod (Coventry)	
Bantam	Archie Downie (Glasgow)	win pts 8	Billy Skelly (Belfast)	
Feather	Matt Fulton (Glasgow)	lost pts 10	Aryee Jackson (Ghana)	
Middle	John McCormack (Glasgow)	win ret 3	Eddie Williams (Tredegar)	
Light Heavy	Dave Mooney (Wishaw)	lost rsf 3	Clark Mellor (New Mills)	

09/05/1957	Govan Town Hall		Promoter – Johnny Murray	
Bantam	Billy Rafferty (Glasgow)	win ko 5	Benny Vaun (Belfast)	
Bantam	Derry Treanor (Glasgow)	win pts 8	Billy Skelly (Belfast)	
Welter	Tommy Cavan (Glasgow)	win pts 6	Cliff Lawrence (Mexborough)	
Middle	John McCormack (Glasgow)	win ko 1	Jack Willis (Belfast)	
Light Heavy	Dave Mooney (Wishaw)	win ko 3	Peter Aldridge (Doncaster)	

22/05/1957	Firhill		Promoter – Sammy Docherty	
Fly	Frankie Jones (Plean)	win pts 10	Jose Ogazon (Spain)	
Bantam	Peter Keenan (Glasgow)	win rsf 6	John Smillie (Fauldhouse)	
	(British and Empire Bantamweight Titles)			
Bantam	Archie Downie (Glasgow)	lost ko 2	Freddie Gilroy (Belfast)	
Light	Guy Gracia (France)	win rsf 7	John McNally (Belfast)	
Middle	John McCormack (Glasgow)	win ko 1	Frank Davis (Gloucester)	
Light Heavy	Dave Mooney (Wishaw)	win ko 2	Danny Wall (Wembley)	

28/05/1957	Leith Eldorado		Promoter – Harry Black
Feather	Bobby Coote (Clydebank)	win rsf 3	Johnny Nearby (Belfast)
Light	Tommy McGuinness (Edinburgh)	win rsf 3	Tony McCrorey (Greenock)
Welter	Walter Black (Edinburgh)	lost ko 4	Roy Alway (Halifax)
Middle	John McCormack (Glasgow)	win rsf 3	Bonny Garraway (Ghana)
Light Heavy	Dave Mooney (Wishaw)	win ko 3	Jim Teasdale (Middlesbrough)

26/06/1957	Firhill		Promoter – Sammy Docherty
Fly	George McDade (Glasgow)	win pts 4	Danny McNamee (Dundee)
Bantam	Peter Keenan (Glasgow)	win pts 10	Robert Tartari (France)
Bantam	Freddie Gilroy (Belfast)	win rsf 5	Jose Alvarez (Spain)
Feather	Jimmy Brown (Belfast)	win dis 6	Belaid Meslem (France)
Middle	John McCormack (Glasgow)	win rsf 5	Wally Scott (West Ham)

15/08/1957	Kelvin Hall		Promoter – Sammy Docherty
Bantam	Chic Brogan (Clydebank)	win rsf 4	Tanny Campo (Phillipines)
Bantam	John Morrissey (Newarthill)	win ret 4	Benny Vaun (Belfast)
Feather	Owen Reilly (Glasgow)	win pts 6	Len Harvey (Cardiff)
Light	Billy Kelly (Derry)	lost pts 10	Willie Toweel (South Africa)
Middle	John McCormack (Glasgow)	win ret 2	Eddie Lennon (London)
Middle	John Woolard (Glasgow)	lost rsf 1	Evie Vorster (South Africa)

21/08/1957	Paisley Ice Rink		Promoter – Jim Gilmour
Bantam	Peter Keenan (Glasgow)	win pts 8	Rudy Edwards (British Guiana)
Feather	Johnny Kidd (Aberdeen)	win rsf 1	Don Flack (London)
Feather	Charlie Hill (Cambuslang)	win pts 8	Alf Drew (Hackney)
Light	Arthur Donnachie (Greenock)	win ret 5	Bobby Neill (Edinburgh)
Light Heavy	Willie Armstrong (Port Glasgow)	win pts 8	Albert Finch (Croydon)

28/08/1957	Hamilton Town Hall		Promoter – Finlay Hannah
Bantam	John Morrissey (Newarthill)	win rsf 3	Billy Adams (Newcastle)
Feather	Owen Reilly (Glasgow)	win ko 3	Reg Jackson (Derby)
Welter	Charlie Currie (Coatbridge)	win rsf 2	Tommy Cavan (Glasgow)
Middle	John Woolard (Glasgow)	lost pts 6	Eddie Phillips (Edinburgh)
Light Heavy	Dave Mooney (Wishaw)	win pts 6	Clark Mellor (New Mills)

12/09/1957	Falkirk Ice Rink		Promoter – Jim Gilmour
Fly	Frankie Jones (Plean)	win pts 10	Christian Marchand (France)
Fly	Alex Ambrose (Glasgow)	win pts 6	Jim Loughrey (Belfast)
Bantam	John Smillie (Fauldhouse)	win pts 8	Pat McCairn (Bethnal Green)
Light	Tommy McGuinness (Edinburgh)	win pts 8	Johnny McLaren (Coatbridge)
Light Heavy	Chic Calderwood (Craigneuk)	win ko 2	Jim Teasedale (Middlesbrough)

18/09/1957	Kelvin Hall	Promoter – Sammy Docherty		
Fly	Dick Currie (Glasgow)	win pts 8	George O'Neill (Belfast)	
Bantam	John Morrissey (Newarthill)	win ko 2	Harry Hunter (Belfast)	
Feather	Owen Reilly (Glasgow)	win rsf 4	Joe Sharp (Belfast)	
Light	Willie Toweel (South Africa)	win pts 10	Mario Calcaterra (Italy)	
Light	George Martin (Bermondsey)	win pts 8	Franco Rossini (Italy)	

25/09/1957	Paisley Ice Rink	Promoter – Jim Gilmour		
Fly	Alex Ambrose (Glasgow)	win rsf 5	Jim Loughrey (Belfast)	
Bantam	Peter Keenan (Glasgow)	win pts 10	Albert Schweer (Germany)	
Bantam	Billy Rafferty (Glasgow)	win pts 8	Jake Tuli (South Africa)	
Light	Arthur Donnachie (Greenock)	win pts 8	Jim McCormack (Belfast)	
Light Heavy	Chic Calderwood (Craigneuk)	win ko 1	Tommy Summers (Bootle)	
Light Heavy	Willie Armstrong (Port Glasgow)	win ret 6	Alex Buxton (Watford)	

16/10/1957	Hamilton Town Hall	Promoter – George Blyth		
Bantam	Billy Rafferty (Glasgow)	win ret 4	Billy Skelly (Belfast)	
Feather	Matt Fulton (Glasgow)	lost pts 8	Spike McCormack (Belfast)	

23/10/1957	Kelvin Hall	Promoter – Sammy Docherty		
Fly	Frankie Jones (Plean) (British Empire Flyweight Title)	lost ko 3	Dennis Adams (South Africa)	
Bantam	Dick Currie (Glasgow)	lost rsf 5	Ken Langford (Slough)	
Bantam	John Morrissey (Newarthill)	win pts 8	Dennis East (Plaistow)	
Middle	John McCormack (Glasgow)	lost rsf 5	Jimmy Lynas (Coventry)	
Light Heavy	Dave Mooney (Wishaw)	win rsf 2	Johnny Williamson (Gloucs)	

06/11/1957	Govan Town Hall	Promoter – Finlay Hannah		
Bantam	John Morrissey (Newarthill)	win ret 3	George O'Neill (Belfast)	
Feather	Owen Reilly (Glasgow)	win ko 4	George O'Brien (Belfast)	
Light	Matt Fulton (Glasgow)	win ko 1	Jim Loughlin (Belfast)	
Welter	Tommy Cavan (Glasgow)	win pts 6	Tommy Young (South Africa)	

13/11/1957	Greenock Town Hall	Promoter – Hugh Ferns		
Fly	George McDade (Glasgow) (Scottish Flyweight Title)	win pts 12	Pat Glancy (Glasgow)	
Bantam	Alex Ambrose (Glasgow)	win ko 1	Harry Hunter (Belfast)	
Middle	Len Mullen (Glasgow)	win rsf 3	Tommy Summers (Bootle)	

28/11/1957	Kelvin Hall	Promoter – Sammy Docherty		
Fly	Peter Walsh (Glasgow)	win ko 2	Charlie O'Neill (Belfast)	
Bantam	Dick Currie (Glasgow)	win pts 8	Antonio Diaz (Spain)	
Bantam	John Morrissey (Newarthill)	win pts 8	Ken Langford (Slough)	
Feather	Owen Reilly (Glasgow)	win ko 3	Dickie Richardson (Belfast)	
Middle	John McCormack (Glasgow)	win rsf 7	Evie Vorster (South Africa)	
Light Heavy	Dave Mooney (Wishaw)	win pts 8	Neville Rowe (Australia)	

1958

15/01/1958	Hamilton Town Hall	Promoter – Sammy Docherty	
Bantam	John Morrissey (Newarthill) (Scottish Bantamweight Title)	win ko 4	Archie Downie (Glasgow)
Feather	Owen Reilly (Glasgow)	win ret 6	Alex McCready (Belfast)
Light	Jim Ballantyne (Johnstone)	win pts 6	Joe Sharpe (Belfast)
Welter	Charlie Currie (Coatbridge)	win pts 8	Sam Thompson (Belfast)
Welter	Tommy Cavan (Glasgow)	lost ret 4	Dougie Johnstone (London)
Middle	Jack Woolard (Glasgow)	win rsf 1	Billy Corbett (Carrickfergus)

05/02/1958	Kelvin Hall	Promoter – Sammy Docherty	
Fly	John Caldwell (Belfast)	win ko 2	Billy Downer (Stoke Newington)
Bantam	Dick Currie (Glasgow)	win pts 8	Guy Schatt (France)
Bantam	John Morrissey (Newarthill)	lost pts 8	Antonio Diaz (Spain)
Bantam	Derry Treanor (Glasgow)	win rsf 5	Eddie Burns (Liverpool)
Middle	John McCormack (Glasgow)	win rsf 7	Vincent O'Kine (West Africa)
Light Heavy	Dave Mooney (Wishaw)	win rsf 4	Ken Rowlands (Luton)

19/02/1958	Hamilton Town Hall	Promoter – Sammy Docherty	
Fly	Peter Walsh (Glasgow)	win ret 4	Bobby Davis (Halifax)
Bantam	Archie Downie (Glasgow)	lost pts 8	Dennis East (Plaistow)
Feather	Chic Brogan (Clydebank) (Scottish Featherweight Title)	win pts 12	Owen Reilly (Glasgow)
Light	Jim Ballantyne (Johnstone)	win ko 2	Ted Arthur (Lancaster)
Light Heavy	Chic Calderwood (Craigneuk)	win pts 6	Joe Walcott (Trinidad)
Light Heavy	Dave Mooney (Glasgow)	win rsf 5	Abe Stanley (Poole)

26/02/1958	Paisley Ice Rink	Promoter – Jim Gilmour	
Fly	Alex Ambrose (Glasgow)	win pts 8	Mick Barone (Brixton)
Feather	Dave Croll (Dundee)	lost pts 8	David Oved (Israel)
Feather	John O'Brien (Glasgow)	lost pts 8	Roy Jacobs (Nigeria)
Light	Arthur Donnachie (Greenock)	win pts 8	Spike McCormack (Belfast)
Light	Johnny Kidd (Aberdeen)	win ko 1	Tony McCrorey (Greenock)

05/03/1958	Kelvin Hall	Promoter – Sammy Docherty	
Fly	John Caldwell (Belfast)	win ko 1	Eddie Barraclough (Rotherham)
Bantam	Peter Keenan (Glasgow)	win rsf 10	Dick Currie (Glasgow)
Bantam	John Morrissey (Newarthill)	win ko 3	Antonio Diaz (Spain)
Bantam	Derry Treanor (Glasgow)	win ret 3	Ken Langford (Slough)
Feather	Jim Ballantyne (Johnstone)	lost pts 6	Glyn Evans (Doncaster)
Light Heavy	Dave Mooney (Wishaw)	lost ko 2	Jack Whittaker (Warwick)

02/04/1958	Paisley Ice Rink		Promoter – Jim Gilmour
Fly	Alex Ambrose (Glasgow)	win ret 6	Len Reece (Cardiff)
Bantam	Peter Keenan (Glasgow) (British Empire Bantamweight Title)	win pts 15	Graham Van Der Walt (South Africa)
Bantam	Billy Rafferty (Glasgow)	win pts 8	Pat McCairn (Bethnal Green)
Feather	Jim Ballantyne (Johnstone)	lost rsf 3	Robbie Wilson (Dagenham)
Light	Arthur Donnachie (Greenock)	lost ko 2	Roy Jacobs (Nigeria)
Light	Johnny McLaren (Coatbridge) (Vacant Scottish Lightweight Title)	win rsf 12	Tommy McGuinness (Edinburgh)

23/04/1958	Kelvin Hall		Promoter – Sammy Docherty
Fly	Peter Walsh (Glasgow)	win pts 6	Barry Ridge (Leicester)
Bantam	Derry Treanor (Glasgow)	win pts 8	Terry Toole (Hackney)
Light	Guy Gracia (France)	win rsf 7	Willie Toweel (South Africa)
Middle	Vincent O'Kine (West Africa)	lost rsf 5	Evie Vorster (South Africa)
Middle	John McCormack (Glasgow)	win pts 8	Johnny Read (Norwood)

21/05/1958	Kelvin Hall		Promoter – Sammy Docherty
Fly	John Caldwell (Belfast)	win pts 8	Moncef Fehri (Tunisia)
Bantam	Freddie Gilroy (Belfast)	win pts 8	Kimpo Amarfio (Ghana)
Bantam	Derry Treanor (Glasgow)	win pts 8	Jose Luis Martinez (Spain)
Bantam	John Morrissey (Newarthill)	win rsf 6	Terry Toole (Hackney)
Feather	Archie Hawkins (Glasgow)	lost ko 3	Billy Whitfield (Cardiff)
Light Heavy	Dave Mooney (Wishaw)	win pts 8	Redvers Sangoe (Cardiff)

28/05/1958	Hamilton Town Hall		Promoter – Jim Gilmour
Fly	Alex Ambrose (Glasgow)	win ret 4	Tommy Armour (Belfast)
Bantam	Billy Rafferty (Glasgow)	win pts 8	Danny McNamee (Dundee)
Feather	Chic Brogan (Clydebank)	win pts 8	John O'Brien (Glasgow)
Welter	Tommy Cavan (Glasgow)	lost pts 6	Colin Moore (Barnsley)
Light Heavy	Chic Calderwood (Craigneuk)	win ret 1	Clark Mellor (New Mills)

18/06/1958	Kelvin Hall		Promoter – Sammy Docherty
Fly	Dennis Adams (South Africa)	win rsf 6	Silas Boko (Nigeria)
Fly	John Caldwell (Belfast)	win ret 4	Michael Lamora (France)
Bantam	Derry Treanor (Glasgow)	win pts 8	Kimpo Amarfio (Ghana)
Bantam	John Morrissey (Newarthill)	win pts 8	Jimmy Carson (Belfast)
Light Heavy	Dave Mooney (Wishaw)	win ko 8	Billy Ellaway (Liverpool)

02/07/1958	Cathkin Park		Promoter – Jim Gilmour
Fly	Alex Ambrose (Glasgow) (Scottish Flyweight Title)	win pts 12	George McDade (Glasgow)
Bantam	Peter Keenan (Glasgow)	win pts 10	Billy Peacock (USA)
Bantam	Billy Rafferty (Glasgow)	lost rsf 5	Eric Brett (Retford)
Feather	Bobby Neill (Edinburgh)	win rsf 6	Owen Reilly (Glasgow)
Feather	Charlie Hill (Cambuslang) (British Featherweight Title)	win ret 11	Chic Brogan (Clydebank)
Middle	John McCormack (Glasgow) (Vacant Scottish Middleweight Title)	win pts 12	Len Mullen (Glasgow)

25/07/1958	Linksfield Park Aberdeen	Promoter – Ralph Townsley	
Fly	Alex Ambrose (Glasgow)	win pts 8	Eddie O'Connor (Dublin)
Bantam	Billy Rafferty (Glasgow)	win pts 8	Danny McNamee (Dundee)
Feather	Johnny Murphy (Glasgow)	lost pts 6	Johnny Jerrett (Belfast)
Light	Johnny Kidd (Aberdeen)	win ko 9	Johnny McLaren (Coatbridge)
	(Scottish Lightweight Title)		
Light	Ricky Kiernan (Glasgow)	win pts 6	Tommy Houston (Belfast)

28/08/1958	Paisley Ice Rink	Promoter – Jim Gilmour	
Fly	Alex Ambrose (Glasgow)	win pts 8	Pat Glancy (Glasgow)
Bantam	Peter Keenan (Glasgow)	lost rsf 6	Derry Treanor (Glasgow)
Bantam	Tommy Miller (West Lothian)	win pts 8	Eric Brett (Retford)
Bantam	Billy Rafferty (Glasgow)	win rsf 5	Terry Spinks (West Ham)
Middle	Len Mullen (Glasgow)	lost ko 8	Jim Reilly (Twechar)
Middle	John McCormack (Glasgow)	win pts 8	Jimmy Lynas (Coventry)

17/09/1958	Kelvin Hall	Promoter – Sammy Docherty	
Fly	John Caldwell (Belfast)	win pts 8	Dennis Adams (South Africa)
Bantam	Jimmy Carson (Belfast)	lost ret 2	Eric Brett (Retford)
Bantam	John Morrissey (Newarthill)	lost ret 8	Freddie Gilroy (Belfast)
Light	Guy Gracia (France)	win rsf 9	Billy Kelly (Derry)
Light Heavy	Dave Mooney (Wishaw)	lost ko 3	Eddie Wright (Mile End)
	(British Light Heavyweight Title Eliminator)		

16/10/1958	Paisley Ice Rink	Promoter – Jim Gilmour	
Fly	Jackie Brown (Edinburgh)	win rsf 3	Mark Quinn (London)
Bantam	Peter Keenan (Glasgow)	win pts 15	Pat Supple (Canada)
	(British Empire Bantamweight Title)		
Bantam	Tommy Miller (West Lothian)	win rsf 6	Billy Rafferty (Glasgow)
Feather	Charlie Hill (Cambuslang)	win pts 8	Joe Quinn (Belfast)
Middle	John McCormack (Glasgow)	win pts 8	Jean Ruellet (France)

29/10/1958	Kelvin Hall	Promoter – Sammy Docherty	
Fly	Frankie Jones (Plean)	win pts 8	Dennis Adams (South Africa)
Fly	John Caldwell (Belfast)	win ko 5	Juanito Cid (Spain)
Fly	George McDade (Glasgow)	win pts 8	Silas Boko (Nigeria)
Bantam	Freddie Gilroy (Belfast)	win pts 8	Jose Luis Martinez (Spain)
Light Heavy	Chic Calderwood (Craigneuk)	wn rsf 5	Dave Mooney (Wishaw)
	(Scottish Light Heavyweight Title)		

19/11/1958	Kelvin Hall	Promoters – Sammy Docherty and Jim Gilmour	
Fly	George McDade (Glasgow)	win rsf 8	Dennis Adams (South Africa)
Fly	Frankie Jones (Plean)	lost rsf 4	Pancho Bhatachaji (India)
Feather	Derry Treanor (Glasgow)	lost rsf 7	Roy Jacobs (Nigeria)
Feather	Arthur Donnachie (Greenock)	win rsf 6	Percy Lewis (Trinidad)
Middle	Jack Woolard (Glasgow)	lost pts 8	Paddy Delargy (Galway)

25/11/1958	Leith Eldorado	Promoter – Andy Neill	
Fly	Alex Ambrose (Glasgow)	win pts 8	Eddie Barraclough (Rotherham)
Bantam	Danny McNamee (Dundee)	lost pts 8	Hugh Riley (Edinburgh)
Feather	Dave Croll (Dundee)	win pts 8	Junior Cassidy (Nigeria)
Feather	John Smillie (Fauldhouse)	win pts 8	Andy Hayford (Ghana)

1959

31/01/1959	Whiteinch Town Hall	Promoter – Jim Gilmour	
Fly	Jackie Brown (Edinburgh)	win pts 6	Eddie Barraclough (Rotherham)
Bantam	Hugh Riley (Edinburgh)	win pts 8	Billy Skelly (Belfast)
Feather	Dave Croll (Dundee)	win pts 6	Junior Cassidy (Nigeria)
Feather	Ollie Wylie (Aberdeen)	win pts 6	Benny Vaun (Belfast)
Light	Arthur Donnachie (Greenock)	lost pts 8	Spike McCormack (Belfast)

05/02/1959	Kelvin Hall	Promoter – Sammy Docherty	
Fly	Frankie Jones (Plean) (British Flyweight Title)	win pts 15	Alex Ambrose (Glasgow)
Fly	John Caldwell (Belfast)	win pts 8	Henri Schmid (France)
Bantam	Billy Rafferty (Glasgow)	win pts 8	Dennis East (Plaistow)
Feather	Floyd Robertson (Ghana)	win pts 8	Roy Jacobs (Nigeria)
Light	Ricky Kiernan (Glasgow)	win pts 4	Cecil Martin (Belfast)
Middle	Pat Byrne (Glasgow)	win rsf 1	Vincent O'Kine (West Africa)

25/02/1959	Kelvin Hall	Promoter – Jim Gilmour	
Fly	Alex Ambrose (Glasgow) (Scottish Flyweight Title)	drew 12	George McDade (Glasgow)
Bantam	Tommy Miller (West Lothian)	win pts 8	Eddie O'Connor (Dublin)
Bantam	Graham Van der Walt (South Africa)	lost pts 8	Ron Jones (West Ham)
Feather	Ollie Wylie (Aberdeen)	win pts 4	Benny Vaun (Belfast)
Middle	John McCormack (Glasgow)	win ret 6	Paddy Delargy (Galway)
Light Heavy	Chic Calderwood (Craigneuk)	win ret 2	Burke Emery (Canada)

18/03/1959	Paisley Ice Rink	Promoter – Peter Keenan	
Fly	Alex Ambrose (Glasgow)	lost rsf 8	Derek Lloyd (Chingford)
Fly	Jackie Brown (Edinburgh)	win pts 8	Malcolm McLeod (Coventry)
Light	Ricky Kiernan (Glasgow)	win rsf 4	Jackie Davidson (Belfast)
Middle	John McCormack (Glasgow)	win pts 10	Michel Diouf (France)
Light Heavy	Chic Calderwood (Craigneuk)	win ko 10	Yoland Pompey (Trinidad)

15/04/1959	Kelvin Hall	Promoter – Sammy Docherty	
Fly	John Caldwell (Belfast)	win pts 8	Pierre Rossi (France)
Bantam	Freddie Gilroy (Belfast)	win ko 2	Charles Sylla (France)
Bantam	Billy Rafferty (Glasgow)	win pts 8	George Dormer (West Ham)
Bantam	John Morrissey (Newarthill)	win ko 3	Gerry Jones (Wigan)
Welter	Freddie Tiedt (Dublin)	win pts 6	Terry Lake (Morden)
Middle	Orlando Paso (Nigeria)	win pts 8	Alan Dean (Birkinhead)
07/05/1959	Paisley Ice Rink	Promoter – Peter Keenan	
Fly	Alex Ambrose (Glasgow)	win pts 8	Pancho Bhatachazi (India)
Fly	Jackie Brown (Edinburgh)	win rsf 8	Frankie Spencer (Wolverhampton)
Bantam	John Morrissey (Newarthill)	win pts 8	Ron Jones (West Ham)
Middle	John McCormack (Glasgow)	win pts 10	Gene Johns (USA)
Light Heavy	Chic Calderwood (Craigneuk)	win rsf 7	Charlie Forrest (USA)
14/05/1959	Central Hotel, Glasgow	Promoter – Jerry Lever	
Bantam	Billy Rafferty (Glasgow)	win pts 8	Graham Van Der Walt (South Africa)
Feather	Owen Reilly (Glasgow)	lost rsf 1	Terry McManus (Belfast)
Light	Ricky Kiernan (Glasgow)	lost ko 1	Pat Loughran (Belfast)
Light	Arthur Donnachie (Greenock)	lost pts 8	Roy Jacobs (Nigeria)
28/05/1959	Kelvin Hall	Promoter – Jim Gilmour	
Fly	Frankie Jones (Plean)	win pts 8	George McDade (Glasgow)
Fly	Alex Ambrose (Glasgow)	lost dis 4	Pat Glancy (Glasgow)
Bantam	Tommy Miller (West Lothian)	lost pts 8	Pierre Cossemyns (Belgium)
Feather	Owen Reilly (Glasgow)	drew 8	John Smillie (Fauldhouse)
Middle	John McCormack (Glasgow)	win rsf 6	Remo Carati (Italy)
17/06/1959	Firhill	Promoter – Sammy Docherty	
Fly	John Caldwell (Belfast)	win pts 10	Giacomo Spano (Italy)
Bantam	Billy Rafferty (Glasgow)	win pts 8	Mohamed Zarzi (France)
Feather	John O'Brien (Glasgow)	win pts 8	Eric Brett (Retford)
Light	Dave Charnley (Dartford)	win dis 6	Billy Kelly (Derry)
Welter	Freddie Tiedt (Dublin)	win rsf 7	Billy Wadham (London)
Middle	Pat Byrne (Glasgow)	lost pts 8	Derek Liversidge (Retford)
22/07/1959	Deveronvale Park, Banff	Promoter – Peter Keenan	
Feather	Ollie Wylie (Aberdeen)	win ko 5	Archie Hawkins (Glasgow)
Light	Johnny McLaren (Coatbridge)	win ret 5	Ricky Kiernan (Glasgow)
28/08/1959	Greenock Town Hall	Promoter – Hugh Ferns	
Bantam	Alex Ambrose (Glasgow)	win rsf 2	Billy Skelly (Belfast)
Feather	Dave Croll (Dundee)	win ko 3	Johnny Murphy (Glasgow)
Light	Bobby Kane (Greenock)	win pts 6	Johnny McLaren (Coatbridge)
Light	Ricky Kiernan (Glasgow)	win pts 6	Jim Ballantyne (Johnstone)

10/09/1959	Paisley Ice Rink	Promoter – Peter Keenan	

Fly	Jackie Brown (Edinburgh) (Scottish Flyweight Title)	win ret 10	Alex Ambrose (Glasgow)
Bantam	John Morrissey (Newarthill) (Scottish Bantamweight Title)	win ret 5	Tommy Miller (West Lothian)
Feather	George Judge (Glasgow)	win rsf 6	Ollie Wylie (Aberdeen)
Light	Bobby Kane (Greenock)	win pts 6	Ricky McMasters (Jamaica)
Light Heavy	Chic Calderwood (Craigneuk)	win ret 7	Sam Langford (Nigeria)

21/10/1959	Paisley Ice Rink	Promoter – Peter Keenan	

Fly	Jackie Brown (Edinburgh) (British Flyweight Title Eliminator)	win rsf 5	Derek Lloyd (Chingford)
Feather	George Judge (Glasgow)	win rsf 3	Ron Jones (West Ham)
Feather	John Smillie (Fauldhouse)	win pts 8	Junior Cassidy (Nigeria)
Welter	Jim McGuinness (Wishaw)	win pts 8	Ted Batterham (Peterborough)
Light Heavy	Chic Calderwood (Craigneuk)	win pts 10	Ron Redrup (West Ham)

28/10/1959	Kelvin Hall	Promoter – Sammy Docherty	

Fly	John Caldwell (Belfast)	win rsf 6	Salvatore Manca (Italy)
Bantam	Billy Rafferty (Glasgow) (British Bantamweight Title Final Eliminator)	win pts 12	Len Reece (Cardiff)
Bantam	John Morrissey (Newarthill)	win pts 8	Peter Lavery (Belfast)
Feather	Floyd Robertson (Ghana)	win pts 8	Pentti Rautiannen (Finland)
Welter	Freddie Tiedt (Dublin)	lost pts 8	Tommy Tagoe (Ghana)

11/11/1959	Caird Hall, Dundee	Promoter – Peter Keenan	

Bantam	Alex Ambrose (Glasgow)	win rsf 3	Danny McNamee (Dundee)
Feather	Dave Croll (Dundee) (Scottish Featherweight title)	win ko 2	Chic Brogan (Clydebank)
Feather	George Judge (Glasgow)	win pts 6	Eddie Burns (Liverpool)
Middle	Jimmy Croll (Dundee)	dnc6	Dennis Patrick (Ghana)

09/12/1959	Paisley Ice Rink	Promoter – Peter Keenan	

Fly	Jackie Brown (Edinburgh)	win pts 8	John Agwu (Nigeria)
Bantam	Billy Rafferty (Glasgow)	win pts 10	Dwight Hawkins (USA)
Bantam	John Morrissey (Newarthill)	win pts 8	Hugh Riley (Edinburgh)
Feather	George Judge (Glasgow)	win ret 5	Kenny Thomas (London)
Light Heavy	Chic Calderwood (Craigneuk) (British Light Heavyweight Title Final Eliminator)	win rsf 7	Jack Whittaker (Warwick)

1960

28/01/1960	Paisley Ice Rink	Promoter – Peter Keenan	

Bantam	Alex Ambrose (Glasgow)	win rsf 6	Len Reece (Cardiff)
Feather	Dave Croll (Dundee)	lost pts 8	Derry Treanor (Glasgow)
Feather	George Judge (Glasgow)	win pts 6	Junior Cassidy (Nigeria)
Light	Jimmy Gibson (Dunfermline)	win pts 6	Pat Aaron (Nigeria)
Light	Bobby Kane (Greenock)	lost pts 6	Dave Coventry (Liverpool)
Light Heavy	Chic Calderwood (Craigneuk) (Vacant British Light Heavyweight Title)	win rsf 13	Arthur Howard (Islington)

09/03/1960	Kelvin Hall		Promoter – Peter Keenan
Bantam	John Morrissey (Newarthill)	win dis 5	Dwight Hawkins (USA)
Feather	John Smillie (Fauldhouse)	win rsf 7	George Judge (Glasgow)
Light	Jimmy Gibson (Dunfermline)	win rsf 2	Arthur Burley (Wolverhampton)
Light	Dave Coventry (Liverpool)	win pts 8	Jimmy Norcott (Stepney)
Middle	John McCormack (Glasgow)	win rsf 3	Tommy Tagoe (Ghana)
Light Heavy	Ron Redrup (West Ham)	lost pts 8	Donnie Fleeman (USA)

10/03/1960	Central Hotel, Glasgow		Promoter – Jerry Lever
Fly	George McDade (Glasgow) (Scottish Flyweight Title Eliminator)	win pts 10	Pat Glancy (Glasgow)
Light	Bobby Kane (Greenock)	win pts 8	Ray Ashie (Ghana)
Light	Ricky Kiernan (Glasgow)	win pts 6	John Bacon (Middlesbrough)
Welter	Jim McGuinness (Wishaw) (Scottish Welterweight Title)	win pts 12	Tommy McGuinness (Edinburgh)

28/04/1960	Leith Eldorado		Promoters – Peter Keenan and Harry Black
Fly	Jackie Brown (Edinburgh)	win ko 7	Billy Walker (Kings Cross)
Feather	John Smillie (Fauldhouse)	win pts 8	Moses Edeki (Nigeria)
Light	Jimmy Gibson (Dunfermline) (Scottish Lightweight Title Eliminator)	win pts 8	Johnny McLaren (Coatbridge)
Light	Ricky Kiernan (Glasgow)	lost rsf 2	Tony Barry (Birkenhead)
Middle	Andy Barry (Glasgow)	win rsf 2	Tommy Cavan (Glasgow)

19/05/1960	Irvine Meadow Ground		Promoter – Pat Hughes
Fly	John McGeough (Glasgow)	win pts 6	Jim Cresswell (Glasgow)
Fly	George McDade (Glasgow)	win pts 6	Barry Adgie (Derby)
Bantam	Alex Ambrose (Glasgow)	win pts 8	John Agwu (Nigeria)
Feather	John Smillie (Fauldhouse)	win pts 6	Moses Edeki (Nigeria)
Light	Jimmy Gibson (Dunfermline)	win pts 6	Pat Aaron (Nigeria)
Middle	Andy Barry (Glasgow)	win rsf 2	Tommy Cavan (Glasgow)

27/05/1960	Dumfries Drill Hall		Promoter – George Brown
Feather	George Judge (Glasgow)	win pts 8	Tommy Tiger (Leicester)
Light	John Bacon (Middlesbrough)	win ko 1	Harry Shaw (St Helens)
Middle	Andy Barry (Glasgow)	win ko 1	Billy Johnston (Ulverstone)
Middle	Tommy Cavan (Glasgow)	win pts 6	Jimmy Lawson (Middlesbrough)

02/06/1960	Coatbridge Greyhound Stadium		Promoter – Ernie Rea
Feather	John Smillie (Fauldhouse)	win rsf 7	George Judge (Glasgow)
Light	Bobby Kane (Greenock)	win pts 8	Jim McCormack (Belfast)
Light	Johnny McLaren (Coatbridge)	win rsf 4	Ricky Kiernan (Glasgow)
Welter	Tony Barry (Birkinhead)	win rsf 6	Ron Jackson (Newcastle)

09/06/1960	Firhill Stadium		Promoter – Peter Keenan
Fly	Jackie Brown (Edinburgh)	win pts 10	Mario D'Agata (Italy)
Bantam	Alex Ambrose (Glasgow)	win pts 8	Eddie O'Connor (Dublin)
Bantam	John McGeough (Glasgow)	win pts 6	John Agwu (Nigeria)
Light	Jimmy Gibson (Dunfermline)	win pts 8	Johnny McLaren (Coatbridge)
Middle	Andy Barry (Glasgow)	win pts 6	Vernon Pallai (Ghana)
Light Heavy	Chic Calderwood (Craigneuk)	win rsf 12	Johnny Halafihi (Tonga)
	(Vacant British Empire Light Heavyweight Title)		

10/08/1960	Paisley Ice Rink		Promoter –Peter Keenan
Bantam	Jackie Brown (Edinburgh)	win pts 8	John Morrissey (Newarthill)
Bantam	John McGeough (Glasgow)	win ret 2	Jim Cresswell (Glasgow)
Light	Jim Jordan (Belfast)	win pts 6	Sammy Etioloja (Ghana)
Middle	John McCormack (Glasgow)	win rsf 9	George Aldridge (Market Harborough)
Middle	Andy Barry (Glasgow)	win pts 6	Laurie Homer (Croydon)
Light Heavy	Chic Calderwood (Craigneuk)	win rsf 8	Joey Armstrong (Ghana)

16/09/1960	Kelvin Hall		Promoter – Peter Keenan
Bantam	Billy Rafferty (Glasgow)	win ko 4	Angelo Priami (Italy)
Bantam	George McDade (Glasgow)	lost pts 8	Eddie Barraclough (Rotherham)
Bantam	Danny McNamee (Dundee)	win rsf 2	John McGeough (Glasgow)
Middle	Andy Barry (Glasgow)	win pts 6	Tommy Colcliff (London)
Light Heavy	Alf Barker (Dunfermline)	win ko 2	Bill Bruce (Banff)
Light Heavy	Chic Calderwood (Craigneuk)	win pts 10	Willie Pastrano (USA)

02/11/1960	Paisley Ice Rink		Promoter – Peter Keenan
Feather	Tommy McMillan (Glasgow)	lost rsf 1	Andy Hickson (Bury)
Light	Jimmy Gibson (Dunfermline)	win pts 12	Alex McMillan (Glasgow)
	(Scottish Lightweight Title)		
Middle	John McCormack (Glasgow)	win pts 10	George Benton (USA)
Light Heavy	Chic Calderwood (Craigneuk)	win rsf 4	Rolf Peters (Germany)

1961

22/02/1961	Paisley Ice Rink		Promoter – Peter Keenan
Bantam	Danny Lee (Port Glasgow)	win rsf 5	Pat McCormick (Tipperary)
Light	Owen Reilly (Glasgow)	win pts 6	George Hand (Edinburgh)
Light	Jimmy Gibson (Dunfermline)	lost pts 8	Johnny Cooke (Liverpool)
Welter	Willie Fisher (Craigneuk)	win rsf 5	Andy Barry (Glasgow)
Middle	John McCormack (Glasgow)	win pts 12	Phil Edwards (Cardiff)
	(British Middleweight Title Final Eliminator)		
Light Heavy	Alf Barker (Dunfermline)	lost rsf 7	Gerry McNally (Liverpool)

05/04/1961	Hamilton Town Hall		Promoter – Tommy McGuinness
Bantam	John Morrissey (Newarthill)	win rsf 5	Tommy Burgoyne (Plean)
Light	Jimmy Gibson (Dunfermline)	win rsf 2	Jim Jordan (Belfast)
Light	Owen Reilly (Glasgow)	win pts 8	Billy Skelly (Belfast)
Light	Ricky Kiernan (Glasgow)	lost rsf 5	Sammy McSpadden (Fulham)
Middle	Willie Fisher (Craigneuk)	win pts 6	Maurice Loughran (Belfast)

12/04/1961	Paisley Ice Rink		Promoter – Peter Keenan
Bantam	Jackie Brown (Edinburgh)	lost ko 4	Freddie Gilroy (Belfast)
Bantam	Danny Lee (Port Glasgow)	win pts 6	Gerry Jones (Wigan)
Feather	Johnny Kidd (Aberdeen)	lost pts 8	Derry Treanor (Glasgow)
Feather	George Judge (Glasgow)	lost pts 8	Roy Jacobs (Nigeria)
Feather	Owen Reilly (Glasgow)	win pts 6	Ollie Wylie (Aberdeen)
Welter	Willie Fisher (Craigneuk)	win ret 3	Ken Chadwick (Bournemouth)

02/05/1961	Kelvin Arena		Promoter – Johnny Kelly
Fly	Johnny Mallon (Glasgow)	win rsf 1	Christy Kelly (Limerick)
Feather	Derry Treanor (Glasgow)	win pts 8	Jean Renard (Belgium)
Light	Jimmy Gibson (Dunfermline)	win ko 3	John Bacon (Middlesbrough)
Light	Ricky Kiernan (Glasgow)	win pts 6	Johnny McLaren (Coatbridge)
Middle	Andy Barry (Glasgow)	win rsf 1	Con Morrisey (Liverpool)

10/05/1961	Kelvin Hall		Promoter - Peter Keenan
Bantam	Danny Lee (Port Glasgow)	win rsf 4	Dave Johnson (Belfast)
Feather	George Judge (Glasgow)	win ko 1	Pat Kelly (Belfast)
Feather	Tommy McMillan (Glasgow)	win rsf 1	Bobby Elliott (Belfast)
Light	Johnny Cooke (Bootle)	win pts 8	Roy Jacobs (Nigeria)
Light	Alex McMillan (Glasgow)	win pts 6	George Hand (Edinburgh)
Middle	John McCormack (Glasgow)	win pts 10	Michel Diouf (France)

24/05/1961	Kelvin Arena		Promoter – Johnny Kelly
Fly	George McDade (Glasgow)	drew 8	Don Braithwaite (Caerphilly)
Bantam	Alex Ambrose (Glasgow)	win rsf 7	Hugh Riley (Edinburgh)
Light	Jimmy Gibson (Dunfermline)	win rsf 5	Jim McCormack (Belfast)
Heavy	Jim Cooper (Bellingham)	win pts 8	Jack Whittaker (Warwick)

09/08/1961	Kelvin Hall		Promoter – Peter Keenan
Fly	Walter McGowan (Hamilton)	win ret 3	George McDade (Glasgow)
Fly	Danny Lee (Port Glasgow)	win ko 3	Pancho Bhatachazi (India)
Feather	Jackie Brown (Edinburgh)	win pts 6	Ollie Wylie (Aberdeen)
Feather	George Hand (Edinburgh)	win rsf 3	Kofie Manu (Ghana)
Middle	Willie Fisher (Craigneuk)	win rsf 6	Bob Roberts (Ghana)
Heavy	Chic Calderwood (Craigneuk)	drew 10	Jim Cooper (Bellingham)

22/09/1961	Hamilton Town Hall		Promoter – Peter Keenan
Fly	Walter McGowan (Hamilton)	win pts 8	Eddie Barraclough (Rotherham)
Fly	Danny Lee (Port Glasgow)	win pts 8	Danny Wells (Basildon)
Feather	Bobby Fisher (Craigneuk)	win rsf 1	George Hand (Edinburgh)
Welter	Ian McKenzie (Ayr)	win ret 3	Mick McAdam (Coatbridge)
Middle	Willie Fisher (Craigneuk)	win pts 8	Andy Barry (Glasgow)

25/10/1961	Paisley Ice Rink		Promoter – Peter Keenan
Fly	Jackie Brown (Edinburgh)	win pts 8	Walter McGowan (Hamilton)
Fly	Johnny Mallon (Glasgow)	win pts 6	Eddie Barraclough (Rotherham)
Feather	George Judge (Glasgow)	win pts 8	Bobby Fisher (Craigneuk)
Light	Mick McAdam (Coatbridge)	win rsf 4	Frank McGuinness (Wishaw)
Welter	Ian McKenzie (Ayr)	win pts 6	Eddie McDonnell (Leeds)
Middle	Willie Fisher (Craigneuk)	win pts 8	Malcolm Worthington (Crewe)

29/11/1961	Glasgow Central Hotel		Promoter – Jerry Lever
Feather	Bobby Fisher (Craigneuk)	win ko 2	George Judge (Glasgow)
Middle	Willie Fisher (Craigneuk)	win rsf 6	Ivor Evans (Bournemouth)
Middle	Willie Hart (Glasgow)	win pts 6	Tommy Bolton (Manchester)
Middle	Bernard Rea (Coatbridge)	win ko 3	Roland Mitchell (Coventry)

16/12/1961	Kelvin Arena		Promoter – Peter Keenan
Fly	Walter McGowan (Hamilton)	win pts 8	Brian Bissmire (West Ham)
Bantam	Danny Lee (Port Glasgow)	drew 8	Tommy Burgoyne (Plean)
Welter	Ian McKenzie (Ayr)	win pts 6	Maurice Nichols (Castleford)
Middle	Willie Hart (Glasgow)	win rsf 4	Alan Kaihau (Tonga)
Middle	Bernard Rea (Coatbridge)	win pts 6	Tommy Colcliff (London)

1962

27/02/1962	Govan Town Hall		Promoter – Peter Keenan
Feather	John Morrissey (Newarthill)	win rsf 2	Bobby Fisher (Craigneuk)
Light	George Hand (Edinburgh)	win pts 6	Ricky Kiernan (Glasgow)
Welter	Mick Kane (Glasgow)	win pts 6	Mick McAdam (Coatbridge)
Welter	Ian McKenzie (Ayr)	win pts 6	Joe Sharpe (Belfast)
Middle	Andy Barry (Glasgow)	lost pts 6	Maurice Loughran (Belfast)

26/04/1962	Hamilton Town Hall		Promoter – Peter Keenan
Bantam	Alex Ambrose (Glasgow)	win pts 8	Tommy Burgoyne (Plean)
Light	Sammy McSpadden (Fulham)	win pts 8	Manuel Sosa (France)
Light	Joe Woodhouse (Glasgow)	won ko 3	Dennis Bonsor (Derby)
Welter	Mick Kane (Glasgow)	win pts 6	Fitzroy Lindo (Jamaica)
Welter	Ian McKenzie (Ayr)	lost ko 5	Steve Gibson (South Africa)

14/06/1962	Kelvin Hall		Promoter – Peter Keenan	

Fly	Walter McGowan (Hamilton)	win pts 8	Danny Lee (Port Glasgow)
Bantam	Tommy Burgoyne (Plean)	win pts 8	Danny Wells (Basildon)
Feather	Bobby Fisher (Craigneuk)	win ret 4	George Judge (Glasgow)
Feather	Joe Woodhouse (Glasgow)	win pts 6	Bobby Elliott (Belfast)
Welter	Ian McKenzie (Ayr)	win rsf 4	Teddy Gardner (Croydon)
Middle	John McCormack (Glasgow)	win pts 8	Henry Hank (USA)

13/09/1962	Kelvin Hall`		Promoter – Peter Keenan	

Bantam	Alex Ambrose (Glasgow)	win pts 8	Tommy Burgoyne (Plean)
Feather	Bobby Fisher (Craigneuk)	win ret 5	Kid Irapuato (Mexico)
Welter	Derek Cowper (Glasgow)	win rsf 4	Teddy Gardner (Croydon)
Middle	John McCormack (Glasgow)	win pts 10	Ike White (USA)
Middle	Willie Fisher (Craigneuk)	win pts 8	Orlando Paso (Nigeria)
Middle	Willie Hart (Glasgow)	win pts 6	Panther Cyril (Nigeria)

20/09/1962	Kelvin Hall		Promoter – Jack Solomons	

Fly	Walter McGowan (Hamilton)	win ko 6	Jacques Jacob (France)
Fly	Johnny Mallon (Glasgow)	lost rsf 7	Alex O'Neill (Belfast)
Bantam	Lewie Mackay (Edinburgh)	drew 8	Don Weller (London)
Feather	John Morrissey (Newarthill)	win pts 10	Gene Fossmire (USA)
Light	Sammy McSpadden (Fulham)	win pts 8	Boswell St Louis (Trinidad)
Welter	Ian McKenzie (Ayr)	win ko 2	Charlie Brady (Belfast)

14/11/1962	Kelvin Hall		Promoter – Jack Solomons	

Fly	Walter McGowan (Hamilton)	win rsf 6	Ray Jutras (USA)
Bantam	Tommy Burgoyne (Plean) (Vacant Scottish Bantamweight Title)	win rsf 8	Lewie Mackay (Edinburgh)
Feather	John Morrissey (Newarthill)	win pts 10	Pablo Acevedo (USA)
Welter	Ian McKenzie (Ayr)	win rsf 7	Sugar Gibiliru (Ghana)
Welter	Bob Keddie (Glasgow)	win pts 6	Panther Cyril (Nigeria)
Middle	Willie Fisher (Craigneuk)	win dis 5	Ron Vale (Leamington)

1963

31/01/1963	Kelvin Hall		Promoter – Jack Solomons	

Bantam	Walter McGowan (Hamilton)	win pts 8	Bernard Jubert (France)
Bantam	Johnny Mallon (Glasgow)	win pts 8	Eddie Barraclough (Rotherham)
Feather	John Morrissey (Newarthill) (British Featherweight Title)	lost rsf 11	Howard Winstone (Wales)
Welter	Bob Keddie (Glasgow)	win rsf 5	Teddy Gardner (Croydon)
Welter	Norrie McCulloch (Kilmarnock)	win pts 6	Panther Cyril (Nigeria)
Middle	Ian McKenzie (Ayr)	win ret 4	Clem Winchester (London)

28/02/1963	Kelvin Arena		Promoter – Peter Keenan
Feather	John O'Brien (Glasgow)	win rsf 5	Con Mount Bassie (Jamaica)
Feather	John McDermott (Cambuslang)	win pts 6	Neil Hawcroft (Manchester)
Feather	Bobby Fisher (Craigneuk)	lost ko 10	Billy Calvert (Sheffield)
	(British Featherweight Title Final Eliminator)		
Light	Ricky Kiernan (Glasgow)	lost rsf 4	Al Keen (London)
Welter	Norrie McCulloch (Kilmarnock)	win pts 6	Derek Cowper (Glasgow)
Welter	Jimmy Gibson (Dunfermline)	lost pts 8	Nat Jacobs (Manchester)

21/03/1963	Kelvin Hall		Promoter – Jack Solomons
Feather	George Hand (Edinburgh)	drew 6	Brian Smith (Belfast)
Light	Floyd Robertson (Ghana)	win pts 10	Dave Parsons (London)
Light	John Morrissey (Newarthill)	drew 10	Dennis Adjei (Ghana)
Welter	Norrie McCulloch (Kilmarnock)	win rsf 1	Mike Fleetham (Doncaster)
Welter	Panther Cyril (Nigeria)	win rsf 1	Eddie McDonnell (Leeds)
Light Heavy	Chic Calderwood (Craigneuk)	win pts 10	Tommy Fields (USA)

02/05/1963	Paisley Ice Rink		Promoter – Peter Keenan
Fly	Walter McGowan (Hamilton)	win ko 12	Jackie Brown (Edinburgh)
	(British and Empire Flyweight Titles)		
Feather	Bobby Fisher (Craigneuk)	win rsf 4	Peter Lavery (Belfast)
Feather	John McDermott (Cambuslang)	win rsf 6	Eddie Shaw (Belfast)
Light	Preston McFarlane (Falkirk)	win ko 1	Bobby Elliott (Belfast)
Light	Al Keen (London)	win pts 8	Tommy Atkins (Nigeria)
Welter	Norrie McCulloch (Ayr)	win pts 6	Steve Ako (Liverpool)

30/05/1963	Kelvin Hall		Promoter – Peter Keenan
Fly	John McAllister (Motherwell)	lost ko 4	Ron Elliott (London)
Feather	John McDermott (Cambuslang)	win dis 2	Ray Thompson (London)
Light	Johnny Kidd (Aberdeen)	win ko 2	Dele Majeke (Nigeria)
Welter	Norrie McCulloch (Kilmarnock)	win rsf 2	Mick Kane (Glasgow)
Middle	Ian McKenzie (Ayr)	win pts 10	Willie Hart (Glasgow)
	(Scottish Middleweight Title)		
Light Heavy	Chic Calderwood (Craigneuk)	win pts 10	Von Clay (USA)

27/06/1963	Paisley Ice Rink		Promoter – Peter Keenan
Fly	Walter McGowan (Hamilton)	win rsf 9	Ray Perez (Honolulu)
Light	Preston McFarlane (Falkirk)	win rsf 3	Francis Ibe (Nigeria)
Middle	Don McMillan (Glasgow)	win pts 6	Harry Wheeler (London)
Middle	Willie Hart (Glasgow)	win pts 6	Joe Somerville (Berkhamstead)
Middle	Ian McKenzie (Ayr)	lost rsf 2	Panther Cyril (Nigeria)
Light Heavy	Chic Calderwood (Craigneuk)	lost pts 10	Eddie Cotton (USA)

12/09/1963	Paisley Ice Rink	Promoter – Peter Keenan	
Fly	Walter McGowan (Hamilton) (British Empire Flyweight Title)	win rsf 9	Kid Solomon (Jamaica)
Feather	John O'Brien (Glasgow)	win rsf 2	Bobby Fisher (Craigneuk)
Welter	Andy Wyper (Newmilns)	win rsf 1	Vince Brown (Cardiff)
Welter	Norrie McCulloch (Kilmarnock)	win pts 6	Adam Robertson (Greenock)
Welter	Don McMillan (Glasgow)	win pts 6	Peter McBeth (Burnbank)
Middle	Ian McKenzie (Ayr)	lost rsf 8	Panther Cyril (Nigeria)
28/11/1963	Paisley Ice Rink	Promoter – Peter Keenan	
Fly	Walter McGowan (Hamilton)	win pts 10	Rick Magrano (Phillipines)
Bantam	Jackie Brown (Edinburgh)	win pts 8	Kid Solomon (Jamaica)
Bantam	Evan Armstrong (Ayr)	win ko 1	Candido Sawyer (Nigeria)
Bantam	Sam McIlvenna (Glasgow)	win pts 4	Henry Hoey (Airdrie)
Welter	Andy Wyper (Newmilns)	win ko 5	Don McMillan (Glasgow)
Welter	Peter McBeth (Burnbank)	win pts 6	Patrick Onwuna (Nigeria)
Middle	Willie Fisher (Craigneuk)	win pts6	Ian McKenzie (Ayr)

1964

21/01/1964	Govan Town Hall	Promoter – Peter Keenan	
Bantam	Sam McIlvenna (Glasgow)	win pts 8	Simon Tiger (Nigeria)
Feather	Evan Armstrong (Ayr)	win pts 8	Dele Majeke (Nigeria)
Light	Ricky Kiernan (Glasgow)	lost pts 8	Francis Ibe (Nigeria)
Welter	Andy Wyper (Newmilns) (Vacant Scottish Welterweight Title)	win rsf 7	Don McMillan (Glasgow)
Light Heavy	John McCormack (Glasgow)	win rsf 1	Joe Louis (Nigeria)
19/02/1964	Hamilton Town Hall	Promoter – Mike Geraghty	
Bantam	Henry Hoey (Airdrie)	win pts 8	Sam McIlvenna (Glasgow)
Feather	Jim Jones (Plean)	win pts 6	Billy Graham (Belfast)
Feather	John Morrissey (Newarthill)	win pts 8	Brian Smyth (Belfast)
Light	Ricky Kiernan (Glasgow)	lost pts 8	Preston McFarlane (Falkirk)
Welter	Norrie McCulloch (Kilmarnock)	win rsf 1	Charlie Brady (Belfast)
Welter	Adam Robertson (Greenock)	win rsf 2	Bobby Griffin (Belfast)
04/03/1964	Paisley Ice Rink	Promoter – Peter Keenan	
Bantam	Walter McGowan (Hamilton)	win pts 10	Risto Luukkonen (Finland)
Bantam	Sam McIlvenna (Glasgow)	win pts 8	Tommy Connor (Glasgow)
Welter	Andy Wyper (Newmilns)	win rsf 4	George Palin (Birkenhead)
Welter	Norrie McCulloch (Kilmarnock)	win pts 8	Fitzroy Lindo (Jamaica)
Light Heavy	John McCormack (Glasgow)	win ko 1	Malcolm Worthington (Crewe)
28/05/1964	Kelvin Hall	Promoter – Peter Keenan	
Feather	Evan Armstrong (Ayr)	win pts 8	Con Mount Bassie (Jamaica)
Welter	Andy Wyper (Newmilns)	win ko 5	Jackie Powell (Preston)
Welter	Don McMillan (Glasgow)	win pts 8	Fitzroy Lindo (Jamaica)
Light Heavy	Terry Downes (Paddington)	win pts 10	Eddie Zaremba (USA)
Light Heavy	Chic Calderwood (Craigneuk)	win ret 6	Alan Harmon (Jamaica)

03/09/1964	Paisley Ice Rink	Promoter – Peter Keenan	
Fly	Walter McGowan (Hamilton)	win pts 10	Natalio Jiminez (Dominican Republic)
Feather	Bobby Fisher (Craigneuk)	win rsf 6	Evan Armstrong (Ayr)
Welter	Andy Wyper (Newmilns)	win pts 8	Bob Sempey (Belfast)
Welter	Don McMillan (Glasgow)	win rsf 8	Jackie Powell (Preston)
Middle	Ian McKenzie (Ayr)	lost rsf 1	Milo Calhoun (USA)
Middle	Mick Leahy (Coventry)	win pts 10	Sugar Ray Robinson (USA)
11/11/1964	Paisley Ice Rink	Promoter – Peter Keenan	
Bantam	Jackie Brown (Edinburgh)	drew 10	John Caldwell (Belfast)
Feather	Bobby Fisher (Craigneuk)	lost rsf 1	Joe Rafiu King (Nigeria)
Welter	Don McMillan (Glasgow)	win pts 8	Bob Sempey (Belfast)
Welter	John McMillan (Glasgow)	lost pts 8	Francis Ibe (Nigeria)
Light Heavy	Chic Calderwood (Craigneuk) (British Light Heavyweight Title)	win rsf 7	Bob Nicholson (Farnborough)

1965

04/02/1965	Kelvin Hall	Promoter – Peter Keenan	
Fly	Danny Lee (Port Glasgow)	win pts 8	Sam McIlvenna (Glasgow)
Bantam	Jackie Brown (Edinburgh)	win rsf 6	Baby John (Rhodesia)
Feather	John O' Brien (Glasgow)	lost rsf 5	Joe Rafiu King (Nigeria)
Feather	Evan Armstrong (Ayr)	win rsf 6	Tommy Burgoyne (Plean)
Welter	Don McMillan (Glasgow)	win pts 8	Ivan Whiter (Tooting)
Welter	John McMillan (Glasgow)	lost dis 1	Lex Hunter (Antigua)
29/04/1965	Govan Town Hall	Promoter – Peter Keenan	
Bantam	Jackie Brown (Edinburgh)	win rsf 6	Ramon Casal (Spain)
Bantam	Tommy Connor (Glasgow)	win pts 6	Sam McIlvenna (Glasgow)
Welter	Andy Wyper (Newmilns)	win pts 8	Don McMillan (Glasgow)
Light Heavy	John McCormack (Glasgow)	win rsf 6	Bernard Quellier (France)
10/06/1965	Paisley Ice Rink	Promoter – Peter Keenan	
Bantam	Jackie Brown (Edinburgh)	lost ko 2	Ronnie Jones (USA)
Bantam	Tommy Connor (Glasgow)	win pts 6	Tommy Burgoyne (Plean)
Feather	Evan Armstrong (Ayr)	win pts 8	Johnny Adabesi (Nigeria)
Welter	Don McMillan (Glasgow)	win pts 8	Ernest Musso (Rhodesia)
Middle	Willie Fisher (Craigneuk)	win pts 8	Len Gibbs (Jamaica)
Light Heavy	John McCormack (Glasgow)	win rsf 2	Chic Calderwood (Craigneuk)
20/08/1065	Paisley Ice Rink	Promoter – Peter Keenan	
Bantam	Walter McGowan (Hamilton)	lost rsf 6	Ronnie Jones (USA)
Feather	Evan Armstrong (Ayr)	win ko 7	Johnny Adabesi (Nigeria)
Welter	Bob Keddie (Glasgow)	lost ko 5	George Onwuma (Nigeria)
Welter	Rory O'Shea (USA)	win pts 8	Tommy Saibu (Nigeria)
Middle	Willie Hart (Glasgow)	win ko 8	Ian McKenzie (Ayr)

1966

04/04/1966	Central Hotel, Glasgow	Promoter – Peter Keenan	
Bantam	John McCluskey (Hamilton)	win pts 8	Tommy Connor (Glasgow)
Bantam	George Hind (Glasgow)	win rsf 4	Sam McIlvenna (Glasgow)
Feather	Evan Armstrong (Ayr)	win rsf 3	Tei Dovie (Ghana)
Welter	Andy Wyper (Newmilns)	win rsf 2	Darkie Smith (London)

02/05/1966	Central Hotel, Glasgow	Promoter – Peter Keenan	
Bantam	George Hind (Glasgow)	win rsf 5	Malcolm Lowe (Sheffield)
Bantam	Tommy Connor (Glasgow)	lost pts 8	Winston Van Guylenberg (Ceylon)
Welter	Andy Wyper (Newmilns)	lost rsf 7	Don Davis (Jamaica)
Middle	Derek Cowper (Glasgow)	win pts 6	Dick Griffiths (Chesterfield)

06/06/1966	Central Hotel, Glasgow	Promoter – Peter Keenan	
Fly	John McCluskey (Hamilton)	win pts 10	Winston Van Guylenberg (Ceylon)
Light	John O'Neill (Glasgow)	win pts 4	Jim Whitecross (Edinburgh)
Welter	Don McMillan (Glasgow)	win pts 10	Don Davis (Jamaica)

01/08/1966	Govan Town Hall	Promoter – Peter Keenan	
Fly	George Hind (Glasgow)	win pts 6	Baby John (Rhodesia)
Bantam	Evan Armstrong (Ayr)	win rsf 2	OyeTurpin (Nigeria)
Bantam	Tommy Connor (Glasgow)	win pts 6	Simon Tiger (Nigeria)
Middle	Willie Connolly (Glasgow)	lost pts 6	Joe Somerville (Berkhamstead)

29/08/1966	Central Hotel, Glasgow	Promoter – Peter Keenan	
Fly	George Hind (Glasgow)	win rsf 5	Baby John (Rhodesia)
Bantam	Evan Armstrong (Ayr)	win rsf 2	Angel Chinea (Spain)
Middle	Derek Cowper (Glasgow)	win rsf 1	Joe Somerville (Berkhamstead)
Middle	Jackie Powe (Coatbridge)	win dis 5	Steve Richards (Bermondsey)

19/09/1966	Central Hotel, Glasgow	Promoter – Peter Keenan	
Bantam	Evan Armstrong (Ayr) (Scottish Bantamweight Title)	win ko 4	Jackie Brown (Edinburgh)
Light	John McMillan (Glasgow)	win rsf 3	Paddy Winters (Belfast)
Middle	Derek Cowper (Glasgow)	lost pts 6	Panther Cyril (Nigeria)
Middle	Jackie Powe (Coatbridge)	win pts 4	Jim Stewart (Preston)

10/10/1966	Central Hotel, Glasgow	Promoter – Peter Keenan	
Light	John O'Neill (Glasgow)	win rsf 1	Al Graham (Belfast)
Welter	Don McMillan (Glasgow)	win pts 8	Chris McAuley (Larne)
Middle	Derek Cowper (Glasgow)	win rsf 3	Hugh Gilhooley (Belfast)
Light Heavy	Willie Connolly (Glasgow)	lost pts 4	Paddy Dempsey (Swindon)

28/11/1966	Central Hotel, Glasgow		Promoter – Peter Keenan	

Bantam	George Hind (Glasgow)	win pts 6	Simon Tiger (Nigeria)
Feather	Evan Armstrong (Ayr)	win pts 8	Bobby Davies (West Ham)
Light	John O'Neill (Glasgow)	win ko 2	Denny Baker (Leicester)
Middle	Derek Cowper (Glasgow)	win pts 6	Larry Brown (Leicester)

1967

23/01/1967	Central Hotel, Glasgow		Promoter – Peter Keenan	

Bantam	George Hind (Glasgow)	win pts 6	Simon Tiger (Nigeria)
Bantam	Tommy Connor (Glasgow)	win dis 3	Tommy Burgoyne (Plean)
Light	Ken Buchanan (Edinburgh) (Scottish Lightweight Title)	win pts 10	John McMillan (Glasgow)
Middle	Jackie Powe (Coatbridge)	drew 6	Dervan Airey (West Indies)

20/02/1967	Central Hotel, Glasgow		Promoter – Peter Keenan	

Bantam	Tommy Burgoyne (Plean)	win rsf 5	George Hind (Glasgow)
Feather	Hugh Baxter (Glasgow)	lost pts 8	Brian Cartwright (Birmingham)
Welter	James Stewart (Coatbridge)	win pts 6	George Onwuma (Nigeria)
Middle	Willie Fisher (Craigneuk)	win pts 6	Louis Onwuna (Nigeria)

20/03/1967	Central Hotel, Glasgow		Promoter – Peter Keenan	

Welter	John McMillan (Glasgow)	lost pts 8	Winston Laud (St. Ives)
Middle	Don McMillan (Glasgow)	win pts 8	Mickey Laud (St. Ives)
Middle	Derek Cowper (Glasgow)	win pts 6	Joe Somerville (Berkhamstead)
Heavy	Alex Kelly (Glasgow)	win pts 6	Barry Rodney (Jamaica)

24/04/1967	Central Hotel, Glasgow		Promoter – Peter Keenan	

Bantam	George Hind (Glasgow)	win pts 6	Tommy Burgoyne (Plean)
Bantam	Tommy Connor (Glasgow)	win pts 6	Henry Hoey (Airdrie)
Middle	Derek Cowper (Glasgow) (Scottish Middleweight Title Final Eliminator)	win dis 4	Willie Fisher (Craigneuk)

11/05/1967	Paisley Ice Rink		Promoter – Peter Keenan	

Fly	John McCluskey (Hamilton)	lost pts 10	Fernando Atzori (Italy)
Bantam	Evan Armstrong (Ayr) (British Bantamweight Title Final Eliminator)	win rsf 5	Jim McCann (Belfast)
Feather	John McDermott (Cambuslang)	win pts 8	Tommy Connor (Glasgow)
Light	Ken Buchanan (Edinburgh)	win rsf 3	Franco Brondi (Italy)

30/05/1967	Central Hotel, Glasgow		Promoter – Peter Keenan	

Bantam	Tommy Connor (Glasgow)	dnc 4	Tommy Burgoyne (Plean)
Middle	Derek Cowper (Glasgow)	win rsf 3	Johnny Coombes (Cardiff)
Middle	Willie Fisher (Craigneuk)	win ko 4	Willie Connolly (Glasgow)

1968

30/10/1968	Hamilton Town Hall	Promoter – Sammy Docherty	
Feather	John O'Brien (Glasgow)	win rsf 3	Ray Opoku (Guyana)
Feather	Joe Murphy (Glasgow)	win rsf 2	Brian Smyth (Belfast)
Jnr Light	Bobby Fisher (Craigneuk)	win pts 8	Sean McCafferty (Belfast)
Light	Jim Watt (Glasgow)	win ko 4	Santos Martins (Guyana)
Heavy	Terry Feeley (Glasgow)	win rsf 4	Obe Hepburn (Jamaica)
11/12/1968	Hamilton Town Hall	Promoter – Sammy Docherty	
Bantam	John Kellie (Dundee)	win pts 6	John Mitchell (Kirkcaldy)
Feather	Bobby Fisher (Craigneuk)	win pts 8	Jimmy Bell (Ayrshire)
Feather	Hugh Baxter (Glasgow)	lost pts 8	Gerry McBride (Manchester)
Light	Ken Buchanan (Edinburgh)	win rsf 3	Ameur Lamine (Tunisia)
Light	Jim Watt (Glasgow)	win rsf 2	Alex Gibson (Belfast)

1969

10/04/1969	Govan Town Hall	Promoter – John Ness	
Bantam	Al Hutcheon (Glasgow)	win rsf 4	Bernard Nicholls (Manchester)
Jnr Light	Tommy Glencross (Glasgow)	win rsf 5	Billy Surgenor (Belfast)
Light	Jim Watt (Glasgow)	win pts 8	Victor Paul (Nigeria)
Middle	Dave McCooke (Belfast)	lost rsf 4	Panther Cyril (Nigeria)
Middle	Hugh Gilhooley (Belfast)	win rsf 5	Alison Chico (Liverpool)

Appendix 2

Boxer Records

Alex Ambrose
Flyweight/ Bantamweight
Born 22/04/1936

12/09/1957	Falkirk	win pts 6	Jim Loughrey (Belfast)
25/09/1957	Paisley	win rsf 5	Jim Loughrey (Belfast)
13/11/1957	Greenock	win ko 1	Harry Hunter (Belfast)
18/11/1957	Derby	lost pts 8	Jerry Parker (Nottingham)
02/12/1957	Doncaster	win pts 6	Eddie Barraclough (Rotherham)
28/12/1957	Belfast	win pts 8	Tommy Armour (Belfast)
26/02/1958	Paisley	win pts 8	Mick Barone (Brixton)
20/03/1958	Hull	lost ret 2	Pancho Bhatachaji (India)
02/04/1958	Paisley	win ret 6	Len Reece (Cardiff)
28/05/1958	Hamilton	win ret 4	Tommy Armour (Belfast)
02/07/1958	Glasgow (Scottish Flyweight Title)	win pts 12	George McDade (Glasgow)
25/07/1958	Aberdeen	win pts 8	Eddie O'Connor (Dublin)
28/08/1958	Paisley	win pts 8	Pat Glancy (Glasgow)
25/11/1958	Leith	win pts 8	Eddie Barraclough (Rotherham)
05/02/1959	Glasgow (British Flyweight Title)	lost pts 15	Frankie Jones (Plean)
25/02/1959	Glasgow (Scottish Flyweight Title)	drew 12	George McDade (Glasgow)
18/03/1959	Paisley	lost rsf 8	Derel Lloyd (Chingford)
07/05/1959	Paisley	win pts 8	Pancho Bhatachaji (India)
28/05/1959	Glasgow	lost dis 4	Pat Glancy (Glasgow)
28/08/1959	Greenock	win rsf 2	Billy Skelly (Belfast)
10/09/1959	Paisley (Scottish Flyweight Title)	lost ret 10	Jackie Brown (Edinburgh)
11/11/1959	Dundee	win rsf 3	Danny McNamee (Dundee)
08/12/1959	Leeds	win pts 8	Eddie O'Connor (Dublin)
28/01/1960	Paisley	win rsf 6	Len Reece (Cardiff)
23/02/1960	Wembley	lost ret 3	Roy Beaman (Brixton)
01/05/1960	Cagliari	lost pts 10	Piero Rollo (Italy)
19/05/1960	Irvine	win pts 8	John Agwu (Nigeria)
09/06/1960	Glasgow	win pts 8	Eddie O'Connor (Dublin)
17/04/1961	London	win pts 8	Don Weller (Battersea)
15/05/1961	London	win pts 8	Don Cosheril (Alderney)
24/05/1961	Glasgow	win rsf 7	Hugh Riley (Edinburgh)
29/01/1962	Cardiff	win pts 10	Michel Lamora (France)
03/03/1962	Stockholm	lost pts 8	Risto Luukkonen (Finland)
26/04/1962	Hamilton	win pts 8	Tommy Burgoyne (Plean)
27/06/1962	Wolverhampton	lost pts 8	Brian Cartwright (Birmingham)
13/09/1962	Glasgow	win pts 8	Tommy Burgoyne (Plean)
18/09/1962	London	drew 8	Bobby Davies (West Ham)
23/10/1962	London	lost pts 8	Bobby Davies (West Ham)
05/11/1962	London	lost pts 8	Brian Bissmire (West Ham)
21/03/1963	Paris	lost pts 10	Felix Brami (Tunisia)

40 contests, won 25, drew 2, lost 13.

Evan Armstrong (Ayr/Tarbolton)
Bantamweight/ Featherweight
Born 15/02/1943

28/11/1963	Paisley	win ko 1	Candido Sawyer (Nigeria)
21/01/1964	Govan	win pts 8	Dele Majeke (Ghana)
11/02/1964	London	win ko 3	Dele Majeke (Ghana)
24/02/1964	Manchester	win rsf 3	Billy Williams (Cannock)
09/03/1964	Manchester	win rsf 5	Mick Carney (Wakefield)
12/05/1964	Wembley	win ko 4	Mick Greaves (Leicester)
28/05/1964	Glasgow	win pts 8	Con Mount Basie (Jamaica)
03/09/1964	Paisley	lost rsf 6	Bobby Fisher (Craigneuk)
27/10/1964	Wembley	win pts 8	Ali Juma (Kenya)
16/11/1964	London	lost pts 8	Brian Cartwright (Birmingham)
04/02/1965	Glasgow	win rsf 6	Tommy Burgoyne (Denny)
22/03/1965	London	win pts 8	Peter Lavery (Belfast)
10/06/1965	Paisley	win pts 8	Johnny Adebisi (Nigeria)
12/07/1965	London	lost pts 6	Tony Riley (Coventry)
20/08/1965	Paisley	win ko 7	Johnny Adebisi (Nigeria)
13/09/1965	London	win rsf 5	Tony Riley (Coventry)
01/11/1965	London	win rsf 3	George Bowes (Hesleden)
08/12/1965	London	win rsf 7	Johnny Mantle (Battersea)
17/01/1966	London	lost pts 8	Brian Cartwright (Birmingham)
04/04/1966	Glasgow	win rsf 3	Tei Dovie (Ghana)
28/06/1966	London	win rsf 8	Monty Laud (St. Ives)
01/08/1966	Govan	win rsf 2	Oye Turpin (Nigeria)
29/08/1966	Glasgow	win rsf 2	Angel Chinea (Spain)
19/09/1966	Glasgow	win ko 4	Jackie Brown (Edinburgh)
	(Scottish Bantamweight Title)		
17/10/1966	London	win ret 3	Orizu Obilaso (Nigeria)
28/11/1966	Glasgow	win pts 8	Bobby Davies (West Ham)
30/01/1967	London	win rsf 2	Benny Lee (Ghana)
11/05/1967	Paisley	win ret 5	Jim McCann (Belfast)
	(British Bantamweight Title Final Eliminator)		
23/10/1967	London	drew 8	Patrick Mambwe (Zambia)
23/01/1968	London	win rsf 6	Pornchai Poppraigam (Thailand)
05/03/1968	London	win rsf 2	Patrick Mambwe (Zambia)
11/03/1968	London	win rsf 7	Jose Bisbal (Spain)
31/03/1968	Mexico	lost pts 10	Jose Medel (Mexico)
28/08/1968	Inglewood	lost rsf 2	Jesus Castillo (Mexico)
12/11/1968	Wembley	lost rsf 4	Bob Allotey (Ghana)
24/02/1969	London	win pts 8	Billy Hardacre (Liverpool)
09/06/1969	Manchester	lost ret 11	Alan Rudkin (Liverpool)
	(British Bantamweight Title)		
08/12/1969	London	win ko 2	Reg Gullifer (Dagenham)

38 contests, won 29, drew 1, lost 8.

Bobby Boland (Dundee)
Bantamweight/ Featherweight
Born 04/04/1929

02/01/1950	Dundee	win pts 10	Norman Tennant (Dundee)
02/02/1950	Liverpool	win pts 10	Amleto Falcinelli (Italy)
15/02/1950	Dundee	win rsf 3	Roy Ball (Pontypool)
21/02/1950	London	win pts 10	Fernando Gagnon (Canada)
08/03/1950	Glasgow	lost pts 8	Maurice Sandeyron (France)
24/04/1950	Liverpool	drew 10	Alvaro Nuvoloni (Italy)
01/05/1950	London	win pts 8	Jimmy Webster (Canning Town)
14/06/1950	Dundee	win dis 5	Alvaro Nuvoloni (Italy)
30/06/1950	Manchester	lost pts 10	Black Pico (Cuba)
04/09/1950	Newcastle	lost dis 5	Tommy Proffitt (Droylesden)
(British Bantamweight Title Eliminator)			
10/10/1950	London	win pts 10	Danny O'Sullivan (Finsbury Park)
21/11/1950	London	lost rsf 3	Gaetan Annaloro (Tunisia)
27/12/1950	Paisley	win pts 8	Theo Medina (France)
03/04/1951	London	win pts 8	Ron Johnson (Bethnal Green)
09/05/1951	Glasgow	win pts 10	Gaetan Annaloro (Tunisia)
21/05/1951	Paris	lost dis 4	Maurice Sandeyron (France)
27/06/1951	Glasgow	lost rsf 12	Peter Keenan (Glasgow)
(British Bantamweight Title)			
01/09/1951	Johannesburg	lost ko 1	Vic Toweel (South Africa)
01/02/1952	Blackpool	lost pts 10	Denny Dawson (Sheffield)
11/02/1952	London	win pts 8	Hugh Mackie (British Giuana)
20/02/1952	Glasgow	lost dis 6	Benny Chocolate (Gold Coast)
07/03/1952	London	win pts 8	Reuben Carl (Ghana)
31/03/1952	London	win ko 8	Johnny Barclay (Ickenham)
17/04/1952	Liverpool	lost ko 5	Hogan Bassey (Nigeria)
11/07/1952	Madrid	lost ret 5	Luis Romero (Spain)
11/09/1952	Liverpool	lost pts 8	Manny Francis (Gold Coast)
27/10/1952	Derby	lost pts 8	Jackie Fairclough (Preston)
10/11/1952	London	win pts 8	Jimmy Cardew (Holloway)
15/12/1952	Manchester	lost rsf 5	Hogan Bassey (Nigeria)
17/04/1953	Rhyl	win pts 8	Hugh Mackie
18/05/1953	West Hartlepool	lost pts 8	Glyn Evans (Askern)
03/08/1953	Jersey	drew 8	Gene Caffrey (Glasgow)
25/08/1953	London	lost pts 8	Sammy Bonnici (Malta)
11/06/1954	Belfast	lost pts 8	John McNally (Belfast)
17/07/1954	Belfast	drew 8	Joe King (Belfast)
11/10/1954	Bristol	lost ko 1	Teddy Peckham (Bournemouth)
20/02/1956	London	win pts 8	Malcolm Ames (Croydon)
05/03/1956	Leicester	lost dis 4	Freddie Hicks (Bermondsey)

38 contests, won 16, drew 3, lost 19.

Chic Brogan (Clydebank)
Bantamweight/ Featherweight
Born 18/01/1932

15/11/1950	Paisley	win pts 4	Benny Lacey (Glasgow)
13/12/1950	Paisley	win pts 4	Mickey King (Belfast)
10/01/1951	Belfast	lost pts 6	Pat Marley (Belfast)
20/01/1951	Glasgow	lost dis 3	Pat Dunlop (Belfast)
07/02/1951	Belfast	lost dis 2	Billy Skelly (Belfast)
10/03/1951	Glasgow	win ko 1	Joe Lancaster (Rochdale)
17/03/1951	Glasgow	win ko 6	John Kenny (Glasgow)
31/03/1951	Glasgow	win pts 6	John Kenny (Glasgow)
13/09/1951	Liverpool	win pts 6	Colin Clitheroe (Preston)
26/01/1952	Johannesburg	lost pts 4	Kalla Persson (South Africa)
05/04/1952	Glasgow	win ko 2	Johnny Bartles (Nottingham)
19/04/1952	Glasgow	win ko 2	Dickie Gunn (Dundee)
02/05/1952	Falkirk	win pts 6	Ron Perry (Stalybridge)
23/06/1952	West Hartlepool	lost rsf 6	Neville Tetlow (Manchester)
17/09/1952	Glasgow	win ko 3	Charlie Mannion (W Hartlepool)
15/10/1952	Paisley	lost ret 3	Manny Francis (Gold Coast)
28/01/1953	Belfast	lost pts 8	George O'Neill (Belfast)
25/09/1953	Manchester	lost pts 8	Manny Francis (Gold Coast)
25/02/1954	Liverpool	lost pts 8	Billy Ashcroft (Wigan)
02/03/1954	Dundee	win pts 8	Billy Taylor (Stirling)
23/03/1954	Edinburgh	win pts 10	Gene Caffrey (Glasgow)
	(Scottish Featherweight Title Eliminator)		
29/04/1954	Liverpool	lost ko 2	Percy James (Southport)
05/06/1954	Belfast	lost pts 8	Joe Quinn (Belfast)
09/08/1954	Carlisle	drew 8	Neville Tetlow (Manchester)
21/08/1954	Belfast	win pts 8	Jim Fisher (Belfast)
21/09/1954	Paisley	win ko 1	Sammy Fisher (Belfast)
07/12/1954	Paisley	lost pts 12	Charlie Hill (Cambuslang)
	(Scottish Featherweight Title)		
31/01/1955	Nottingham	lost pts 8	Ola Enoch (Nigeria)
24/02/1955	Liverpool	lost pts 8	Joe Quinn (Belfast)
08/03/1955	London	lost rsf 4	Pat McCoy (Galway)
02/05/1956	Glasgow	win rsf 7	Paul Dunne (Manchester)
20/06/1956	Glasgow	lost pts 12	Malcolm Grant (Glasgow)
	(Scottish Bantamweight Title)		
19/09/1956	Glasgow	win pts 12	Malcolm Grant (Glasgow)
	(Scottish Bantamweight Title)		
27/10/1956	Belfast	win ret 5	Ron Currie (Belfast)
12/03/1957	London	win pts 8	George Dormer (East Ham)
29/03/1957	Manchester	win pts 8	Rudy Edwards (Guyana)
15/08/1957	Glasgow	win rsf 4	Tanny Campo (Phillipines)
16/09/1957	Paris	lost ko 2	Alphonse Halimi (Algeria)
19/02/1958	Hamilton	win pts 12	Owen Reilly (Glasgow)
	(Vacant Scottish Featherweight Title)		
28/05/1958	Hamilton	win pts 8	John O'Brien (Glasgow)
02/07/1958	Glasgow	lost ret 11	Charlie Hill (Cambuslang)
	(British Featherweight Title)		
11/11/1959	Dundee	lost ko 2	Dave Croll (Dundee)
	(Scottish Featherweight Title)		

42 contests, won 22, drew 1, lost 19.

Jackie Brown (Edinburgh)
Flyweight/ Bantamweight
Born 02/03/1935

16/10/1958	Paisley	win rsf 3	Mark Quinn (London)
31/01/1959	Glasgow	win pts 6	Eddie Barraclough (Rotherham)
18/03/1959	Paisley	win pts 8	Malcolm McLeod (Coventry)
07/05/1959	Paisley	win rsf 8	Frankie Spencer (Wolverhampton)
10/09/1959	Paisley	win ret 10	Alex Ambrose (Glasgow)
	(Scottish Flyweight Title)		
21/10/1959	Paisley	win rsf 5	Derek Lloyd (Chingford)
	(British Flyweight Title Eliminator)		
09/12/1959	Paisley	win pts 8	John Agwu (Nigeria)
19/01/1960	London	win pts 8	Eddie Barraclough (Rotherham)
02/02/1960	Hanley	win pts 8	John Agwu (Nigeria)
07/03/1960	Manchester	win pts 8	Pancho Bhatachaji (India)
28/04/1960	Leith	win ko 7	Billy Walker (Kings Cross)
09/05/1960	Manchester	win pts 8	Albert Younsi (France)
09/06/1960	Glasgow	win pts 10	Mario D'Agata (Italy)
10/08/1960	Paisley	win pts 8	Johnny Morrissey (Newarthill)
22/11/1960	Wembley	lost ret 5	Derek Lloyd (Chingford)
12/04/1961	Paisley	lost ko 4	Freddie Gilroy (Belfast)
15/05/1961	Newcastle	win pts 8	Brian Cartwright (Birmingham)
12/06/1961	Newcastle	dnc	Eddie Barraclough (Rotherham)
09/08/1961	Glasgow	win pts 6	Ollie Wylie (Aberdeen)
02/09/1961	Cagliari	lost ko 6	Piero Rollo (Italy)
25/10/1961	Paisley	win pts 8	Walter McGowan (Hamilton)
27/01/1962	Birmingham	win pts 15	Brian Cartwright (Birmingham)
	(Vacant British Flyweight Title)		
17/08/1962	Helsinki	lost ko 4	Risto Luukkonen (Finland)
17/09/1962	London	win pts 8	Brian Bissmire (West Ham)
19/11/1962	London	win rsf 7	Ben Laiache (Morocco)
10/12/1962	London	win pts 15	Orizu Obilaso (Nigeria)
	(Vacant British Empire Flyweight Title)		
14/01/1963	Manchester	win rsf 7	Alex O'Neill (Belfast)
02/05/1963	Paisley	lost ko 12	Walter McGowan (Hamilton)
	(British and Empire Flyweight Titles)		
30/09/1963	Paris	lost rsf 3	Felix Brami (Tunisia)
28/11/1963	Paisley	win pts 8	Kid Solomon (Jamaica)
24/02/1964	London	win pts 10	Tommy Burgoyne (Denny)
28/07/1964	Porthcawl	win pts 8	Glyn Davies (Llanelly)
11/11/1964	Paisley	drew 10	John Caldwell (Belfast)
04/02/1965	Glasgow	win rsf 6	Baby John (Rhodesia)
08/03/1965	London	win rsf 6	Don Weller (Battersea)
29/04/1965	Govan	win rsf 6	Ramon Casal (Spain)
10/06/1965	Paisley	lost ko 2	Ron Jones (USA)
02/11/1965	Belfast	win dis 5	Jim McCann (Belfast)
22/11/1965	London	win pts 8	Glyn Davies (Llanelly)
09/02/1966	Cardiff	win pts 8	Terry Gale (Cardiff)
09/05/1966	London	lost ret 2	Bob Allotey (Ghana)
06/08/1966	London	win pts 8	Carl Taylor (Richmond)

Jackie Brown (Edinburgh) - continued

19/09/1966	Glasgow	lost ko 4	Evan Armstrong (Ayr)
	(Scottish Bantamweight Title)		
24/10/1966	Newcastle	lost rsf 2	George Bowes (West Hartlepool)

44 contests, won 32, drew 1, lost 10, no contest 1.

Ken Buchanan (Edinburgh)
Lightweight
Born 28/06/1945

20/09/1965	London	win rsf 2	Brian Tonks (London)
18/10/1965	Manchester	win rsf 2	Vic Woodhall (Mexborough)
01/11/1965	London	win rsf 2	Billy Williams (Cannock)
22/11/1965	London	win rsf 3	Joe Okezie (Nigeria)
13/12/1965	London	win pts 8	Junior Cassidy (Nigeria)
24/01/1966	London	win pts 8	Tommy Tiger (Nigeria)
07/03/1966	London	win rsf 4	Manley Brown (Bournemouth)
04/04/1966	London	win pts 8	Tommy Tiger (Nigeria)
19/04/1966	London	win pts 8	Chris Elliott (Leicester)
11/05/1966	Manchester	win pts 8	Junior Cassidy (Nigeria)
12/07/1966	Aberavon	win rsf 1	Brian Smyth (Belfast)
06/08/1966	London	win pts 8	Ivan Whiter (Tooting)
06/09/1966	London	win pts 8	Mick Laud (St. Ives)
17/10/1966	London	win pts 10	Antonio Paiva (Brazil)
29/11/1966	Leeds	win pts 8	Al Keen (Fulham)
19/12/1966	London	win pts 10	Phil Lundgren (Bermondsey)
23/01/1967	Glasgow	win pts 10	John McMillan (Glasgow)
	(Scottish Lightweight Title)		
14/02/1967	London	win pts 10	Tommy Garrison (USA)
11/05/1967	Paisley	win rsf 3	Franco Brondi (Italy)
28/06/1967	London	win pts 8	Winston Laud (St. Ives)
26/07/1967	Aberavon	win pts 10	Rene Roque (France)
14/09/1967	London	win rsf 7	Al Rocca (Manchester)
30/10/1967	London	win pts 12	Spike McCormack (Belfast)
	(Final Eliminator British Lightweight Title)		
19/02/1968	London	win ko 11	Maurice Cullen (Shotton)
	(British Lightweight Title)		
22/04/1968	London	win pts 8	Leonard Tavarez (Senegal)
10/06/1968	London	win pts 8	Ivan Whiter (Tooting)
23/10/1968	London	win pts 10	Angel Garcia (Cuba)
11/12/1968	Hamilton	win rsf 3	Ameur Lamine (Tunisia)
02/01/1969	London	win pts 10	Frankie Narvaez (Puerto Rico)
17/02/1969	London	win rsf 4	Mike Cruz (Puerto Rico)
05/03/1969	Solihull	win pts 8	Jose Luis Torcida (Spain)
14/07/1969	Nottingham	win rsf 1	Jerry Graci (USA)
11/11/1969	London	win rsf 2	Vincenzo Pitardi (Italy)

33 contests, won all 33.

Chic Calderwood (Craigneuk)
Light Heavyweight
Born 09/01/1937

Date	Venue	Result	Opponent
12/09/1957	Falkirk	win ko 2	Jimmy Teasdale (Middlesbrough)
25/09/1957	Paisley	win rsf 1	Tommy Summers (Bootle)
14/11/1957	Liverpool	win rsf 4	Johnny Hunt (Northampton)
25/11/1957	Leicester	win rsf 3	Gordon Corbett (Birmingham)
02/01/1958	Liverpool	win pts 4	Jackie Scott (Preston)
06/02/1958	Liverpool	win rsf 3	Jackie Scott (Preston)
19/02/1958	Hamilton	win pts 6	Joo Walcott (Trinidad)
25/03/1958	London	win rsf 1	Johnny Cole (Bow)
28/05/1958	Hamilton	win ret 1	Clark Mellor (Barnsley)
16/06/1958	West Hartlepool	win pts 8	Neville Rowe (Australia)
04/09/1958	Liverpool	win pts 8	Ted Williams (Huddersfield)
18/09/1958	Birmingham	win ko 1	Stan Cullis (Bristol)
09/10/1958	Liverpool	win ret 6	Billy Ellaway (Liverpool)
29/10/1958	Glasgow	win rsf 5	Dave Mooney (Wishaw)
	(Scottish Light Heavyweight Title)		
08/12/1958	Manchester	win ret 6	Neville Rowe (Australia)
12/01/1959	London	win rsf 5	Redvers Sangoe (Cardiff)
16/02/1959	Birmingham	win pts 8	Harry Dodoo (Ghana)
25/02/1959	Glasgow	win ret 2	Burke Emery (Canada)
18/03/1959	Paisley	win ko 10	Yolande Pompey (Trinidad)
07/05/1959	Paisley	win rsf 7	Charlie Forrest (USA)
10/09/1959	Paisley	win ret 7	Sam Langford (Nigeria)
21/10/1959	Paisley	win pts 10	Ron Redrup (West Ham)
09/12/1959	Paisley	win rsf 7	Jack Whittaker (Warwick)
	(Final Eliminator British Light Heavyweight Title)		
28/01/1960	Paisley	win rsf 13	Arthur Howard (Islington)
	(Vacant British Light Heavyweight Title)		
09/06/1960	Glasgow	win rsf 12	Johnny Halafihi (Tonga)
	(Vacant Empire Light Heavyweight Title)		
10/08/1960	Paisley	win rsf 8	Joey Armstrong (Ghana)
16/09/1960	Glasgow	win pts 10	Willie Pastrano (New Orleans)
02/11/1960	Paisley	win rsf 4	Rolf Peters (Germany)
22/11/1960	Wembley	win pts 10	Sonny Ray (USA)
07/03/1961	Wembley	lost pts 10	Von Clay (USA)
06/07/1961	Liverpool	win rsf 7	Dave Rent (Liverpool)
09/08/1961	Glasgow	drew 10	Jim Cooper (Bellingham)
15/12/1961	Detroit	lost pts 10	Henry Hank (USA)
12/02/1962	London	win ko 9	Stan Cullis (Bristol)
	(British and Empire Light Heavyweight Titles)		
04/06/1962	Newcastle	win pts 15	Johnny Halafihi (Tonga)
	(British Empire Light Heavyweight Title)		
28/09/1962	Rome	lost pts 15	Giulio Rinaldi (Italy)
	(Vacant European Light Heavyweight Title)		
14/02/1963	Manchester	win pts 10	Ray Shiel (St. Helens)
21/03/1963	Glasgow	win pts 10	Tommy Fields (USA)
30/04/1963	Glasgow	win pts 10	Von Clay (USA)
27/06/1963	Paisley	lost pts 10	Eddie Cotton (USA)
30/07/1963	Blackpool	win ret 11	Ron Redrup (West Ham)
	(British and Empire Light Heavyweight Titles)		
16/11/1963	Dortmund	lost pts 10	Gustav Scholz (Germany)

Chic Calderwood (Craigneuk) - continued

28/05/1964	Glasgow	win ret 6	Alan Harmon (Jamaica)
28/07/1964	Porthcawl	win pts 8	Freddie Cross (Nuneaton)
09/11/1964	Paisley	win rsf 7	Bob Nicholson (Farnborough)
	(British Light Heavyweight Title)		
12/01/1965	London	win ret 8	Otha Brown (USA)
03/02/1965	Wolverhampton	lost ko 8	Freddie Mack (USA)
05/05/1965	Solihull	win pts 10	Johnny Persol (USA)
10/06/1965	Paisley	lost rsf 2	John McCormack (Glasgow)
24/01/1966	London	win rsf 1	Derek Richards (Merthyr)
07/02/1966	London	win rsf 3	Alfredo Vogrig (Italy)
14/03/1966	London	lost rsf 10	Jose Menno (Argentina)
25/04/1966	Newcastle	win pts 10	Dick Hall (USA)
17/08/1966	Lignano	dnc 6	Piero Del Papa (Italy)
	(European Light Heavyweight Title)		
15/10/1966	San Juan	lost ko 2	Jose Torres (Puerto Rico)
	(World Light Heavyweight Title)		

55 contests, won 44, drew 1, lost 9, no contest 1.

Vic Herman (Glasgow)
Flyweight
Born12/02/1929

15/02/1950	Dundee	win pts 10	Norman Tennant (Dundee)
08/03/1950	Glasgow	win pts 8	Norman Tennant (Dundee)
22/03/1950	Paisley	lost pts 10	Louis Sckena (France)
14/04/1950	Glasgow	win pts 8	Jacques Louni (France)
31/05/1950	Glasgow	lost pts 10	Peter Keenan (Glasgow)
25/07/1950	London	win pts 8	Eddie McCormick (Deal)
23/08/1950	Porthcawl	win rsf 10	Norman Lewis (Nantymoel)
	(British Flyweight Title Eliminator)		
19/09/1950	London	drew 8	Honore Pratesi (France)
04/10/1950	Paisley	win pts 8	Tino Cardinale (Italy)
17/01/1951	Paisley	win pts 12	Norman Tennant (Dundee)
	(Scottish Flyweight Title and British Flyweight Title Final Eliminator)		
19/03/1951	Manchester	win ko 2	Juan Cristobal (Spain)
09/04/1951	Leeds	win pts 8	Theo Nolten (Holland)
23/04/1951	Manchester	win pts 10	Dante Bini (France)
11/06/1951	Leicester	lost pts 15	Terry Allen (Islington)
	(British Flyweight Title)		
27/06/1951	London	win rsf 7	Henry Carpenter (Peckham)
08/10/1951	Newcastle	lost pts 12	Teddy Gardner (West Hartlepool)
	(British Flyweight Title Final Eliminator)		
05/11/1951	Newcastle	lost pts 10	Jimmy Pearce (Middlesbrough)
12/11/1951	London	drew 8	Peter Fay (Bournemouth)
04/02/1952	London	win pts 8	Peter Fay (Bournemouth)
25/02/1952	Nottingham	win rsf 1	Billy Gibson (Fishburn)
26/03/1952	London	win ko 2	Jackie Briers (Belfast)
07/04/1952	Manchester	win ret 4	Mickey McKay (South Africa)
21/04/1952	Nottingham	win pts 8	Ogli Tettey (Gold Coast)
04/05/1952	London	win pts 10	Jean Binet (France)
21/05/1952	Glasgow	lost pts 10	Maurice Sandeyron (France)

Vic Herman (Glasgow) - continued

11/06/1952	Porthcawl	win pts 10	Honore Pratesi (France)
20/08/1952	Glasgow	lost pts 12	Joe Cairney (Coatbridge)
	(Scottish Flyweight Title)		
14/11/1952	Manchester	win pts 10	Andre Jasse (France)
02/02/1953	London	win pts 8	Alex Bollaert (Belgium)
27/02/1953	Manchester	lost pts 10	Jake Tuli (South Africa)
31/05/1953	Bangkok	lost pts 10	Chamrern Songkitrat (Thailand)
01/06/1953	Bangkok	win ko 2	Boondam Vitheechai (Thailand)
17/07/1953	Tokyo	lost rsf 10	Yoshio Shirai (Japan)
23/02/1954	London	drew 8	Mickey O'Sullivan (Finsbury Park)
26/05/1954	Glasgow	lost pts 10	Peter Keenan (Glasgow)

35 contests, won 21, drew 3, lost 11.

Charlie Hill (Cambuslang)
Featherweight
Born 20/06/1930

17/06/1953	Glasgow	win pts 6	Art Belec (Manchester)
16/07/1953	Liverpool	lost dis 3	Andy Monahan (Southport)
27/07/1953	West Hartlepool	win ko 5	Ron Hillyard (Leeds)
13/08/1953	Liverpool	win ko 2	Andy Monahan (Southport)
07/09/1953	Newcastle	win pts 6	Bob Hodgson (Seaham)
03/10/1953	Belfast	win ko 4	Jim Fisher (Belfast)
19/11/1953	Liverpool	win ret 6	Peter Fay (Bournemouth)
14/12/1953	Newcastle	win pts 8	Tommy Higgins (Hanley)
26/12/1953	Belfast	win ko 1	Michael Feeney (Banbridge)
24/02/1954	Glasgow	win rsf 5	Billy Smith (Bangor)
30/03/1954	Edinburgh	win ret 5	Bobby Dodoo (Gold Coast)
10/04/1954	Belfast	win ret 5	Eddie McNally (Belfast)
10/05/1954	Newcastle	win ret 5	Steve Trainor (Manchester)
26/05/1954	Glasgow	win pts 8	Freddie King (Wandsworth)
30/06/1954	Motherwell	win ret 6	Jacques Lesseine (Belgium)
24/07/1954	Kilwinning	win pts 8	Gene Caffrey (Glasgow)
21/09/1954	Paisley	win pts 8	Henk Klok (Holland)
07/12/1954	Paisley	win pts 12	Chic Brogan (Clydebank)
	(Scottish Featherweight Title)		
10/05/1955	Glasgow	win pts 8	Flaviano Ciancarelli (Italy)
02/06/1955	Glasgow	win pts 8	Jacques Bataille (France)
30/06/1955	Glasgow	win pts 8	Denny Dawson (Sheffield)
14/09/1955	Glasgow	win pts 8	Ken Lawrence (Southampton)
27/12/1955	Belfast	win pts 8	Jesus Rubio (Spain)
04/02/1956	Belfast	win pts 15	Billy Kelly (Derry)
	(British Featherweight Title)		
28/04/1956	Dundee	win pts 8	Flaviano Ciancarelli (Italy)
27/06/1956	Glasgow	win rsf 10	Ken Lawrence (Southampton)
23/07/1956	West Hartlepool	win rsf 6	Aime Devisch (Belgium)
04/12/1956	London	lost rsf 1	Bobby Neill (Edinburgh)
19/01/1957	Belfast	lost rsf 5	Joe Quinn (Belfast)
20/05/1957	West Hartlepool	win pts 8	Denny Dawson (Sheffield)
21/08/1957	Paisley	win pts 8	Alf Drew (Hackney)

Charlie Hill (Cambuslang) - continued

07/10/1957	Nottingham	win ko 10	Jimmy Brown (Belfast)
	(British Featherweight Title)		
09/12/1957	Nottingham	lost rsf 10	Percy Lewis (Trinidad)
	(British Empire Featherweight Title)		
02/07/1958	Glasgow	win ret 11	Chic Brogan (Clydebank)
	(British Featherweight Title)		
16/10/1958	Paisley	win pts 8	Joe Quinn (Belfast)
13/04/1959	Nottingham	lost rsf 9	Bobby Neill (Edinburgh)
	(British Featherweight Title)		

36 contests, won 31, lost 5.

Frankie Jones (Plean)
Flyweight
Born 12/02/1933

30/06/1955	Glasgow	win pts 6	Ken Langford (Slough)
14/09/1955	Glasgow	win pts 6	Bobby Robinson (Newcastle)
03/11/1955	Paisley	win pts 8	Eddie O'Connor (Dublin)
17/02/1956	Blackpool	win pts 8	Malcolm McLeod (Coventry)
21/03/1956	Govan	win rsf 5	Dave Moore (Belfast)
27/06/1956	Glasgow	win pts 8	Vic Glenn (Stepney)
19/09/1956	Glasgow	win pts 12	Dick Currie (Glasgow)
	(Scottish Flyweight Title and British Flyweight Title Eliminator)		
20/02/1957	Glasgow	win rsf 8	Len Reece (Cardiff)
10/04/1957	Paisley	win rsf 10	Malcolm McLeod (Coventry)
22/05/1957	Glasgow	win pts 10	Jose Ogazon (Spain)
31/07/1957	Porthcawl	win ko 11	Len Reece (Cardiff)
	(British and Empire Flyweight Titles)		
12/09/1957	Falkirk	win pts 10	Christian Marchand (France)
23/10/1957	Glasgow	lost ko 3	Dennis Adams (South Africa)
	(British Empire Flyweight Title)		
24/03/1958	Birmingham	lost pts 8	Terry Toole (Hackney)
19/05/1958	West Hartlepool	win pts 8	Malcolm McLeod (Coventry)
25/09/1958	Middlesbrough	lost ko 1	George Bowes (West Hartlepool)
29/10/1958	Glasgow	win pts 8	Dennis Adams (South Africa)
19/11/1958	Glasgow	lost rsf 4	Pancho Bhatachati (India)
05/02/1959	Glasgow	win pts 15	Alex Ambrose (Glasgow)
	(British Flyweight Title)		
04/05/1959	Manchester	lost pts 8	Derek Lloyd (Chingford)
28/05/1959	Glasgow	win pts 8	George McDade (Glasgow)
20/05/1960	Hanley	win ret 7	Eddie Barraclough (Rotherham
15/08/1960	Aberdare	lost pts 10	Ron Davies (Llanbradach)
31/08/1960	Caracas	lost ko 7	Ramon Arias (Venezuela)
08/10/1960	Belfast	lost ko 3	John Caldwell (Belfast)
	(British Flyweight Title)		

25 contests, won 17, lost 8.

Peter Keenan (Glasgow)
Bantamweight
Born 18/08/1928

18/01/1950	Paisley	win ko 3	Dickie O'Sullivan (Finsbury Park)
07/03/1950	London	win pts 10	Jean Sneyers (Belgium)
10/05/1950	Glasgow	win pts 8	Maurice Sandeyron (France)
31/05/1950	Glasgow	win pts 10	Vic Herman (Glasgow)
06/07/1950	Paisley	win pts 10	Bunty Doran (Belfast)
	(British Bantamweight Title Eliminator)		
15/11/1950	Paisley	win ko 2	Tommy Proffitt (Droylesden)
	(British Bantamweight Title Eliminator)		
13/12/1950	Paisley	win pts 8	Louis Skena (France)
14/02/1951	Paisley	win pts 8	Jose Rubio (Spain)
14/03/1951	London	win rsf 6	Armand Deianna (France)
28/03/1951	Paisley	win pts 10	Amleto Falcinelli (Italy)
09/05/1951	Glasgow	win ko 6	Danny O'Sullivan (Finsbury Park)
	(British Bantamweight Title)		
27/06/1951	Glasgow	win rsf 12	Bobby Boland (Dundee)
	(British Bantamweight Title)		
05/09/1951	Glasgow	win pts 15	Luis Romero (Spain)
	(European Bantamweight Title)		
31/10/1951	Paisley	drew 10	Maurice Sandeyron (France)
26/01/1952	Johannesburg	lost pts 15	Vic Toweel (South Africa)
	(World and Empire Bantamweight Titles)		
21/05/1952	Glasgow	lost ko 5	Jean Sneyers (Belgium)
	(European Bantamweight Title)		
15/10/1952	Paisley	lost ret 5	Amleti Falcinelli (Italy)
28/01/1953	Paisley	win rsf 7	Frankie Williams (Birkinhead)
	(British Bantamweight Title)		
18/03/1953	Glasgow	win pts 10	Stan Rowan (Liverpool)
17/06/1953	Glasgow	win pts 15	Maurice Sandeyron (France)
	(European Bantamweight Title)		
03/10/1953	Belfast	lost pts 15	John Kelly (Belfast)
	(British and European Bantamweight Titles)		
17/11/1953	London	win rsf 7	Ron Johnson (Bethnal Green)
25/01/1954	Nottingham	win pts 8	Robert Meunier (France)
24/02/1954	Glasgow	win pts 12	Eddie Carson (Edinburgh)
	(Scottish Bantamweight Title)		
26/05/1954	Glasgow	win pts 10	Vic Herman (Glasgow)
21/09/1954	Paisley	win ko 6	John Kelly (Belfast)
	(British Bantamweight Title)		
11/12/1954	Belfast	win pts15	George O'Neill (Belfast)
	(British Bantamweight Title)		
22/02/1955	Glasgow	win pts 10	Dante Bini (France)
28/03/1955	Sydney	win pts 15	Bobby Sinn (Australia)
	(Vacant British Empire Bantamweight Title)		
09/05/1955	Sydney	lost pts 12	Andre Vilignat (France)
20/06/1955	Sydney	lost pts 12	Roberto Spina (Italy)
14/09/1955	Glasgow	win ko 14	Jake Tuli (South Africa)
	(British Empire Bantamweight Title)		
03/11/1955	Paisley	win pts 10	Pierre Cossemyns (Belgium)
11/12/1955	Marseilles	lost pts 10	Emile Chemama (France)

Peter Keenan (Glasgow) - continued

22/10/1956	Sydney	win rsf 2	Kevin James (Australia)
	(British Empire Bantamweight Title)		
09/11/1956	Melbourne	win pts 12	Federico Scarponi (Italy)
15/12/1956	Manila	lost ko 9	Al Asuncion (Phillipines)
22/05/1957	Glasgow	win rsf 6	John Smillie (Fauldhouse)
	(British and Empire Bantamweight Titles)		
26/06/1957	Glasgow	win pts 10	Robert Tartari (France)
21/08/1957	Paisley	win pts 8	Rudy Edwards (Guyana)
25/09/1957	Paisley	win pts 10	Alfred Schweer (Germany)
05/03/1958	Glasgow	win rsf 10	Dick Currie (Glasgow)
02/04/1958	Paisley	win pts 15	Graham Van Der Walt (South Africa)
	(British Empire Bantamweight Title)		
02/07/1958	Glasgow	win pts 10	Billy Peacock (USA)
28/08/1958	Paisley	lost rsf 6	Derry Treanor (Glasgow)
16/10/1958	Paisley	win pts 15	Pat Supple (Canada)
	(British Empire Bantamweight Title)		
17/11/1958	Paris	lost pts 10	Alphonse Halimi (Algeria)
10/01/1959	Belfast	lost rsf 11	Freddie Gilroy (Belfast)
	(British and Empire Bantamweight Titles		

48 contests, won 36, drew 1, lost 11.

Jim Kenny (Polmont)
Featherweight
Born 27/03/1928

08/02/1950	Paisley	win ko 3	Tommy Burns (Belfast)
	(British and Empire Featherweight Title Eliminator)		
10/03/1950	Falkirk	win pts 10	Stan Gossip (Hull)
14/04/1950	Glasgow	win pts 10	Stan Rowan (Liverpool)
27/05/1950	Blackpool	win ko 5	Bert Jackson (Fleetwood)
	(British and Empire Featherweight Title Eliminator)		
19/07/1950	Coatbridge	win pts 10	Dai Davies (Skewen)
23/08/1950	Coatbridge	drew 8	Tom Bailey (Liverpool)
14/09/1950	Ayr	win pts 8	Mario Lutti (Italy)
19/09/1950	London	win pts 8	Jean Machtelinck (Belgium)
28/11/1950	London	lost pts 15	Ronnie Clayton (Blackpool)
	(British and Empire Featherweight Titles)		
28/02/1951	Glasgow	lost pts 12	George Stewart (Hamilton)
	(Scottish Featherweight Title)		
30/06/1951	Johannesburg	lost ret 7	Vic Toweel (South Africa)
22/10/1951	Newcastle	lost ret 5	Frank Johnson (Manchester)
05/04/1952	Glasgow	win dis 4	Hugh Mackie (British Guiana)
19/04/1952	Glasgow	win ret 4	Brian Jelley (Bury)
02/05/1952	Falkirk	lost pts 10	Tommy Miller (Lothian)
	(Scottish Featherweight Title Eliminator)		
27/05/1952	London	lost pts 8	Charlie Tucker (Camberwell)
07/07/1952	West Hartlepool	lost dis 5	Stan Skinkiss (Manchester)
17/09/1952	Glasgow	win pts 10	Ronnie Clayton (Blackpool)

Jim Kenny (Polmont) - continued

15/10/1952	Paisley	win pts 8	Rolly Blyce (Trinidad)
11/11/1952	London	lost pts 10	Sammy McCarthy (Stepney)
18/03/1953	Glasgow	win pts 8	Lou Jacob (Belgium)

21 contests, won 12, drew 1, lost 8.

John McCluskey (Hamilton)
Flyweight
Born 23/01/1944

11/10/1965	London	win pts 6	Baby John (Rhodesia)
01/11/1965	London	win rsf 8	Tony Barlow (Manchester)
19/01/1966	London	win pts 6	Simon Tiger (Nigeria)
14/03/1966	London	win ret 6	Tommy Connor (Glasgow)
04/04/1966	Glasgow	win pts 8	Tommy Connor (Glasgow)
02/05/1966	Manchester	win rsf 5	Tony Barlow (Manchester)
06/06/1966	Glasgow	win pts 10	Winston Van Guylenburg (Ceylon)
16/01/1967	Manchester (Vacant British Flyweight Title)	win ko 8	Tony Barlow (Manchester)
13/02/1967	Manchester	win pts 10	Manolin Alvarez (Spain)
21/03/1967	Wembley	win pts 10	Lachy Linares (Domenican Republic)
11/05/1967	Paisley	lost pts 10	Fernando Atzori (Italy)
18/11/1967	Stockholm	win pts 10	Jan Persson (Sweden)
11/03/1968	London	win ko 2	Kid Miller (Zambia)
09/04/1968	Wembley	win pts 8	Fabian Bellanco (Spain)
26/06/1968	Naples (European Flyweight Title)	lost ko 4	Fernando Atzori (Italy)
12/11/1968	Wembley	lost pts 9	Johnny Clark (Walworth)
29/11/1968	Berne	lost pts 10	Fritz Chervet (Switzerland)
03/03/1969	Johannesburg	win pts 10	Mike Buttle (South Africa)
07/05/1969	Solihull (British Flyweight Title)	win rsf 13	Tony Barlow (Manchester)
13/10/1969	London	win ret 5	Glyn Davies (Merthyr)
26/11/1969	San Antonio	win rsf 1	Arturo Leon (Mexico)
26/12/1969	Zurich	win pts 10	Fritz Chervet (Switzerland)

22 contests, won 18, lost 4.

John McCormack (Glasgow)
Middleweight/Light Heavyweight
Born 09/01/1935

26/02/1957	Glasgow	win pts 6	Dudley Cox (Bournemouth)
26/03/1957	Leith	win ko 1	Cliff Garvey (Dundalk)
10/04/1957	Paisley	win ret 3	Eddie Williams (Tredegar)
09/05/1957	Govan	win ko 1	Jack Willis (Belfast)
22/05/1957	Glasgow	win ko 1	Frank Davis (Gloucester)
28/05/1957	Leith	win rsf 3	Bonny Garraway (Ghana)
26/06/1957	Glasgow	win rsf 5	Wally Scott (West Ham)

15/08/1957	Glasgow	win ret 2	Eddie Lennon (London)
23/10/1957	Glasgow	lost rsf 5	Jim Lynas (Coventry)
28/11/1957	Glasgow	win rsf 7	Evie Vorster (South Africa)
05/02/1958	Glasgow	win rsf 7	Vincent O'Kine (West Africa)
15/04/1958	Newcastle	win ko 2	Harry Dodoo (Ghana)
23/04/1958	Glasgow	win pts 8	Johnny Read (Norwood)
05/05/1958	Newcastle	win pts 8	Attu Clottey (Ghana)
02/07/1958	Glasgow	win pts 12	Len Mullen (Glasgow)

(Vacant Scottish Middleweight Title)

28/08/1958	Paisley	win pts 8	Jim Lynas (Coventry)
09/10/1958	Liverpool	win pts 10	Martin Hansen (Liverpool)

(British Middleweight Title Eliminator)

16/10/1958	Paisley	win pts 8	Jean Ruellet (France)
19/01/1959	Newcastle	win pts 8	Orlando Paso (Nigeria)
25/02/1959	Glasgow	win ret 6	Paddy Delargy (Galway)
18/03/1959	Paisley	win pts 10	Michel Diouf (France)
07/05/1959	Paisley	win pts 10	Gene Johns (USA)
28/05/1959	Glasgow	win rsf 6	Remo Carati (Italy)
15/09/1959	Wembley	win dis 8	Terry Downes (London)

(British Middleweight Title)

03/11/1959	Wembley	lost rsf 8	Terry Downes (London)

(British Middleweight Title)

09/03/1960	Glasgow	win rsf 3	Tommy Tagoe (Ghana)
18/06/1960	Milan	win pts 10	Giancarlo Garbelli (Milan)
10/08/1960	Paisley	win rsf 9	George Aldridge (Market Harborough)
19/08/1960	Berlin	lost pts 10	Gustav Scholz (Berlin)
02/11/1960	Paisley	win pts 10	George Benton (USA)
22/02/1961	Paisley	win pts 12	Phil Edwards (Cardiff)

(Final Eliminator British Middleweight Title)

10/05/1961	Glasgow	win pts 10	Michel Diouf (France)
11/07/1961	Wembley	win pts 8	Sandy Luke (Nigeria)
17/10/1961	Wembley	win pts 15	Harko Kokmeyer (Germany)

(European Middleweight Title)

06/01/1962	Frankfurt	win pts 15	Heini Freytag (Germany)

(European Middleweight Title)

08/02/1962	Copenhagen	lost dis 4	Chris Christensen (Denmark)

(European Middleweight Title)

14/06/1962	Glasgow	win pts 8	Henry Hank (USA)
13/09/1962	Glasgow	win pts 10	Ike White (USA)
26/11/1962	Manchester	lost ko 6	George Aldridge (Market Harborough)

(Vacant British Middleweight Title)

10/09/1963	Wembley	lost rsf 5	Harry Scott (Liverpool)
21/01/1964	Govan	win rsf 1	Joe Louis (Nigeria)
04/03/1964	Paisley	win ko 1	Malcolm Worthington (Crewe)
29/04/1965	Govan	win rsf 6	Bernard Quellier (France)
10/06/1965	Paisley	win rsf 2	Chic Calderwood (Craigneuk)
28/06/1966	London	lost pts 10	Young McCormack (Dublin)

(British Light Heavyweight Title Eliminator)

45 contests, won 38, lost 7.

Walter McGowan (Hamilton)
Flyweight/ Bantamweight
Born 13/10/1942

09/08/1961	Glasgow	win ret 3	George McDade (Glasgow)
22/09/1961	Hamilton	win pts 8	Eddie Barraclough (Rotherham)
25/10/1961	Paisley	lost pts 8	Jackie Brown (Edinburgh)
16/12/1961	Glasgow	win pts 8	Brian Bissmire (West Ham)
14/06/1962	Glasgow	win pts 8	Danny Lee (Port Glasgow)
20/09/1962	Glasgow	win ko 6	Jacques Jacob (France)
16/10/1962	Wembley	win rsf 6	Rene Libeer (France)
14/11/1962	Glasgow	win rsf 6	Ray Jutras (USA)
31/01/1963	Glasgow	win pts 8	Bernard Jubert (France)
02/05/1963	Paisley	win ko 12	Jackie Brown (Edinburgh)
	(British and Empire Flyweight Titles)		
27/06/1963	Paisley	win rsf 9	Ray Perez (Honolulu)
12/09/1963	Paisley	win rsf 9	Kid Solomon (Jamaica)
	(British Empire Flyweight Title)		
28/11/1963	Paisley	win pts 10	Ric Magrano (Phillipines)
04/03/1964	Paisley	win pts 10	Risto Luukkonen (Finland)
24/04/1964	Rome	lost pts 15	Salvatore Burruni (Italyl
	(European Flyweight Title)		
03/09/1964	Paisley	win pts 10	Natalio Jiminez (Domenican (Republic)
25/11/1964	Solihull	win rsf 2	Luis Rodriguez (Spain)
20/01/1965	Solihull	win rsf 3	Mick Hussey (London)
23/02/1965	London	win pts 10	Felix Brami (France)
23/04/1965	Rome	win pts 10	Benny Lee (Ghana)
01/06/1965	London	lost rsf 6	Jose Medel (Mexico)
20/08/1965	Paisley	lost rsf 6	Ron Jones (USA)
03/12/1965	Rome	drew 15	Tommaso Galli (Italy)
	(European Bantamweight Title)		
06/01/1966	London	win rsf 6	Nevio Carbi (Italy)
28/03/1966	London	win pts 8	Ernesto Miranda (Argentina)
14/06/1966	London	win pts 15	Salvatore Burruni (Italy)
	(World Flyweight Title)		
06/09/1966	London	win pts 15	Alan Rudkin (Liverpool)
	(British and Empire Bantamweight Titles)		
16/11/1966	London	win ret 5	Jose Bisbal (Spain)
30/12/1966	Bangkok	lost rsf 9	Chartchai Chionoi (Thailand)
	(World Flyweight Title)		
15/03/1967	London	win pts 10	Osamu Miyashita (Japan)
10/05/1967	London	win pts 10	Giancarlo Centa (France)
10/07/1967	London	win pts 10	Antoine Porcel (France)
19/09/1967	Wembley	lost rsf 7	Chartchai Chionoi (Thailand)
	(World Flyweight Title)		
13/05/1968	Manchester	lost pts 15	Alan Rudkin (Liverpool)
	(British and Empire Bantamweight Titles)		
23/10/1968	London	win rsf 4	Gerald Macrez (France)
26/11/1968	Belfast	win rsf 7	Marc Van Domme (France)
17/12/1968	Brighton	win pts 8	Messaoud Boussaboua (Algeria)
28/04/1969	London	win rsf 4	Michel Houdeau (France)

Walter McGowan (Hamilton) - continued

13/08/1969	San Remo	win pts 8	Umberto Simbola (Italy)
11/11/1969	London	win pts 8	Antonio Chiloiro (Italy)

40 contests, won 32, drew 1, lost 7.

Sammy McSpadden (Hamilton)
Lightweight/Welterweight
Born 16/05/1941

07/11/1960	London	win pts 6	Dave Chandler (Battersea)
16/11/1960	London	win ret 2	Alf Thomson (London)
09/12/1960	London	drew 6	Dave Parsons (Northolt)
30/03/1961	Bristol	win pts 6	Tommy Kansas (Bristol)
05/04/1961	Hamilton	win rsf 5	Ricky Kiernan (Glasgow)
28/04/1961	Birmingham	win pts 6	Gus Harry (Trinidad)
11/05/1961	Bristol	win pts 8	Stan Bishop (Birmingham)
29/05/1961	London	win rsf 6	Teddy Carter (Guisborough)
20/06/1961	London	win pts 6	Vic Andreetti (Hoxton)
12/09/1961	London	win pts 8	Pat Aaron (Nigeria)
23/10/1961	London	win pts 8	Dave Parsons (Northolt)
14/11/1961	London	win pts 8	Vic Andreetti (Hoxton)
27/11/1961	London	win pts 8	Bobby Kelsey (Forest Gate)
19/12/1961	London	win rsf 7	Dave Stone (Battersea)
23/01/1962	Wembley	win rsf 1	Peter Heath (Coventry)
05/02/1962	London	win pts 8	Byron Hollingsworth (Trinidad)
26/02/1962	London	win pts 8	Brian Jones (Nottingham)
21/03/1962	London	win pts 10	Maurice Cullen (Shotton)
26/04/1962	Hamilton	win pts 8	Manuel Sosa (France)
20/09/1962	Glasgow	win pts 8	Boswell St. Louis (Trinidad)
16/10/1962	Wembley	win pts 8	Kenny Field (Hoxton)
12/03/1963	London	win pts 8	Junior Cassidy (Nigeria)
26/03/1963	Wembley	win rsf 5	Jean Dantas (France)
24/08/1963	New York	lost pts 10	Johnny Bizzarro (USA)
16/09/1963	London	win pts 8	Spike McCormack (Belfast)
22/10/1963	Wembley	lost rsf 2	Sugar Ramos (Cuba)
02/11/1963	Johannesburg	lost pts 10	Stoffel Steyn (South Africa)
17/01/1964	Capetown	lost pts 10	Stoffel Steyn (South Africa)
14/02/1964	Durban	win rsf 9	Charlie Els (South Africa)
20/07/1964	Bristol	win pts 8	Rick McMasters (Jamaica)
12/11/1964	Southport	win pts 10	Johnny Cooke (Bootle)
01/06/1965	Wembley	win pts 10	Nessim Max Cohen (Morocco)
17/07/1965	Johannesburg	lost pts 10	Willie Ludick (South Africa)
17/08/1965	Johannesburg	lost pts 10	Fraser Toweel (South Africa)
25/11/1965	Cardiff	lost rsf 12	Brian Curvis (Swansea)
	(British and Empire Welterweight Titles)		
15/06/1966	Gothenburg	lost pts 8	Stig Walterson (Sweden)
06/08/1966	London	lost pts 8	Obletey Commey (Ghana)
25/10/1966	London	lost rsf 6	Ralph Charles (West Ham)

38 contests, won 27, drew 1, lost 10.

Johnny Morissey (Carfin/Newarthill)
Bantamweight/ Featherweight
Born 17/08/1937

15/08/1957	Glasgow	win ret 4	Benny Vaun (Belfast)
28/08/1957	Hamilton	win rsf 3	Billy Adams (Belfast)
18/09/1957	Glasgow	win ko 2	Harry Hunter (Belfast)
23/10/1957	Glasgow	win pts 8	Dennis East (Plaistow)
06/11/1957	Govan	win ret 3	George O'Neill (Belfast)
28/11/1957	Glasgow	win pts 8	Ken Langford (Slough)
15/01/1958	Hamilton	win ko 4	Archie Downie (Glasgow)
	(Scottish Bantamweight Title)		
05/02/1958	Glasgow	lost pts 8	Antonio Diaz (Spain)
05/03/1958	Glasgow	win ko 3	Antonio Diaz (Spain)
21/05/1958	Glasgow	win rsf 6	Terry Toole (Hackney)
18/06/1958	Glasgow	win pts 8	Jimmy Carson (Belfast)
17/09/1958	Glasgow	lost ret 8	Freddie Gilroy (Belfast)
	(British Bantamweight Title Eliminator)		
15/04/1959	Glasgow	win ko 3	Gerry Jones (Wigan)
07/05/1959	Paisley	win pts 8	Ron Jones (West Ham)
10/09/1959	Paisley	win ret 5	Tommy Miller (Lothian)
	(Vacant Scottish Bantamweight Title)		
28/10/1959	Glasgow	win pts 8	Peter Lavery (Belfast)
09/12/1959	Paisley	win pts 8	Hugh Riley (Edinburgh)
09/03/1960	Glasgow	win dis 5	Dwight Hawkins (USA)
31/05/1960	Wembley	win pts 8	Roy Beaman (Brixton)
10/08/1960	Paisley	lost pts 8	Jackie Brown (Edinburgh)
21/11/1960	Nottingham	lost pts 8	George Bowes (Hesladen)
05/04/1961	Hamilton	win rsf 5	Tommy Burgoyne (Halton)
30/05/1961	Wembley	lost pts 8	Kenny Field (Hoxton)
27/02/1962	Govan	win ko 2	Bobby Fisher (Craigneuk)
09/04/1962	Manchester	win ret 8	Floyd Robertson (Ghana)
05/06/1962	Wembley	win pts 8	Rene Barriere (France)
20/09/1962	Glasgow	win pts 10	Gene Fossmire (USA)
16/10/1962	Wembley	drew 8	Phil Lundgren (Bermondsey)
14/11/1962	Glasgow	win pts 10	Pablo Acevedo (USA)
31/01/1963	Glasgow	lost rsf 11	Howard Winstone (Wales)
	(British Featherweight Title)		
21/03/1963	Glasgow	drew 10	Dennis Adjei (Ghana)
19/02/1964	Hamilton	win pts 8	Brian Smyth (Belfast)

32 contests. Won 24, drew 2, lost 6.

Bobby Neill (Edinburgh)
Featherweight
Born 10/10/1933

10/05/1955	London	win rsf 2	Denny Dennis (Plumstead)
31/05/1955	London	win rsf 1	Albert Stokes (Battersea)
19/07/1955	London	win rsf 4	George Clay (Nottingham)
22/09/1955	London	win pts 6	Percy James (Southport)
04/10/1955	London	win rsf 4	Peter Fay (Bournemouth)
15/11/1955	London	win ret 2	Jim Fisher (Belfast)
29/11/1955	London	win ko 3	Eddie McCormick (Islington)

Bobby Neill (Edinburgh) – continued

07/02/1956	London	win pts 8	Denny Dawson (Sheffield)
21/02/1956	London	win ko 1	Billy Ashcroft (Wigan)
13/03/1956	London	win pts 8	Ken Lawrence (Southampton)
05/06/1956	London	win rsf 3	Freddie Reardon (Downham)
19/06/1956	London	win rsf 4	Juan Alvarez (Belgium)
19/09/1956	Glasgow	win ret 8	Matt Fulton (Coatbridge)
	(Scottish Featherweight Title/ British Featherweight Title Eliminator)		
02/10/1956	London	win ret 5	Ray Famechon (France)
04/12/1956	London	win rsf 1	Charlie Hill (Cambuslang)
22/01/1957	Belfast	lost ko 8	Jimmy Brown (Belfast)
	(Final Eliminator British Featherweight Title)		
19/02/1957	London	win rsf 7	Dos Santos (Portugal)
09/04/1957	London	lost pts 10	Victor Pepeder (France)
16/07/1957	London	win rsf 4	Edouard Roelandt (Belgium)
21/08/1957	Paisley	lost ret 5	Arthur Donnachie (Greenock)
29/05/1958	London	win ko 1	Arthur Devlin (Millwall)
11/06/1958	London	win ret 4	Con Mount Bassie (Jamaica)
17/06/1958	London	win dis 4	Andy Hayford (Ghana)
02/07/1958	Glasgow	win rsf 6	Owen Reilly (Glasgow)
15/07/1958	London	win rsf 5	George Dormer (East Ham)
09/09/1958	London	win rsf 6	Aime Devisch (Belgium)
13/04/1959	Nottingham	win rsf 9	Charlie Hill (Cambuslang)
	(British Featherweight Title)		
02/06/1959	Wembley	win ko 9	Terry Spinks (West Ham)
20/10/1959	Wembley	lost rsf 1	Davey Moore (USA)
01/02/1960	Nottingham	win pts 10	Albert Serti (Italy)
26/04/1960	Manchester	win rsf 5	Germain Vivier (Italy)
02/06/1960	Liverpool	win ko 3	Jimmy Carson (Belfast)
21/06/1960	London	lost rsf 5	Johnny Kidd (Aberdeen)
27/09/1960	London	lost rsf 7	Terry Spinks (West Ham)
	(British Featherweight Title)		
22/11/1960	Wembley	lost ko 14	Terry Spinks (West Ham)
	(British Featherweight Title)		

35 contests. Won 28, lost 7.

John O'Brien (Glasgow)
Featherweight
Born 20/02/1937

15/10/1956	Newcastle	win pts 6	Arthur McGregor (Newcastle)
02/11/1956	Blackpool	win pts 6	Jackie Tiller (Manchester)
19/11/1956	Middlesbrough	win pts 6	Johnny Bamborough (West Hartlepool)
04/03/1957	Newcastle	win pts 6	Len Harvey (Cardiff)
15/07/1957	West Hartlepool	win rsf 3	Jack Richards (Middlesbrough)
21/10/1957	Middlesbrough	win ko 1	Tommy Houston (Belfast)
08/11/1957	Blackpool	win pts 6	George Mason (Bootle)
23/11/1957	Belfast	win pts 8	Gil Neill (Belfast)
26/02/1958	Paisley	lost pts 8	Roy Jacobs (Nigeria)
25/03/1958	London	lost pts 8	George Dormer (East Ham)

John O'Brien (Glasgow) - continued

20/05/1958	London	win pts 8	George Dormer (East Ham)
28/05/1958	Hamilton	lost pts 8	Chic Brogan (Clydebank)
16/06/1958	West Hartlepool	lost pts 8	Roy Jacobs (Nigeria)
15/04/1959	Cardiff	lost pts 8	Aryee Jackson (Ghana)
27/04/1959	Newcastle	win pts 8	Con Mount Bassie (Jamaica)
05/05/1959	London	win pts 8	Johnny Howard (Islington)
17/06/1959	Glasgow	win pts 8	Eric Brett (Retford)
15/09/1959	Wembley	win pts 12	Terry Spinks (West Ham)
	(British Featherweight Title Eliminator)		
07/12/1959	Nottingham	lost ko 2	Percy Lewis (Trinidad)
	(British Empire Featherweight Title)		
05/06/1962	Wembley	lost rsf 3	Kenny Field (Hoxton)
05/09/1962	London	lost rsf 6	George Bowes (Hesleden)
15/10/1962	London	win rsf 2	Andy Doherty (Derry)
12/11/1962	Croydon	win rsf 6	Phil Lundgren (Bermondsey)
07/02/1963	Blackpool	win rsf 6	George Bowes (Hesleden)
28/02/1963	Glasgow	win rsf 5	Con Mount Bassie (Jamaica)
05/04/1963	Milan	lost pts 10	Lino Mastellaro (Italy)
12/09/1963	Paisley	win rsf 2	Bobby Fisher (Craigneuk)
09/12/1963	London	lost pts 15	Howard Winstone (Wales)
	(British and European Featherweight Titles)		
07/12/1964	Manchester	win rsf 7	Dennis Adjei (Ghana)
04/02/1965	Glasgow	lost rsf 5	Rafiu King (Nigeria)
07/09/1965	London	win ko 4	Jesus Saucedo (Mexico)
11/12/1965	Mexico City	lost rsf 8	Mario Diaz (Mexico)
03/02/1967	Accra	win ret 12	Floyd Robertson (Ghana)
	(British Empire Featherweight Title)		
24/11/1967	Melbourne	lost rsf 11	Johnny Famechon (Australia)
	(British Empire Featherweight Title)		
23/09/1968	London	win rsf 5	Daniel Vermandere (France)
30/10/1968	Hamilton	win rsf 3	Ray Opoku (Guyana)
24/03/1969	London	lost rsf 5	Jimmy Revie (Stockwell)
	(Vacant British Featherweight Title)		
30/08/1969	Johannesburg	win pts 10	Arnold Taylor (South Africa)
08/09/1969	Durban	win ret 4	Ernie Baronet (South Africa)

39 contests, won 25, lost 14.

Billy Rafferty (Glasgow)
Bantamweight
Born 14/08/1933

27/03/1956	Leith	win pts 6	Danny McNamee (Glasgow)
16/05/1956	Glasgow	win rsf 6	Jack Sala (Nigeria)
27/06/1956	Glasgow	win pts 6	Jim Cresswell (Glasgow)
05/09/1956	Greenock	win pts 8	Jim Cresswell (Glasgow)
14/12/1956	Leith	win pts 6	Derry Treanor (Glasgow)
09/05/1957	Govan	win ko 5	Benny Vaun (Belfast)
29/07/1957	West Hartlepool	lost pts 6	George Bowes (West Hartlepool)
27/08/1957	London	win pts 8	Ron Jones (West Ham)
25/09/1957	Paisley	win pts 8	Jake Tuli (South Africa)
08/10/1957	London	win pts 8	Len Reece (Cardiff)

Billy Rafferty (Glasgow) - continued

16/10/1957	Hamilton	win ret 4	Billy Skelly (Belfast)
02/12/1957	Doncaster	drew 8	Eric Brett (Retford)
28/02/1958	Rotherham	win pts 8	Kimpo Amarfio (Ghana)
02/04/1958	Paisley	win pts 8	Pat McCairn (Bethnal Green)
28/05/1958	Hamilton	win pts 8	Danny McNamee (Glasgow)
02/07/1958	Glasgow	lost rsf 5	Eric Brett (Retford)
25/07/1958	Aberdeen	win pts 8	Danny McNamee (Glasgow)
28/08/1958	Paisley	win rsf 5	Terry Spinks (London)
16/10/1958	Paisley	lost rsf 6	Tommy Miller (Lothian)
05/02/1959	Glasgow	win pts 8	Dennis East (Plaistow)
15/04/1959	Glasgow	win pts 8	George Dormer (East Ham)
14/05/1959	Glasgow	win pts 8	Graham Van Der Walt (South Africa)
17/06/1959	Glasgow	win pts 8	Mohamed Zarzi (France)
28/10/1959	Glasgow	win pts 12	Len Reece (Cardiff)
	(British Bantamweight Title Eliminator)		
09/12/1959	Paisley	win pts 10	Dwight Hawkins (USA)
19/03/1960	Belfast	lost rsf 13	Freddie Gilroy (Belfast)
	(British, Empire and European Bantamweight Titles)		
09/06/1960	Manchester	win pts 10	Ignacio Pina (Mexico)
16/09/1960	Glasgow	win ko 4	Angelo Priami (Italy)
30/10/1960	Cagliari	lost pts 15	Piero Rollo (Italy)
29/04/1961	Belfast	win pts 12	George Bowes (West Hartlepool)
	(Final Eliminator British Bantamweight Title)		
03/03/1962	Belfast	lost ko 12	Freddie Gilroy (Belfast)
	(British and Empire Bantamweight Titles)		

31 contests, won 24, drew 1, lost 6.

John Smillie (Fauldhouse)
Bantamweight/Featherweight
Born 12/11/1933

17/03/1955	Glasgow	win ko 1	Benny Vaun (Belfast)
22/04/1955	Leith	win pts 6	Ernie Savery (Dunstable)
10/05/1955	Glasgow	win rsf 3	Billy Gibson (Fishburn)
02/06/1955	Glasgow	win pts 6	Dave Robins (Camberwell)
30/06/1955	Glasgow	win rsf 5	Jimmy Brewer (Kings Cross)
18/07/1955	West Hartlepool	win rsf 2	Tommy Gillen (Hayes)
08/08/1955	West Hartlepool	win pts 8	Mickey Roche (Dublin)
06/09/1955	London	drew 8	Ron Johnson (Bethnal Green)
21/11/1955	Middlesbrough	win pts 8	Don Coshirel (Alderney)
04/02/1956	Belfast	win ret 5	George O'Neill (Belfast)
27/06/1956	Glasgow	win pts 10	George Dormer (East Ham)
	(British Bantamweight Title Eliminator)		
13/08/1956	West Hartlepool	win pts 8	Jimmy Carson (Belfast)
07/09/1956	Manchester	win rsf 5	George O'Neill (Belfast)
16/11/1956	Manchester	win pts 8	Pat McCairn (Bethnal Green)
04/12/1956	London	win rsf 4	Alan Sillett (Acton)
19/01/1957	Belfast	lost pts 8	Jimmy Carson (Belfast)
22/05/1957	Glasgow	lost rsf 6	Peter Keenan (Glasgow)
	(British and Empire Bantamweight Titles)		

John Smillie (Fauldhouse) - continued

09/07/1957	London	win dis 5	George Dormer (East Ham)
12/09/1957	Falkirk	win pts 8	Pat McCairn (Bethnal Green)
09/12/1957	Nottingham	win ret 3	Rudy Edwards (British Guiana)
23/01/1958	Liverpool	lost ret 4	Eddie Burns (Liverpool)
17/02/1958	Newcastle	win pts 8	Eddie Burns (Liverpool)
05/05/1958	Newcastle	win pts 8	Andy Hayford (Ghana)
30/06/1958	West Hartlepool	lost rsf 4	Ola Michael (Nigeria)
25/11/1958	Leith	win pts 8	Andy Hayford (Ghana)
10/01/1959	Belfast	lost ko 1	Floyd Robertson (Ghana)
28/05/1959	Glasgow	drew 8	Owen Reilly (Glasgow)
07/09/1959	Newcastle	win ret 7	Charles Odumasi (Nigeria)
21/10/1959	Paisley	win pts 8	Junior Cassidy (Nigeria)
16/11/1959	Carlisle	win pts 8	Billy Calvert (Sheffield)
05/01/1960	London	lost ret 5	Sexton Mabena (South Africa)
09/03/1960	Glasgow	win rsf 7	George Judge (Glasgow)
28/04/1960	Leith	win pts 8	Moses Edeki (Nigeria)
09/05/1960	Manchester	lost rsf 6	Chris Elliott (Leicester)
19/05/1960	Irvine	win pts 6	Moses Edeki (Nigeria)
02/06/1960	Coatbridge	win rsf 6	George Judge (Glasgow)
14/06/1960	Merthyr	lost rsf 2	Harry Carroll (Cardiff)
22/08/1960	Carlisle	lost rsf 1	Ronnie Calvert (Sheffield)

38 contests, won 27, drew 2, lost 9.

Derry Treanor (Glasgow)
Bantamweight/Featherweight
Born 17/07/1937

19/06/1956	London	win pts 4	Dennis East (Plaistow)
24/07/1956	Dartford	lost pts 6	Billy Downer (Stoke Newington)
14/12/1956	Leith	lost pts 6	Billy Rafferty (Glasgow)
01/04/1957	Nottingham	lost pts 6	Eric Brett (Retford)
09/05/1957	Govan	win pts 8	Billy Skelly (Belfast)
21/06/1957	Manchester	win pts 8	Eric Brett (Retford)
09/12/1957	Newcastle	win pts 8	Billy Skelly (Belfast)
13/01/1958	Newcastle	lost pts 8	George Bowes (West Hartlepool)
05/02/1958	Glasgow	win rsf 5	Eddie Burns (Liverpool)
05/03/1958	Glasgow	win ret 3	Ken Langford (Slough)
23/04/1958	Glasgow	win pts 8	Terry Toole (Hackney)
21/05/1958	Glasgow	win pts 8	Jose Luis Martinez (Spain)
18/06/1958	Glasgow	win pts 8	Kimpo Amarfio (Ghana)
28/08/1958	Paisley	win rsf 6	Peter Keenan(Glasgow)
19/11/1958	Glasgow	lost rsf 7	Roy Jacobs (Nigeria)
23/05/1959	Derby	win pts 8	Eric Brett (Retford)
01/09/1959	London	win pts 8	Terry Spinks (West Ham)
28/01/1960	Paisley	win pts 8	Dave Croll (Dundee)
08/07/1960	Surbiton	win pts 8	Hugh O'Neill (Walworth)
12/04/1961	Paisley	win pts 8	Johnny Kidd (Aberdeen)
02/05/1961	Glasgow	win pts 8	Jean Renard (Belgium)
10/11/1961	Manchester	win rsf 7	Freddie Dobson (Manchester)
10/04/1962	Wembley	lost rsf 14	Howard Winstone (Wales)
	(British Featherweight Title)		

23 contests, won 17, lost 6.

Appendix 3

Some Boxer Profiles

Alex Ambrose

Alex Ambrose was born at the Round Toll in Glasgow in April 1936, close to Oakbank Hospital and just south of Possilpark. He attended Rockvilla School and Keppochhill School and became an apprentice fitter with NB Loco when he left school. In 1955, he was called up for national service but recalls spending much of his time in the gym and boxing for the army. He had become friends with Peter Keenan prior to his call-up and turned to Keenan for help and advice when his national service stint ended. He turned professional in September 1957.

Alex fought 24 of his 40 professional contests in Scotland, losing only 4 and drawing 1. His efforts in the remainder of the UK yielded 6 wins, 6 losses and a draw. He lost all 3 of his overseas fights on points but these contests were against top quality opponents Piero Rollo, Risto Luukkonen and Felix Brami and he felt that he had won two of them.

He won the Scottish flyweight title in 1958 against George McDade. In a rematch for the title, he drew with McDade before losing the title in the next year to Jackie Brown. The highlight of his career was his British flyweight title fight against Frankie Jones in 1959. Alex thought that he was in front in that fight and had opportunities to finish off the champion but it was Jones who got the decision.

Following defeat by the tough Felix Brami in Paris, Alex gave up boxing in 1963 and spent many years as a publican. He is now retired and lives with his mother in Maryhill.

Evan Armstrong

Evan Armstrong was born in Ayr but moved to Tarbolton in 1964 when he got married. His early passion was to play snooker before he became seriously involved with boxing. He was employed by the Electricity Board before he turned professional in late 1963.

Evan began professional life as a featherweight and won his first 7 contests. However, he was stopped in his next contest by his old amateur foe, Bobby Fisher. Two months later, he was outpointed by Brian Cartwright. He returned to winning ways in 1965, losing only 1 of 8. He had moved up the featherweight rankings by stopping top challenger George Bowes. However, following another defeat at the hands of Brian Cartwright, Evan moved down to bantamweight. He was quickly elevated to British number 3 behind McGowan and Rudkin following his victory over Monty Laud. He confirmed his new status by knocking out Jackie Brown to take the Scottish bantamweight title in September. Cartwright was his only defeat in 8 contests in 1966.

Evan's 13-fight unbeaten sequence lasted from April 1966 to March 1968. He had won a British bantamweight title final eliminator against Jim McCann in May 1967 but it was some time before he fought for the title. Evan spread his wings in 1968 and took fights in Mexico and Los Angeles against world-class opposition. Unfortunately, he lost both fights but his profile had been raised. The British title fight against Alan Rudkin took place in June 1969 but Evan was forced to retire in the eleventh round.

Evan Armstrong continued to box in the seventies. As a featherweight, he became Scottish champion in 1970 and British champion by defeating Jimmy Revie in 1971. He was unsuccessful in his attempts for the Empire title in 1971 and the European title in 1972. However, he won the Empire title in Brisbane in 1974. He successfully defended his British title in 1972 before losing the title to Tommy Glencross in the same year. However, he regained the title from Glencross in 1973. He further won a British and Empire title defence in 1974. In his subsequent and final professional contest, Evan was stopped in Accra in Ghana and decided to quit boxing while he was still at the top.

Evan returned to life at the Electricity Board and continues to live at Tarbolton.

Bobby Boland

Bobby Boland was born in Dundee in 1929. His first professional fight was just before his seventeenth birthday. By the end of 1949, Boland had lost only 3 of 37 fights and was a top contender for the British bantamweight title. He had been outpointed by European bantamweight champion, Luis Romero, in Barcelona. He was disqualified against Tommy Proffitt whom he knocked out in the rematch and he was knocked out by Ron Bissell whom he outpointed in the rematch.

In 1950, he fought Tommy Proffitt in a British bantamweight title eliminator and was again disqualified. This major blow to Boland spurred him on in his next fight when he defeated British bantamweight champion, Danny O'Sullivan. He also defeated Theo Medina, Fernando Gagnon and Amleto Falcinelli who were the bantamweight champions of France, Canada and Italy respectively. He turned down the chance to fight Eddie Carson for the Scottish bantamweight title as his sights remained on the British title. His record for 1950 was 8 wins, 4 losses and one draw.

Boland was ranked number 2 in the UK behind Peter Keenan at the beginning of 1951. He began the year with two wins but there followed a further disqualification, this time following a clash of heads against Maurice Sandeyron in Paris. He then fought Peter Keenan for the British bantamweight title but was stopped in the twelfth round. Boland had fought courageously but had a bad cut and was floored in the tenth following slack defensive work and was unable to get back into the fight. A trip to South

Africa followed but Boland was knocked out in the first round by world bantamweight champion Vic Toweel.

In his first fight of 1952, Boland weighed just over 9 stones. Although he did shed some weight in subsequent fights, he was undoubtedly a featherweight by the end of the year. His 1952 record was 4 wins in 11 contests and his UK bantamweight ranking had dropped to 8 by the end of 1952. He fought and lost twice to future world featherweight champion Hogan Bassey.

Boland had 9 further fights between 1953 and 1956 but won only twice. He did not feature in the UK rankings after 1952. In his final fight against Freddie Hicks, he was disqualified for going in with his head low. His overall professional record was 75 contests, won 48, lost 22, drew 5. Five of the losses were by disqualification.

Chic Brogan

Chic Brogan was born in Clydebank in 1932 and was an apprentice joiner when he turned professional at the age of 18 in 1950. As a bantamweight, he won 6 of his first 9 contests. 2 of his 3 losses were on disqualifications. He was close to Peter Keenan and was his training partner in South Africa in December 1951/ January 1952 when Keenan fought Vic Toweel for the world bantamweight title. Brogan fought on the same bill but lost a points decision to South African flyweight champion, Kalla Persson. By March 1954, Brogan had won 11 and lost 9 of his 20 contests, had moved up to featherweight but had not penetrated the UK rankings. In his next contest, he outpointed Gene Caffrey in a Scottish featherweight title eliminator. The run up to his Scottish title fight with Charlie Hill was unremarkable and he won only 2 of 5 contests. In his biggest fight to date, he was outpointed by Hill.

He fought and lost three times in 1955 and reverted to bantamweight in 1956. He fought Malcolm Grant for the Scottish bantamweight title, losing the first time but winning the return to become Scottish bantamweight champion. There followed a 4-fight unbeaten sequence and a UK bantamweight ranking of 4. Fights against Dick Currie and Peter Keenan did not materialise but, in September 1957, he travelled to Paris to face world bantamweight champion, Alphonse Halimi. Halimi was too strong for the Scottish champion and knocked him out in the second round. The fight had been at 8 stones 6 pounds and Brogan had to work hard to make the weight.

In 1958, Brogan moved back to featherweight and in his first outing of the year he defeated Owen Reilly on points to win the Scottish featherweight title. In his next fight, he narrowly outpointed John O'Brien. These wins catapulted Brogan up the UK featherweight rankings and he was matched with Charlie Hill for the British featherweight title in July 1958. Hill retained his title when Brogan had to retire in the eleventh with a bad cut over his right eye.

Brogan did not fight again until November 1959. He travelled to Dundee to defend his Scottish featherweight title against Dave Croll. Croll won by a knockout in the second round and Chic Brogan retired after 9 years of professional boxing.

Jackie Brown

Jackie Brown was born in the south side of Edinburgh in 1935. In his youth, he was a keen cyclist but took up boxing following a chance visit to Gilmerton Amateur Boxing Club. His boxing career was in doubt following several mastoid operations and the loss of hearing in one of his ears but he was to make a full recovery.

Jackie Brown turned professional in October 1958 and, within a year, he was Scottish flyweight champion. In his fifth contest, he stopped Alex Ambrose to take the Scottish title. In his next contest, he defeated Derek Lloyd in a British flyweight title eliminator but it would be some time before he would contest the title. By August 1960, Brown had won all of his 15 professional fights. He had defeated former world bantamweight champion Mario D'Agata and Johnny Morrissey in the course of his amazing progress but his winning sequence was about to end.

In his next fight, he retired with a damaged wrist against Derek Lloyd. He was then knocked out by the much heavier and more powerful Freddie Gilroy. He won two of his next three contests but his reputation was damaged by a no contest result against Eddie Barraclough in Newcastle. He was then stopped by future European bantamweight champion, Piero Rollo. He ended 1961 with a narrow but well-earned points victory over Walter McGowan.

In 1962, Brown won the British flyweight title vacated by John Caldwell when he outpointed Brian Cartwright. Later in the year, he won the Empire title by outpointing Orizu Obilaso. He lost only 1 of 5 contests in 1962, against former European flyweight champion Risto Luukkonen.

In May 1963, Jackie Brown lost both titles to the much improved Walter McGowan. He moved up to bantamweight and won the Scottish bantamweight title against Tommy Burgoyne in 1964. In the same year, he boxed a draw with former world bantamweight titleholder, John Caldwell. In June 1965, Brown suffered his first defeat for 21 months when he was knocked out by world ranked Ron Jones.

Brown lost his Scottish bantamweight title to Evan Armstrong in 1966 and retired shortly afterwards. Brown had fought professionally for eight years and had lost only 10 of 44 contests. Not one of these defeats was on points and most of them were against heavier opponents. As a successful flyweight, he had to take on bantamweights if he wanted regular boxing. He fought three times abroad against top bantamweight opposition but lost inside the distance on each occasion. A thoughtful man who enjoyed singing and dancing, Jackie Brown was one of the finest Scottish boxers of this era.

Ken Buchanan

Ken Buchanan was born just outside of Portobello and was interested in boxing from a very early age. He was already a member of the Sparta Boxing Club when he left Towerbank Primary School for Portobello Secondary. On leaving Secondary school, Ken trained and qualified as a carpenter in Edinburgh. He turned professional when aged 20 in 1965. Bobby Neill had wanted to manage the young Buchanan but a suggested change of style and a permanent move to London were not on the Buchanan agenda.

Buchanan fought and won 16 contests between 1965 and 1966. He won the Scottish lightweight title in his 17th professional fight and his first in Scotland. In his 24th fight, he won the British lightweight title from Maurice Cullen in February 1968. By the end of the sixties, Buchanan had extended his winning sequence to 33 and was ranked number 6 in the world. Only 3 of his professional fights had taken place in Scotland.

Ken Buchanan went on to greater things in the seventies. In his first outing of the decade, he fought outside of the UK for the first time. He also suffered his first professional defeat. He was narrowly defeated over 15 rounds in his European title fight against Miguel Velazquez in Madrid. He returned to winning ways with 3 wins in the UK including the retention of his British title against Brian Hudson. Next stop was Puerto Rico for a WBA world lightweight title fight against the battle-hardened holder Ismael Laguna. Buchanan won the world title in September 1970 with a superb display in the sweltering heat of San Juan.

A win at Madison Square Garden was followed by a successful WBA/WBO unification in February 1971 against Ruben Navarro. Buchanan then outclassed Laguna in a world title return at Madison Square Garden in September 1971. He returned to the Garden in June 1972 to defend his world title against Roberto Duran. Duran landed a low blow after the bell at the end of the thirteenth round. Buchanan went down holding his groin and did not answer the bell for round 14. The referee stated that he had stopped the fight because Buchanan did not answer the bell for round 14. Ken Buchanan was probably robbed of his world title by dirty tactics but he had been fighting in the dirty tactic capital of the world.

Buchanan had two further successes at the Garden in 1972. In his next outing, he defeated Jim Watt in Glasgow to retain his British lightweight title. There followed a period on the road where he recorded victories in Miami, New York, Toronto and Copenhagen. He won the European lightweight title in Italy in May 1974 and retained the title in Paris in December 1974. In February 1975, Buchanan fought for the WBC lightweight title. He lost a unanimous points decision in Japan to Ishimatsu Suzucki. Duran remained the WBA title holder and had previously stopped Suzucki. Buchanan subsequently defended his European title in Italy. However, as a result of damage that he had received to his eyes, Ken decided to retire from boxing.

Following financial difficulties, Ken returned to the ring in 1979 and after two winning contests, he was defeated by Londonderry's Charlie Nash in a match for the European title. There were further fights between 1980 and 1982 but Ken Buchanan had seen his best days.

Chic Calderwood

Chic Calderwood was born in Craigneuk in January 1937. He was unbeaten in his first 29 fights in the 4-year period September 1957 to August 1961. He won the Scottish light heavyweight title against Dave Mooney in 1958. He then won the British and Empire light heavyweight titles against Arthur Howard and Johnny Halafihi respectively in 1960. In December 1961, he suffered his first professional defeat against Henry Hank in Detroit.

In 1962, all of his 3 fights were title fights. He retained his British and Empire titles against Stan Cullis and then his Empire title against Johnny Halafihi. He then contested the vacant European light heavyweight title against Giulio Rinaldi in Rome but was defeated on points.

In 1963, he won 4 of 6 fights. He retained his British and Empire titles against Ron Redrup but lost points decisions to Eddie Cotton in Paisley and Gustav Scholz in Germany. Chic was imprisoned for 3 months at the end of 1963 for assault. Following a subsequent suspension, he won 3 of 3 in 1964. He won back the British light heavyweight title against Bob Nicholson in November 1964.

He lost 2 of 4 in 1965, to heavyweight Freddie Mack to whom he conceded 10 pounds and to his old foe Cowboy McCormack. He won 3 of 4 in 1966 before ending his career with two further title fights. His European bid against Piero Del Papa was declared no contest because of appalling and dangerous weather conditions and Del Papa retained the title. His final fight was for the world light heavyweight title against Jose Torres of Costa Rica on 15th October 1966 when he was knocked out in the second round

Few got to know Chic Calderwood. To outsiders, he appeared dour and sullen and seldom smiled. However, he played the accordion and the trumpet, loved horses and animals and walking in the countryside and had thought of becoming a farmer. Unfortunately, he did not live to achieve this ambition. Chic Calderwood was killed in a car crash at Fiddler's Bridge between Carluke and Lanark on 12th November 1966, just 4 weeks after he fought for the world title. Hundreds turned out to witness his funeral at Wishaw Old Parish Church.

Chic fought for the British title 4 times, the Empire title 4 times, the European title twice and the world title once. He won all of his British and Empire title fights but was unsuccessful in his European and world attempts. No one had taken his British or Empire titles from him in the ring. He had fought only 2 fellow Scots in his professional career and Cowboy McCormack was the only UK fighter to have beaten him.

Vic Herman

Vic Herman was born in Manchester in 1929 but moved to Glasgow as a young boy. He was one of four boxing brothers and stepped into the professional ring for the first time in 1947. In his professional career, Herman fought 57 times, winning 38, losing 16 and drawing 3. In his thrilling encounter with Peter Keenan in 1949, he put Keenan through the ropes in the fifth and Keenan had to scramble back into the ring to beat the count. Keenan was promptly put on the canvas but the bell sounded when the count reached seven. Keenan's boxing skills gained him a narrow verdict over eight rounds.

The dynamic little battler from the Gorbals was a favourite of local fight fans. His growing reputation won him contests at the Royal Albert Hall and Earls Court Arena in 1949. He won and held the Scottish flyweight title from January 1951 until August 1952. Perhaps his finest achievement was to come through the series of British flyweight title eliminators against Norman Lewis and Norman Tennant and to take former world champion Terry Allen the distance in his fight for the British title. Allen had won the world title against Honore Pratesi in 1950. Herman had drawn with Frenchman Pratesi in 1950 and beat him in a rematch in 1952.

Herman undertook a Far East tour in 1953 where he lost to world flyweight champion Yoshio Shirai and future world bantamweight contender Chamrern Songkitrat. His final contest was a return and another points defeat against Peter Keenan at the Kelvin Hall. Herman had fought at the top of his profession with limited success.

Outside the ring, Vic Herman was a prolific oil painter and played both the violin and bagpipes. He was a character and, on occasion, piped himself into the ring before his contest. Vic Herman died on 7th March 2002 aged 73.

Charlie Hill

Charlie Hill was born in 1930. Following the end of the Second World War, he developed a passion for cycling and could often be found pedalling his bicycle through the country lanes around Cambuslang. After leaving school, he became a shipyard electrician by trade and it was during his apprenticeship that he became involved in boxing.

Hill was almost 23 when he turned professional in June 1953. In his second professional contest, Hill was well ahead when he was disqualified because of a low blow. He was rematched with his opponent, Andy Monahan, in the following month and knocked him out in the second round. The disqualification was to be the only blemish on Hill's fight record until December 1956 at which time his record read 26 wins, 1 defeat. He won the Scottish featherweight title in December 1954. In 1955, he was due to meet Sammy McCarthy in a British featherweight title eliminator. Due to various illnesses, the fight did not go ahead and McCarthy was matched with Billy Kelly for the title. This decision infuriated Hill but when McCarthy was unable to make the weight, Hill was given the fight against Kelly whom he outpointed to take the British featherweight title in February 1956.

In December 1956, he accepted a non-title fight with Bobby Neill and was knocked out in the first round. A second defeat followed in the next month but Hill was back on song by October 1957 when he knocked out Jimmy Brown to retain his British title. In December, he was stopped by Percy Lewis as he tried to win the Empire featherweight title. In 1958, he notched up his third successive British title win and a Lonsdale Belt by stopping Chic Brogan.

The long awaited title defence against Bobby Neill took place at Nottingham in April 1959. The referee stopped the fight in favour of Neill and Charlie Hill retired from boxing.

Charlie Hill may not have achieved his full potential as a professional. He was due to fight Jean Sneyers for the European featherweight title in 1954 and although he had the support of the Scottish Area Council, the fight was vetoed by the British Boxing Board. It is a pity that this contest did not materialise as it would have meant a step up in class when Hill was at his best. He also turned down potential money-spinning fights with Peter Keenan, Hogan Bassey and Cherif Hamia at this time. A victory over any of this trio would have enhanced his reputation and confidence considerably.

Charlie Hill was a professional for just under six years but never fought outside the UK. He won 31 fights and lost 5. He fought 17 times in Scotland and won each time. He won 5 of 6 contests in Belfast. He lost 4 of 13 fights in England. Following his retirement, Charlie Hill trained John McDermott for a time before he emigrated to Australia.

Frankie Jones

Frankie Jones was born in Larkhall in 1933. On leaving school, he became a coal miner and was employed at Plean Colliery in Stirlingshire. He did his National Service with the RAF and became a professional boxer under manager Joe Gans in 1955.

Following 6 straight wins, Frankie fought Dick Currie for the Scottish flyweight title. The match also doubled as an eliminator for the British flyweight title. Jones won the Scottish title on points and, following 3 further victories, took his record to 10 wins in 10 starts. He had already beaten Len Reece whom he had to fight for the vacant British and Empire titles in July 1957. He won both titles in style. Following win number 11, he defended his Empire title against Dennis Adams in October and was surprisingly stopped.

He lost 3 of his next 5 fights but one of the victories was in a non-title fight against Dennis Adams. He then successfully defended his British title against Alex Ambrose but future world champion John Caldwell was his next challenger. He lost 2 of his next 4 fights and then took a fight in Venezuela where he was knocked out. His final contest was for the British title against

John Caldwell and again he was knocked out. There was no future for Frankie in professional boxing and he retired.

Frankie Jones died on 1st January 1991 at the age of 57.

Peter Keenan

Peter Keenan was born in Scotstoun in 1928. He left school when aged 14 and knew immediately that he wanted to work for himself. He graduated from selling coal briquettes from a barrow to becoming an entrepreneur and successful businessman throughout his life in Glasgow.

Peter Keenan turned professional on 17th September 1948. By the end of 1949, he had fought and won his first 18 contests. In May 1951 at Firhill, he lifted the British bantamweight title by defeating Danny O'Sullivan. Back at Firhill, he retained the title against Bobby Boland in June 1951 and won the European bantamweight title against Luis Romero in September. His winning sequence was now 31 but disappointment was around the corner.

He ended 1951 with a draw against Maurice Sandeyron. He then travelled to South Africa to fight Vic Toweel for the world and Empire bantamweight titles. He suffered his first professional loss to Toweel on points over 15 rounds. At Firhill in May, he lost his European title to Jean Sneyers when he had to retire in the fifth round. He completed a dismal year with a defeat by Amleto Falcinelli.

He was back to winning ways in 1953. He retained his British title against Frankie Williams and regained the European bantamweight title by beating Maurice Sandeyron. However, he lost both titles to John Kelly in Belfast. In 1954, he beat Eddie Carson to win the Scottish bantamweight title, regained the British title from John Kelly and defended the title against George O'Neill.

In 1955, he won the Empire bantamweight title by defeating Australian Bobby Sinn in Sydney. Later in the year, he successfully defended the Empire title against Jake Tuli following a magnificent comeback. In 1956, he again travelled to Australia and defeated Kevin James to retain his title. However, in his global travels in 1955 and 1956 he was defeated four times and these defeats halted his chance of another world title fight.

In 1957, he retained his British and Empire titles against John Smillie. In 1958, he retained his Empire title against Graham Van Der Walt and Pat Supple but was stopped by Derry Treanor and outpointed by world champion Alphonse Halimi. He lost his British and Empire titles to Freddie Gilroy in January 1959 and immediately retired.

Keenan fought 66 times, won 54, drew 1 and lost 11. He won 6 of his 8 British title fights and was the only Scot to win two Lonsdale belts outright. He also won 6 of his 8 Empire title fights and 2 of his 4 European title fights. He was dedicated to the sport and was the leading Scottish boxer in the fifties by a considerable distance. He was also the leading Scottish promoter in the sixties but turned to wrestling promotion which offered a better financial return.

Peter Keenan has been described as cocky, controversial, impatient, outspoken, arrogant, belligerent, generous, charitable, single-minded, ambitious, innovative, stubborn and determined. He upset many people in his lifetime and had many famous clashes with the Scottish Area Council. However, he was undoubtedly the Scottish boxing personality of this era and a true Scottish boxing legend.

Peter Keenan died at Gartnaval Hospital on 27th July 2000 after a long illness.

Jim Kenny

Gentleman Jim Kenny was born in Polmont, just outside of Falkirk, in 1928 and turned professional in 1947 when he was 19. By the end of 1949, he had fought 32 times, winning 27, losing 4 and drawing one. He won the Scottish featherweight title in 1949 with a win over Jackie Robertson. At the beginning of 1950, he was ranked 2 in the UK behind British champion, Ronnie Clayton.

1950 was a wonderful year for the Gentleman. He won both his semi final and final eliminator for the British and Empire featherweight titles by knockout. In February, he knocked out Irishman, Tommy Burns, in the third round and in May, he knocked out Bert Jackson of Fleetwood in the fifth round. He had three further wins against good opposition in the period to July. In August, he was surprisingly held to a draw against Tom Bailey but followed up with two points wins against continental opposition. In November 1950, he fought Ronnie Clayton for the British and Empire featherweight titles. Although he was floored in the fourth round, he fought back well and put up a good show but it was Clayton who took the points verdict.

In 1951, Kenny lost his Scottish title to George Stewart, and was stopped by Frank Johnson and world bantamweight champion, Vic Toweel, in South Africa. After two wins in 1952, he lost to Tommy Miller in an eliminator for the Scottish featherweight title. There followed two defeats but then he upset the form book by outpointing Ronnie Clayton over 10 rounds. He had three further fights before retirement, losing only to future British featherweight champion, Sammy McCarthy.

John McCluskey

John McCluskey was born in Burnbank in 1944 and attended school in Hamilton where he still lives. On leaving school, he trained as a hairdresser at Stow College in Glasgow. He lost his job in East Kilbride village when he took time off to take part in the Tokyo Olympics in 1964. On his return from Tokyo, he worked as a driver for Scottish Special Housing Association.

John turned professional in 1965. Having won his first 7 fights, he fought and won the British flyweight title against Tony Barlow in fight number 8. He turned his attention to overseas opponents and following two further victories, he tasted defeat for the first time against European flyweight champion Fernando Atzori. He had three further victories against overseas opposition before he travelled to Naples to take on Atzori for the European flyweight title but was knocked out in the fourth round. Two further defeats followed.

1969 was a much better year for John McCluskey. He was unbeaten in 5 fights and notched up wins in South Africa, USA and Switzerland. He also retained his British flyweight title by again defeating Tony Barlow. The Swiss win was particularly sweet as he reversed the disputed loss to Fritz Chervet of the previous year.

In the seventies, John won and lost the Empire flyweight title in Melbourne. He also fought twice for the European flyweight title and once for the European bantamweight title. He lost each of these fights which were all held at the Hallenstadion in Zurich. He retained his British flyweight title against Tony Davies in 1974. John retired from professional boxing in 1975 whilst he was British champion. His overall professional record was 23 wins and 15 losses in 38 contests. He fought overseas 15 times, in England and Wales 18 times but only 5 of his fights were in Scotland.

In 2000, John was knocked down by a car and suffered a blood clot. He was ill for some time but has made a full recovery. He is a member of the Scottish Area Council and takes local boxing classes twice per week. He remains a close friend of Walter McGowan and regularly visits him.

John McCormack

John McCormack was born in Maryhill in 1937. He lived in Bantaskin Street and attended nearby St. Mary's school. He spent some time in the RAF alongside fellow middleweight Len Mullen and Lisbon Lion Bertie Auld. He was a proficient footballer as well as a skilled boxer. He played for Maryhill Harp and almost signed for Third Lanark. In 1957, however, he got married and became a professional boxer.

The Cowboy won his first 8 professional fights in a 6-month period. He then unexpectedly lost to Coventry's Jim Lynas. He won his next 5 and then the Scottish middleweight title when he defeated Len Mullen in July 1958. He then won his return against Jim Lynas and defeated Martin Hansen in a British middleweight title eliminator. Further victories took his impressive record to one loss in 23. In September 1959, he became British middleweight champion when he defeated Terry Downes on a disqualification. He held the title for 49 days as Downes stopped him in the return.

Cowboy began 1960 with 3 wins including a win in Milan. He was the first British fighter to win in Italy for 14 years. There followed a trip to Berlin to face Gustav Scholz whose only defeat in 12 years had been in Paris. Predictably, the points decision went to the German. There followed 4 more victories including an eliminator for the British middleweight title against Phil Edwards.

In October 1961, Cowboy won the European middleweight title against Harko Kokmeyer. In 1962, he successfully defended against Heini Freytag in Frankfurt but then lost the title on a disqualification to Chris Christensen in Copenhagen. The Copenhagen defeat was a travesty and Cowboy was robbed of his title which he had agreed to defend against Laszlo Papp.

He got back to business with two wins in Glasgow, including a very pleasing win over Henry Hank. In November, he fought George Aldridge for the British middleweight title and was surprisingly defeated. He moved up to light heavyweight and won 3 of his next 4. In June 1965, he stopped Chic Calderwood. In his final contest, he was defeated on points by Young McCormack in a British light heavyweight title eliminator.

Cowboy feels that he has had a great life, thanks to boxing.

Walter McGowan

Walter McGowan was born in Burnbank in 1942. The second youngest of 5 sons and 5 daughters, his father was Joe Gans, a former boxer, who ran a local gym. Walter was introduced to the sport whilst still in his formative years and was 13 when his occasional housemate and future sparring partner, Frankie Jones, became British flyweight champion. On leaving school, Walter rejected a jockey apprenticeship and went on to qualify as a car mechanic at a Hamilton garage.

Walter turned professional in 1961. After two wins, he came unstuck in his third contest, against seasoned professional Jackie Brown who won the British flyweight title three months later. After a 6-fight winning sequence, he again met Brown in May 1963 for the British and Empire flyweight titles and this time he was the victor. His winning sequence was extended to 11 following an Empire title defence and a win against European bantamweight champion Risto Luukkonen. In April 1964, there followed his first overseas trip as a professional against the vastly experienced Salvatore Burruni who was unbeaten in more than 4 years and had been European flyweight champion for almost 3 years. Although Walter was defeated narrowly on points, he put up a brave fight and had grown immensely in stature.

He won his next 5 fights but then suffered successive defeats in 1965 to world top 10 bantamweights Jose Medel and Ron Jones. A second trip to Rome completed 1965. He was unable to take the European bantamweight title from Tommaso Galli who somehow achieved a draw verdict despite being completely outboxed by McGowan.

1966 was a great year for Walter. In June, he outpointed Salvatore Burruni to win the world flyweight title and in September, he won the British and Empire bantamweight titles against Alan Rudkin. He was now the British and Empire champion at both flyweight and bantamweight and world champion at flyweight. However, he had to relinquish his British and Empire flyweight titles and he then, in December, defended and lost his world title against Chartchai Chionoi in Bangkok.

Walter remained British and Empire bantamweight champion. On his return to the UK, he chalked up 3 good wins before he was rematched with Chionoi for the world title in London. An accidental head clash robbed McGowan of winning back the title. He was well ahead when the referee had to stop the fight because of another eye injury. Eight months later, Walter put up his remaining titles against Alan Rudkin and he was narrowly outpointed by the Liverpudlian.

Walter had been to the pinnacle but now he had no title to defend. He fought again three times in 1968 and three times in 1969 and won all of these fights. Walter had however lost interest in his profession and when a rematch with Rudkin was not forthcoming, he called it a day.

Following his retirement from the ring, Walter moved first to Prestwick and then emigrated to New Zealand. He returned to Scotland and bought a pub in Carluke. There followed marital and drink problems and Walter has now been ill for some years and resident in a nursing home. Walter was undoubtedly a Scotland great. Without cut eyes, he could have been the greatest of all time.

Sammy McSpadden

Sammy McSpadden was born in Hamilton in 1941 and subsequently lived in Newarthill. He was a training partner of Walter McGowan and trained by Joe Gans. As he was unable to get many fights in Scotland when he turned professional in November 1960, he moved to Fulham in London with his brother George who fought as Al Keen and was also a good lightweight.

By the end of 1961, McSpadden was unbeaten in 14 fights. All of these fights had been in England other than one appearance at Hamilton Town Hall when he beat Ricky Kiernan, a man that Al Keen would later defeat twice. By the end of 1962, McSpadden was ranked number 3 lightweight in the UK behind Dave Charnley and Maurice Cullen whom he had previously beaten. Two more victories followed in the early part of 1963, taking his unbeaten tally to 23. He could not resist a trip to New York for fight 24. In August, he lost his unbeaten record on points to Italian-American Johnny Bizzarro who had fought for the world featherweight title earlier in the year but who was only a quarter of a pound lighter than McSpadden when they fought. This was a step up in class for Sammy which he handled well. Following the fight, he was inundated with offers from Australia, South Africa and the United States.

He beat Spike McCormack on his return to London. Dave Charnley had beaten Maurice Cullen in May and McSpadden was surely next in line to challenge for the title. McSpadden was matched with world featherweight champion Sugar Ramos at Wembley in October but was stopped in 2 rounds. Perhaps the referee had been a tad hasty but the gulf in class was apparent.

Sammy next fought in South Africa. He lost twice to South African champion Stoffel Steyn but defeated the former South African title holder, Charlie Els. McSpadden had a splendid record as a lightweight but it was now time to move to welterweight and a fight with Dave Charnley would not now happen. He had two UK wins towards the end of 1964, the most impressive being his defeat of the number 1 welterweight challenger, Johnny Cooke. McSpadden was now number 1 welterweight challenger to Brian Curvis.

McSpadden defeated Jewish Moroccan, Nessim Max Cohen, at Wembley in June 1965 and returned to South Africa. There, he lost to world number 4 welterweight Willie Ludick and to number 2 South African welterweight, Fraser Toweel. In November 1965, he travelled to Cardiff to face Brian Curvis for the British and Empire welterweight titles. He fought courageously but was well beaten by Curvis and the referee halted the fight in the twelfth round.

Sammy had peaked and his career was almost at an end. He fought three times in 1966 but lost each fight and decided to retire. He was a wonderful prospect as a lightweight with unlimited stamina and determination but seemed to lose something when he moved to welterweight. He had boundless energy and durability, he was not afraid to travel and did not shirk world class opposition but he had probably reached his limit when he lost to Curvis.

Johnny Morrissey

Johnny Morrissey was born in Carfin in 1937 but moved to next-door Newarthill when he married his wife Margaret. He was one of five children all of whom have remained in the area. He was a plumber to trade and spent some time working on the oilrigs with Cowboy McCormack. He avoided National Service supposedly because of an ear infection but he is sure that his future manager Sammy Docherty had some influence on this outcome.

He made his professional debut just before his twentieth birthday in August 1957 on a Sammy Docherty bill. Within 12 months, he had won 10 of 11 contests. His sole defeat had been emphatically reversed when he knocked out Antonio Diaz. In his twelfth contest, he faced Freddie Gilroy in a British bantamweight title eliminator. Gilroy won in the eighth and broke Johnny's jaw in the process. Johnny recalls being taken to hospital by boxing correspondent James Sanderson. It was only when Johnny won the Scottish bantamweight title against Tommy Miller one year later that he was able to box without worrying about his jaw.

By 1962, Johnny had moved up to featherweight and began the year by beating his local rival and friend, Bobby Fisher. He then stopped Empire champion Floyd Robertson in 8 rounds in his best win to date. There were 4 further good performances in 1962 before he met Howard Winstone for the British featherweight title in 1963. Johnny admits that he was never at the races against future world champion Winstone and got such a doing that he was never the same again.

After his next fight against the awkward Dennis Adjei, he decided to call it a day. He did fight again in early 1963 but is at a loss to understand how he managed to scale 9 stones at the weigh-in. He insists that he was definitely overweight and that he had no chance of ever fighting as a featherweight again.

26 of Johnny Morrissey's 32 contests were fought in Scotland. He fought in England 6 times, losing only 2.

Bobby Neill

Bobby Neill was born in Ibrox but moved to Edinburgh when he was five years old. He was educated at Trinity Academy in Edinburgh and became a trainee commercial artist in the city when he was 16. On his way home from work one evening, he was hit by a motor cycle and this put paid to his career as a commercial artist and put his boxing ambitions on hold for some time. Doctors managed to save his crushed left leg but Bobby spent 18 months encased in plaster from feet to chest. When he recovered, he resumed boxing and became a trainee actuary with the British Oxygen Company in Pall Mall, London. His studies meant that he had to attend night school three times a week. Such demands on his time proved too much as he felt that he was not devoting sufficient time to his boxing. He was fortunate to find a new job in the accounts department of Lex Garages in Piccadilly and his new employer allowed him time off to go the gym

Bobby had intended to turn professional when he became 18 but due to his serious accident, he did not become a professional until he was 21 in 1955. He quickly made his mark on the London scene with twelve straight wins in his first thirteen months as a professional. He then fought Matt Fulton for the Scottish featherweight title at Firhill and stopped him in eight rounds. He was to relinquish the title nine months later due to lack of opposition.

He returned to London to meet 32-year-old Frenchman Ray Famechon who had previously held the European featherweight title for more than eight years and who had lost a world featherweight title fight on points to Willie Pep. This was the classiest opponent Bobby had met to date and he stopped him in five rounds. In his next fight, he stopped the British featherweight champion Charlie Hill in the first round. By the end of 1956, Bobby Neill was a box office attraction with a great future.

In January 1957, he fought Jimmy Brown in a final eliminator for the British featherweight title in Belfast. Bobby had to lose a few pounds to make the weight but it was still a surprise to everybody that he was knocked out in the eighth round by the tough Irishman. Bobby recalls being jeered and spat upon by the Belfast fans as he entered the King's Hall but he was unaffected by this greeting and indeed he was confident that he would win the fight going into the eighth round. Bobby bounced back with a win but then suffered a points defeat. After one more win, he returned to Scotland to meet Arthur Donnachie at Paisley Ice Rink. Donnachie fought as a lightweight and the match was made at 9 stone 4 pounds. Bobby recalls that Donnachie was a strong fighter and it was a good contest. Bobby was robbed of a win by a cut above his eye but he thinks that he was ahead on points at the time. A few days later, Bobby was badly injured in a car crash on the road between

Glasgow and Edinburgh. He remained in Edinburgh Royal Infirmary for two weeks and was in plaster for three months as a result of breaking his left knee again. It was thought that this would be the end of Bobby's career. The boxing fraternity rallied round Bobby Neill and a benefit promotion was held on his behalf. The promotion provided desperately needed cash to see him through the difficult days.

Nine months after the horrendous accident, Bobby returned to the ring in London and won three fights in the space of three weeks. He then returned to Scotland and stopped Owen Reilly in the sixth round at Cathkin Park. A further win in London and then a match with Belgian champion Aime Devisch followed. Devisch hit Bobby with a right in the first round and he knew immediately that his jaw had been broken. This did not deter Bobby Neill who fought on and stopped Devisch in the sixth. The broken jaw meant another enforced absence from the ring and Bobby did not fight again for seven months.

In April 1959, the long-awaited contest against Charlie Hill for the British featherweight title was his next fight. In a memorable contest, Bobby Neill stopped Hill in the ninth round but received cuts to both eyes, one of which required eight stitches. He had at last become British featherweight champion despite the numerous setbacks that he had received in his career.

Later that year, Bobby was well beaten by world champion Davey Moore. In the following year, he controversially lost his British title to Terry Spinks when the referee stopped the fight because of a small cut above his left eyebrow. Bobby's last fight was the rematch with Spinks. He was knocked out in the fourteenth round. In the aftermath, he recalls feeling dehydrated and drinking tea. He felt sick and then collapsed and was rushed to hospital with a blood clot on his brain and he underwent immediate surgery which saved his life.

27 of Bobby's 35 professional contests were in the London area and he fought only 3 times in Scotland. Bobby went on to manage and train such British boxing greats such as Johnny Pritchett, Alan Minter and Alan Rudkin.

John O'Brien

John O'Brien was a plumber from the east end of Glasgow. He was a mean footballer but opted for boxing as his main sport. He was 19 when he turned professional in October 1956. By the end of the following year, he had fought and won eight times and was ranked number 3 featherweight in the UK. In 1958, he won only one of 5 contests and his ranking dropped to 5. After a reverse in his first fight of 1959, he won his next three and then defeated Terry Spinks in a British featherweight title eliminator. Before the end of the year, he took on Percy Lewis for the British Empire featherweight title but a major error by O'Brien resulted in a second round defeat. He ended 1959 as number 2 British featherweight after Bobby Neill whom he was due to meet for the British title in the new year. However, John grew tired of constantly training and decided to retire from boxing and the match with Neill did not take place.

John came out of retirement in 1962. He lost his first two comeback fights with cut eyes but won the next two and was ranked number 5 British featherweight by the end of the year. Following one reverse in 4 in 1963, he improved his ranking to 3 and was matched with Howard Winstone in December 1963 for the British and European featherweight titles. O'Brien fought with considerable courage but Winstone was a classy champion and he retained his titles on points.

O'Brien had one fight in 1964, outpointing the leading Empire challenger Dennis Adjei. He fought three times in 1965, losing two to world ranked opponents. He won the third fight against Jesus Saucedo but was distraught to learn that Saucedo had died of injuries sustained in the fight. O'Brien was inactive in 1966.

John O'Brien's finest moment arrived in February 1967. In Ghana, he destroyed Floyd Robertson to win the British Empire featherweight title. This was a major victory against a man whose previous fight had been for the world featherweight title and had been long time world ranked. O'Brien now had a number 12 world ranking. However, O'Brien lost the title in Melbourne to Johnny Famechon on a cut eye stoppage in his next fight in November.

He won his only two fights of 1968 and, in March 1969, he fought Jimmy Revie for the British featherweight title. He lost in the fifth round, the referee stopping the fight, again because of damage to his eyes. After two subsequent victories in South Africa and another victory in London, John O'Brien departed the British boxing scene.

John emigrated to Melbourne in 1970 with his wife and two children. He fought 7 times in Australia, winning the first 4 and losing the next 3. He retired in July 1971 and died on 30th March 1979 at the age of 42. John O'Brien was a tough and talented boxer who would travel anywhere and take on the best. If he had not had a two and a half year break in the early sixties, he may have achieved more. However, to fight for major titles five times between 1959 and 1969, it could have been six, and to win the Empire title in Africa is the mark of a successful boxer and he was a credit to Scotland.

Billy Rafferty

Billy Rafferty was born in Glasgow in 1933. He did not take up boxing until he was 21 and spent only 18 months as an average amateur before he turned professional in 1956. He clocked up six straight wins on the Scottish circuit before losing on points to George Bowes in his first contest south of the border. By the middle of 1959, he had lost only 3 of 23 fights and had beaten leading boxers such as Jake Tuli, Terry Spinks, Len Reece, Derry Treanor and Graham Van Der Walt. In October 1959, he outpointed Len Reece in a final eliminator for the British bantamweight title and ended the year with a points victory over Californian bantamweight champion, Dwight Hawkins.

In March 1960, Billy fought Freddie Gilroy in Belfast for the British, Empire and European bantamweight titles. A superb display of guts was not enough to win the title but Rafferty was only slightly behind when the referee stopped the fight following serious damage to Rafferty's eye. Rafferty was a battler and was back in the ring within three months. A wonderful display in Manchester saw him defeat Ignacio Pina on points. Pina had ended Freddie Gilroy's unbeaten professional record just six weeks earlier. Billy was buzzing again. He was now one of the leading bantamweights in the world and the world title was vacant. Unfortunately for Billy, Freddie Gilroy and Alphonse Halimi were nominated to fight for the title. Billy was matched against top European Piero Rollo in Cagliari but lost the fight on points.

After a six-month break, Billy defeated George Bowes in a final eliminator for the British bantamweight title. In March 1962, ten months later, Billy returned to the King's Hall in Belfast to face Freddie Gilroy for the British and Empire bantamweight titles. This time Rafferty was knocked out by Gilroy and retired from boxing.

Red haired Billy Rafferty hailed from Easterhouse in Glasgow and was a van driver and a scrap metal dealer when he was not boxing. He was a popular, all action fighter who received tremendous crowd receptions wherever he fought. He was tough and courageous and a dedicated trainer. Although he won no titles either as an amateur or professional, he was a model professional who was a credit to the sport.

John Smillie

John Smillie came from the mining village of Fauldhouse in West Lothian. His sole interest was boxing and he joined the local boxing club when he was young. On leaving school, he became a coal miner in a local pit. He was an outstanding amateur boxer and turned professional in 1955.

In 1955, he won 8 and drew one of 9 contests and ended the year as British number 7 bantamweight. He won all of his 6 fights in 1956. In June, he defeated George Dormer on points in a British bantamweight title eliminator after a remarkable fightback that showed tremendous guts and courage. He ended 1956 as number one challenger to Peter Keenan. In January 1957, he lost his unbeaten professional record to Jimmy Carson in Belfast. His next fight in May was against Peter Keenan for the British and Empire bantamweight titles. Smillie was leading after 5 rounds but the ruthless Keenan proved too wily for the youthful Smillie and stopped him in the sixth round.

Smillie had 3 further fights and 3 wins before the end of the year. He ended the year as number 3 bantamweight behind Keenan and Carson. He announced at the end of the year that he was going to emigrate and work in a gold mine in Ontario. However, this move fell through.

He had struggled to make the weight against Peter Keenan and it was no surprise when, in 1958, he moved up to featherweight. He won 3 of 5 contests in the year and was ranked number 7 UK featherweight. His only loss in 5 in 1959 was to future Empire champion, Floyd Robertson, but his UK ranking did not improve. In 1960, Smillie won 4 of 8 contests and ceased to box in the UK.

He later emigrated to Australia. He fought 8 times in Melbourne in 1962, winning 5, and retired just before his 29th birthday. Smillie seemed to lose interest after the Keenan defeat. He performed well as a bantamweight but did not fight anyone of true class other than Keenan. When he fought at featherweight, that division was rich with Scottish talent but he did not meet Hill, Neill, O'Brien, Kidd or Croll. He did meet Floyd Robertson but was knocked out in the first round. Perhaps John Smillie knew his limitations as a professional and deliberately avoided the top fighters to prolong his career.

Derry Treanor

Derry Treanor was born in Monaghan in the Republic of Ireland in 1937. He came to Glasgow to find work in 1954 when he was only 16. He stayed in Kennedy Street in Townhead before moving to join the Irish contingent in the Gorbals. Derry turned professional in 1956 when he was signed by Arthur Boggis. He moved to Dartford in Kent where his sparring partners included Dave Charnley and Joe Lucy. After 2 fights in England, Derry returned to the Gorbals and was looked after by Joe Aitchison in Dalmarnock. After one fight, he moved to Los Angeles where he trained hard for 2 months in a rough area at the beginning of 1957. On his return to Scotland, he won 3 of 4 fights in 1957.

His career took off in 1958 when, following a controversial loss to George Bowes in Newcastle, he won his next 6 fights. This last victory in this winning sequence was against the mighty Peter Keenan. After a setback against Roy Jacobs, Derry won all 7 contests between 1959 and 1961 including a victory over Terry Spinks. In April 1960, Derry's application for British citizenship had been approved and he could now fight for a British title. He had moved up to featherweight by this time and was the number one contender for the British featherweight title throughout 1961.

The British title fight with Howard Winstone went ahead at Wembley in April. Derry put up a brave fight but was well beaten in what was both the pinnacle and conclusion of his professional boxing career. Derry now lives in Bishopbriggs and is a Representative Steward with the British Boxing Board of Control.